THE GEORGE GUND FOUNDATION
IMPRINT IN AFRICAN AMERICAN STUDIES

The George Gund Foundation has endowed
this imprint to advance understanding of
the history, culture, and current issues
of African Americans.

The publisher and the University of California Press Foundation gratefully acknowledge the generous support of the George Gund Foundation Imprint in African American Studies.

Tip of the Spear

*Black Radicalism, Prison Repression,
and the Long Attica Revolt*

Orisanmi Burton

UNIVERSITY OF CALIFORNIA PRESS

University of California Press
Oakland, California

© 2023 by Orisanmi Burton

Cataloging-in-Publication data is on file at the Library of Congress.

ISBN 978-0-520-39631-9 (cloth : alk. paper)
ISBN 978-0-520-39632-6 (pbk. : alk. paper)
ISBN 978-0-520-39633-3 (ebook)

Manufactured in the United States of America

32 31 30 29 28 27 26 25 24
10 9 8 7 6 5 4

Contents

Acknowledgments   *vii*

Introduction   *1*

PART ONE. THE LONG ATTICA REVOLT

1. Sharpening the Spear
   Strategies and Tactics of Revolutionary Action   *23*

2. Black Solidarity Under Siege
   Three Terrains of Protracted Rebellion   *50*

3. Attica Is
   Revolutionary Consciousness and Abolitionist Worldmaking   *79*

PART TWO. PRISON PACIFICATION

4. Gender War
   Sexual Revenge and White Masculine Repair   *119*

5. Hidden War
   Four Strategies of Reformist Counterinsurgency   *150*

6. The War on Black Revolutionary Minds
   Failed Experiments in Scientific Subjugation   183

Epilogue   223
Notes   231
Bibliography   273
Index   301

Acknowledgments

I could not have written this book without support from a vast network of ancestors, elders, teachers, mentors, colleagues, and friends, nor without the raging fire fueled by our enemies.

Profound gratitude goes to Jalan Burton, whose love, encouragement, and sacrifice throughout the entirety of this process kept me going. And to my children—Z, M, and O—who teach me new things about life each day. Thank you to Aukram and Nefertiti Burton for setting me on my path and showing me how to use my Ori. Gratitude to my family, who laid the foundation for me to do this work.

Thank you to all the childcare providers who took care of my babies while I worked on this project.

This work was nurtured and enriched by a community of scholars and comrades: Charles R. Price, Dylan Rodriguez, Damien Sojoyner, Sarah Haley, Savannah Shange, Joy James, Ruth Wilson Gilmore, Craig Gilmore, Emani Davis, Jack Norton, Maya Berry, Manissa Maharawal, Zoltan Gluck, Sarah Ihmoud, Mubbashir Rizvi, Delio Vasquez, Willie J. Wright, Bianca Williams, Ryan Jobson, Ashanté M. Reese, Garrett Felber, Amaka Okechukwu, Stuart Schrader, Ilana Feldman, David Vine, David Kaib, Heath Pearson, Megan French, Michael Bolds, Toussaint Losier, Roberto D. Sirvent, Robin D. G. Kelley, Alvaro Reyes, and Dorothy Holland.

Thank you to the staff at the University of California Press, especially Kate Marshall, Chad Attenborough, Julie Van Pelt, and Catherine R.

Osborne. Thank you to my colleagues in the Anthropology Department at American University and to my former colleagues in the Department of Criminal Justice at the University of the District of Columbia.

This book would not exist if Kyung-Ji Rhee hadn't hired me to work at the Prison Moratorium Project all those years ago. Thank you, and to Eddie Ellis, Chino Hardin, Divine Pryor, and the Center for NuLeadership on Human Justice and Healing.

Additional gratitude goes to Jared A. Ball, Patricia J. Williams, Yousuf Al-Bulushi, Dan Berger, Samar Al-Bulushi, Judah Schept, Matt Birkhold, Jared Ware, Monica Kim, Juli Grigsby, Ruth Gomberg-Muñoz, Shanya Cordis, James Kilgore, Dána-Ain Davis, Shaun Lin, Karanja Keita Carroll, Kazembe Balagun, Micol Seigel, Christopher Harris, Amanda Huron, Matt Hooley, Susan B. Hyatt, Michael Hull, Amy Jordan, Kareem Rabie, Barbara Ransby, Leila Pourtavaf, Keeanga-Yamahtta Taylor, Powerful, Adam Bledsoe, Phillip B. Williams, Mariame Kaba, Victoria Law, Derecka Purnell, Che Gossett, Kiese Laymon, Chinua Thelwell, Harmony Holiday, Sara Kaplan, Charmaine Chua, Angélica Cházaro, Nicole Fabricant, Christina Hanhardt, Akinyele Umoja, Vincent Joos, Traci Curry, Chris Tinson, Carlos "REC" McBride, Catherine Besteman, Bertin Louis, Alexis Pauline Gumbs, Liz Gaynes, Perry Zurn, Deborah Boehm, Darrick Hamilton, Kristin Doughty, Joshua Dubler, Ashon Crawley, Ericka Edwards, Jeremy Levinson, Shana Redmond, Ben Rubin, Elif Babul, Jasmine Syedullah, Amy Jordan, Michelle Bigenho, Kara Lynch, Stevie Wilson, Corey Green, Richard Jackson, Justin Hosbey, Peter Redfield, Karla Slocum, Connie Wun, Christina Heatherton, Jordan Camp, Jean Dennison, Reuben Jonathan Miller, Lilly Wong, Josh Myers, Mali Collins, Garrett Graddy-Lovelace, Alice Green, Brandon Proia, Claude Marks, Ain Grooms, Shelia Wilson, Brenda Tapia, Clarence Washington, Sheila Washington, Angela Craghead, Khary Lazarre-White, Zahara Duncan, Charles Curtis, Chuck Holden, Junauda Petrus, Paul Grant, Tim Lovelace, Daisy Lovelace, Victorious Hall, Malik Duncan, Hanifa Hakim, Aichi Kochiyama, Akemi Kochiyama, Stephen Hines, Susan Wilcox, John Chenault, Preston Smith, Lynda Pickbourn, Valerie Caesar, Mark Swier, Abby Vaughn, Eris Johnson-Smith, Coco Killingsworth, Joan Morgan, and Ted Barco.

A number of people helped with my research: Sam Menefee-Libey, Maia McCall, Farah Afify, Jade Woods, Delande Justinvil, Bethany Zaiman, Miho Watabe, Shannon Clark, Penina Meier-Silverman, Kathy Kaib, Brad Schreiber, Colin A. Ross, Greg deGiere. Thank you to the various librarians, archivists, records managers, and court clerks who helped me pull this off. Special thanks to the American University librarians, particularly the Interlibrary Loan staff who indulged my exploration of various rabbit holes.

I sharpened my analysis in dialogue with a number of intellectual networks: The Critical Prison Studies Caucus of the American Studies Association, the Critical Ethnic Studies Association, the Freedom Scholars, the Palestinian American Research Center, Rochester Decarceration Initiative, the Institute for Critical Social Inquiry, the Association of Black Anthropologists, the Association of American Geographers, the Freedom Archives, the Abolition Collective, Pan-African Community Action, the Carceral Subjects Workshop, Black Power Media, and Millennials Are Killing Capitalism.

My research received material support from the Association of Black Anthropologists, the Society for Applied Anthropology, the UNC-CH Anthropology Department, the American University College of Arts and Sciences, the Wenner-Gren Foundation, the UNC-CH Institute of American Research, the Radcliffe Institute for Advanced Study, and the Marguerite Casey Foundation. Thank you.

Last but certainly not least, many thanks to movement elders who have nurtured my political and intellectual development: Queen Mother Moore, Yuri Kochiyama, Muhammad Ahmad, Alkamal Duncan, Dhoruba bin-Wahad, Masia A. Mugmuk, Hassan Gale, Kwando M. Kinshasa, Kathleen Cleaver, George Prendes, Basir Mchawi, Tony Menelik Van der Meer, Daniel Sheppard, Tyrone Larkins, James Killebrew, Kareem C'Allah, Laura Whitehorn, Sekou Odinga, Robert J. Boyle, Ashanti Alston, Jalil Muntaqim, Larry White, Tanaquil Jones, Denise Oliver-Velez, Jihad Abdulmumit, Blood McCreary, Mae Adams, Joseph "Jazz" Hayden, David Gilbert, Kathy Boudin, and so many others.

Introduction

On August 18, 1973, Queen Mother Audley Moore, a stalwart Communist and Pan-Africanist revolutionary, traveled to Green Haven Prison and delivered a remarkable keynote address. A video of the event shows stylishly dressed Black men, women, and children seated in rows of folding chairs, standing in small groups, eating, laughing, talking, and embracing.[1] Were it not for the massive concrete walls encircling the gathering, one might easily mistake it for a typical picnic or celebration. However, the peaceful and bucolic scene belied the profound violence simmering just beneath the surface. The inaugural years of the 1970s were among the most explosive and lethal in US prison history, due in no small measure to militant rebellions that ruptured carceral institutions across the nation. The two-year anniversary of Attica, the most infamous of these conflicts, was less than a month away. Hundreds of "Attica Brothers"—the incarcerated rebels who seized the prison and endured the state-orchestrated massacre that followed—had been transferred to Green Haven, and many now gathered to hear Moore speak.

Standing before a modest podium, Moore explained that Green Haven's imprisoned men were enduring "re-captivity." Offering an analysis made popular by her political mentee Malcolm X, she argued that prison walls made visible a condition of incarceration that is constitutive of Black life in America.[2] Black people are a "captive nation"; the physically imprisoned had therefore been captured "doubly so." Moore then explained that it was not the captives, but the White Man who was "the real criminal." She reminded her audience—comprised of people variously convicted of robbery, assault, rape, murder, and drug-related crimes—that none of them had ever stolen entire countries, cultures, or peoples, or sold human beings into slavery for profit. Although some of them had tried to imitate the White Man, she continued, they had never *really* stolen and neither had they ever really murdered. "Have you taken mothers and strung them up by their heels?" she asked. "And took your knives and slit their bellies so that their unborn babies can fall to the ground? And then took your heel and crushed those babies into the ground? . . . Have you dropped bombs on people and killed whole countries of people, have you done that brothers?" Given that American empire is constituted through apocalyptic violence and incalculable theft, Moore argued that "crimes" committed by the human spoils of war were necessarily derivative of the organized crime of the state.[3]

Moore explained that as a student of Marcus Garvey and a veteran of the Black liberation struggle since the 1930s, she had accumulated valuable insight into the "science" of white supremacy. With the horror of the Attica massacre fresh in the audience's mind, she told the appalling story of her grandfather's lynching, explaining that prisons function in tandem with other tactics of white patriarchal domination. The aim of the White Man's science was to "denature" African people: to crush their spirits, destroy their cognitive autonomy, and transform them into obedient "negroes" with no knowledge of their history or will to resist. Moore likened this process to the taming of lions, who can be caged and conditioned to "purr like kittens" at the crack of a whip. She concluded her address by enjoining the captive population—the formally imprisoned as well as the nominally free—to reject this oppressive science, to nurture a sovereign Black consciousness, to embrace armed struggle, and to rely on each other for the battles that lay ahead. For only then would the captive nation be able to decisively liberate itself from the prisons ensnaring it.

Queen Mother Moore's unconventional analysis unsettles commonsense notions of crime, violence, imprisonment, the state, politics, science, temporality, and the idea of the human itself. Her narrative method dislodges these concepts from criminology, sociology, anthropology, and other liberal formations of knowledge, repurposing them for Black revolutionary ends. By theorizing Black prisoners as re-captives and situating prisons within the *longue durée* of European colonialism, she forces a reckoning with non-linear, fractured, and cyclical understandings of historical movement.[4] Her visceral rendering of gendered racial violence disrupts past and present attempts to construct the Attica massacre—

during which state actors slaughtered *at least* thirty-nine people and sexually tortured hundreds more—as aberrational or exceptional. Rather, without ever mentioning it directly, she calls attention to the resonance between this recent spectacle of violence and supposedly bygone regimes of chattel slavery, racial apartheid, and settler colonialism. Moreover, her argument that the White Man's allegedly objective "science" involves methods of "taming" Black rebellion is suggestive of concurrent efforts by CIA-affiliated behavioral psychologists, physicians, and others to "neutralize" political radicality by chemically, surgically, and electronically altering brain function.[5] Conveyed during a moment in which the struggle behind the walls was taking on a less combative posture, Moore's oratory challenged the state's authority to criminalize and incarcerate Black communities, while affirming the captives' right, indeed their duty, to struggle against the carceral world. These ideas, thematic concerns, and political imperatives prepare us for the narrative that follows.

Tip of the Spear argues that prisons are war. They are state strategies of race war, class war, colonization, and counterinsurgency. But they are also domains of militant contestation, where captive populations reject these white supremacist systems of power and invent zones of autonomy, freedom, and liberation. The book's major tasks are threefold. One, I analyze what I term the *Long Attica Revolt*, a genealogy of Black radical and revolutionary struggle that emerged among New York's captive population during the early 1970s. Two, I illuminate what I call *prison pacification*, a campaign of racist and political repression, white supremacist science, and organized violence advanced by a network of state actors variously located within penal hierarchies, police agencies, foreign theaters of war, counterinsurgency think tanks, universities, the FBI, and the CIA. Three, I examine how the protracted *collision* of these projects gave rise to new formations of consciousness, politics, sociality, gender, and being, as well as new—which is to say *renewed*—technologies of racial-colonial domination, dehumanization, and extraction.

The war of which I write is fundamentally asymmetrical, not only in terms of each side's capacities and methods, but also in terms of their goals. Through prison pacification, state actors wage a war of conquest on a subject population as part of broader efforts to accumulate capital and preserve the dominance of White Man. Their mode of combat combines siege warfare and counterinsurgency warfare. Through siege warfare, an antagonist surrounds an enemy fortification and institutes blockades on the flow of resources in an attempt to starve the surrounded population into submission.⁶ In this context, *to starve* must be understood capaciously as the calculated denial of the material, social, cultural, and political nutrients necessary for reproducing defiant Black life and consciousness across generations. Counterinsurgency, according to the US Army, is a style of warfare that involves "military, paramilitary, political, economic, psychological, and civic actions taken by a government to defeat insurgency."⁷ As will become clear, the planners and administrators of this carceral siege aimed to crush the Revolt by deploying a range of techniques, both "hard" and "soft," across these terrains of intervention.

In contrast to this carceral warfare project, the Long Attica Revolt was not a war of conquest or accumulation. Against carceral siege, revolting captives waged a people's war, a counter-war, or what exiled Black revolutionary Robert F. Williams called "a guerrilla war of self-defense."⁸ Popularly characterized as "a war of the weak against the strong," guerrilla warfare involves irregular, small-scale attacks that aim to disrupt the social order, raising the cost of business as usual to a level that is unsustainable for the ruling authority, forcing them to relinquish control. Within and against captivity, rebels employed diverse methodologies of attack: political education, critique, protest, organizing, cultural production, litigation, subversion, refusal, rebellion, retaliation, hostage-taking, sabotage, armed struggle, and the intimate labor of care.⁹ Like Moore, they saw prison walls not as boundaries between freedom and unfreedom, but as material demarcations of different intensities of captivity, vulnerability, and rebellion.

Attica was, and is, a multiracial structure of Revolt led by people who self-identified as Black. However, the Blackness they claimed was as much, if not more, a collective *political* designation as an individual identity. Through this rubric, Black skin is insufficient for Blackness, as Moore's derision for Black-skinned "negroes" makes clear. For decades, combatant-theorists and politically engaged academics have conceptualized political Blackness as a mode of consciousness emerging from a collective historical experience of oppression and struggle.¹⁰ Attica erupted out of this context, a historical moment in which people whose African ancestors were enslaved in what became known as Latin America increasingly embraced their African heritage.¹¹ Moreover, conditions of extreme carceral duress coerced some imprisoned and destitute whites into Black modalities of rebellion: "Authority itself may be going down a fast track toward the Niggerization of everyone," explained a white Attica survivor.¹² Forged within cauldrons of racial, sexual, and class oppression, the Long Attica Revolt threatened the existence of prisons, the social order, and the very coherence of White Man, a coercively universalized paradigm of human being.[13]

Contrary to most academic scholarship on prison-based movements and rebellions, *Tip of the Spear* decenters incarcerated peoples' formal demands to improve prison conditions. Though struggles over access to decent food, clothing, shelter, medical care, visitation privileges, humane parole policies, and so on are an important site of political contestation, these appeals constitute the prison movement's *minimum demands:* calls for bare survival amid genocide.[14] Investigations of prison insurgency tend to focus on this rational and pragmatic class of demands, while ignoring, dismissing, or downplaying calls to "tear down the walls" and "free all political prisoners" as unrealistic, hyperbolic, immature, or too extreme. Moreover, as Dylan Rodríguez has shown, even these minimum demands, which tend to be articulated in the form of the petition to the state, are routinely analyzed in unsophisticated ways that circumscribe the horizon of incarcerated people's ambitions to a desire for full incorporation within existing regimes of citizenship, rights, and humanity.[15] I am not arguing against the common refrain that incarcerated people *just want to be treated as human beings*. In many cases this is certainly true, but in others, it is the conception of the human itself that is seen as the problem.[16] As the dominant way of interpreting anticarceral struggle, the focus on external demands on the state narrows the scope of people's actual desires and facilitates the mystification of prison abolition's revolutionary and anticolonial origins.

Tip of the Spear argues that the Long Attica Revolt was itself a demand. Uttered through what Rev. Dr. Martin Luther King Jr. famously termed "the language of the unheard,"[17] this riot, this rebellion, this revolutionary upheaval was an *internal* demand, a call to arms directed not toward the state, which did not have the capacity to comprehend or satiate the rebellion's most fulsome desires, but toward allied communities across prison walls and beyond US territorial boundaries. The content of this maximum demand was the abolition of prisons, the abolition of war, the abolition of racial capitalism, the abolition of White Man, and the emergence of new modes of social life not predicated on enclosure, extraction, domination, or dehumanization. In the pages that follow, I carefully excavate incarcerated people's protracted and often fatal struggles to realize their most unruly, unreasonable, and irrational demands. In doing so, I reframe our understanding of Attica and Black rebellion more broadly.

At the tail end of our conversation, Che Nieves, the former Minister of Education for a prison-based formation of the Young Lords Party and a veteran of the Attica rebellion, articulated a version of the maximum demand with rare clarity. We had covered the highs and lows of his life of struggle behind the walls: the relentless brutality of prison existence, the trajectory of his political radicalization, the ecstasy of achieving the rebellion's illegal freedom, and the unspeakable horrors of the massacre he survived. Like most of the interviews I conducted while researching this book, it was a heavy discussion that was filled with rage, tears, laughter, and the wonderment that surfaces when someone rediscovers a lost thread of memory that had lain dormant for decades. As we prepared to go our separate ways, I thanked Che for entrusting me with his memories and analysis. He responded: "Listen, all I could say is, we brothers, man. We need each other. It's not only me, but you. That's what keeps us going. Exchange, it keeps the spirit going, and it keeps us moving toward freedom. The more you acquire, the more I acquire. And without you, it's not me. You make me and I make you."[18]

Che's poetic reflection illuminates the abolitionist ethical philosophy at the core of the Revolt. Though immediately triggered by carceral repression and violence, Attica signifies a positive demand that exceeds normative frameworks of the political and challenges hegemonic norms of individualism that are at the heart of capitalism, patriarchy, and white Western humanism. Decades before the term entered the popular lexicon, where it has been diluted and co-opted, Attica rebels engaged in a praxis of abolition, generating abolitionist knowledge, theory, and practice amid conditions of carceral war. They not only imagined and dreamed a world without prisons, but put their bodies and lives on the line to materialize their vision in the face of determined opposition. The shape of the world they began to build in place of what they began to tear down was not predetermined. Rather, it was improvised through the unfolding of the Revolt, a collective movement toward freedom. Theirs was a freedom that was not only material and political, but cognitive and metaphysical, a freedom nurtured within and between people who came to understand themselves as new kinds of beings for a new kind of world, a freedom that could not be granted, that could only be seized. The Long Attica Revolt, in other words, *is* abolition. It is a paradigm and a blueprint, imperfect to be sure, but invaluable nonetheless, for creating an abolitionist world.

Che's assertion that the power of our principled brotherhood exceeds the sum of its parts points to another major theme of this book: manhood, masculinity, patriarchy, and gendered life under domestic warfare. *Tip of the Spear* focuses on struggles enacted by people incarcerated in prisons designated for men, who by and large understood incarceration as a process that attacked their manhood, and who engaged in rebellion as a humanizing and indeed a masculinizing process.[19] As such, it analyzes the complex ways that claims to manhood are constructed, contested, and violently negated in the process of struggle, and shows that the content of the manhood proclaimed by the rebels was radically different from that enacted by their captors. Across years of learning with and from progressive, radical, and revolutionary Black men who rebelled within and against the racist and patriarchal state, I have learned that a gendered struggle, a struggle to redefine manhood itself, to create an ethical and life-giving manhood, was (and is) indispensable to this Revolt.[20]

MAKING THIS BOOK

Tip of the Spear is my response to an intergenerational assignment that Eddie Ellis and others gave me nearly a decade ago. I met Ellis in 2009 while facilitating political education workshops with the Prison Moratorium Project, an organization he helped establish after spending twenty-three years behind the walls. In 2014, when I began conducting research for what evolved into this book, I interviewed Eddie, hoping to learn about his life as a journalist for the magazine *The Liberator*, his role in the Harlem Black Panther Party, his experience in Attica during the rebellion, and his work as part of the Green Haven Think Tank, a prison-based formation whose research influenced multiple generations of activists, scholars, and policymakers, often in unacknowledged ways.[21] During our interview, which lasted upward of six hours, Eddie shared his feeling that he and those with whom he was in community had failed to theorize, document, and contextualize the movements they led behind prison walls. "We have never been able to use the tools of academia to demonstrate that our analysis is a better analysis," he said.[22] He then suggested that perhaps I could play that role, that I make it my mission to use the resources of academic scholarship to rigorously elaborate a genealogy of knowledge production that today largely remains criminalized, pathologized, and intentionally hidden from public view. It was a transformative interview in many ways, but unfortunately it was our last. Ellis died of cancer shortly after that conversation.

The arguments and narratives that follow are the result of intensive research in institutional and personal archival collections combined with repeated, extended, and open-ended oral history interviews I conducted with more than sixty people, most of them Black and Latinx men and women who participated in radical social movements within and beyond prisons between the 1960s and the 1990s. As such, this work extends a legacy of anthropological research carried out in service of anticolonial, liberatory, and abolitionist projects.[23] It operationalizes scholar Michel-Rolph Trouillot's insight that non-academics are critical producers of historiography: that not only do such subjects engage in concrete struggle to transform material reality, they also strive to "define the very terms under which some situations can be described."[24] It also builds on the work of theorist Cedric Robinson, who shows us that to contend with Black radicalism on its own terms, we must unshackle our analytical frameworks from the cognitive prison of (white) Western rationality and refuse to impose knowledge paradigms developed to justify the current social order upon movements that aim to unmake that order.[25] Generated by deep and long-term relationships of trust, my analytical method takes the Black radical epistemologies, narratives, and modes of argumentation of those with whom I am in community as both a point of departure and lodestar. Moreover, it employs an ethnographic approach to historical narration in which I, the reflexive authorial subject, remain present in the story, thinking and theorizing with the protagonists of this struggle to collectively scrutinize the meanings of key ideas, decisions, tensions, and events.[26]

It is this relation of accountability to the intellectuals and combatants of this undeclared war, both living and dead, and to the ancestral traditions that nurtured them, that distinguishes this book from previous treatments of Attica and from the growing body of academic scholarship on Black radicalism within and beyond prisons.[27] The dominant understanding of Attica as a four-day event that was confined to a single prison and primarily aimed to ameliorate oppressive conditions is facilitated by interpretive practices that prioritize knowledge yielded by state sources over knowledge produced and archived by rebels.[28] In contrast to the imperatives of this counterinsurgent historiography, Black radical ways of knowing constitute the primary sources of this study. To gather these sources I have pursued, excavated, and analyzed the recollections, letters, treatises, manuals, journalism, testimony, and even the rumors, legends, and "conspiracy theories" generated by people who understood themselves, and were understood by the state, to be revolutionaries.[29]

The Long Attica Revolt names a protracted accumulation of rebellion that circulated within and beyond New York prisons for at least thirteen months prior to what ultimately *culminated* in Attica prison between September 9 and 13, 1971. As Trouillot asserts, "The historical narrative within which an actual event fits could precede that event itself, at least in theory, but perhaps also in practice."[30] Indeed, the narrative practices of the people I spoke to troubled coherent, linear, and bounded notions of the Attica rebellion. Rather, these figures narrated their involvement in multiple rebellions, both large and small, some preceding the September rebellion in Attica, others emerging in its wake, some confined to a single prison, others dispersed across multiple carceral sites: city jails, state prisons, mental institutions, urban streets, foreign territories, and so on. From this perspective, "Attica" functions as a metonym for a temporally, geographically, and politically diverse structure of Revolt to which many roots and branches connect and extend in different, sometimes contradictory directions. So said Gary McGivern, imprisoned in Green Haven when Attica erupted, who authored a poem claiming, "Attica is our heritage and our beginning."[31]

My decision to organize this book around the paradigm of war arose from listening to movement elders and taking what they had to say seriously. "We are the tip of the spear," wrote Jalil Muntaqim in a letter to me years ago. A veteran of the Black Panther Party (BPP) and Black Liberation Army (BLA) who, in the early years of the 1980s, was accused of attempting to foment "another Attica," Muntaqim had been incarcerated for over four decades on a range of intensely politicized charges, including a conviction for the assassination of two New York City Police Department (NYPD) patrolmen back in 1971, a conviction that was facilitated by the FBI's anti-Black Counterintelligence Program (COINTELPRO). I was captivated by this phrase, which is commonly used in military parlance to refer to combat forces deployed to penetrate an enemy's first line of defense. Initially, I interpreted it as a reference to the leading role that politicized prisoners have played in challenging the state.[32] That is, I interpreted the statement as a historical claim. It later occurred to me that in using this martial idiom, Muntaqim could also have been pointing to the location of incarcerated people "behind enemy lines," such that their effective organization could catalyze movements beyond the walls. In other words, maybe he was deploying this phrase as a tactician, much like Frantz Fanon was when he wrote, "It is among these masses, in the people of the shanty towns and in the lumpenproletariat that the insurrection will find its urban spearhead."[33]

However, there is a more chilling possibility. The war paradigm means that it is also possible to interpret Muntaqim's statement from the point of view of the state. This would make incarcerated people, and especially incarcerated Black revolutionaries, the tip of a counterinsurgency spear that has pierced through the front line of its opposition on its way toward striking a more essential target, "us." As a story about war, *Tip of the Spear* mobilizes these various interpretations of the term, analyzing the cutting edge of carceral struggle as seen from both sides of the blade.

CARCERAL WAR

"As soon as all this became clear to me and I developed the nerve to admit it to myself, that we were defeated in a war and are now captives, slaves or actually that we inherited a neoslave existence, I immediately became relaxed, always expecting the worst, and started working on the remedy."[34] George Jackson offered this reflection from Soledad Prison in a 1967 letter to his mother. Six years earlier, an eighteen-year-old Jackson had been given an indeterminate sentence of one-year-to-life for robbing a gas station at gunpoint. It was behind the walls of the California prison system, where racism was "in its pure state, gathering its forces, pulsing with power, ready to spring," that Jackson mutated into a revolutionary.[35] He studied martial arts, read voraciously, co-organized underground formations of resistance, became Field Marshal of the BPP, wrote incisively and prodigiously, and engaged in physical combat against the state.[36]

Jackson's insight about the relationship between prisons, war, and slavery is a useful point from which to begin our examination of carceral war. Dominant understandings of prisons as neoslavery are typically grounded in critical interpretations of US jurisprudence.[37] For activist scholars and politically engaged academics, two primary sources have been particularly influential: the exception clause in the 13th Amendment to the US Constitution, which abolished slavery and involuntary servitude *except as punishment for a crime*, and *Ruffin v. Commonwealth*, the 1871 case in which the Virginia Supreme Court declared incarcerated people "slaves of the state." I am sympathetic to neoslavery arguments that cite these sources, particularly when slavery is understood as a violent relation of domination that often involves, but does not require, the exploitation of labor for profit.[38] I myself was politicized through this mode of historical narration, that compelled me to embrace abolition as the only ethical response to slavery. However, as I researched this book, I grew increasingly critical of this approach—not of the neoslavery analytic per se, but of how its alleged basis in law is endlessly deployed, as though slavery exists because the law allows it to.

George Jackson's assertion that Black people are captives and slaves not because of law, but because we are historical *Prisoners of War*, invokes the paradigmatic rationale for slavery.[39] This rationale is embedded within classical liberal theory, the philosophical substrate of capitalist social relations. Against the dominant understandings of liberalism as a political order that expands peace, political philosopher Mark Neocleous argues that liberalism is a self-conscious doctrine of a war "exercised in permanent fashion against rebellious slaves, antagonistic Indians, wayward workers, and of course, the criminal more broadly defined."[40] Analyzing the thought of classical liberals like John Locke, an investor in the Royal African Company, he finds that claims about the liberal state's power to punish are drawn from international theories of war, in which criminals are "beasts" who have declared war on the state and slavery, an appropriate response to criminality.[41]

Decades before the 13th Amendment and *Ruffin v. Commonwealth*, the so-called Antelope case of 1825 enshrined the link between war and slavery in US jurisprudence. Deciding on the legitimacy of the transatlantic slave trade, which had already been formally outlawed, Supreme Court Chief Justice John Marshall, a slave owner, wrote that it was universally accepted that "the victor might enslave the vanquished" and that slavery "is a legitimate result of force." "The state of things which is thus produced by general consent, cannot be pronounced unlawful," he continued.[42] The Antelope case established the sanctity of property over the supposedly natural right of liberty and shows how the basis of neoslavery lies in war, not law. Rather political and economic elites weaponize law as the continuation of war by other means.[43]

Enslaved Africans argued that slavery *is* war. "When you make men slaves," wrote Olaudah Equiano in 1789, you "compel them to live with you in a state of war."[44] Critically, however, slavery represents a particular moment in the life and death cycle of war, a moment in which one antagonist has imposed their will with near totality upon the other. I say "near" because regimes of domination are never total, riddled as they are with contradictions, fissures, vulnerabilities, and what fugitive slave Harriet Jacobs called "loopholes of retreat."[45] Antebellum plantocracies lived in constant fear of rebellion, a term that etymologically means the renewal of war. To rebel is to repudiate the master/slave relation and inaugurate new movements toward freedom, to create ruptures and breaches through which repressed ways of knowing and being overrun violently imposed boundaries. This is why throughout the Western Hemisphere, self-organized formations of Black rebellion—maroon resistance, general strikes, slave insurrections, urban rebellions, prison revolts—often take on an overtly martial character.[46]

Prison pacification names a historically specific articulation of this permanent war, one that was forged amid tectonic shifts in US political economy during the second half of the twentieth century. Black radical intellectuals like James Boggs understood that something drastic was coming. In 1963, this Detroit autoworker saw that technological changes in industrial production—computerization, automation, and offshoring—were ensuring that more and more workers would find themselves without meaningful ways to make a living. For Boggs, this raised a critical question that would only intensify as the years wore on: What would happen to those whose labor was no longer needed by the capitalist system?[47] In her 2007 book *Golden Gulag*, abolitionist geographer Ruth Wilson Gilmore offers an answer. She shows that beginning in the 1970s, state actors and bourgeois elites pursued "the prison fix" as a solution to the compounding crises of capitalism. They usurped state capacity that could have been used to expand the "social wage," instead deploying it to criminalize and cage what were deemed "surplus populations." As Gilmore explains, this move amounted to "the abandonment of one set of public mandates in favor of another—of social welfare for domestic warfare, if you will."[48]

Tip of the Spear zeroes in on the political dimensions of this war, which began in the so-called "free world" then erupted through prison walls. In July of 1964, four months after New York Governor Nelson Rockefeller passed the nation's first "stop and frisk" law empowering police to question and detain anyone "reasonably" suspected of criminalized activity, a rebellion erupted on the streets of Harlem and Brooklyn.[49] Sparked by a lethal act of racist police violence, it was among the first of hundreds of urban uprisings that shook US cities between 1964 and 1972.[50] Inspired by the anticolonial struggles sweeping Asia, Africa, Latin America, and the Caribbean, Black radicals in the United States sought to harness this energy into an organized force for overturning the status quo.[51] In doing so, the framework of Civil Rights was increasingly supplanted by "revolutionary nationalism," the idea that Black and other racially oppressed groups in the United States constituted domestic colonies, and that national liberation and socialist revolution were the correct path forward.[52] Although the strategy of nonviolence was never as hegemonic as anointed histories of Black struggle make it out to be,[53] revolutionary nationalist formations positioned self-defense and armed struggle as central to their praxis. As BPP cofounder Huey P. Newton wrote in 1967, "An unarmed people are slaves or subject to slavery at any given moment."[54]

A constellation of repressive state agencies responded to these developments through counterinsurgency strategies developed in global laboratories of empire. Local police "red squads" like the Bureau of Special Services and Investigation in New York hunted radicals under the pretext of law enforcement.[55] In August of 1967, FBI Director J. Edgar Hoover launched "Black Nationalist-Hate Groups," a project collected under COINTELPRO that infamously deployed a range of illegal methods to "expose, disrupt, misdirect, discredit, or otherwise neutralize the activities" of Black radical organizations in general and the BPP in particular.[56] Days later, the CIA inaugurated Operation CHAOS, a lesser-known initiative that aimed to sever links between social movements in the United States and those abroad.[57] Having recently declared a "war on crime," President Lyndon Johnson established the Law Enforcement Assistance Administration (LEAA) in 1968. Modeled after the Office of Public Safety (OPS), a CIA-connected unit within the US Agency for International Development whose mission was to combat global communist revolution, the LEAA bolstered the repressive capacity of the domestic warfare state by dispensing block grants and technical assistance to law enforcement agencies and by working alongside OPS to facilitate the repatriation of counterinsurgency expertise.[58]

One of the unforeseen consequences of this state strategy of repression was that it transformed prisons into key sites of this domestic war and a primary zone of militant Black resistance through what activist Stevie Wilson calls "the imprisoned Black radical tradition."[59] In addition to assassinating political activists and facilitating internecine conflict within leftist organizations, partisans of this carceral warfare project deployed agent provocateurs, political frame-ups, and excessive bail to imprison activists they deemed threatening, thereby removing them from circulation.[60] However, this use of incarceration to "solve" the problem of urban rebellion created the conditions for a new problem: carceral rebellion. It can scarcely be a coincidence that a massive uptick in prison rebellions emerged amid the state's intensified campaign to criminalize Black resistance. Extending the trajectory that emerged in urban zones, prison rebellions proliferated: Ohio in 1968, Minnesota and New Jersey in 1969, New York City and Upstate New

York in 1970, and California and Western New York in 1971. According to one study, forty-eight prisons erupted in 1972, the most in a single year in US history up to that point.[61]

Compelled to update its riot control manual for the first time in more than a decade, the American Correctional Association (ACA) noted new developments in the form as well as the content of these new eruptions. Regarding form, they were increasingly "contagious," an idea that mirrored the anxieties of seventeenth- and eighteenth-century plantocrats who feared that if allowed to develop, slave resistance would spread, infecting otherwise orderly geographies.[62] Regarding content, the ACA found that post-1970 prison rebellions were less likely to emerge as spontaneous outbursts of anger and more likely to be "organized, calculated movements of massive resistance supported and assisted by outside groups and led by intelligent inmates using revolutionary tactics."[63] Moreover, alluding to their maximum demands, the ACA wrote that these new eruptions were increasingly "motivated by a conscious desire to bring about revolutionary improvements in the American social system and to put an end to the devaluation of certain elements of the population by those who are in positions of power."[64] Thus, we see that it was not only rebels but also the state that understood this era of carceral struggle as being about much more than prison conditions and prison reform. Although they erupted within prisons, these rebellions looked beyond them. As I will show, the fact that this is not widely understood today is an effect of prison pacification.

Authored by some of "the best minds in American corrections," the ACA manual sought to reorient carceral systems toward the administration of political warfare. The organization advised prisoncrats to maintain well-equipped riot squads capable of "splitting up the rioters into manageable groups," detailed maps of the physical layout to facilitate the tactical reassertion of control, and updated logs of available weapons and supplies. Based on the theory that all rebellions contain elements of leadership, the manual stressed that rebel leaders should be swiftly identified, "eliminated or rendered ineffective." It also advocated the use of psychological warfare, instructing prisoncrats to be at least as concerned with controlling the public's *perception* of riots as they were with controlling the riots themselves. As such, it urged administrators to cultivate "mutual confidence and understanding" with media outlets to achieve sympathetic coverage. It further indicated that public perception, and not a regard for human life, should be the primary determinant in dealing with hostage situations. Although "a reckless disregard for a hostage's life would not be excused by the public or by his fellow employees," the ACA stressed that prison guards accepted the same risks associated with being a police officer or a soldier. Therefore, determinations about the fate of captured guards should be based on political rather than moral calculations.[65] Published in 1970, the manual reflects the insinuation of counterinsurgency into the normalized routines of prison management, a process that would only intensify over time.

While the FBI's use of illegal covert actions to neutralize movements outside prison walls have been well documented, its use of similar methods inside prison walls are not well known. On August 21, 1970, one year to the day before George Jackson was assassinated in San Quentin Prison, Hoover launched a program of *carceral* counterintelligence. What became known as the Prison Activists Surveillance Program (PRISACTS) was first exposed by the legal team of Dhoruba bin-Wahad, a BPP/BLA political prisoner who the FBI helped frame for the attempted murder of two NYPD patrolmen in 1971. As a result of protracted lawsuits against the Bureau, the NYPD, and the New York Department of Correctional Services (NY DOCS), bin-Wahad, along with attorneys Elizabeth Fink,[66] Robert J. Boyle, and others, proved that the conviction was secured through the prosecution's illegal withholding of exculpatory evidence.[67] Not only did this result in a reversal of bin-Wahad's conviction and his release from prison in 1990,[68] it yielded more than three hundred thousand pages of documents pertaining to clandestine government repression of domestic dissent, including the Bureau's targeting of those whom incarceration had failed to "neutralize." After safeguarding these materials for decades, bin-Wahad and Boyle entrusted me with several boxes from this massive archive.

Since the rigorous study of war necessitates attention to both sides of the struggle, *Tip of the Spear* pulls extensively from archives of white supremacy and repression. Acquired from the personal collections of veterans like bin-Wahad and others, as well as state repositories and Freedom of Information Act requests, these documents attest to a constantly mutating statecraft of counterinsurgency across prison walls. Recognizing that the state seeks to criminalize and incarcerate Black radical knowledge while stabilizing its own legitimacy, I analyze these hostile sources through a rebellious and disloyal interpretive paradigm.[69] Just as the effective conduct of revolutionary war demands mobility, flexibility, and creativity, so too does its historical interpretation. I therefore deploy carceral sources—surveillance files, official investigations, prison records, police reports, and mainstream journalism—in varied ways depending on context. In some moments I cite them to corroborate what people have told me. In others, I invoke them to expose silences, distortions, and redactions in narratives of domination or to demystify the racist and patriarchal logics of the permanent war machine.[70] In any case, my simultaneous reading of carceral and Black radical sources—a method I call archival war—generates epistemic antagonisms that I make no effort to resolve. To the contrary, I underscore these antagonisms as evidence of a war that unfolds on material, cognitive, narrative, and epistemological terrains.[71]

By expropriating evidence from carceral archives, I am able to illuminate prison pacification in the process of formation. Frantically reacting to the crisis his FBI helped create, Hoover explained to a Special Agent in Albany that top priority should be given to what he termed "Black Extremist Activities in Penal Institutions," a term that discloses the structuring anti-Blackness of this carceral war. In a March 9, 1971, memo, he wrote: "There is no question that a definite link is being established between the extremely dangerous black [sic] extremist organizations such as the BPP and black extremist groups operating within the penal system in this country. Likewise, there is no doubt regarding the fact that the black extremists in our penal institutions are increasingly responsible for fomenting discord within the penal system including extortion, blackmail, rioting and the holding of hostages in furtherance of their revolutionary aims."[72] It was imperative, Hoover stressed, that agents "develop sources of information among prison officials in each penal institution" and ascertain "the identity of all suspect black revolutionary extremists" as well as "details regarding their revolutionary activities and the forming of any black extremist groups similar to the BPP." Moreover, "arrangements should be made to be advised in advance of the release of any revolutionary black extremists" to enable the Bureau to "open [an] investigation to follow his activities immediately after release."[73]

The operations of state power and secrecy preclude us from obtaining proof of illegal government activity.[74] However, an abundance of evidence suggests FBI involvement in assassinating imprisoned revolutionaries just as it does with their counterparts in the "free world."[75] Moreover, captive rebels have long argued that many who evaded physical assassination were subjected to technologies of "living death," including sensory deprivation, behavior modification, "brain warfare" and "mind control" experiments.[76] Entitled "The War on Black Revolutionary Minds," chapter 6 discusses episodes that are often dismissed as conspiracy theories or examples of "racial paranoia."[77] And yet this hesitancy to pursue seemingly outlandish or unprovable claims has hindered our understanding of historical development and the political dynamics in play. Many of the events explored throughout this book cannot be "proven" according to positivist standards of Truth because powerful actors strove to conceal their actions.

Critically, coercion is not the only weapon in the arsenal of this carceral war machine. Authors of counterinsurgency doctrine stress the imperative of calibrating terror-inducing violence with solicitous reforms. The US Army *Counterinsurgency Field Manual* notes that "auxiliaries might be co-opted by economic or political reforms, while fanatic combatants will most likely have to be killed or captured."[78] Measures designed to rectify "genuine grievances" and "increase prosperity" deprive insurgents of issues that can be exploited to foment popular unrest, explains Frank Kitson, a British counterinsurgency expert whose *Low Intensity Operations: Subversion, Insurgency and Peacekeeping* was central to the development of COINTELPRO and PRISACTS.[79] "They [intelligent inmate leaders] can be neutralized to a considerable extent by prompt management attention to widespread correctable grievances," notes the ACA.[80] *Tip of the Spear* engages with repression and reform as complementary tactics of war that facilitate what scholars have variously termed "movement absorption," "movement capture," "movement channeling," and the "institutionalization of dissent." These terms describe the strategy of encapsulating the potentially disruptive claims, demands, and tactics of movements within liberal institutions and discourses, which transform them into routinized processes that legitimize rather than challenge established authority.[81] Without an understanding of this critical aspect of counterinsurgency theory and practice, weaponized reforms will continue to thwart the development of revolutionary and abolitionist projects as well as their analysis and historicization.

In many cases reform, a hallmark of liberalism, involves little more than the use of obfuscating language that aims to reshape the political and epistemological terrain of struggle.[82] Operating in a context of anticommunist counterinsurgency at the height of the Cold War, expert propagandist Paul Linebarger dubbed this "nomenclatural reform."[83] In 1970, nearly twenty years later, New York's carceral system underwent what Ricardo DeLeon, an imprisoned Black Panther, called a "euphemistic baptism."[84] Prisons became "Correctional Institutions," guards "Correctional Officers," and Wardens "Superintendents," with similar rhetorical shifts occurring at the national level.[85] These nomenclatural reforms and euphemistic baptisms were part of a broader strategy of psychological warfare through which counterinsurgency intellectuals aimed to present a benign public image of prisons without in any way altering their repressive and dehumanizing function within the social order. Readers will notice my obdurate refusal to normalize those reformist vernaculars. This is a rhetorical strategy of counter-war that strives to destabilize the epistemic dominance of the state.

Interestingly, the event that brought Queen Mother Moore to Green Haven emerged out of this context of reformist counterinsurgency. Introduced as a direct response to Attica, prison-based Community Day events were among a constellation of "humanizing reforms" that incorporated the Revolt's minimum demands in order to pacify rebellion. After Attica, as I show in chapter 5, New York prisoncrats began opening their prisons to outsiders as a tactic of control. Although publicly celebrated as a "win" for movements behind the walls, this tactic was essentially a bribe. It allowed prison authorities to dangle the opportunity for captives to commune with their loved ones and partake in these periodic "bursts of gaiety," as the *New York Times* described such events, in exchange for their compliance with administratively defined standards of "good behavior."[86] That Moore entered this allegedly humanized space and nurtured a Black militant consciousness that authorities sought to tame demonstrates her political acuity and illustrates a difficult to perceive psychological layer of this war.

These multifaceted tactics of state repression index the dynamism of the movements they aimed to contain, signifying the extent to which the prison rebellions of the 1970s posed a material and symbolic threat to the social order. These highly politicized, self-organized, anti-carceral eruptions demonstrated that the most despotic institutions in US society could not contain a rising tide of collective striving for liberation. Moreover, national and international support for these movements signaled a widespread view of the state as illegitimate, as lacking the authority to criminalize populations and banish them from the realm of rights, humanity, and civilization.

By recasting the prison as war and tracing the collision of the Long Attica Revolt against imperial technologies of pacification, *Tip of the Spear* provides a counter-history of the contemporary carceral landscape. Readers will not be rewarded with a comforting resolution, nor will they find prescriptions for future action. To seek any such prescription in an academic book is a fool's errand. What this text provides is an archive and a theory-driven narration exposing a war that has been intentionally concealed. Although its geographic focus is New York

State, it yields a wealth of new insights about Black radical politics and state repression that are global in scope and critical to understanding the current political moment. It shows that without understanding carceral spaces as zones of undeclared domestic war, zones that are inextricably linked to imperial and officially acknowledged wars abroad, we cannot fully understand how and why the United States became the global leader of incarceration that it is today. It is my belief that with a consciousness that they, that we, inhabit war, communities of struggle will be in a better position to live through, organize against, and abolish it.

PART ONE

The Long Attica Revolt

CHAPTER 1

Sharpening the Spear

*Strategies and Tactics of
Revolutionary Action*

During the late afternoon of October 2, 1970, six incarcerated men marched across the interior courtyard of the Long Island City branch of the Queens House of Detention, known commonly as "Branch Queens," and approached a cluster of microphones perched atop two folding tables. In front of them stood a phalanx of print, radio, and television journalists, police officers, Department of Correction (DOC) guards, elected officials, and community leaders, as well as DOC Commissioner George F. McGrath. Behind them, anonymous faces were visible through broken but still barred windows. What could not be seen were the six DOC guards who had been taken hostage and sequestered somewhere in the jail's interior. The jail's entire captive population—335 human beings—had exploded in rebellion the previous day. Over the next several hours, captives in four more New York City jails would rebel and in ensuing months, an anticarceral Revolt would traverse the Empire State.

Recorded by CBS-TV, the public statements of Victor Martinez, an elected rebel spokesman, demystify the political stakes of this unfolding struggle. Martinez, a member of the Young Lords Party (YLP), situated this militant collective action within the longue durée of resistance to racial-colonial violence. "This system . . . has oppressed us for the last 400 years and we're here to put a stop to it," he proclaimed, his voice quivering with rage.[1] Martinez's analysis contradicted that of DOC officials, who preferred to frame the "disorder" as a reaction to jail conditions, especially overcrowding. While the brutal density of the environment—the fact that human beings were packed two, three, and sometimes four to a cage designed for one—no doubt stoked their discontent, Martinez and others understood themselves to be engaged in a struggle that exceeded the spatial boundaries of a given institution and the temporal confines of the historical present. They conceptualized their captivity as only the latest iteration of a regime that had ensnared colonized people for centuries. By relocating the rebellion's historical point of origin from jail conditions to the violence at the core of Western modernity, Martinez constructed the rebels as legitimate political actors, indeed as anticolonial revolutionaries who had taken bold and necessary steps to halt a transgenerational onslaught.

In what follows I trace the rise and fall of the New York City jail rebellion, the opening chapter of the Long Attica Revolt. I explore how figures like Martinez and many others—the Revolt's organic intellectuals, elected spokesmen, and hidden engineers—labored to steer the collective rage of the wretched in a revolutionary direction. I analyze their public-facing demands while ultimately looking beyond them, toward the internal dynamics of their insurgent organization, processes of self-governance, and anticarceral strategy. I also explore how the rebels and the state negotiated the role of violence in achieving their objectives.

As I have already argued, "tip of the spear" is a military idiom for that which creates a breach in the enemy's defenses. Forced behind enemy lines, behind walls erected to preserve the existing social order, incarcerated people possess a latent insurgent potential. Detailing a process I call "sharpening the spear," this chapter shows how jail captives began to pull themselves together, honing their capacity to act as a unit, preparing themselves to strategically engage in a war that had surrounded them and saturated their very being. Making their tactical victories legible, I show how this besieged population managed to exert political leverage from within one of the most repressive institutions in US society, succeeded in radicalizing populations on both sides of the walls, and inaugurated a paradigm of revolutionary struggle that intensified over time.

DISPATCHES FROM THE TOMBS

The August 11, 1970, edition of the *New York Times* featured a list of demands authored in the Manhattan House of Detention, an infamous jail popularly known as the Tombs. The carefully worded statement assailed the city courts for allowing legions of the poor to languish in decrepit cages for months without trial and for ignoring their writs and petitions seeking legal redress. It accused the Legal Aid Society, a nonprofit organization charged with defending them, of encouraging the accused to accept plea deals that railroaded them to prison. The authors framed the judiciary as a rationalized instrument of violence, from which "we cannot receive any justice and can only suffer threat, coercion and intimidation disguised as law and justice."

Their dispatch denounced jail conditions: moldy food, lack of clothing, restricted access to law books, overcrowding, infestations of lice, roaches, mice, and rats. They accused their keepers of subjecting them, and especially the Blacks and Puerto Ricans, to incessant physical violence. It was common practice, they wrote, for guards to "beat ... defenseless inmate[s] into unconsciousness, often injuring [them] for life physically and mentally or both." Demanding the immediate cessation of this "system of brutality and dehumanization and injustice," they signed the document, "WE ARE ONE PEOPLE."[2] As we will see again and again, this statement is the core aspiration of the Long Attica Revolt.

Though authored in a specific institution, this document was relevant across the jail system, a network of institutions distributed across four city boroughs and Rikers Island. Written for a general audience, it was a *measured* critique of what was seen in radical circles as a concentration camp system that aimed to dehumanize and liquidate the racialized poor. In the wake of the rebellion, a jail official who was far from a radical declared, "If we kept our animals in the Central Park Zoo in the way we cage fellow human beings in the Tombs, a citizens committee would be organized and prominent community leaders would be protesting the inhumanity of our society."[3]

Discourses of "criminal justice" legitimized this race and class war. Between 1967 and 1970, the jail population nearly doubled; a system built for fewer than eight thousand people now confined more than fourteen thousand.[4] Although a moral panic about rising crime suggested otherwise, misdemeanor and discretionary arrests drove this growth.[5] Moreover, the majority of the city's captives were "pretrial detainees," meaning they had not been convicted of the crimes of which they were accused. Rather, they were in jail because they were either denied bail or, as was more often the case, could not afford to pay the bail set by a judge.[6]

The official purpose of bail is to ensure that the accused appear at trial, while also protecting their civil liberties before the trial takes place. However, as historian Toussaint Losier has argued, this moment was increasingly characterized by the political use of bail as a strategy of "preventive detention": a means of incapacitating economically surplus and politically restive populations.[7] Bail enabled judges to remove people from circulation and preempt certain behaviors deemed threatening.[8] A clear attack on the poor; it was common for pretrial detainees to languish behind bars for six, twelve, or eighteen months on bail amounts as low as $100.[9] Those lucky enough to reach their scheduled hearing date were handcuffed and marched from the jail to a courthouse, where they were crammed into court detention pens, another set of dark, hot, filthy, cages, and forced to wait for several hours to be called for arraignment. And even then, their proceedings could be delayed, forcing their return to the jail. One captive likened it "to being suspended in reality for an indefinite period of time."[10]

Amid conditions of extreme duress, the dregs of the capitalist order began to fashion themselves anew. Out of the necessity of survival, they organized political formations that built on their diverse experiences in street gangs, crime syndicates, the US military, and groups like the BPP and the YLP. Through radical study, deliberation, and debate—a process often described as "iron sharpening iron"—they began to forge solidarity across various lines of difference and collectively analyze the deep structures that produced their incarceration within these hellish human zoos. By 1970, "a new spirit" had emerged within the jail.[11] As one of the rebellion's survivors later told the press, "The other times I was in, prisoners were sort of conditioned to accept brutality. . . . There was a feeling that if you said something or complained, you were a punk. It's different now. People were not giving in."[12]

Among the many who nurtured this new spirit, who helped sharpen the spear and fuse the population into one people, was a ghostly figure named Casper Baker Gary. We will take a closer look at Casper in chapter 4, but for now let us note that he was radicalized through his incarceration in Clinton and Attica during the 1960s. Prisoncrats labeled him a Muslim, a Panther, a "black militant agitator and political activist."[13] He was a nonconformist, a practitioner of what I call "mad science," whose ethical philosophy, political ideology, and system of knowledge did not cleave to established paradigms of thought. In November of 1969, while languishing in the Tombs on a parole violation, Casper authored the "Prisoners Injustice Resistance and Survival Manual," a secret document that aimed to foster "a spirit of UNITY and SOLIDARITY based on the reality of a common OPPRESSION."[14]

The manual delineates an ambitious vision for the development of a new organization called the Prisoners Liberation Front (PLF). Casper imagined the PLF as a disciplined formation capable of coordinating political activities among people held captive across city jails and state prisons, as well as hospitals, where rebellions were also emerging, and "all other institutions in which any person is made to unwillingly remain."[15] As per the manual, each carceral site would develop its own PLF chapter; each chapter would be divided into branches, which in turn would be further subdivided into sections. Sections were to consist of "two or more prisoners residing in the same side, tier, or dorm . . . and shall be named after the institution in which it functions, as for instance: Tombs Prisoners Liberation Front—8th floor—C Side Section." The organization would be administered by officers tasked with clearly defined roles pertaining to political education, intelligence gathering, communications, propaganda, healthcare, finance, and security. Casper laid out the expectations of each role with meticulous attention to detail. For example, the Information Officer was expected to "keep, in secret codes, essential records for the SECTION, and for transmission elsewhere. Will be responsible for the obtaining of news items, articles and essays for publication in the NEWSPAPER. Will also concern himself with obtaining and circulating Revolutionary literature."[16]

The development of autonomous capacities for acquiring, preserving, and transmitting knowledge are indispensable to the conduct of revolutionary warfare and, as I will show in the second part of this book, these capacities were seen as especially threatening to the state.

PLF membership was to be extended to those who took an oath swearing to support the ideas contained in the manual. This is highly significant, as oathtaking has been a core feature of insurgent movements across a range of contexts. Oaths figured prominently in the conduct of maroon resistance of the seventeenth century, the French Revolution of the eighteenth century, the so-called Mau Mau Emergency of the twentieth century, and in the far-right Oath Keepers movement of our contemporary moment.[17] Oaths signify the consecration of an individual's loyalty to a collective and their active withdrawal of support from opposing forces. By introducing this oathtaking process into the prison, Casper sought to force captives to formally declare which side of the war they were on and to constantly demonstrate that commitment. PLF members were enjoined to always greet each other with "the CLENCHED FIST SALUTE" while declaring "ALL POWER TO THE PEOPLE!"[18]

Casper was transferred to the state prison system before the Tombs erupted in rebellion, but not before his ideas left their mark on the population. Not only would PLF chapters later emerge throughout the state prison system, but six months later, Victor Martinez helped organized a similarly named organization that performed many of the functions set forth in Casper's manual. As Martinez told *The Black Panther*, the Inmates Liberation Front (ILF) "began as a committee of two people, which grew to four and then kept multiplying until we were able to organize the complete ninth floor."[19] ILF branches spread to other floors and eventually to the world outside the walls, where they were incorporated into the YLP. Tombs ILF members facilitated study groups under the guise of playing innocuous card games. They also established and surreptitiously circulated a handwritten newspaper called *The Inmates Forum*, which had an estimated circulation of two hundred at its peak.[20] While the relationship between the PLF and the ILF is unclear, what is clear is that on the eve of the jail rebellion, captives increasingly saw themselves as political agents capable of transforming their material conditions and the broader world.

Though it began with these furtive processes of sharpening the spear, the Long Attica Revolt announced itself to the world on August 10, 1970. On that day, Tombs captives on the ILF stronghold of the ninth floor captured five hostages and demanded an audience with the authorities. Hours later, Commissioner McGrath entered the jail and participated in what a mayoral aide called a "long, loud and angry face-to-face meeting" with Victor Martinez and others, including Herbert X Blyden, who would later be elected as a spokesman in Attica. After extracting promises that DOC would not retaliate, and that the captives' long-ignored grievances would be published by the elite press, the rebels released their hostages unharmed. A writer for *The Black Panther* recognized that although their most legible demands were for rights, their tactics signified a much deeper demand. "Finally, the accumulated frustration, desperation and rage of the prisoners was transferred into a flaming determination to better their plight by taking the only form of action that the pigs of the power structure relate to—revolutionary action."[21]

The grievances appeared in the *New York Times* the following morning. As if to punctuate their urgency, that afternoon captives confined to the psychiatric unit on the fourth floor accosted three guards by leaping on them from a catwalk twelve feet above.[22] Rebellion then spread to the fifth, seventh, and eighth floors, until more than eight hundred rebels were in control of most of the facility. They swarmed throughout the jail assaulting the physical expression of their degradation: they set fire to bedding, destroyed their medical records, smashed windows, and threw handwritten messages, burning trash, and dead rats onto the downtown Manhattan streets. After reiterating their demands they again released their hostages unharmed.[23] These actions were demonstrations of the captives' capacity to inflict what Huey P. Newton called a "political consequence."[24] They were warnings about what was to come if the minimum demands for ameliorating jail conditions were not addressed.

Although they no longer held leverage over the lives of hostages, the rebels remained in control of portions of the Tombs for ten more days. During this period of limited self-rule, they continued to sharpen the spear, discussing ways of exercising power despite their physical incapacitation. One idea involved taking their case before the United Nations, where the captives would argue their conditions violated the Geneva Convention relative to the Treatment of Prisoners of War, the Statement on the Treatment of Criminal Offenders, and the provisions related to the crime of genocide. While this plan never came to fruition, its ideation was indicative of an "abolitionist internationalism" that would reach its fullest expression in Attica (chapter 3).[25]

Experimenting with another form of leverage, the rebels organized a boycott of the courts. As Melvin Alston, a surviving jail rebel, told me: "Our strategy was to completely withdraw our participation. We felt that if none of us went to court, we could back the system up even more than it already was and force them to concede to our demands."[26] The move received coverage in the elite press, with the *New York Times* reporting that on August 17, only 94 out of the 190 detainees scheduled for hearings appeared in court. The action also spread across the East River to Branch Queens, which had an even lower court turnout, with only 13 out of 100 people on the schedule appearing before a judge. An enthusiastic participant in the boycott, Melvin recalls how he was tricked into appearing in court. He was told his parents had come to see him, but when he arrived at what he thought was a visiting area, he was greeted by a judge, who summarily sentenced him to ten years in prison. From there he was loaded onto a bus and shipped upstate.[27]

The opening salvo of the Long Attica Revolt concluded on August 20, when eighty state agents stormed the Tombs and violently reasserted control.[28] Commissioner McGrath then authorized a mass transfer in which two-thirds of the Tombs's population, including Martinez, were transferred to Branch Queens. He later cited the fact that captives were no longer forced to sleep in the hallways and on floors as evidence that his administration was following through on its promises to improve conditions. However, a captive named Curtis Brown saw things differently. For Brown, who would play a key role in the rebellion's next phase, DOC didn't solve the problem. "What they did was transfer the problem from the Tombs to Queens."[29]

TURNABOUT DAY

The Revolt developed in dialectical relation to state tactics of domestic war against radical social movements. In 1969, the same year that J. Edgar Hoover infamously deemed the BPP "the greatest threat to the internal security of the country," armed agents of the state intensified their efforts to "neutralize" radical left movements, especially the BPP.[30] One study calculated that by year's end, 749 Panthers were arrested and jailed, 24 were killed by police, and scores more were injured.[31] As planned, this strategy deprived the Party of some of its most dedicated members. However, the incarcerated targets of COINTELPRO repression continued to organize behind the walls, fueling anticarceral rebellion. Responding to this development the day after DOC reasserted control in the Tombs, Hoover urged the Bureau to pay closer attention to carceral institutions: "Recruiting activities of black extremist groups, establishment of such groups within penal institutions, plans made for violent action by these groups and overall racial picture within penal institutions are of definite interest to Bureau and many other agencies."[32]

The state employed the preventive detention strategy that it used in a generalized way against populations deemed "surplus" in a targeted fashion against Black revolutionaries. On April 2, 1969, the NYPD executed coordinated predawn raids, capturing several members of New York's BPP. Each of the Panther 21, as they came to be known, were held on $100,000 bail and indicted on a range of fabricated charges, including conspiring to assassinate police officers and bomb police stations, the subway system, department stores, and other public places. A prosecutor later explained that the indictment was intentionally worded to paint the Panthers as terrorists, disseminate prejudicial information to potential jurors, and "legitimize warlike responses by the state."[33] Reflecting on the absurdity of this ordeal, BPP/BLA member Assata Shakur would later write, "It was well known by everybody in the movement that the New York police had kidnapped the most experienced, able, and intelligent leaders of the New York branch and demanded $100,000 ransom for each one."[34] Four months later, in a lesser-known case dubbed the "mini-Panther trial" by the press, four more New York Panthers were captured, charged with conspiracy, and held on $50,000 bail, this time for a planned expropriation of the New Duston Hotel, a known Harlem drug market.[35]

Kuwasi Balagoon, one of the Panther 21, later called the commencement of the Branch Queens rebellion "turnabout day."[36] This statement was fitting, not only because the rebellion reversed the relations of power within the institution, relations between the keepers and the kept, but also because the Branch Queens rebels were responding to the broader strategy of state repression that had produced their incarceration. It began at noon on October 1, 1970, when captives on the fourth floor forced their way through a gate, rammed a guard against the concrete wall, and demanded his keys. After incarcerating him and others on what Balagoon called "the right side of the bars for a change," they uncaged the entire population, including nine members of the Panther 21, who DOC had been holding in political quarantine in an isolated wing of the jail.[37]

Upon seizing power, the rebels began to discipline their movement into a durable form of organization. They held elections, selecting as their leaders three members of the Panther 21—Balagoon, Lumumba Shakur, and Kwando Kinshasa—along with Victor Martinez and two politically unaffiliated captives, one Black, the other white. With their leadership committee intact they fortified their positions, barricaded entry points, established guard posts, assigned rotating sentries, and developed a system for carrying messages to different areas of the jail. Announcing an incipient challenge to US territorial sovereignty, they hung a red, black, and green flag out of the top floor window. It represented Pan-African unity and a declaration of what anticolonial revolutionaries in Mozambique called "semi-liberated zones," spaces from which colonial forces had been expelled and where insurgent self-governance could be actively nourished.[38]

The Branch Queens demands reflected the captives' desire to engage with broader political struggles. In addition to affirming the published Tombs demands, the rebels demanded an end to censorship and asserted their right to read *The Black Panther* and *Palante*, the YLP's official organ. They also called for more Black people to be assigned to the Panther 21 jury and for the release of Panther 21 member Afeni Shakur, whose bail from the Women's House of Detention had recently been revoked. Rehearsing a strategy that would later be used in Attica, they called for the presence of neutral observers to oversee any future negotiations and pressure DOC to keep its promises. Finally, in an effort to

FIGURE 1. Rebels incarcerated in Branch Queens standing below a sign that reads "We don't want token pacification. We want 1-reasonable bails, 2-hearings, 3-fast speed and fair trials NOW!" Photo: Getty Images.

communicate with the public on their own terms, they called for a press conference.[39]

These demands reflected a key tension within the Long Attica Revolt: the co-existence of ameliorative and revolutionary yearnings. These often-contradictory ambitions were evident in Martinez's remarks, his appeal to liberal-democratic values at one moment, and his transgression of those values at another. He stressed the demand for "basic rights of dignity, respect, and justice," then invoked an irrational and utopian aspiration. "This is not a protest. This is not a riot. This is a whole *thing*," he explained. "We are going to create a paradise out of this hell!"[40] The rebellion was at once a struggle for recognition within the existing social order and a struggle to upend that order. Drawing a distinction between this rebellion and the one back in August, where hostages were released soon after they were captured, Martinez let it be known that he and his comrades were prepared to make the ultimate sacrifice: "We are ready to die and *kill* until you pigs give us back our rights."[41]

The press conference marked a turning point in the rebellion. As it was taking place, captives in the Tombs seized hostages for the third time in as many months. Curtis Brown later explained that upon catching live news coverage of the Branch Queens rebellion, captives in the Tombs decided to expand the struggle to a second site.[42] As they were in transit on the eleventh floor a small group sprang out of line, split into two formations, and seized physical control of the guards. Ricardo DeLeon explained to the *Village Voice*, "The actual take-over was executed perfectly, like clockwork. It was a complete surprise—a classic guerrilla operation."[43] DeLeon was a Vietnam veteran and a defendant in the mini-Panther trial. He and Brown were elected to a "revolutionary committee" and, following the lead of their counterparts in Manhattan, they captured hostages, erected defensive fortifications, and affirmed the minimum demands.[44]

Later that night, captives in another jail, the Queens House of Detention at Kew Gardens (QHD), opened a third front of struggle. At 9:00 p.m. a torrent of enraged humanity sabotaged state property, set several fires, and tore through the tiers. Though they took no hostages, roughly 900 rebels seized six of the jail's eight floors. The *New York Times* described the situation as "one of the most serious crises in the history of the city prisons. More than 1,400 inmates in three jails were in command of scores of cellblocks and were holding a total of 23 hostages—including three guard captains, 14 guards and six civilian employees."[45] And the crisis continued to deepen. On October 3, nearly 1,500 rebels in the Brooklyn House of Detention (BHD) seized three more hostages and gained control of seven out of the institution's nine floors.[46] The American Correctional Association's warning about the dangers of "contagious" rebellions had come to fruition.[47]

Although they had declared themselves "one people," this multisited rebellion was riddled with internal contradictions. DeLeon explained that while the revolutionary committee was "hassling with the administration, developing lines of communication with the outside through various reporters and interested parties who came to the roofs of the buildings facing the jail," disruptive elements emerged from within: "All the divisive influences began to make themselves manifest; quarrels and fights were developing in the ranks about the dumbest things—food, cigarettes, candy, and pills. Some of the committee members were on ego trips; the pill heads were running around creating confusion, fighting. Ethnic animosity between blacks and Puerto Ricans was smoldering, fanned by ignorance and fear of the oppressor. . . . Between dealing with pigs and trying to maintain a united front, all our efforts were being dissipated on ineffectual activity."[48]

Curtis Brown agreed that drugs were a major barrier to organization. He was a recovering addict who had kicked his habit by handcuffing himself to a radiator, subsequently making it his mission to help others free themselves of addiction by teaching them how to "replace drugs with politics." He told a producer at WBAI-FM that he "didn't sleep at all while we was up there"—that during the rebellion, most of his time was spent confiscating drugs from the population. Notably, this antidrug policy ran contrary to the jail's normal operation; according to an investigation of the Tombs, "pills [were] dispensed like popcorn at a bad movie."[49]

There was also an important contradiction between the pretrial majority and the roughly three thousand captives who had been convicted of crimes and were serving short sentences. Many from the latter category were employed in jobs to perform the "reproductive labor" of the jail—that is, they cooked the food and did building maintenance and custodial services. Unlike the detainees, who were held in limbo, the "Time Men," as they were called, had set release dates to look forward to and often lived in their own section of the jail where conditions were substantially better than for the general population. Following the takeover, the Time Men of QHD smuggled out a letter pleading with prisoncrats to allow them safe passage out of the jail or at least to send in sandwiches to keep them from going hungry. They assured the authorities, "We stand in a neutral position as not one time man has participated in any act of aggression against the institution."[50] The Time Men's desire to be recognized as a neutral party exposes one of the many fault lines between differently situated fractions of the population.

Balagoon wrote of an incident over bean pies that were delivered to the Branch Queens rebels by the Nation of Islam. The popular desserts arrived at night, while most were asleep. "The thought was that it would be best to pass them out to those who were awake, since 90 percent of those awake had been carrying the burden of most of the responsibilities," he explained. There were enough to go around, but a few people devoured the remaining pies such that "a sizable amount of inmates did not receive any."[51] In a context where food is characteristically deployed as a technology of control, a weapon of war, this culturally significant dessert represented a meaningful source of sustenance and pleasure in an otherwise drab environment.[52]

In his autobiography Balagoon, who would soon declare himself an anarchist, did not elaborate on the impact this affront had on the morale of the rebels and if or how those who took more than their fair share were held accountable. However, the fact that he discusses this challenge at all evinces an interest in the mechanics of self-governance and the equitable distribution of resources.[53] If the rebellion was going to succeed and evolve into a full-blown revolution, as Balagoon, Martinez, and others hoped it would, the rebels would have to develop autonomous systems capable of meeting their needs. In this way, the seemingly trivial bean pie incident signified deeper challenges for how the rebels would organize the world they sought to build from the ground up.

These fissures and tensions clarify the significance of Casper Baker Gary's manual. His attempt to forge discipline and unity through organization, education, and oathtaking reflected an understanding that in the face of opposition, solidarity had to be nurtured, defended, and indeed enforced. "Any PRISONER who actively opposes the REVOLUTION should be eliminated as soon as possible. Otherwise, they will corrupt all meaningful progress," his manual states.[54] As will soon become clear, the inability of the rebels to develop the level of unity Casper called for contributed to the rebellion's collapse.

A LEGAL JAILBREAK

It was in this context that Branch Queens became the site of a bail review hearing unlike any that had occurred previously or since. During the press conference, the rebels announced their plan to expose the violence of the bail system. They released two hostages as a show of good faith and promised to release two more if New York State Supreme Court judges were brought to the jail to review their cases. If this did not happen, however, the rebels announced their readiness to carry out executions.[55]

The authorities conceded, a decision that took them into uncharted legal territory. As one official noted, "We were being asked . . . to set a legal precedent that was logistically impossible and probably illegal."⁵⁶ Figuring things out on the fly, a coterie of judges, mayoral aides, and attorneys convened in the Manhattan office of Frank Hogan, prosecutor in the Panther 21 case. There they examined the case files and court records of forty-seven bail candidates who had been selected by the rebels.⁵⁷ As per a previous agreement, none of the Panther cases would be reviewed, nor would any involving homicide, armed robbery, or kidnapping.⁵⁸

And so it was that for several hours on October 3, 1970, a three-judge panel held court on the grounds of a jail controlled by criminals, radicals, and revolutionaries. Lawyers, police, media, and the elected spokesmen of the rebellion packed the small anteroom. One by one the judges, seated at the end of a long conference table, called the names on their list. Fresh out of law school, Gerald Lefcourt, a young white attorney for the Panther 21, had no doubt that his clients would have killed the remaining hostages had the hearings not taken place. "They were all so serious," he recalled. "And the Panthers were facing life and assumed that they would do life."⁵⁹

Gilberto Jimenez was the first name called. Like all who came after him, he stepped forward and named Lefcourt as his legal counsel. Jimenez had been awaiting trial on a charge of possessing stolen property. The judges reviewed his case file and criminal record, conferred briefly with each other, and summarily reduced his bail from $500 to zero. Although he was still facing charges, he was now free to leave on his own recognizance. The sound of the gavel rapping against the table signified the finality of the decision. Jimenez was then escorted out of the gates of Branch Queens, but not before embracing each of the organizers in a show of gratitude. He immediately joined the Young Lords Party and continued to support the Revolt as part of the ILF.⁶⁰

The judges reached the same conclusion in eight other cases, reducing established bails to zero and cutting captives loose on the spot. An additional four men had their bails reduced to $25 each and were also able to walk out the front gates after the supporters amassed outside pooled the $100 necessary to post the bails.⁶¹ All told thirteen men, many of whom had languished in jail for more than a year, were set free in a matter of hours. This was an astonishing confirmation, not only of the captives' long-standing indictment against the state for conspiring to keep them locked up, but also of the legitimacy of their rebellion and their use of political violence. A local politician was convinced that "had the judges stayed to hear all 460 cases, at least 400 of those men would have been freed on the spot."⁶² This did not happen. Instead, after presiding over these initial cases, the judges disregarded the other thirty-five names on the list, terminating the hearings. While he was pleased to see Jimenez and the others leave, Balagoon saw the reductions as a token gesture. "[They] didn't dig submitting to anything close to justice, but just did as much as they had to," he wrote later.[63]

As we sat in his Manhattan office and discussed these events nearly fifty years after they occurred, Lefcourt said the experience was "one of the most unusual things I've ever lived through or heard about. It was the first ever 'legal' jailbreak."[64] His apt pairing of the antonyms "legal" and "jailbreak" exposes how the rebels' mobilization of collective disorder and lawbreaking produced a favorable outcome that was sanctioned by law. In that small anteroom, the objects of law destabilized the state's monopoly over the legitimate use of violence and exerted power over and through the agents of law. Under the threat of violence from below, the legal system surmounted its massive backlog and circumvented the "procedural inefficiencies" that were supposedly the cause of the ballooning detention population. The event had a profound impact on Lefcourt's political development and that of a whole generation of "radical lawyers," who increasingly came to understand themselves as the legal support arm of a revolutionary movement unfolding on the streets and within the jails of the United States.[65]

Imprisoned revolutionaries approached the hearings as a means of delegitimizing the state. Given the rebels' incapacity to win a Gramscian war of maneuver against a militarily and technologically superior enemy,[66] they organized the hearing as an act of political theater, dramatizing the legal system's dereliction of its duty to provide equal protection under the law for a sizable fraction of its subjects. As a result of their militant action, human beings were released from the teeth of the state, exposing the violence of judicial discretion and affirming the rebels' claims that they were being subjected to a genocidal conspiracy. Yet there was a contradiction here too. By forcing the judiciary to adhere to its own standards—that the criminally charged should be presumed innocent, be granted due process of law, and receive speedy trials—their legal jailbreak could be viewed as an acquiescence to state authority. As legal theorist Isaac D. Balbus explains, "Those who would argue that delegitimation can result from the failure of law to live up to its 'promises' . . . fail to understand that the legitimation of the legal order is not primarily a function of its ability to live up to its claims or 'redeem its pledges' but rather of the fact that its claims or pledges are valued in the first place."[67]

From this perspective, one might be tempted to view the hearing as an appeal for the system to reform itself in accordance with its stated principles. While many within and beyond the rebellion saw the movement in this way, it is critical to understand that this struggle unfolded amid a robust revolutionary culture. Two years earlier, Queen Mother Moore and other citizens of the newly formed Provisional Government of the Republic of New Afrika, a Black revolutionary formation that sought to secede from the United States, signed a Declaration of Independence. In the spring of the following year, BPP chapters began organizing People's Tribunals, makeshift court proceedings in which community members adjudicated conflicts, determined the guilt or innocence of the accused, and handed down penalties on their own authority. The Party organ described these tribunals as "the only legitimate and just recourse that Black people have to redress their grievances."[68] At the same time, the Party was in the early stages of organizing a Revolutionary People's Constitutional Convention where they planned to convene representatives from various radical left organizations on the campus of Howard University in Washington, DC, in order to author and ratify a new constitution that reimagined the United States as a democratic and anti-imperialist formation. The bail review hearing must be understood within this broader revolutionary imaginary in which efforts to hold the state accountable to its own law coexisted with attempts to delegitimize established law and efforts to establish new law.[69]

CONCERNING VIOLENCE

Violence lay at the core of this conflict and both sides had important considerations concerning its use. When captives, an already criminalized and dishonored population, attacked jail infrastructure, seized hostages, and threatened them with execution, they defied the moral and legal norms that granted the state a monopoly on legitimate violence. Their revolutionary action gave rise to an alternate political, ethical, and moral universe where established terms like "murder" and "killing" failed to convey the meaning of taking lives that many believed *deserved* to be taken. As one of the rebels explained to a radio journalist: "What do you call killing a man who really deserves to die? Because they deserve to die. They *should* be killed. . . . They are more guilty than we are, if anybody is. They have done ten times worse than we have ever done, than we could ever do. . . . They are the real criminals for allowing this system to perpetuate."[70] As the enforcers of this carceral war, guards were seen as the facilitators of a genocidal process. It is therefore nothing short of remarkable that at least some of them were not immediately executed, either as a tactical move to maximize negotiating leverage or simply as accountability for past violence.

As we will see across the ensuing chapters, participants in the Long Attica Revolt exercised immense restraint. Social theorist Cedric Robinson identified "the absence of mass violence" as a characteristic feature that is "always indicated in the histories of the [Black] radical tradition."[71] Analyzing slave revolts in the United States and the Caribbean, Robinson claims that "Blacks have seldom employed the level of violence that they (Westerners) understood the situation required." He sees this generalized refusal among African-descendant populations to fully reciprocate violence as they struggle against enslavement, colonialism, and captivity as evidence of their embeddedness within alternate formations of consciousness, a way of being that was not a simple reaction to oppressive conditions. Rather, it was "a revolutionary consciousness that proceeded from the whole historical experience of Black people and not merely from the social formations of capitalist slavery or the relations of production of colonialism."[72]

Robinson's argument is provocative, and the content of this book seems to support his theory. However, as I will show, the question of violence was just that: a question. And it was fiercely contested. Historical analysts of Attica in general and the prison movement more broadly have tended to produce fetishized portrayals of Black victimization while obscuring these internal debates and the forms of violence the rebels considered, planned, and often enacted. Moreover, the decision to exercise restraint was viewed by many, especially those later associated with the Black Liberation Army, not as a reflection of revolutionary historical consciousness but as a deep-seated pathology that facilitates Black peoples' continued subjugation amid a carceral and colonial war.

State actors were also grappling with the question of violence, specifically as it related to the public relations crisis the rebellion created. Since August, the rebellion had obtained sympathetic coverage in elite media. The *New York Times* and other major outlets had published their demands and run stories about the abysmal state of the jails and courts. The public understood that most of the rebels had not been convicted of the crimes for which they were imprisoned and were therefore formally presumed innocent. Moreover, the rebellion had begun to generate massive protests and other solidarity actions from outside organizations. Within this context, state actors feared that a public display of official violence might alienate Mayor John Lindsay's liberal base, further radicalize the rebels, and enlarge their support network. This explains why they had taken a largely conciliatory approach during the first stages of the Revolt.

Following a string of victories for the rebels that included the geographic expansion of the rebellion, the press conference, and the bail hearings, authorities resolved to retake the jails by force. Dozens of officers from the Tactical Patrol Force, a specially trained "crowd control" unit of the NYPD, were brought in to perform additional violence work.[73] From the outset, hostage deaths were seen as an acceptable form of collateral damage. "We're just going to have to consider the hostages expendable," said a high-level DOC official, in a view that echoed the American Correctional Association's position that the value of hostages' lives should be tactically assessed in relation to public perception.[74]

Unlike the state response to Attica eleven months later, an assault force did not breach the jails with live ammunition. Police and prison guards were instead outfitted with body armor, riot shields, batons, clubs, bats, ax handles, gas masks, and tear gas. However, the commonly held view that the state incursion of Attica represented a moment of exceptional violence misrecognizes the dynamics of domestic warfare under liberal democracy. The Attica massacre was not a departure from the norm, but its revelation in an intensified form. As political prisoner Martin Sostre wrote, "Attica defrocked the vicious outlaw murderers who were passing themselves off as lawful authorities."[75] As I will argue later, the massacre was an experiment in the public exhibition of state violence, an attempt to radically recalibrate public understandings of how Black rebellion in the United States could and should be managed. The reassertion of state control over the jails mobilized similar discourses, tactics, and technologies of subjugation, but did so in ways designed to seem like measured liberal governance. At this point in the struggle, the state strategy was to conceal the fact that a war was unfolding, whereas later it would shift toward dramatizing the state's war-waging superiority.

Prisoncrats surmised that since the BHD and QHD were the most recent jails to erupt, they would be the least organized and ill-prepared to fend off attack.[76] In fact, as they developed their plan to retake the jails, guards had already forcefully suppressed an incipient rebellion in the Adolescent Remand Shelter on Rikers Island in which captives briefly took three hostages.[77] So it was that during the late afternoon hours of October 4, 1970, armed agents of the state flooded the Brooklyn jail with tear gas and forced their way onto the fifth floor, swiftly wresting the prison from the rebels and freeing the hostages unharmed.[78] They then traveled to Kew Gardens, where the rebels had been in control for thirty hours. They fired tear gas onto the fourth floor and used blowtorches to cut through the door hinges and locks. The press later reported that the assault force met "heavy resistance" from rebels armed with steel pipes, forcing them to respond in kind. However, in a civil rights lawsuit subsequently filed on the captives' behalf, the rebels maintained that they were incapacitated by the gas and tried to surrender. They further claimed that upon reaching the fourth floor, a supervising officer announced, "Kill them all," at which point the assault force commenced ferociously beating them into submission.[79]

Although more battles lay ahead, state actors had swiftly recaptured three jails, decisively shifting the momentum in their favor. Following these victories, they regrouped to reevaluate their strategy in preparation for the Tombs and Branch Queens, the rebellions that posed the greatest potential to meet them with organized resistance. The state adopted an approach that foreshadowed what would become a normalized aspect of carceral strategy after Attica: psychological warfare. The assault force was instructed to encircle the jails, using a siege tactic to publicly demonstrate its superior capacity for violence, while a recorded ultimatum from Mayor Lindsay was played on local radio stations. The recording informed the rebels that they had one hour to release their hostages and face no reprisals "or face other courses of action." Not only did this message aim to degrade the rebels' resolve, it was a clever public relations maneuver that enabled the public to hear their mayor offering the rebels an opportunity to surrender peacefully. If the rebels refused and people were seriously injured or killed, the casualties could be easily attributed to rebel intransigence and not the state's disregard for life.

This strategy was effective. As Ricardo DeLeon recalls, when the rebels heard Lindsay's ultimatum over the radio, "pandemonium" ensued. While the rebellion had endured for more than two days, DeLeon, Brown, and others on the revolutionary committee had not managed to solidify organizational discipline. Rather, just as the state intended, the promise of protection and the threat of violence exacerbated already-existing fissures. "Immediately," recalled DeLeon, "all the waverers, fence sitters, and opponents started shouting, 'Let them go! Let them go,'" setting off an extended argument about strategy. Before a consensus could be reached, a vocal faction "steamrolled the surrender" and released the hostages. By midnight on October 5, 1970, the Tombs rebellion was over, and the rebels were again caged.[80]

The Branch Queens rebels had followed the developments in the Tombs on the radio and in anticipation of the same technique being used against them, also debated surrendering or fighting. According to Balagoon, who named himself after a West African deity of iron and war, the debate occurred between two factions: the "warriors" and "non-warriors." The central questions were first, whether the rebels were going to surrender or fight, and second, whether they were actually prepared to execute their prisoners. For Balagoon, the non-warrior faction was as irrational as it was immoral. He believed that as colonial subjects, most of whom were raised in poverty, the rebels should have known from experience that Lindsay could not be trusted and that even if his no-reprisal promise had been sincere, he would not be able to enforce it once the steel cages clanged shut and the rebels were back at the mercy of their captors. They would all suffer consequences, he explained. As the warriors saw it, the only question was whether they would do so alone.

Balagoon was also distressed by those who refused to kill in order to defend their own existence. He interpreted this phenomenon, not as a radically different "shared order of things,"[81] as does Cedric Robinson, but in the tradition of Queen Mother Moore, as symptomatic of a pathological plantation mentality that had been inculcated in Black people through generations of racial terror. "Black people have been conditioned to die behind any old bullshit for so long," he wrote, "that taking those white pigs' lives in response for murders of ourselves seemed to be incomprehensible to them. A crime against God, and three other white men."[82] Like theorist Frantz Fanon, whose ideas were profoundly influential to this movement, Balagoon suggests that the primary barrier to the liberation of the colonized was within their own minds—a combination of fear of death, respect for state authority, and deference to white power that had been hammered into the population from birth.[83] Liberation would remain an impossibility as long as colonized subjects respected the taboos put in place by their oppressors.

Theorizing this pivotal moment at the level of ontology, Balagoon argued that what was at stake was beyond even questions of life and death; it involved the very existence of colonized people as beings in the world. He believed that through rebellion the captives had asserted a masculine humanity that disrupted the existing order. He was inimically opposed to the thought of *not* defending that humanity out of awe of the White Man or fear of death. Speaking directly to the readers of his autobiography in an interrogatory manner, he employs the blues as a mode of theorizing Black life:[84]

> Do you—*you* who is reading this, here and now, know how it is to feel like nothing? Can you dig how it feels to be tired of feeling like nothing, a piece of shit? Can you dig how it feels to be a human being? A man? A man with a will and a purpose and a quest for justice? Can you relate to being a man for four days—then stepping back into a cage, that houses a hollow shell, a bundle of blues, a being who receives whatever a treacherous society throws at him, who has been forgotten by so many people that he's forgotten his damn self, on your own accord? For the sake of an unjust peace? And a continuation of non-existence?[85]

Balagoon's existential meditation conceptualizes violence as a process that demarcates the boundary between ungendered nothingness and masculine being in the world.

In later chapters I explore in greater detail how such claims to masculine humanity should not be confused with a desire to achieve parity with the White Man. To the contrary, I argue that by reading and listening to the living practices of this masculine anticarceral insurgency we can apprehend the emergence of a gendered humanity unshackled from white patriarchal norms. For now, it is important to note that Balagoon's personal biography, and that of many other rebels, illustrates the incommensurability of their notion of manhood with hegemonic white masculinity. Balagoon himself, who died of AIDS in prison in 1986, is remembered by his comrades as a "gender rebel" and for several years of his life was in a relationship with a transgender woman.[86]

In contrast to the non-warriors, members of the warrior faction proclaimed their preparedness to accept the terms of war imposed upon them by the state and to respond to that violence in kind. In an open letter attributed to the entire Panther 21, but which was primarily authored by Balagoon, Lumumba Shakur, and Kwando Kinshasa months after this ordeal, these key organizers of the Branch Queens rebellion offer an unvarnished endorsement of political violence as a productive force for revolutionary transformation. Published in *The East Village Other*, the infamous letter is most often discussed in historical scholarship for its trenchant critique of the BPP's turn away from armed struggle under the leadership of the Oakland-based Central Committee.[87] This critique exacerbated ideological tensions within the BPP, tensions that the FBI exploited and deepened to cause a split within the Party. Although the central purpose of the letter was to criticize the Party's perceived pivot toward reformism, the analysis it offers is relevant to the jail rebellion.

"Revolution is ARMED STRUGGLE—revolution is VIOLENCE—revolution is BLOODSHED—and the duty of a revolutionary is to make revolution."[88] Following the theoretical trail blazed by Fanon, these engineers of rebellion argued that the violence of the colonized was a rational response to a condition of collective abjection and that contrary to their portrayal as "extremists," they were not initiating force but "counter-force," not advocating violence but "counter-violence" against the normalized and entirely predictable violence of the state. They argued that this counter-violence should be strategically employed to level the field of battle. "We must match the enemy AT LEAST blow for blow—AT LEAST! You see—for us things are critical—every day—every hour—how many of our people are suffering? How many die?" They believed that the philosophy of nonviolence facilitated genocide: that police, prison guards, and other agents of the state routinely subjected Black people to abuse because they had no reason to fear retaliation. Within this context, they saw revolutionary counter-violence as a violence reduction strategy. Its aim was to make the wagers of war think twice before dispensing abuse.[89]

While it is easy to dismiss these ideas as immature expressions of far-left adventurism, they demand to be taken seriously if we jettison liberal modes of analysis and understand what was unfolding as an actual war. From this perspective, the Panthers' unequivocal endorsement of counter-violence is legible as a rational political strategy, a diagnosis of actually existing conditions at an acute moment of confrontation. The warrior faction knew that their small band of incarcerated rebels could not militarily defeat an incursion by agents of the state and that a battle would mean that many of the rebels would be badly injured, some even killed. However, the Panthers theorized incarcerated people as the tip of the spear. Not only would their determined resistance ensure that casualties were recorded on both sides, it would inspire others to take militant action. "To rumble then would have pulled the mass of us together in a truly revolutionary fashion. A victory—that is, to turn back the charge of the pigs—would have produced an army out of prisoners of war, who would then be drafted by their incarceration."[90] For Balagoon, all Black people in America are prisoners of war, but most are not conscious of this fact. To engage in combat against the carceral state would heighten their consciousness and draw them into the Black Liberation Army.

Balagoon's vision did not materialize. The question of violence was put to a vote, resulting in the non-warriors winning by a margin of one. Members of the warrior faction considered launching an internecine battle for control of the hostages but decided against impeding the will of the majority. Instead, they watched as the rebels demobilized, voluntarily returning themselves to nonexistence. As some men broke down the barricades, others uncaged the hostages, covered their heads with pillows to protect them from harm, brought them down to the street level, and released them. Then, in small groups, most of the rebels walked down the steps of Branch Queens and turned themselves in. However, thirty-nine of the rebels, including the Panthers and Victor Martinez, refused to willingly enter into police custody where they knew they would be abused. Instead, they barricaded themselves on the top floor of the jail and promised to continue resisting until their lawyers were able to ensure they could surrender safely.

Upon cutting their way into the fourth floor of QHD, a guard captain reportedly announced, "The war is over . . . You have lost, this is now a concentration camp."[91] This openly fascist declaration of genocidal intent contextualizes the Panthers' embrace of political violence as the only sufficient means of defending their existence. A lawsuit filed on behalf of those who survived the QHD rebellion offers a glimpse of what recaptured rebels across the jail system endured. As Balagoon predicted, despite Lindsay's no-reprisals promise, they were immediately subjected to a surplus of trauma. Captives were stripped naked and made to stand at attention, only to be sprayed with fire extinguishers, shot at point-blank range with tear gas canisters, and savagely beaten with clubs, chains, and ax handles. At the street level, in front of QHD's lower C gate, spectators observed uniformed men dragging their captives out of the jail and collecting their beaten and bloodied bodies into a writhing pile, estimated by various witnesses to number between twenty-five and sixty people. Guards then jumped on the pile, kicking and clubbing the defenseless men in full view of the media. Offering a glimpse into the violent processes of psychological conditioning through which the killing of white authority figures becomes unfathomable, the guards forced the recaptured rebels to chant "Power to the Correction Officer," "the Correction Officer is our God," and other affirmations of their mastery and deification.[92]

These nominally illegal inflictions of white supremacist violence were tacitly sanctioned by the federal government. While the FBI generated extensive surveillance of the rebellions, especially those involving Panthers, it was curiously disinterested in tracking abuse of the incarcerated. As a tactic of archival power, indeed of archival war, this active silencing attempts to weaponize history, to preserve a one-sided narrative as seen through the eyes of the state. Their surveillance conjures an

FIGURE 2. Supporters of the rebellion protesting outside the Branch Queens House of Detention, October 4, 1970. Photo: *People's World*.

image of bloodthirsty "black extremists," while revealing little about the racial terror that supports the established order.[93] Moreover, at the same time that the FBI was going to great lengths to crush the Black liberation movement, it was hospitable to the consolidation of organized white supremacy within the police, the prisons, and the military, leading us to the historical present in which white nationalism and homegrown fascism are flourishing in the open.[94]

Casualties were immense. At least one captive, a Black man named Thomas "Shorty" Hines, was beaten to death, his lifeless body left lying in a cage for over twenty-four hours.[95] At least fifty-nine QHD captives were hospitalized for serious injuries, including broken bones, lacerations, and skull fractures.[96] In the weeks following the rebellion four captives, all of whom were Black/Puerto Rican men, were found hanged in New York City jail cages. While official investigations disputed accusations leveled by the Young Lords that these deaths were political assassinations, state actors conceded that the jail system was ultimately responsible for letting them die, indicting the prison as a normalized site of "necropolitics." Whether by outright murder or malign neglect, the carceral system consumes the lives of the most vulnerable but does so in ways that register as justice administration.[97]

It was not until 12:30 a.m. on October 6, with the assistance of Gerald Lefcourt, that the thirty-nine Branch Queens holdouts allowed themselves to be lowered to the ground in groups of three in a fire department cherry picker, with their fists raised triumphantly. Lumumba Shakur was the last to exit the jail. As he descended, a crowd of over two hundred supporters cheered him on. He responded with a symbolic gesture of liberation. He raised his arm, revealed the keys to the jail, and tossed them into the crowd.[98]

Balagoon maintained that love and support from outside groups and organizations energized the rebellion and prevented the rebels from martyrdom. However, in their open letter, the Panther 21 criticized these same supporters for not taking advantage of the opportunities the rebellion created. Organizations such as the BPP, the YLP, the Women's Bail Fund, and Youth Against War and Fascism had organized citywide rallies that drew hundreds of people. While employing militant rhetoric, most of these outside supporters studiously abided the law and remained corralled behind police barricades. The jail rebellion's "warriors" saw this as a missed opportunity.

> When we were in the Long Island City (Branch Queens) jail rebellion—we felt that the people outside could have supported us in the fullest revolutionary manner in two or three simultaneous ways. 1) Mass demonstrations at each of the prisons involved. 2) While the pigs—quite a large percentage—were surrounding the prisons—and if there had been mass demonstrations—while leaving the city vulnerable—in this case for five days—for some righteous urban guerrilla military actions, and 3) if the chance occurred—to liberate the prisoners at any jail that the opportunity presents itself. Thus you see—the best tactics in revolution is in CONTINUOUS CONFRONTATION AND STRUGGLE.[99]

The Panthers argued that lawful and peaceful mass demonstrations were necessary but radically insufficient for revolutionary struggle against a system engaged in genocidal war. Their critique radically disrupts hegemonic understandings of what solidarity between those within and beyond prison walls can and should look like. While the rebels had successfully organized guerrilla counteroffensives and "legal jailbreaks" from within, they were calling on those outside the walls to engage in militant acts of strategically organized lawbreaking. Only through criminalized activity on both sides of the walls could their insurgency succeed.

State actors had attempted to minimize their public displays of violence so as not to encourage greater involvement of those beyond the immediate scope of the conflict. Yet, toward the end of the rebellion, urban guerrilla military actions showed signs of developing. According to the *New York Times*, as state actors were preparing to recapture the BHD, the police were harassed by an estimated three thousand people who gathered on rooftops adjacent to the jail and pelted them with rocks and bottles.[100] The police responded by shooting at them, heightening the possibility of a more generalized insurgency.[101] Had a rebellion outside the BHD matured, the opportunities for struggle inside would have shifted dramatically.

Following the collapse of the rebellion, an abstracted form of combat continued in the courts. On May 13, 1971, after two years of litigation, the Panther 21 were acquitted on all 156 counts. Five months later, DeLeon and others in the mini-Panther trial were acquitted of the most serious charges against them.[102] In both cases, the prosecution relied on evidence and testimony provided by undercover agents of NYPD's antisubversive unit, which had infiltrated the Panthers in order to gather intelligence and act as agents provocateurs.[103] Of the forty-five captives indicted for their alleged role in the various sites of the jail rebellion, only the case of the so-called "Tombs 3" made it to trial. In August of 1972, DeLeon, Curtis Brown, and a Black Muslim named Nathaniel Ragsdale were acquitted of all charges related to the rebellion.[104]

These acquittals inaugurated a debate around the role of law in state repression and radical resistance. The jail rebels, the Panthers, and other radical groups viewed law as an instrument of race and class war. Liberals viewed it as an instrument of justice, albeit one that was vulnerable to corruption. If the United States was truly a racist empire engaged in war on colonized populations, as many on the left maintained, then (liberal critics argued) it should have been impossible to obtain victory in the courts.[105] Of course, this logic neglected the fact that although they did not result in convictions, these criminal cases succeeded in weakening radical organizations. Legal support for the Panther 21 trial drained the Party of resources, incapacitated many of its key members for over two years, and exacerbated internal tensions. For this reason, DeLeon soundly rejected the notion that the acquittals were victories. "How can we say we won a *victory* when the pigs still have my brothers, when the farce still goes on, when we are still slaves, still victims—this is just a small step. . . . We have only won a skirmish on the m.f.'s terms. The battle lies ahead."[106]

For many, this chapter was just one in a much longer biography of anticarceral struggle. Although he beat the conspiracy rap, DeLeon was convicted on a weapons charge and spent the next several years behind prison walls, most in Unit 14, a complex of "torture and bestiality" within Clinton Prison, where intractables like Casper Baker Gary, Martin Sostre, and many others were routinely isolated. There DeLeon continued to resist intense carceral repression under the banner of the BPP.[107] Following his experience in the Panther 21 and the jail rebellion,

Kuwasi Balagoon concluded that "to survive and contribute I would have to go underground and literally fight." He joined the Black Liberation Army, a clandestine formation that, as I show in later chapters, was central to the protracted Revolt.[108]

DeLeon's contention that the battle lay ahead was prescient. Eager to relieve crowded conditions and cool the jails, Governor Nelson Rockefeller arranged for three thousand sentenced jail captives to be offloaded to state-run prisons, expanding the state prison population by nearly 25 percent in a matter of months. This sudden influx of new captives, many of whom had survived the jail rebellion, provoked massive shifts in the composition of New York's prison population. As wardens in Sing Sing, Clinton, Eastern, and elsewhere made space available to accommodate the transferees, they seized the opportunity to purge their own institutions of "troublemakers" and "militants." Many of these undesirables landed in Auburn, resulting in what one prisoncrat called "a critical mass of revolutionaries" within that facility.[109] Just as the deployment of prisons to contain revolutionary action on the streets backfired in the jails, the imposition of carceral war continued to create conditions conducive to rebellion. One month after the jail rebellion's collapse, captives in Auburn rebelled, and it is to this new, woefully undertheorized site of the Long Attica Revolt that we now turn.

CHAPTER 2

Black Solidarity Under Siege

Three Terrains of Protracted Rebellion

Prisons are archives in literal and figurative ways.[1] When Auburn was constructed in 1816, penal architects introduced a design and management innovation allowing them to collect human beings within prison walls, subdivide them into "convict companies," and further subdivide them into individuated cells, each labelled with unique identification numbers. Described by one analyst as "a human filing system," this physical ordering allowed penal experts to efficiently identify, observe, classify, access, sort, describe, sequester, silence, release, destroy, and extract knowledge from their targets.[2] As theorist Michel Foucault notes, prison-based surveillance "leaves behind it a whole meticulous archive," "situates [individuals] in a network of writing," and "engages them in a whole mass of documents that capture and fix them."[3] The sources generated by this carceral archive become the epistemic infrastructure for dominant narratives about the prison and those forced to dwell within it, as elite media look to these records and the state actors who produce them to establish architectures of Truth.[4]

Although Auburn was designed to reform wayward white men, by the late 1960s and early 1970s it was increasingly weaponized against Black insurgency. Captive populations accumulated during this era increasingly aimed to subvert the prison's control over their physical bodies as well as their bodies of knowledge. Auburn and Attica rebel Jomo Omowale wrote that when he first landed in Auburn in 1970, "the efforts of the Panthers and other groups was beginning to grow in prison as more of us were being imprisoned and taking our books and experiences with us."⁵ Prohibited from literally transporting his physical library inside the walls, Jomo's phrasing is suggestive of African oral traditions and scholar Sonia Vaz Borges's concept of *walking archives*, embodied forms of knowledge that reveal themselves through dynamic interaction and inquiry.⁶ The Auburn rebellion reveals that the prison as archive is incapable of containing or disciplining the walking archives and Black radical knowledges it holds.

In the preceding chapter, I narrated the rise and collapse of the New York City jail rebellion in order to analyze the political strategies and tactics of its central figures. I now turn to Auburn, another key site of the Long Attica Revolt, and analyze its unfolding across three overlapping terrains. The physical struggle was only the most visible form of a manifold rebellion. In what follows, I also illuminate a *narrative* rebellion. I show that through an insurgent letter-writing praxis, incarcerated combatants contested the state's control over the story of Auburn: its genesis, temporality, intensity, meaning, and demands. Finally, examining what I call the epistemic layer, I show how the captives cultivated Black radical ways of knowing and thinking that rebelled against Western conceptions of political rationality. Unearthing these layers of rebellion through unconventional archival strategies, I demonstrate that at the core of this struggle was the category of the human. I show that imprisoned Black radicals were not struggling solely to achieve diminutive notions of reform or rights, or even for assimilation into the existing regime of humanity. Drawing on Black radical and decolonial theory, I argue, to the contrary, that they were struggling to realize and preserve new definitions of what it means to be human.

As a white Western discourse that developed in dialogue with colonial conquest, the liberal humanist project attempts to define and demarcate the boundaries of humanity.⁷ Across the longue durée of Western modernity, Black and other colonized populations have functioned as the nonhuman Others existing beneath and beyond humanity's normative paradigm. In *The Wretched of the Earth*, which the rebels employed as a kind of manual, Frantz Fanon famously explains that racial-colonial domination "divided," "compartmentalized," and "sealed" the modern world into mutually exclusive zones, each inhabited by distinct species reified by colonialism itself. The colonized zone is a disreputable geography inhabited by objectified things, by "niggers" and "towelheads," those representing a "corrosive element," the very "negation of values." By contrast, "the ruling species" inhabits the zone of white civilization, of European culture, of historical progress, as defined by those who created the world in their own image. These zones are policed by a border of violence, a border that incarcerates the colonized within a "regime of oppression." And yet despite inhabiting the zone of Enlightenment—of official freedom, justice, and equality—the colonizer also suffers a deformed existence, an existence secured by genocide.[8] As Aimé Césaire explains, "The West has never been further from being able to live a true humanism—a humanism made to the measure of the world."[9]

As I will argue more forcefully in the following chapter, the Long Attica Revolt was a revolutionary struggle for decolonization and abolition at the site of the US prison. Although Auburn was a key zone of this struggle, it has been largely forgotten, and what little scholarly literature exists reflects the state's deceptive framing of the event. This framing largely confines the rebellion to the eight-hour period during which the rebels held hostages; imposes a partial understanding of their demands; and treats the confrontation as a relatively minor prelude to the much more well-known rebellion in Attica, which has also been memorialized through a counterinsurgent historiography that fixates on the spectacle of anti-Black violence that repressed the rebellion, while ignoring the forms of abolitionist worldmaking that made it such a threat.[10] It is often said that the central contribution of Auburn was that it taught captive rebels not to trust state promises regarding reprisals—as if this lesson had not already been learned, as if their political praxis crested at petitioning authority. Disrupting established understandings of Auburn and the prison movement more broadly, I demonstrate that Auburn was a protracted struggle that endured for at least eight months, during which members of the captive and colonized species transformed themselves into revolutionary subjects who ruptured the humanist paradigm and injected new rhythms of Black radical being into the world.

The content of this new rhythm, this new *genre* of human being, to use theorist Sylvia Wynter's formulation, was not determined in advance but was, rather, actively produced through the process of collective struggle. The Auburn rebels wrote extensively about their multifaceted Revolt and did so through the rubric of protracted war. But unlike the state-initiated war to which they were responding, theirs was a war of becoming. Elucidating this point through prose conditioned by violence, Charles Leon Hill wrote: "We are engage in protracted struggle at Auburn Concentration Camp. Often clashes of force, verbal confrontation, but never retreat, open conflict, war till the death. Either we who dare to fight, to resist, to demand human treatment or succumb to the wrath of tyranny and forsake the cause of human dignity or our bodies will be crushed but our spirit prevail. For we maintain no illusions of superhuman victory behind these walls we but keep aflame the spirit of the freedom fighter."[11]

Excerpted in the *New York Times*, Leon's intervention clarifies the stakes of the rebellion while demonstrating the salience and inseparability of the various terrains examined in this chapter. Auburn was a life and death contest that unfolded simultaneously on corporeal and discursive terrains. The physical "clashes of force" are only legible because captives were also engaged in a struggle to narrate these clashes. Both were shaped by such a profound asymmetry that achieving a decisive victory seemed beyond the rebels' physiological capacities as earthly beings.[12] And yet, fully aware that their bodies would be "crushed," they continued to resist. In doing so they struggled on a third terrain, one that nurtured a being beyond the body, a "spirit," a social consciousness, an affective state that is largely beyond representation. Although Leon demanded "human treatment" and "human dignity," he noted that his spirit burned for a form of freedom that the captors had no ability to grant, a freedom that could only be taken, or more accurately, one that had to be invented. And invent they did. As Fanon explains, a "new humanism is written into the objectives and methods of the struggle."[13]

In the sections that follow, I analyze the protracted Auburn rebellion as it unfolded across these interlocking terrains. First, I show how rebels narrated their Revolt against material and symbolic obliteration. Next, I analyze their implacable will to physically resist. I show that the rebels refused their compartmentalized dehumanization by enacting an *insurgent counter-humanism* that aimed to redistribute a fraction of the violence that assailed them. Yet, within, against, and beyond this totalizing spiral of violence, I show them evolving on an altogether different terrain. They were cultivating intra- and inter-corporeal modalities of collectivity, intimacy, love, tenderness—modalities that reveal the smoldering core of the Revolt's revolutionary content.

TO WHOM IT MAY CONCERN

The protagonists of the Long Attica Revolt contested a carceral and counterinsurgent narrative. "And what the ruling power, the administration of the penitentiary, and the reactionary newspapers have published must be considered as 'war communiques,'" wrote the French-based Prisons Information Group, adopting the analysis of imprisoned revolutionaries in the United States. This methodological intervention demands that analysts interpret dominant narratives, not as reflections of Truth, but of power, as propaganda intended to "fulfill some tactical exigencies" and "serve a specific purpose."[14]

Official sources position the Auburn "disturbance" within a linear temporality that begins on November 2, 1970, reaches its climax two days later, and is swiftly brought under control, leaving a deafening silence in its wake. The rebellion's alleged genesis was the administration's refusal to allow the Black population to celebrate Black Solidarity Day, a recently established holiday on which Black people refused to work. The story begins with a strike, in which captive rebels collectively withdraw their labor from Auburn's license plate shop, tobacco packing plant, textile shop, and metal bed shop.[15] Later that day, while the population convened in the yard, a group of so-called "extremists" associated with the BPP, the YLP, and the Five Percenters—an offshoot of the Nation of Islam—forcibly took control of Auburn's public address system and announced that the strike was occurring in observance of Black Solidarity Day. Rather than inflame an already tense situation, Warden Harry J. Fritz declared November 2 a "half-holiday."[16]

Over the next two days—November 3 was an election day and thus a planned holiday—prison guards surveilled the various meetings, discussions, and speeches that captives self-organized in Auburn's yard. An affidavit from Fritz noted that Black militants "harangued the inmates" with the message that "instead of the administration maintaining control, that *they* would determine the destiny of the black men within the institution."[17] A DOCS official told the *New York Times* that captives increasingly "have a consciousness of themselves as victims or political prisoners. They preach this and through coercion or force they pick up a following."[18] An administrative "Misbehavior Report" charged one captive with "making inflammatory speeches urging assembled inmates to take militant action against the institution."[19] Fritz noted that militant rhetoric notwithstanding, on both nights "virtually all the inmates peacefully partook of the evening meal" and voluntarily returned to their cages at the regularly scheduled time. Nonetheless, he ordered his subordinates to isolate the thirteen "ringleaders" deemed most responsible for these disruptions.[20]

A state investigation later concluded that had Fritz not taken this preemptive action, "the November 4 uprising might not have occurred when it did."[21] That morning hundreds of captives, most of whom were Black, again refused to participate in Auburn's routines, demanding the immediate release of their isolated comrades. The protest then "escalated into a rampage," the investigation noted. Prisoncrats claimed that roughly four hundred "black militants" coerced a population of sixteen hundred into participating, preventing them from leaving by "bodily sealing off exits from the yard."[22] The rebels overran the entire prison, released their comrades from isolation, and captured between thirty-five and fifty hostages, whom they bound, gagged, and assembled in the center of the yard. At least four were brutally attacked with their own clubs and later had to be hospitalized. Others were doused with gasoline and threatened with immolation.[23] "There is no doubt that the prisons are under attack," a DOCS official told the press.[24]

Echoing the conclusion of the Tombs insurgency, the Auburn rebels relinquished their hostages in exchange for a promise that authorities would consider their demands and abstain from retaliation. Little is known about the content of the demands beyond what state authorities tell us. Specifically, a prominent New York Republican who investigated Auburn produced a list of what he understood to be their key grievances, including the lack of Spanish-speaking guards, culturally relevant programming, abysmal conditions, high commissary prices, parole reform, and more.[25] While I have no doubt that these points were among their existential concerns, what we know of the demands presents a conceptual impasse: the filtering of Black radical discourse through a white liberal imagination that necessarily delimits consciousness to terms legible within its knowledge paradigm. The result is the reduction of their thought to either a purely destructive nihilism or a desire for equality within the liberal humanist regime.

Because of its dominance on the narrative terrain, the state was able to shape public perception of the struggle in real time and condition our historical forgetting. Consciously aware that they were engaged in a narrative contest, the rebels deployed the limited means at their disposal to generate counter-narratives, counter-archives, and counter-memory that radically alters our understanding of the conflict.[26] "What occurred at Auburn Concentration Camp on November 2–4, 1970, was not a 'disturbance' as the racist department of correction termed it, nor was it a 'riot' as the sensationalist news media labeled it, but a 'legitimate rebellion,' a revolt against corrupt conditions and oppressive racist policies," they wrote.[27]

Indebted to the political analysis of the BPP, their discursive labor constructed prisons as zones of invisibilized race war, class war, and genocide that were constitutive of the US social formation. Actively pushing back against the conceptual incarceration of their struggle within the domain of rights, they explained that contrary to the official story, "the causes of the rebellion were not isolated or singular demands for Black Solidarity Day" or other institutional reforms, "although all of these and numerous other grievances were voiced."[28] Rather, "the main demands of the Auburn rebellion were for freedom to control our own destinies, the freedom not to be treated like animals, not to be turned into mindless, spineless robots."[29] In other words, the intended effects of their anticarceral praxis exceeded prison walls, posing a challenge to the "sadistic, perverted, racist system [that] is compelled to oppress [the People] so it can survive."[30]

Although the state enjoyed outsized control over the narrative terrain, the captives had recently gained access to a critical means of fighting back. Six months before Auburn erupted, imprisoned revolutionary Martin Sostre secured a legal victory that forced prisoncrats to liberalize their correspondence policies. Prior to *Sostre v. Rockefeller*, DOCS regulated written correspondence in ways that all but ensured that captives were incapable of nurturing meaningful relationships beyond the walls. All letters had to be handwritten in English on an institutional template that provided minimal space for content. Captives were prohibited from discussing "prison news" and were only allowed to exchange letters with "immediate blood relations." Furthermore, expressions of intimacy, even between those within the state's narrowly defined understanding of kinship, were censored. As an Auburn and Attica rebel named Mariano "Dalou" Gonzalez explained, "If your mother wrote something, or [you] wrote something affectionate, they're going to take scissors and literally cut it out and put a piece of . . . tape across the letter and give it to you like that."[31] The *Sostre* ruling formally overturned this oppressive arrangement, enabling captives to employ the epistolary form with greater autonomy, establishing a new arena of anticarceral Revolt.

The state marked the surrender of the hostages on November 4 as the Auburn rebellion's end. Governor Rockefeller issued a press release claiming that prison guards and State Police had "swiftly restored order," re-caging all captives "without confrontation." Auburn's local paper, the *Citizen-Advertiser*, regurgitated this official line, as did the *New York Times*, which declared the prison "quiet after outbreak."[32] In its brief discussion of Auburn, the New York State Special Commission on Attica makes no mention of official retribution or ongoing resistance, only allowing that the state's promise of no-reprisals was broken when the thirteen "ringleaders" were shipped out of Auburn and put in solitary confinement elsewhere.[33] Heather Ann Thompson's history of Attica does slightly better, noting that captives were "beaten and forced to run gauntlets of angry COs with their batons after their surrender," that over one hundred rebels were placed in long-term isolation in Auburn, and that six were indicted for criminal acts committed during the rebellion. Yet, despite being titled "Voices from Auburn," Thompson's narrative is largely told from the perspective of DOCS Commissioner Russell G. Oswald and affords readers few opportunities to hear from the rebels themselves.[34]

For several months after their tactical surrender, the Auburn rebels waged a discursive insurgency that ruptured the narrative incarceration of their praxis. It started slowly, with few, if any, letters reaching their intended recipients for nearly two months. Between January and May of 1971, however, their letters reached family members, federal judges, and community organizers. They were subsequently published in a variety of left outlets, including *Palante*, *The Black Scholar*, the *Village Voice*, and *Right On*.[35] Six months after reporting that Auburn was "quiet," even the *New York Times* was forced to concede that the prison remained "turbulent": their offices were overwhelmed with what a journalist described as "hundreds of letters that pour forth weekly from the isolated galleries," some of which were penned in blood.[36]

In response to the captives' desperate calls for support, a Marxist group called Youth Against War and Fascism launched the Prisoners Solidarity Committee (PSC), an explicitly abolitionist formation. Established in February of 1971, the PSC functioned, in one member's words, as "a vehicle whereby the prisoners themselves could speak to the people outside, could generalize their struggle, fuse their grievances and their hopes into the main current of rebellion that is rising in the country as a whole."[37] Comprised mostly of white university students and activists, the PSC provided the rebels with invaluable financial, moral, and legal support; created a transportation program to convey family members from New York City to Auburn; and organized protests outside the Cayuga County Courthouse, the site of the rebellion's legal aftermath. They even managed to infiltrate the prison by getting one of their members assigned as a legal assistant for the Auburn 6, who were indicted for their role in the November takeover.[38]

The PSC's political labor left behind a rich, yet largely untapped archive of abolitionist journalism, now memorialized in periodicals such as *Worker's World*, *The Activist*, and *Battle Acts*; in pamphlets

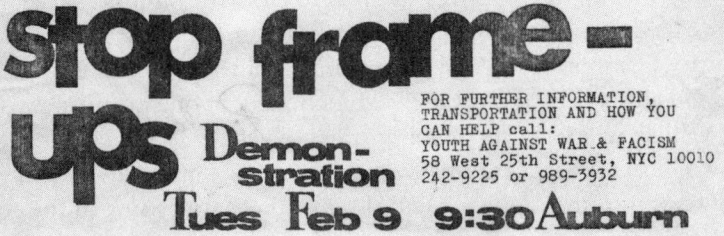

FIGURE 3. A flyer produced by Youth Against War & Fascism in support of the Auburn rebels. Photo: New York State Archives.

such as *Fight for Freedom: It Is the Only Thing Worth Fighting For* and *Prisoners Call Out: Freedom*; and across numerous fliers and other promotional materials. It is largely because the PSC valued and amplified the rebels' letter-writing praxis that an alternative discourse of the rebellion can be constituted. In contrast to that of the state, this narrative does not claim to tell the whole story. It does not pretend to be dispas-

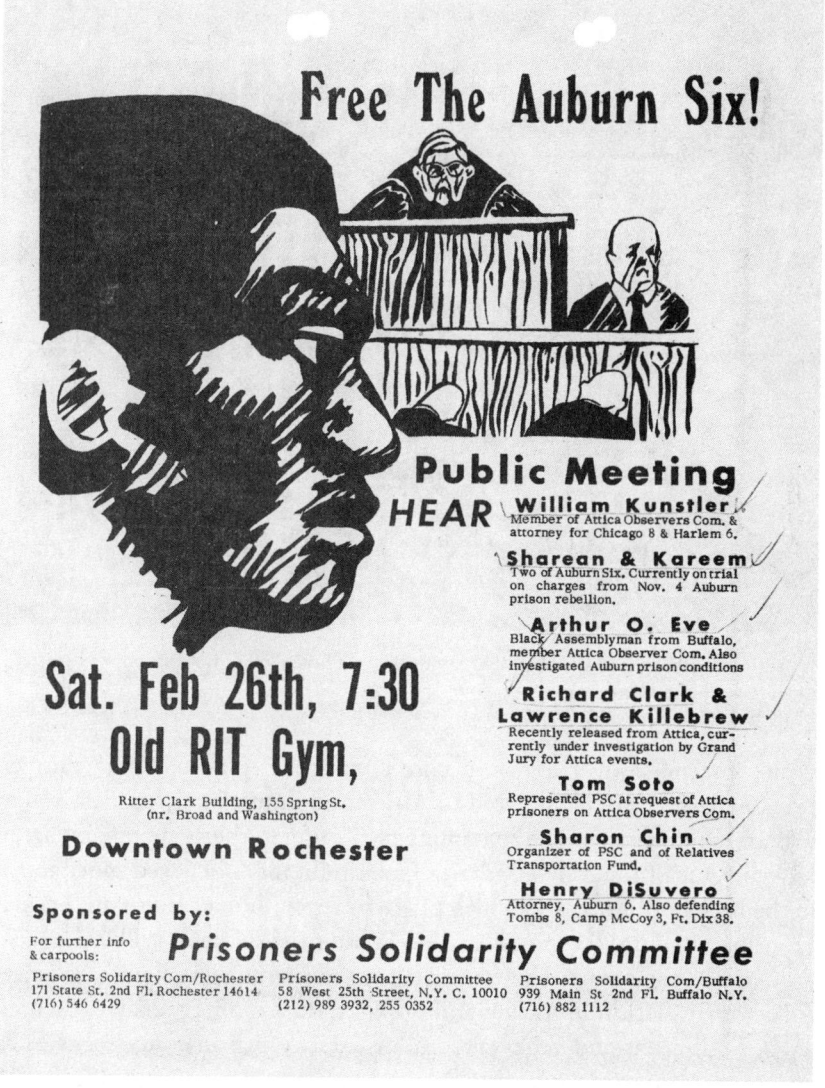

FIGURE 4. A flyer produced by the Prisoners Solidarity Committee in support of the Auburn 6. Photo: New York State Archives.

sionate or objective. It is explicit in its antagonism toward capital, white supremacy, and imperialist war, both foreign and domestic.

After regaining control, Warden Fritz enacted a plan to isolate, silence, and punish the rebels. Declaring a "state of emergency," he placed the prison on total lockdown, indefinitely suspending all programming,

FIGURE 5. Auburn Cell Block in Old South Wing. Photo: Eastern Kentucky University, Correctional Photograph Archives.

visits, internal movement, and correspondence. Eleven of the thirteen "ringleaders" were transferred to Attica and immediately sequestered in solitary confinement. The remaining two suffered the same fate in Green Haven. Out of the four hundred "black militants" believed most active in the rebellion, Fritz isolated eighty captives within a gallery of "Special Housing Unit" (SHU) cages on the top floor of Auburn's cellblocks, also known as "the roof." The remaining malcontents were kept in twenty-four-hour isolation in the general population, pending transfer to Comstock,[39] Clinton, and other maximum-security prisons once more SHU space could be made available.[40]

Rebel letters authored during this period are saturated with meditations on communicative failure: the limitations of the epistolary form, the vicissitudes of illegal prison censorship, and the impossibility of conveying the scope and intensity of the violence they endured. "If I were to relate even some of the major deprivations suffered and still continued in this letter then you would never receive it," wrote one captive.[41] "To put my situation on paper is impossible because things keep building up each and every day, leaving nothing to my imagination,"

FIGURE 6. Cover of Prisoners Solidarity Committee pamphlet supporting the Auburn rebels and entitled "Fight for Freedom! It Is the Only Thing Worth Fighting For!" Photo: New York State Archives.

wrote another.[42] Besieged by inscrutable terror and dehumanization, their letters marked an existential rupture with dominant systems of knowledge production and representation, puncturing state-imposed silences without fully transcending them.[43] "We are the voices of Black inmates who have been relegated into the obscure microcosm of ultra-punitive segregation (the roof) behind the iron curtains of Auburn Prison. Nobody beyond these iron curtains, shaded by a huge wall, can hear the constant cries echoing our agonies because the racist penal 'brutocracy' (i.e., Rockefeller, Oswald and Fritz) has insidiously concealed the atrocities inflicted on us daily."[44]

In a confidential DOCS report, an investigator concluded that his "diligent search" yielded no evidence that the rebellion was "the brutal outcome of months or years of sadistic treatment, of color discrimination, of bad food, of senseless withdrawal of privileges and of denial of proper civil rights."[45] And yet according to rebel letters, even as this investigation was taking place the population was enduring arcane forms of racial terror. They wrote about being stripped naked, beaten, and made to endure the freezing cold; of gassings, macings, and forced druggings; of being sprayed with water hoses; of being starved or alternatively of being served food that was intentionally contaminated with dead insects, feces, phlegm, poison, and shards of glass, sometimes from a wagon also used for hauling garbage.[46] Exposing the radical insufficiency of terms like "solitary confinement" and "punitive segregation," they wrote of being forced into "dark cells" and "strip cells": barren concrete enclosures with no lights, plumbing, or furnishings, in which denuded men were suspended in space and time until they "barely exist," as one victim of this practice explained.[47] Conceptualizing the prison as a space beyond legality, another wrote, "So many crimes have been committed by the officials hereof that we no longer even know whether or not the United States Constitution is the Law of Amer-rikkka, or the martial decrees arbitrarily enforced by Harry Fritz and his agents."[48]

Within and against this "iron clad atmosphere of racist hate,"[49] captive rebels engaged in autopoetic experiments that narratively engendered radical mutations of their being. In *Prisoners Call Out: Freedom* Leon, also known as Writer for the People, and whose articulation of protracted war opened this chapter, explains that he was politicized in the Tombs by Dhoruba bin-Wahad and Kwando Kinshasa of the Panther 21. Following the developmental arc of figures like Malcolm X, Eldridge Cleaver, and George Jackson, Leon traces his metamorphosis from what he called a "ghetto rat"—a subject that "identified with all the Establishment advocated as legitimate," that "did not strive to be a man and to be human, and most of all to be free"—into a revolutionary. Leon writes about studying the revolutionary tactics of Mao Tse-Tung and Che Guevara, but explains that a deeper shift occurred at the level of consciousness and affect. From the Panthers he learned that "revolution has to be within the body of the person—that the revolution is a process of rearranging one's values—to put it simply, the death of the nigger and the birth of the Black man after coming to grips with being proud to be one's self." Echoing Fanon's theorization of how anticolonial struggle leads to the death of colonized being and the opening of new humanist horizons, Leon writes, "I learned to stretch out my hands and be part of all mankind."[50] In the following chapter, I offer a more thorough engagement with how this form of human being was lived, including a speculative interpretation of the meaning behind its masculine ascription.

For now, let us dwell on the myriad ways that imprisoned Black radicals deployed letter-writing as discursive technology of counter-war. Their epistolary praxis ruptured their "narratively condemned status,"[51] enabling them to constitute themselves as actors and chroniclers of a world historical event. Against the narrow framing of the conflict as an unprovoked outburst of extremist violence that disturbed an otherwise tranquil institution, they narrated the rebellion as a repudiation of genocidal atrocity. Moreover, at the underside of Western civilization's enlightened embrace, they narrated formations of Black radical becoming that simultaneously critiqued and overran the boundaries of the human project. As they always do, the foot soldiers of carceral war responded to these movements by ratcheting up repression, zealously policing the borders of the existing hierarchy. However, their violence had lost its determinative power. For the rebels resolved that it would now flow both ways.

INSURGENT COUNTER-HUMANISM

The corporeal terrain of struggle is the terrain of physical violence. Prisoncrats legitimated their violence by hiding it, mystifying it beneath obfuscating language, and by labelling the rebels as the extremist initiators of violence. However, as Fanon explains, it is the colonist who speaks in the language of violence, the colonist who relegates the colonized to a status of lower "species," and thus, it is the colonist who "has always shown them [the colonized] the path they should follow to liberation."[52]

Black captives were seen as beyond the pale of humanity, as beasts who needed to be contained. As a high-level prison official explained in 1974, many of the guards felt they were a "special kind of breed of animal [that has] very little hope for rehabilitation."[53] Against this normalized dehumanization, the Auburn rebels enacted an insurgent counter-humanism. Into this atmosphere of totalizing violence, they introduced a counter-violence that communicated their willingness to *universalize* the disposability of life, if no other options were available. Barred from accessing the trappings of humanity, the colonized sought to reduce the colonizer to a state of equality revealing, in Fanon's words, that "his life, his breathing and his heartbeats are the same as yours."[54] Coupled with its epistolary narration, this reciprocation of violence reflected the rebels' militant refusal of the epistemic and ontological arrangement of the world.

Prisons had long served as cauldrons of martial Black radicalism. Behind the walls there was no shortage of people who engaged in the disciplined study and practice of unarmed combat, weaponizing their bodies by doing thousands of push-ups per day, executing weighted punches, and hardening the bottoms of their feet by running barefoot in the prison yard. During the late 1960s, Black radicals regularly organized secret fighting competitions in an abandoned area of Green Haven Prison. Attended by various Black nationalist formations, these underground contests provided opportunities for captives to hone their martial prowess in an environment oriented toward collective survival and liberation. They employed East Asian styles such as karate and judo, as well as their own fighting systems. With names like "Mental Boxing" and "Kill the Enemy Within," captives developed these techniques to preserve bodily autonomy while fighting on the internal terrain of war: the conquest of fear, doubt, and the inferiority complex imposed by the colonizing process. "Whenever possible we will avoid antagonizing the Pig," notes the Rules and Regulations of the Auburn BPP. And yet members were instructed to arm themselves with "knives, karate, [and] brute strength" so that "if the Pig should make it apparent that he intends to take you off this Planet, you may get the opportunity to take at least one Pig with you."[55]

Isolated on the roof, the Auburn 80 responded to carceral siege with ever more rebellion. On December 20, 1970, for example, they launched an attack from within the most secure section of the prison. A memo from Warden Fritz limns this insurgency through the drab vernacular of state bureaucracy.

> Whereas, a number of inmates in one of the Special Housing Units participated in a second uprising on December 20, 1970 in that when staff released them from their cells in order to provide outdoor exercise, these inmates armed themselves with a variety of weapons made from cell furniture destroyed for this purpose and mop handles and brooms, broke the windows in the Special Housing Unit, removed the control levers used to open and close the windows, and armed themselves with such levers as weapons, and then refused to return to their cells upon order of institution officials, making it necessary to use tear gas, mace, and other physical force to [compel] inmates to return to their cells and to submit [to a search] for weapons, all of which created a grave threat to [the] safety and security of the Facility.[56]

Fritz frames the SHU rebellion as an unprovoked guerrilla ambush against unwitting guards who were only performing their duty to ensure their captives received their legally mandate hour of recreational time outside their cages. Unresponsive to rational speech, this bloodthirsty horde left the guards with no choice but to beat them back with defensive force and tear gas, which they dispensed with the utmost restraint.

Six months after this confrontation, *The Black Scholar* published a letter that indicts Auburn prisoncrats for consigning the rebels to a realm beyond humanism's protective embrace. According to Jalil Abdul Alim, he and other members of the Auburn 80 were caged twenty-four hours per day in "cruel and inhuman conditions." He wrote that in response to "trivial things like demanding our human rights, hot meals, clean clothes, constitutional guarantees, showers, etc," they were subjected to physical, psychological, and sexual attacks that assailed the surfaces and the interiority of their bodies: the flesh, the vital organs, the nervous system, the respiratory system, the senses. "My first beating came after 38 of us were *gassed* and *maced* and I refused to submit to a '*rectal examination.*' I was deaf in my left ear for more than two weeks, and received lacerations on my legs, arms and head."[57] By placing "rectal examination" in scare quotes, Alim demystifies this commonly used technique of sexualized conquest that is normally cloaked in rationalistic jargon.

The rebels were not passive recipients of these treacheries but rather historical agents who analyzed what was being done to them and consciously fought back. Although they numerically outnumbered their tormentors, they were technologically outgunned and physically immobilized in carceral space. Responding to increasingly militaristic siege tactics, they employed a form of carceral guerrilla warfare. As George Jackson explains, guerrilla warfare is "not fought with high-tech weaponry, or state-of-the-art gadgets. It's fought with whatever can be had—captured weapons when they can be had but often antiquated firearms, homemade ordnance, knives, bows and arrows, even slingshots—but mostly through the sheer will of the guerrilla to fight and win, no matter what."[58] The Auburn rebels actualized this insight, fighting to maintain a modicum of autonomy with no conceivable path to victory. "During the onslaught of these pigs, we were being gassed and forced to break up our toilet bowls, sinks and beds in order that we might defend ourselves to a degree, from those space-men looking pigs with their clubs, mace, and array of gasmasks, oxygen cans and teargas guns, with which we were vamped on. The racist pigs left 20 and 30 gas canisters behind, that we were left to deal with."[59] For their ongoing rebellion they paid a high price, not only in blood and bone, but also in financial debt for the damage incurred to the prison. "I have to pay $87.74 before I'll be able to buy the bare necessities—toothpaste, soap, etc," Alim wrote. "I hate to even mention how much prison time and wages it would take for me to pay that price."[60]

"We was crazy," Brother A explained to me over the phone. "We used to like cursing at them, calling them pigs, spitting on them, and throwing our piss and shit on them."[61] I had asked him why he and others on the roof had organized such strong resistance. Rather than responding through the rubric of politics—radical, revolutionary, or otherwise—he attributed their protracted rebellion to a psycho-affective disorder. He explained that the rebels were not "in their right mind," were not operating as rational, self-owning subjects, but rather as the bearers of madness, of ungovernable cognitive schemas. "And some of us *were* extremists," he continued. His adoption of a term that is often hurled by the state as a delegitimizing gesture resonates with this proclamation by Jackson: "I am an extremist. I call for extreme measures to solve extreme problems."[62]

It is telling, however, that the examples Brother A uses to illustrate rebel "extremism" and "craziness"—the hurling of offensive language, bodily fluids, and feces—again reflect the profound asymmetry of this struggle.[63] A prison psychiatrist who testified at a federal hearing noted that the rebels were struggling through severe trauma, resulting in a sharp increase in suicidal ideation and incidents of self-harm.[64] And yet prisoncrats were in a position to weaponize mental health. Numerous letters accuse the state of having captives forcibly committed to the Dannemora State Hospital for the Criminally Insane and of deploying drugs to reduce them to a vegetative state.

What does it mean to be crazy, to be extreme, to be mad, amid a condition that is itself beyond "reason"? A letter from James Kato Dunn dated January 5, 1971, echoes Fanon, positing that it was the carceral environment that was crazy and extreme. Inscribed in beautifully ornate penmanship, the letter accuses prisoncrats of subjecting captives to "uncivilized acts of insane punitive maltreatments." Hoping to curtail the "abuses and denials of certain guaranteed rights under the US Constitution," Kato's letter pleads for legal support.[65] However, as time wore on, and these abuses intensified, he grew more belligerent, developing a reputation for grabbing patrolling guards through the bars of his cage and choking them out whenever he caught one getting too close. These attacks would invariably result in Kato being singled out for special brutalities, humiliations, and violations. Yet the guards understood that they could not abuse him without incurring a consequence, and so they began to give the area in front of his cage a wide berth.[66] In a letter published months later in *Right On!*, Kato seems to have abandoned any aspiration for inclusion into normative humanity or citizenship. Gone are the references to the US Constitution, human rights, or attorneys. In their stead, Kato demands "equal weapons not equal rights!"[67] Outside of the social contract and the polity, the only way to ensure survival and secure the preconditions for being human was the capacity to inflict what Fanon called a "reciprocal homogeneity" of violence.[68]

Determined physical rebellion overflowed into the Cayuga County Courthouse, where rebels noted the irony in the fact that affixed to the building's exterior was a plaque commemorating Harriet Tubman, the militant abolitionist who lived in Auburn for a time and is buried in its cemetery. The rebels narrated themselves as Tubman's progeny, employing a range of abolitionist and counter-humanist tactics reflecting their desire for disengagement with the carceral regime. A surveillance report notes that the six captives charged with crimes stemming from the November 4 takeover "had to be carried from their cells to vehicles and forced into the courtroom." During their arraignment the Auburn 6, as they came to be known, refused to answer to their slave names and declined to enter pleas, demanding instead that the federal government launch a probe into ongoing carceral violence. "They pounded tables, shouted obscenities, kicked doors and were completely and positively uncontrollable," noted an agent for the New York State Police.[69] At one point a fight broke out in the courtroom itself. After being assaulted by a uniformed officer, Auburn rebel Kareem C'Allah retaliated, executing a double snap kick to the officer's chest and using his manacles to choke him until his face "turned purple." Kareem relented only after another officer put a gun to his head, cocked the hammer and promised to "blow his head off."[70]

Convinced that they would not receive a fair trial, the Auburn 6 accepted a plea bargain for reduced sentences. "We realize that any amount of time in any prison is no 'bargain,'" wrote their legal defense team. "But we felt that a decision ought to be based on the chances we had of an acquittal, and the chances we had of using the trial to expose the conditions which existed at Auburn, and which continue to exist in every penitentiary in New York, as you well know."[71] But rather than turn themselves in and willingly return to their tormentors, two of the Auburn 6 jumped bail, inhabiting an illegal freedom that extended the Auburn rebellion more than two years beyond its officially declared end.[72]

On May 8, 1971, the isolated rebels launched another collective rebellion from Auburn's SHU. This one occurred simultaneously with a protest in which over 100 PSC members marched in the rain outside the prison. As chants denouncing prison slavery, class warfare, and homegrown fascism seeped through the concrete exterior, Brother A and others used the metal springs from their bedframes to pick the locks of their cages, then armed themselves with razor-sharp shards of porcelain obtained from shattering the sinks affixed to the cell walls. They then emerged from their cages and ambushed the guards, slashing them with their self-fashioned blades. The attack yielded a predictable result.

"They beat us damn near to death and threw us back in our cells," Brother A recalled in a manner chilling in its matter-of-factness. And yet, the guards were beaten and bloodied too. In the absence of victory, the production of mutual suffering would have to do.

The Auburn rebellion exposed the inadequacy of existing carceral infrastructure to contain Black insurgency. A confidential DOCS report noted that "the single yard is an open invitation for a few militants to take over."[73] Warden Fritz, meanwhile, complained to the commissioner that "the physical plant is not so designed to provide the necessary supervision for inmates who are bent and determined upon rebellion."[74] Brother A recalls that one of the immediate legacies of the Auburn rebellion was that DOCS shored up these structural vulnerabilities, henceforth soldering stainless-steel sinks, toilets, and bedframes directly onto the surfaces of its enclosures. After Attica, as I will discuss in the second part of this book, so-called Control Units, Maxi-Maxi, and Supermax prisons exploded. Because of struggles like Auburn, carceral institutions of the future were increasingly designed for war.

As a protracted collision between opposing forces, Auburn radically disrupted the normative paradigm of humanism. The rebels responded to the living lie of human universality by exposing the physical and symbolic violence that relegated them to its underside. Through implacable resistance, noncooperation, and epistolary insurgency, their counter-humanist praxis appropriated and redistributed a fraction of the violence that encircled them, seeped into their pores, and assailed their psyches. In doing so, they communicated their refusal to be dominated and their desire to be liberated *from* humanity as embodied by their captors. Engaging Fanon's dialectics of violence and liberation, George Jackson had written, "Two men die with the stroke that slays the slave-master: the slave-master dies in a way that he can do no man any further harm; and then the slave mentality of the former victim dies."[75] But what then? In the final section, I examine some of the positive experiments with new modes of Black radical being that the Auburn rebels created.

"THE SOUND OF A DIFFERENT DRUMMER"

"I have nothing to say, sir." This enunciation of silence is attributed to Eric Thompson 26385. However, at the top of the transcript of this exchange, in a small act of defiance, his chosen name is written in cursive lettering: Jomo Sekou Omowale. Jomo offered his courteous but decisive answer in response to Vincent Mancusi's question: "Were you served with the charges today . . .?" Mancusi was the warden of Attica, where Jomo and other Auburn "ringleaders" were transferred immediately after relinquishing their hostages.[76] They were placed in solitary confinement, where they endured many of the same atrocities visited upon those still in Auburn. It was January of 1971 and legal actions initiated by the rebels had forced prisoncrats to adhere to their own protocols and grant the isolated rebels a disciplinary hearing in compliance with *Sostre v. Rockefeller*. "Do you admit or deny these charges?" Mancusi asked, as if no other response was possible. Jomo remained silent. "Do you refuse to sign this paper?" Mancusi continued, and Jomo again gave no reply.

Recognizing that his inquiry was leading nowhere, Mancusi ordered Jomo out of the room and called on two Auburn guards to testify. They claimed that on November 2, Jomo and others had approached their post, forcibly commandeered the public address system, and announced that a strike was occurring in observance of Black Solidarity Day. This action, they claimed, precipitated the prison-wide "disturbance" that followed. Jomo was called back into the room and retold the narrative just outlined. "Do you admit or deny the charge?" Mancusi asked again. "I plead the 5th on the entire thing," said Jomo. Mancusi affirmed the charges, punishing Jomo by wielding his power to manipulate time. He eliminated 270 days from Jomo's "good behavior" credits and sentenced him to 60 days in solitary confinement, time that he in fact had already served. Mancusi then concluded the proceeding with finality: "That is all."[77]

To close this chapter, I explore the modes of Black radical consciousness that overrun the boundaries of liberal humanism and rational self-ownership. Against the grain of the state's narrative dominance, such an experiment necessitates analyzing Black rebellion through different architectures of reality. To excavate these alternate universes of aspiration, desire, and dreaming beyond inclusion, I deploy conceptual tools that are unavailable within normative paradigms of Western knowledge.[78] Toward this end, my methodological approach to this epistemological and affective terrain of struggle decenters visual and textual evidence and instead privileges *listening* to the sounds, silences, and rhythms of rebellion beyond the body. For it is here that we can perceive what theorists Stephen Best and Saidiya Hartman have called *Black noise*, "the kinds of political aspirations that are inaudible and illegible within the prevailing formulas of political rationality" and as such are "always already barred from the court."[79]

What happens when we actively listen for those expressions of being that exceed the strictures of scientific positivism and "rational" thought? How might this speculative and provisional approach help us fathom the significance of rebellious silence? Into the void we could impose the rational motivation of avoiding self-incrimination, a motivation that almost certainly played a role in Jomo's refusal to engage. But could not there also be layers to his refusal to speak? What if his silence reflected a rejection of the question itself, a rejection of the terms through which the official narrative was being constructed? *Do you admit or deny these charges?* To answer using either word would have legitimized this process and the social order that it produces.[80]

Jomo Sekou Omowale: the handwritten name on the top of the page is a noise that points to an otherwise concealed genealogy of Black radical struggle. Thompson 26385 adopted "Jomo," a Kikuyu name meaning "burning spear," and "Sekou," a Fula name meaning "wise," from anticolonial nationalists-cum-statesmen in Kenya and Guinea, respectively. Omowale, meaning "the child has returned home," is of Yoruba origin and was bestowed upon Malcolm X during his visit to Nigeria. This "self-determining onomastic practice," as Edward Onaci has termed the renaming customs of Black Americans, disturbs the official temporality and geography of Black Solidarity Day, politicizing it in ways that invoke indigenous African traditions, Pan-Africanism, revolutionary nationalism, Third World decolonization, and what Adom Getachew calls "anticolonial worldmaking."[81] From this vista, Jomo's contemplative silence is perceptibly charged with a range of radical possibilities that the carceral archive can neither fully register nor contain.[82]

Unfortunately for me, I did not have an opportunity to meet Jomo and discuss his philosophy before he passed away in 2017. However, I have engaged with his intellectual bequest by listening to and learning from the people to whom he was closest. My conversations with Jomo's daughter Emani Davis, a theorist and scholar-activist in her own right, have been transformative. During one of our discussions, I asked Emani to discuss the significance of being the keeper of her father's knowledge. Her answer foregrounded intimacy, intuition, care, and love as ways of inhabiting a liberated humanity:

> Because in real life there was no real justice or healing for them [the Auburn and Attica Brothers], I feel like they didn't get to fully distill or process what happened. Their whole lives became very reactive. By the time they were able to create any theory from what happened many of them were too unwell either mentally or physically but the people that were close to them had a lot

of access to their thought. I didn't really understand until my dad was transitioning and I was trying to gather all the hundreds of letters he had sent me since like 1986. I would be up all night with him and I would be reading through his letters. And it was as if he was trying to create a blueprint for everything, things that, in the moment, I didn't really understand why he was saying it. He wrote me a book on a legal pad and it's like, everything I should know since the beginning of time—ancient Kemet, the Vikings. There are other things, like which flowers do what. Something like forty pages. I think he realized that he was never going to get to a place of being the old storyteller man that I think he wanted to become and that prison had afforded him the solitude to really think about what he wanted to continue and what he wanted people to know. Most of our conversations were not political, most of our conversations were about healing, wellness, care, patience, compassion. Our relationship was a constant distilling of what he learned in here [rubs chest].[83]

Emani foregrounds how state-inflicted trauma conditioned her father's thought, largely preventing him and others from developing what they had learned as a generalizable social and political theory. At the same time, through physical proximity, emotional intimacy, and by reading and rereading her father's letters in the context of his transition across the threshold of life and death, she managed to access and distill his thought. Reading those letters in this context, she became conscious, in ways she had not before, that her father had been trying to convey his deepest desires, to articulate a vision for what he wanted her and the world in which she lived to be. This positive vision was not reducible to "resistance," "the political," or "rebellion." Rather, it prioritized health, spirituality, internal character development, and authentic self-actualization beyond our present humanity. Her description of this knowledge as a possible "blueprint for everything" resonates with Cedric Robinson's assertion that the Black radical tradition is "the continuing development of a collective consciousness informed by the historical struggle for liberation and motivated by the shared sense of obligation to preserve the collective being," a condition he terms "the ontological totality."[84]

Years after surviving Auburn and Attica, Jomo broke his silence, locating the rebellion's genesis in the struggle to "[revolutionize] the minds of the prisoners," to help them "understand that we as prisoners must join together for our common objectives—an end to capitalism, imperialism, racism, and providing adequate food, housing and shelter for our people—all people, really."[85] In sharp contrast to the state's framing of Auburn as a site of normative peace that was "disturbed" by a violent outburst, Jomo frames the prison as the institutionalization of violence, indeed as a flesh-eating monster: "When the administration of the Auburn flesh-pit refused to let us commemorate Black Solidarity Day in November of 1970," he wrote, "[we] joined forces, took over the prison, and the controls of our own lives."[86] His invocation of this term "flesh" is evocative of Hortense Spillers's canonical theorization of Black enfleshment as the violent "severing of the captive body from its motive will, its active desire," an attempt to transform the captive into a "being for the captor."[87] For Jomo, the Auburn rebellion emerged as part of a historical process in which subjects with no sovereignty over their bodies or lives began to transform their consciousnesses, their understandings of what it meant to be in the world.

Larry "Luqmon" White remembered his time in Auburn during the late 1960s and early 1970s as a turning point in his intellectual and political development. Luqmon was politicized in Auburn by Jomo and the others who organized the Black Solidarity Day strike. In and out of youth "reformatories" for much of his childhood, Luqmon looked to these comrades for political mentorship. During one of our many conversations, I asked him to tell me about the rebellion and he responded not with stories of hostage-taking, property destruction, or torture, but with a discourse on self-realization:

> Auburn is where I realized I could think. I began to understand that I could write. I never tried to. But I remember, I sat down and I starting writing things down and I was shocked, like where did this shit come from? So I began to write and read stuff about the Young Lords and the Black Panthers and I began to integrate their stuff into my thinking and I began to hang out with them and then it just began to evolve. I would gather us all in the back room of the library and hold secret meetings and break down the political stuff [the Panthers] was teaching, especially as it applied to prisons.[88]

For Luqmon, Jomo, and others, the Auburn rebellion was fundamentally a cognitive rebellion, one that was already in process within and between bodies and minds prior to the moment in which hostages were captured. Indeed, that the captives' first overtly rebellious act was the seizure of a public address system—an instrument that facilitates communication through the amplification of sound and voice—supports this interpretation, as does the shape of the rebellion's early stages, a refusal to work and a series of self-organized gatherings.

My question about what happened on the roof during the state of emergency elicited a more taciturn response: "After the rebellion, when they put us up in the box they treated us horribly." This simple string of words conceals the depth of their meaning, a depth conveyed not through the words themselves but in how they were uttered. Luqmon extended the word "hooorrrrribly" into a moan that finally trailed into silence. Seated on a couch across from me, he shook his head slowly and let his eyes drop to the ground. We sat there together with the heavy silence filling the room for what felt like an eternity. Just as I was about to change the subject, largely out of my own discomfort, he broke the silence. Flashing a broad smile, he changed the subject from the torture—the negation of being—to theater, its invention. "We had a dude up there who used to put on little plays. He would invent stories with different characters and do all their voices and sound effects." He told me about how brothers were always yelling across the bars, how they were banging on whatever made the most noise, doing any and everything to disturb the tranquility of the surrounding town. However, "everyone would get quiet and listen" when the thespian performed. "It used to sound so real," he explained.[89]

Luqmon's refusal to re-narrate terror, and to instead transmit that which brought him and others joy, intimates an affective condition that the racial-colonial violence of the state could neither penetrate nor extinguish. For those ensnared within, this war zone was also a site of intimacy, care, and *poesis*, of narrative and subjective innovation. While defending their living, breathing bodies, this formally dehumanized population authored new practices of knowledge and sociality into existence. These practices constitute and reflect the "spirit" of rebellion about which so many of the rebels wrote. It is through these fleeting and improvisational labors of Black speculative production that demands for a departure from normative humanity are made and remade at the interstices of war.

As an experiment in archival interpretation, I brought Luqmon and his son Todd together to read "First Letter to My Son," which Luqmon authored after he was shipped from Auburn to Green Haven. Among the numerous accounts of state violence and militant refusal that comprise *Prisoners Call Out: Freedom*, Luqmon's entry stands out as the compendium's only love letter. While others mentioned love, they wrote about a truncated and incarcerated love, a love that was eclipsed by intense hatred of their keepers. By contrast, Luqmon leans into the love he felt toward his four-year-old son, whom he had not yet met: "And even now as I suffer the loss of freedom, my heart sings with the secret knowledge that now there is a part of me that does not suffer or feel the pain, and which is free and alive—and above all young and growing."[90] The three of us sat in the community room of Luqmon's Harlem apartment discussing this document, which Luqmon had not seen in five decades and which Todd could not remember ever hearing about.

Though I initially interpreted "First Letter to My Son" as a fairly transparent expression of paternal longing and affection, after Todd asked his father to read the following passage a second time, a new meaning began to take shape:

> I know without being told that you and your stubbornness are many and they are surely mine. That in your silence you see the countless thousands of things that is the world around you, and rather than speak or express your awareness of them in words, you feel them deep inside. And what you feel is like the notes of music, each different yet somehow related to each other so that they seem to create a sound. But the sound they make is strange and different that the music that you hear in your mind. So they will say, "oh he is so silent, so quiet," and they will not know that you see and hear, and are aware, but do not understand how or why they make the strange sounds they make. And later when you are older and able to express yourself you will try to tell them that they are making the wrong sounds, that what they make is not music. But they will tell you that you are stubborn and do not understand. This is what you will always have between you and the world, for you hear the sound of a different drummer.[91]

In a profound moment of recognition, Todd turned to his father and said, "You wrote this in '71, when I was four years old and you knew exactly who I was."[92] As Luqmon smiled and nodded knowingly, I too had a moment of recognition, realizing that this discourse on sound and silence, rhythm and language, expression, and affect, could also be read as a meditation on the Long Attica Revolt. Our collective reading of the letter unlocked hidden layers of meaning, invoking what anthropologists Sarah Ihmoud and Shanya Cordis call "a poetics of living rebellion": a method that "call[s] on us to think with the fugitive acts of everyday people struggling to survive the shifting terrains of white supremacy, settler-colonial, and capitalist power, and ecological devastation while also tending to the forms of expansion, imagination, and rearticulation that inherently exist beyond this frame.[93]

This poetics of living rebellion mobilizes its own rationality, a way of seeing "the thousands of things that is the world" not through reason, or logic, or by even by *looking*, a mode of apprehension that is structured through the episteme of racial-colonial power.[94] Rather, it acquires meaning through feeling and listening, by engaging with sonic frequencies, pulsing cadences, and the quiet spaces in between. And as Luqmon explains, he could feel the world making the wrong sounds, he sensed its disharmony and arrhythmia in his body and soul, yet no amount of rational communication could make the world hear what he heard.

In her analysis of how Black life is made and remade under conditions of imposed non-being, Katherine McKittrick highlights the importance of sound: "waveforms—the beats, rhythms, acoustics, notational moods, frequencies that undergird black music—affirm, through cognitive schemas, modes of being human that refuse antiblackness just as they restructure our existing system of knowledge."[95] For Luqmon and others, sound was an essential conduit of knowledge. Captives throughout the carceral system had access to the radio and could sometimes absorb the sounds of Black music. The radio became a technology of revolutionary struggle through which listeners engaged in the process of reinventing themselves, developing sonic epistemologies that nourished resistance, contemplative practices, theatrical productions, and Black radical imaginings. Before the takeover and the state of emergency, their secret meetings in the library and other furtive spaces involved discussions of revolutionary politics and culture such that these domains became inseparable. An Attica Brother told me that he authored a manual for carceral guerrilla warfare while immersed in the spiritual jazz of Alice Coltrane.[96] After seizing Attica, the rebels announced to the world that "what has happened here is but the sound before the fury of those who are oppressed."[97] The Long Attica Revolt was a piercing sound, one that, as Fanon tells us, "infuses a new rhythm, specific to a new generation of men, with a new language and a new humanity."[98]

"First Letter to My Son" is at once a love letter, a method of Black radical interpretation, and an index pointing to other source material. Luqmon confirmed that the last line of the above stanza is a reference to William Melvin Kelley's 1962 novel *A Different Drummer*, a citation that enriches the document's surplus of meaning. At their best, explains Joshua Myers, novels are much more than "a literary phenomenon"; they are, like sound an episteme, an alternative "way of knowing."[99] In Kelley's text, which circulated widely within New York prisons during this period,[100] the Black population of a fictional southern town embarks on a massive exodus after Tucker Caliban, the protagonist, suddenly destroys his crops, kills his livestock, and sets his own house ablaze. Caliban is the descendant of "The African," a mythical figure who, generations earlier, escaped from a slave auction block and led a protracted campaign to liberate his people in the tradition of maroon resistance. The African was eventually hunted down and killed, but his son survived and for a century thereafter, The African's descendants labored as slaves, sharecroppers, and servants for the descendants of the slavecatcher that killed him.

Caliban incinerated his house, breaking this cycle of subservience soon after obtaining a stone that his ancestor was said to be praying over before he was killed. The recovered stone represents Caliban's reconnection to a deliberately suppressed tradition of Black ancestral communion, and yet we never fully understand the inner thoughts and motivations that drove him and others, to leave the town. This is because Kelley narrates the novel entirely through the eyes of the white townspeople who conspired to keep Caliban and others in their place. Much like this chapter, then, *A Different Drummer* and "First Letter to My Son" are critiques of the Western episteme's incapacity to comprehend Black rebellion.[101]

When liberal humanist fixations with rights and incorporation into imperialist regimes are dislodged, a remarkable truth becomes evident: the Auburn rebels were never defeated. The incomprehensible violence of the state failed to divest them of their will to resist and become. Across their protracted and multifaceted struggle, they saw themselves as prisoners only in a material sense. In their minds they were already free. They aligned their actions with this belief and charted their own path on the cutting edge of carceral war. When we peel back the many layers of rage, and suffering, and revenge fantasy, when we listen for the rhythms in the heartbeats of struggle and read the text of unwritten and unspoken demands, when we strive for intimacy with the inner logic of Revolt, what we find is neither a desire for incorporation into their world nor dominance over it. Instead, we find an active desire for a new regime of human and a new world where it can thrive.

It was not until June 9, 1971, when the last of the Auburn rebels were transferred to Attica, that prisoncrats finally announced that Auburn had returned to normalcy.[102] However, rebellion continued to seethe just beneath the surface. As with their "solution" to Black rebellion on the streets and in the city jails, the administration merely displaced this insurgency to other prisons. In Green Haven, Luqmon and others became involved in efforts to establish "aboveground" political formations, including a labor union and, as I show in chapter 5, an important "inmate organization" called the Think Tank. Several were shipped to Clinton, otherwise known as "Klinton Koncentration Kamp" (KKK), where, according to Ricardo DeLeon of the Tombs rebellion, they developed "BPP, YLP, Weathermen cells . . . underground prison newspapers, and carried [out] persistent organizational and propaganda work."[103] And of course, several were shipped to Attica.

Litigation forced prisoncrats to release Jomo and the original Auburn transferees into Attica's general population. Veterans of the jail rebellion, and those who had rebelled in large and small ways elsewhere, welcomed them into a giant human circle staged in Attica's A yard. The circle represented an ongoing effort to organize and politicize Attica's population, to break down the internal divisions that kept them divided.[104] An informer later told state investigators he had witnessed "numerous meetings and discussions in the yard" between "inmates who had been involved in the outbreaks at the Tombs and Auburn." Among the topics of discussion, he continued, were "mistakes that were made in the Tombs and Auburn with a view towards implementing new techniques when a disturbance occurred at Attica."[105] Authorities would later cite documents such as this to try to prove that Attica was a preplanned conspiracy, an assertion that sanitizes the repression that made a rebellion inevitable.

Then, on August 21, 1971, California prisoncrats assassinated George Jackson. The chain of events that led to him being shot with a high-powered rifle is shrouded in mystery and disinformation. Painting him as bloodthirsty and demented, the official story is that after initiating a bloodbath that resulted in the deaths of three guards and two captives, Jackson made a mad dash for the prison's outer wall, which he planned to demolish using a vial of liquid he thought was nitroglycerin, but which was actually diluted sulfuric acid.[106] A lesser-known counter-narrative is that Jackson sacrificed himself out of revolutionary love for those he cared about. According to people who survived the ordeal in San Quentin's ultra-punitive "Adjustment Center," where the conflict took place, Jackson knew the guards were planning to snuff him out and fled the prison's interior to protect them from meeting the same fate.[107]

Through words and deeds, Jackson theorized "a prison movement" that was intimately linked to global struggles against capital, white supremacy, and empire. His bold life and premature death had a profound influence on captives struggling in New York and beyond. The immediate response of Attica's population was to organize a memorial in remembrance of their fallen comrade. They organized a daylong silent fast and wore black armbands as a symbol of mourning. "This had an effect," noted one of the organizers. "We noted that if the people could come together for this, then they could come together for other things."[108]

Let us, then, finally turn our attention to the Attica rebellion, a story that we only think we know. As should by now be clear, the events in Attica Prison were the result of a protracted accumulation of anticarceral struggle. The possibilities, perils, and contradictions that were present in earlier moments of the Revolt intensified in Attica. In what follows, I decarcerate our understanding of that rebellion, revealing a Black radical praxis of abolitionist worldmaking.

CHAPTER 3

Attica Is

*Revolutionary Consciousness and
Abolitionist Worldmaking*

Recovered by state investigators from the detritus of the Attica rebellion, an errant sheet of notebook paper outlines three categories of political actors. *Pragmatists* "ask for practical, institutional reforms without challenging the very foundations of the established order." *Existentialists* "no longer believe in institutionalized reform but . . . rebel culturally rather than politically." And "finally come the *revolutionary* protesters, i.e. the militant minority which believes that the Amerikkkan society is so corrupted by its military-industrial governing class and its imperialist foreign policy that only a revolutionary upheaval could bring meaningful change."[1] Penned by an unknown hand, the document evinces the diverse political currents circulating among the rebels, currents representing multiple genealogies, epistemologies, of ontologies of struggle.

This invitation to engage with the Attica rebellion's political multiplicity destabilizes its overrepresentation as merely a critique of brutality, a rational negotiation between the state and its subjects, and a demand for prison reform. *Blood in the Water: The Attica Uprising and Its Legacy*, Heather Ann Thompson's history of Attica, is emblematic of this prevailing approach. Thompson's account deradicalizes the prison movement by relying heavily on state sources and by interpreting those sources through a carceral epistemology that foregrounds questions of recognition, rights, humane treatment, government transparency, legal redress, and reform, all of which stabilize, rather than challenge, the "foundations of the established order."[2] She writes that in the lead-up to the rebellion, "not only had [the prisoners] been developing a critique of poor prison conditions, but they also had begun to discuss how they might reform their institution—what they might do, concretely, to get the state to treat them as human beings who were serving their time, not as monsters deserving of abuse and neglect."[3] While this is certainly true, the aforementioned schema of protest establishes that the understandings, discussions, and aspirations of many within Attica exceeded these pragmatic concerns. Nonetheless, across nearly seven hundred pages of text and footnotes, Thompson never once evokes the powerful abolitionist tendency that flourished among the rebels. When Thompson mentions "revolutionaries," she does so almost exclusively in quoting statements by prison commissioner Russell G. Oswald, New York Governor Nelson A. Rockefeller, and other white antagonists of the rebellion. In doing so, Thompson analyzes state sources on their own terms without extending the same respect to Black radical sources that the state can neither legitimate nor control. The result, as I have argued elsewhere, is the erasure of Attica's abolitionist legacy and the silencing of the revolutionary theories, visions, subjectivities, and desires that it generated.[4]

Our collective understanding of Attica and Black rebellion more broadly is further impeded by the apparent need of analysts to pander to white audiences that devalue, criminalize, and assail complex and protracted Black insurgency while craving explosive spectacles of Black suffering and death. The rebellion was savagely crushed when a state assault force shot thirty-nine people to death (rebels and hostages) and wounded/tortured countless others. Across the various journalistic, cinematic, and scholarly narrations of Attica, we have been led to believe that what is most important about the event is its repression—the way in which the state deployed, then attempted to conceal, overwhelming violence against it. While I offer an extended exegesis and theorization of the massacre in the following chapter, I agree with the Institute of the Black World (IBW) who, just days after the massacre, wrote that "it is much easier for us to grasp the despicable treachery of the state officials of New York . . . than it is to digest the meaning of Attica."[5] I would go further and suggest that explications of official malfeasance and trickery are not only easier to convey but more comforting, because they hold out the possibility of redress, whereas the revolutionary, abolitionist, and anticolonial content of the rebellion, which I endeavor to elaborate here, constitutes a terrifying antagonism with the known world.

Understandings of anti-prison struggle as *revolutionary* struggle were shaped by conceptions of the prison as a microcosm of broader world order. For Attica captives like John "Dacajeweiah" Hill, the dehumanization of imprisoned people was unique in intensity, but not in form. The Atticas of the world were distillations of colonialism's living legacy. In those who operated them, Dacajeweiah saw the same "angry, distrustful, and deathly being[s]" that perpetrated genocide and enslavement against Indigenous and Black people across the globe. The primary difference between Attica and "the average ghetto," Dacajeweiah wrote in an unpublished open letter, was that in Attica "the people who controlled your life were free to racistly harass, attack and murder you [and] . . . the public would never hear a sound."[6]

Dacajeweiah and others abhorred prison: the dreadful food, the medical neglect, the brutal working conditions, and the intensity of racism and brutality it inflicted upon them. Addressing these minimum demands at the onset of the rebellion, the rebels submitted the 15 Practical Proposals, calling for, among other reforms: higher wages, political freedom, religious freedom, an end to censorship, parole reform, better food, educational programs, and improved medical care.[7] However, Dacajeweiah was uninterested in pleading for what he called "antidotes" for the population's suffering. Rather, he and others desired a remedy for that which caused the disease in the first place. In his own words this was "the complete abolition of prisons and the revolutionary overthrow of the system that needs them—capitalism."[8]

This chapter adopts Dacajeweiah's conceptualization of abolition and revolution as overlapping yet distinct ruptures from the carceral world. At the same time, it is indebted to James and Grace Lee Boggs's useful differentiation between revolution and rebellion. Drawing on their experience in the Detroit Rebellion of 1967, the Boggses argue that rebellions tend to be reactive, localized, negative, and fixated on wresting antidotes from outside entities. A rebellion "disrupts the society but it does not provide what is necessary to establish a new social order." By contrast, they conceptualize revolution as a positive social and political project, a collective process that draws on the internal resources of the people engaged in revolutionary struggle, propelling humanity toward a radically new future while enhancing its capacity for creativity, consciousness, cooperation, and moral evolution.[9] The Long Attica Revolt was revolutionary, not only because people like Dacajeweiah and other members of the "militant minority" understood themselves as such, but also because the communal, internationalist, and autonomous practices that emerged presaged a new social order, a new ethics, and new forms of human sociality. This perspective corrects misleading, state-centered approaches that predominate the historiography of carceral rebellion and instead centers a revolutionary abolitionist Black speculative futurity.

Although it lasted only four days and was largely confined to a small patch of sand and gravel enclosed by a concrete wall, we must not allow the event's geographically and temporally limited scale to detract from its significance as an epochal act of abolitionist worldmaking. The Attica rebellion elaborated revolutionary and abolitionist poetics that were profoundly creative. When the captives rebelled, they ruptured an acute site of racial-colonial domination and sowed the seeds of something entirely new. In doing so they embodied, rehearsed, and struggled through a constellation of radical and revolutionary tactics, dynamics, and contradictions. They developed ethical practices of solidarity, interdependence, place-based struggle, self-actualization, internationalism, care, and militant defiance, including experimentation with underground infrastructures of guerilla warfare capacitation.

The prefigurative implications of their praxis were apprehended by the IBW, who called Attica "The Revolution That Was/The Revolution That Is to Be," and by the Prisoners Solidarity Committee, who wrote, "Under these bizarre conditions, [the Attica rebels] projected onto that arena a glimpse of what is possible—class solidarity, the overthrow of racism, the ingenuity and initiative of the masses, their iron self-discipline and their humanness even to the lowest of their tormentors."[10] Many on both sides of the struggle believed that if the dispossessed could organize themselves, seize power, and radically transform social relations in Attica, one of the most repressive sites in the United States, then revolution on a much larger scale was possible.[11]

This chapter constitutes the most ambitious effort to date to elaborate Attica's abolitionist and revolutionary content. For this reason, it largely forgoes retreading the well-worn "negotiations" between the rebels and the state around what Martin Sostre termed the "Attica reform demands."[12] Instead, it amplifies the political and intellectual labor of the abolitionists, revolutionaries, and gangsters who developed a political culture that was inimical to reformism. Less than a month before the prison's eruption, Samuel Melville, a key figure in the rebellion, wrote a letter where he opined in his unique writing style that captives in Attica needed to "avoid [the] obvious classification of prison reformers." He continued: "When u come right down to it of course, there's only one revolutionary change as far as t prison system in Amerika is concerned. But until t day comes when enough of our brothers & sisters realize what that one revolutionary change is, we must always be certain our demands will exceed what the pigs are able to grant."[13] Achieving an abolitionist future—the obvious alternative to prison reform—depended not on forcing the state to concede to pragmatic demands, which the captives should have already enjoyed as nominal US citizens, but on legitimating their movement, nurturing the consciousness of communities in struggle, and helping them recognize that those in power were unwilling and unable to satiate their political aspirations.

The rebellion's development reflected anarchistic practices inherent in Black resistance.[14] Upon seizing the prison, disproving the widespread belief that Attica was "riot-proof," the rebels organized themselves into what George Jackson called "The Black Commune."[15] Thinking with Black radical and revolutionary formations across time and space—precolonial African communities, marronage in the era of chattel slavery, the "semi-liberated zones" of Guinea-Bissau and Mozambique, and the "survival pending revolution programs" of the BPP—Jackson theorized the Black Commune as an autonomous site of self-organization capable of nurturing revolutionary culture and alternative modes of collective life. The bleeding edge of the rebellion was not a demand for inclusion and recognition, but for escape, resurgence, and autonomy. It was an internal demand for complete divestment from the norms of white culture, liberal capitalist ideology, property relations, and respectability.[16] Angela Davis compared Attica to the Paris Commune, which emerged exactly a century earlier, and what Marx wrote of nineteenth-century Paris is equally true of Attica: "the great social measure of the Commune was its own working existence."[17]

In what follows I offer a never-before-told account of the rebellion's eruption and escalation into a form of carceral guerrilla warfare from the perspectives of the captives who participated in it. I then narrate the shift from spontaneity to organization, showing how the rebels transformed their negation of the carceral regime into a communal space, reordering the prison's social geography and establishing a new political order. Next, I elaborate what I call the "Attica Underground." I show how the rebels fostered a clandestine culture of militant self-defense, strategic retaliation, and warfighting capacity with formal and informal links to the Black Liberation Army, the Weather Underground, and other underground formations. Then I turn to the ecstatic, intimate, and erotic experiences of social life in the commune. Invoking Sylvia

Wynter's notion of "genres of human being," I demonstrate that beneath the hard outer layer of war, the inner core of the rebellion was constituted by radically new forms of human sociality and care. Finally, I close by explicating the rebellion's transnational dimensions, theorizing the commune as itself a demand for a new world, one that was not addressed to the state but to revolutionary and progressive forces in solidarity with the rebellion.

TOTAL DISORDER

After five decades of calculated obscurity, a former captive who I'll call "Bugs" offered a narrative that significantly reshapes our understanding of Attica. A streetwise Harlem native imprisoned for selling dope, Bugs witnessed the spark that ignited the prairie fire; he then fanned the flames, helping to set the inferno ablaze. On the morning of September 9, 1971, Bugs had a rare opportunity to travel from Attica's C Block, where he lived and worked, to A block.[18] Escorted through C tunnel by two guards, he reached Times Square, the point at which the prison's four major quadrants intersect. On a typical day, the console officer stationed within Times Square would have spoken to Bugs's escort or inspected his pass, but this day would soon prove the antithesis of typical.

The console officer, William Quinn, was distracted by a confrontation brewing on the other side of the A tunnel gate, where Bugs had been planning to go. Peering through Times Square, Bugs saw a very large Black man facing off with a much smaller white guard. Behind them, a ragged line of men in grey jumpsuits were looking on. He recognized them as "5 Company," otherwise known as "Idle Company," where the most disruptive and oppositional of Attica's captives were thrown together. These "combatants," as Bugs calls them, were "the guys who were ready to mix it up with the police at the drop of a hat." A day earlier, some of them had been involved in a melee during which a guard and a captain were struck, and two captives had been badly beaten. Rumors had circulated since the previous night that the men had been killed, causing insurrectionary fantasies and whispers of retaliation to emanate from the captives' quarters. When Bugs stepped closer, so that he was now almost touching the C gate, he discerned the identity of the combatant. It was Idle Company's unofficial leader, the infamous Tommy "Kilimanjaro" Hicks.

Hicks is somewhat of a mythical figure for those knowledgeable about New York prisons during this era. A brief write-up in the underground press claims that he hated all symbols of state authority due in no small measure to a confrontation in which a beat cop shot his two front teeth out through his face. Depending on who you ask, a picture will emerge of a genius, a brute, a menace, a killer, or a revolutionary. Hicks was one of BPP/BLA veteran Sekou Odinga's first political mentors. Odinga, a legend is his own right, described Hicks as a "George Jackson-like figure," an autodidact, polyglot, scholar, and a pugilist of the highest order. Apparently, he was known for provoking prison guards into attacking him just so he could knock them out two and three at a time. Legend has it that Hicks inspired such fear and anxiety among them that one warden instituted a rule forbidding his subordinates to open the gate to Hicks's cell unless accompanied by an administrator. Hicks inflicted major damage during the Comstock Prison riot of 1963, in which Blacks banded together to violently retaliate against white captives and guards who had long colluded in subjecting them to a Jim Crow-style apartheid regime. After joining the Panthers in prison, Hicks became one of the original thirteen "ringleaders" of the Auburn rebellion. On the fifth and final day of the Attica rebellion, when the state assault force embarked upon their killing spree, several survivors witnessed Hicks charge a state trooper, strike him in the face, and attempt to take his weapon. The story goes that Hicks was seized upon by several agents, thrown in a ditch, and filled with bullets, retribution not only for what he had done in Attica but for his long biography of rebellion.[19]

Though aware of Hicks's outsized reputation, nothing could have prepared Bugs for what happened next. In an instant, Hicks unleashed a brutal punch to the guard's face and followed it with a roundhouse kick to his body. Bugs saw the guard collapse then watched others from Idle Company, along with men from 9 Company, who were lined up farther down the corridor, run into the fray. They mercilessly attacked the other guards, availing themselves of their billy clubs, handcuffs, and keys. Dacajeweiah, who was among the riot-starters, claims that Samuel Melville, a white revolutionary affiliated with the Weather Underground, was there as well. Dacajeweiah, who was of Native American ancestry, wrote in his autobiography: "A black, white, and red man were unified with one instinctive impulse—to defiantly engage the brutal regime."[20]

Dacajeweiah's conceptualization of the rebellion's initiation as *defiant engagement* with a "brutal regime" reconfigures liberal discourses of "violence," "resistance" and even "self-defense" that permeate most historical accounts of Black insurgency. The word *engage* has overlapping connotations: to expose oneself to risk; to entangle, entrap, or interlock with; to enter; or to bind or pledge, as with marriage. Already ensnared at the fulcrum of a brutal regime, these captives, who formally occupied distinct rungs of the racial-colonial order, willingly hurled themselves deeper into the carceral war zone, exposing themselves to greater suffering in order to momentarily redistribute the violence.

Upon beating the guards into submission, rebels from both companies turned their attention to A gate, the only barrier preventing their insurgency from spreading to the rest of the prison. As they struck the gate with their bodies, clubs, and an industrial mop wringer made of solid steel, Bugs could hear Officer Quinn—confident that the Times Square gate that shielded him would remain unyielding—hurling racial epithets and threatening the rebels with retribution. Then it happened: the contingent development that could not have been foreseen nor planned for. Bugs still remembers the loud "pop" that echoed through C tunnel when the bolt holding A gate in place gave out. A flood of enraged beings instantaneously poured into Times Square. In that moment, Quinn represented the empire, the state, the police; he represented Attica itself. He represented all the humiliation and pain that oppressed people had endured for centuries. "The melee that followed was one of the most incredible displays of unbridled hatred ever unleashed against the enemies of humanity," wrote Dacajeweiah. "It could only be compared to a nuclear explosion."[21] The group seized upon Quinn, subjecting him to repeated blows that crushed his skull. He died two days later, the only prison guard to be killed by prisoners during the Long Attica Revolt.

When A gate fell, Bugs turned and saw that one of his escorts had fled in the opposite direction. The other stood petrified, mouth agape, showing a mixture of terror, curiosity, and disbelief on his face. Without thinking, Bugs snatched his baton and gave him a firm slap across the face. Had he done this just sixty seconds earlier, Bugs would have paid a severe price, but in that time conditions had changed drastically. At that moment, with no backup in sight and nothing standing between him and the onslaught, the guard fell to his knees and began to sob. The fragility of the guard and the gate symbolizes the fragility of empire and exposes the public transcript of its impermeability as mythology. Attica was not riot-proof, as its architects claimed. Its gates could be broken, and its guards were neither gods nor masters. They were mere men who bled, cried, and died like any other; this was the proof.

As had become standard operating procedure across this protracted Revolt, the rebels tore through the prison, causing massive destruction and multiplying their ranks by opening everything that was locked.

They charged into Attica's various corridors, offices, halls, shops, and vented their fury against the infrastructure of their captivity. They shattered everything made of glass, ripped the telephones out of the walls, destroyed the plumbing system and the radiators, damaged the cell-locking and electrical systems. They used a forklift to break down the door to the metal shop and other gates separating various areas of the prison. They broke into the armory and seized two gas guns, which they used to launch gas grenades down corridors and into offices where guards were hiding. They used these weapons to physically attack the captured guards, many of whom they stripped naked and marched down the corridors under threats of death, a Manichean reversal of the humiliating ritual that they had been subjected to so many times before. A government report found that thirty-two prison employees sustained injuries ranging from "bruises, cuts, and tear-gas burns to severe lacerations requiring numerous stitches, concussions, and broken bones."[22]

Enveloped in the chaos, Bugs felt a visceral urge to join in the destruction, to attack, rend, and disable Attica's built environment. But ripping pipes out of the wall, breaking windows, and smashing metal surfaces with sticks, as had been done in past rebellions, seemed inadequate for what the situation called for. "They were causing destruction, but it wasn't *my* kind of destruction," he recalled. "I wanted to blow the joint up!" Bugs's expressed desire conjures Fanon, who wrote that in the opening stages of anticolonial war, "to blow the colonial world to smithereens is henceforth a clear image within the grasp and imagination of every colonized subject."[23]

Seizing this opportune moment to materialize his abolitionist imagination, Bugs drew on his existing knowledge of the terrain, organizing a small crew of rebels to carry out an audacious act of carceral guerrilla warfare. He knew that the welding shop contained several canisters of gas and that there was a stove in the clerk's room above the prison chapel. Amid the pandemonium of the rebellion, he and his crew appropriated three industrial sleds, loaded them each with roughly twenty canisters of gas, and wheeled them down the hall toward the chapel. Then they created a human daisy chain, transporting the canisters up the stairs leading to the chapel. As others saw what was happening, they joined in.

> Each man took a canister and handed it to the next man, all the way up to the top, and stacked them in that room. It was filled with old hymnals and bibles, what I call a pyromaniac's dream [laughs]. And we stacked all that stuff in there and we had kerosene from the paint shop. We just doused that room with flammable liquids and went down where they had a ship's mast

head of Jesus Christ made from ebony wood. The thing was massive. We doused it and we trailed that kerosene out, broke the gas line, and when we got downstairs, we lit the kerosene and it raced back up the stairs to the room and when the fire got going we ran back out into the yard and waited. About maybe twenty minutes later the explosion rocked the prison. I mean I think it blew the steeple off the damn building.[24]

Bugs's detailed account reveals how the spontaneity and chaos of collective rebellion created an opportunity for forethought, plotting, cooperation, and self-organization. Wondering about his targeting of a religious institution that figured so prominently in colonial conquest, I asked Bugs why he blew up the chapel. He responded that the church had no significance whatsoever, that he targeted it simply "because it was there." When I asked him why he sought to cause so much damage, why he wanted to blow the joint up, he said, "because I was a New York State prisoner and I was full of rage, so when I got a chance to show what I thought, that's what I thought to do." Empowered by the context of rebellion, Bugs was able to honestly convey the depths of his anticarceral animus.

This criminalized praxis exists in tension with much of contemporary abolitionist discourse, which seems to actively avoid dealing with destructive "engagements" of this sort. A notable exception can be found in the scholarship of Sarah Haley, who offers the concept of *sabotage* for thinking about calculated, agentic, targeted acts such as the leveling of Attica's chapel. Haley writes that although sabotage mobilizes "the will to break and transform rather than to tweak," it not reducible to the destructive act, nor is it solely about attaining a rational notion of victory over oppression. "Instead, it is about the practice of life, living disruption, rupture, and imagined futures; it is about the development of epistemologies of justice and collectivity, contestation of the binaries produced through Western juridical doctrine and the individualizing ethos of criminal punishment."[25] Enacted against infrastructures that deform, constrain, and incarcerate life, a new theory of living is inherent in the act of sabotage. It disables the existing regime and enables the emergence of new forms of being that had previously been impossible.

By the time the chapel exploded, Bugs had made his way to D yard, where the rebels had gathered their hostages and begun to congregate. He remembers the eerie silence that befell the ensemble as they watched thick plumes of black smoke pouring from the roof. Attica's siren was now blaring, meaning that the walls that surrounded them would soon be surrounded by armed agents of the state. Bugs recalls this as a threshold, a moment where the rebels realized that a line had been irrevocably

FIGURE 7. Smoke emanating from Attica's chapel. Photo: Attica Brothers Foundation.

crossed. None of them knew where their rebellion was headed, but it was clear that they could not turn back.

BUILDING THE BLACK COMMUNE

Although Roger Champen was more of a pragmatist than a revolutionary, his intervention at a critical point in the rebellion helped set it on a revolutionary trajectory. Imprisoned for armed robbery, Champ, as he was called, was well-respected throughout the population. He was an Army vet who had done tours in Korea, the Philippines, and Japan, a skilled quarterback on the football field, and an exceptional legal scholar who had helped dozens of men overturn their cases and win their release from prison. Champen had left his cell only after the chaotic opening moments of the rebellion subsided. As he made his way through D yard, he beheld a mass of uncaged people with no purpose, direction, or objective. Most were just milling about, but others were fighting, having sex (some men were reportedly raped), devouring the available food, vandalizing the prison walls, and getting high on seized drugs. Belligerents wanted to do further harm to hostages but were prevented from doing so by the NOI. Fearing racial revenge for their history of collusion with the guards, several white captives had formed their own clique and were preparing to defend themselves from attack.

Overwhelmed by the gravity of the situation, Champen sat for several moments of silent contemplation. On the one hand, he knew that if left to remain on its current trajectory, D yard would implode and the prison would be swiftly retaken before the captives could accomplish something more. On the other hand, he had only a few years left on his sentence and knew that if he got involved, his chances of being paroled anytime soon would be dashed. Ultimately, deciding that the collective good was more important than his individual desires, Champen grabbed a bullhorn, stood on a picnic table, and addressed the assembly. Although his exact words have been lost to history, witnesses recall him demanding discipline, organization, and unity. He told those in D yard that "the wall surrounds us all," that it was time to "eliminate fights among ourselves and focus our hostilities outside."[26]

A participant later testified that after Champen's internal demand, no one had to be directed or told what to do, that "everyone just fell into position."[27] The hostages were moved to the center of the yard and encircled by a ring of NOI guards. Multiple lunch tables were pulled together to serve as the site of official political discourse and above this, a wooden canopy and lights were erected. The rebels rigged a public address system to allow speakers to address the commune directly. They rationed food and water and prepared meals such that between September 10 and 12, three meals a day were provided for more than twelve hundred people.[28] They demarcated a medical area with a sheet and a white cross. There they dispensed prescriptions and offered basic care to the rebels as well as the hostages.[29] They dug a latrine and established cleanup details to remove waste. When it got dark, they brought their sheets and blankets into the yard and set up tents and lean-tos along the periphery of the prison's inner walls. They named the passageway beyond their control—the barred gate separating A Tunnel, the site of the rebellion's eruption, from Times Square—the Demilitarized Zone (DMZ).[30]

As the rebels demarcated new spaces for being in common, they constructed what Ruth Wilson Gilmore calls an "abolition geography."[31] The organized disorder of the rebellion's opening moments had weakened the prison's material integrity. Now, they exerted kinetic energy and intellectual labor to remap their world, literally "changing places" without ever leaving the walls. Archived video surveillance footage of occupied D yard offers a glimpse of the collective labor they poured into the commune. As the camera's frame pans across the densely populated yard, the voice of a state trooper can be heard over the pervasive sound of hammers driving nails into wood. With a sense of utter bewilderment, he says: "They seem to be building as much as they are destroying!"[32] Carved out from within the sphere of racial-colonial domination, the commune became a zone of epistemological antagonism with the state and an infrastructure of collective self-creation. Comprised of embodied consciousness and collective physical, intellectual, and emotional labor, the captives developed this infrastructure not only to meet their immediate needs, but as a model for the political forms that would be needed in the future. As such, they became what Joy James calls "architects of abolition," creating a historical blueprint for an abolitionist world that future generations can study and learn from.[33]

Dacajeweiah's maternal ancestors belonged to the Haudenosaunee Confederacy, otherwise known as the Iroquois Confederacy, and were indigenous to the land upon which Attica was built. He experienced the commune's emergence as the creation of a decolonized space-time. Refracting the Indigenous concept of the Medicine Wheel through Black and Red Power rhetorics, Dacajeweiah wrote, "On September 9–13, 1971, a new nation was born, a time when all four walks of this earth came together to make a change for social and human dignity, at any cost even if it meant our lives."[34] D yard became an exuberant space of disalienation, liberation, and oneness, an example of what solidarity and revolutionary struggle could produce.

The rebels established a new political order within D yard's abolition geography. Elections were held in which representatives from each cellblock were chosen to serve on a committee of spokesmen. Their

FIGURE 8. Commissioner Russell G. Oswald (seated, bottom left corner) meeting with elected spokesmen, including Frank "Big Black" Smith (standing with sunglasses), Herbert X Blyden (to Big Black's right, looking directly into camera), Richard X Clark (seated, with glasses), Roger Champen (to Big Black's immediate left), and L. D. Barkley (to Champen's left, with glasses). Photo: Associated Press.

insistence on calling themselves "spokesmen," rather than "leaders," resonates with Fanon's assertion that contrary to Western bourgeois ideology, ordinary people-in-struggle are capable of governing themselves. For Fanon, the political party must serve as "the vigorous spokesperson and the incorruptible defender of the masses."[35] Otherwise, anticolonial movements will be vulnerable to neocolonial retrenchment. Among the spokesmen were Roger Champen; Herbert X Blyden, who had served on the negotiating committee during the Tombs rebellion; Richard X Clark, a prominent member of the NOI; and L.D. Barkley, an orator of enormous power.[36] To preserve the integrity of their new order, they also established a security force. Frank "Big Black" Smith, a well-known football player and coach, was voted its chief. Over the course of the rebellion's four days, as many as three hundred rebels participated in security. They patrolled the yard, the catwalks, the tunnels, and cell blocks, ensuring the safety of the rebels, the hostages, and the outside observers who were later sent in to aid the "negotiations" with the state.[37]

During subsequent investigations of the rebellion, the New York State Special Commission on Attica and other government entities exhibited an abiding interest in the commune's decision-making structure and security imperatives. In its final report, the commission concluded that the commune relied heavily on coercion, that it lacked effective democratic decision-making processes, and that the majority of those in the yard feared violence if they voiced unpopular opinions. Echoing the counterinsurgent analysis of carceral rebellion promulgated by the FBI and others, the commission argued that most of the rebels were forcibly "herded" into D yard and could only leave if granted a pass, the very same pass that prison authorities had used when they were in control. The report quotes a local white surgeon who was allowed into the yard to check on the health of the hostages and who later called the commune a "dictatorship." According to Dr. Warren Hanson, the security force was an implement for a small group of militant leadership, who deployed the group to lord it over the voiceless and powerless masses. "In many respects," the commission concluded, "the inmates' society in D yard was arranged in the same way that the authorities, against whom they were rebelling, ran Attica."[38]

The state's characterization of the rebellion as a dictatorial regime contrasts sharply with the recollections of many who were intimately familiar with its inner dynamics. Spokesmen were selected based on their respect within the population and appointed through a consensual process.[39] According to Champen, time constraints often forced the spokesmen to make unilateral decisions. However, he maintained that he and others were elected because the masses trusted them to make these decisions, and that they always informed the commune of such decisions after the fact. Moreover, when faced with major decisions such as those involving the content of their written demands, the spokesmen communicated the issue to the commune and opened the floor for debate. In these instances, anyone who wanted to have a voice in the decision-making process needed only to approach the negotiating table, ask for the microphone, and address the yard. This included those who did not speak English, as Young Lord and Auburn "ringleader" Dalou Gonzalez remained on hand to perform Spanish translation. When debates arose, decisions were reached by simple majority, as indicated by the volume of applause issued in favor of a given course of action. Multiple outside observers would later refer to D yard not as a dictatorship, but as a "true democracy."[40]

In a document written to the surviving Attica Brothers in 1973, Jomo Omowale took exception to the media portrayal of the Attica spokesmen and the security force as a coercive apparatus and the rendering of the commune's majority as "zombies and fools who only move when they're told, who can't think for their own selves."[41] At the time, over sixty of them, including Jomo, were facing charges for their role in the rebellion and the core function of the trial, as Jomo saw it, was to criminalize Black resistance, to portray the rebels as warmongers, and to demonstrate that an autonomous social order established by Black "convicts" and revolutionaries could not possibly be more just or egalitarian than capitalist democracy. He argued that this had to do with the authoritarianism and violence inherent in Western democracy. "It is difficult for people who are familiar with the dictatorship form of government to accept the fact that a group of a couple hundred people could decide things or move on things in a collective or democratic manner." He argues that security was not an instrument of coercion but rather a means of preserving the integrity of the commune and the well-being of each of its members:

> Security was mainly responsible for the food, medical care, clothing ... what have you; to keep people from getting ripped off sexually or keep the water supply, to see that everyone have mattresses, blankets at night—mainly that everybody stay together and recognize one another as brothers, under the same roof, same conditions, being able to look above the 1/1000 of an inch difference such as skin, not to get hung up in the racial thing and not let it grow in to a racial riot—this is one of the main things we tried to prevent.[42]

Through security, the commune protected itself from regressing back toward the culture of exploitation, racism, and atomization that defined the normalized carceral regime.

However, the D yard commune was not a utopian zone free of contradiction, conflict, or coercion. When I asked an Attica survivor if it was true that otherwise unwilling captives were herded into D yard and prevented from leaving, he said, "Let me put it to you like this, everybody wasn't down."[43] Others represented a counterinsurgent element from within. In 1972 Thomas Hughes published an acerbic essay in the conservative *National Review* under the pseudonym Frederick Wiggins. He argued that the rebellion was orchestrated by a small band of communist, anti-white fanatics, who "did not speak for the more rational element of the inmate population."[44]

On September 10, a small group of white captives was ordered to dig the commune's latrine as punishment for flying a white flag above their tent, an apparent signal to the state that they were on the side of the enemy. Later that day, two white men—Barry Schwartz and Kenneth

Hess—were observed giving an unauthorized interview to a reporter who had been allowed into the yard. A tribunal was held in which the pair were found guilty of treason and incarcerated in what the rebels called the "Peoples Prison." Michael Privitera, who was also white and had been suffering from a mental episode so severe that he was unable to remember who he was or control his motor functions, was also incarcerated in this prison within a prison. Three days later, when state investigators were picking through the ruins of the commune, the bodies of Schwartz, Hess, and Privitera were recovered from the yard. One or more of the rebels had stabbed them multiple times and slashed their throats.[45]

The incarceration and execution of these men by the rebels complicates Attica's abolitionist legacy and exposes a tension within abolitionist genealogies. Prison abolition tends to be framed as an ethical practice in which reliance on violence and carceral techniques is discarded in service of building a "world without prisons."[46] What then are we to do with the fact that the Attica rebels erected a prison within what I have already called an abolition geography, and summarily executed three men for violating an unspoken code of conduct and being difficult to manage? It is important to note that while several of the rebellion's revolutionaries identified as abolitionists, others did not. Dalou Gonzalez, a Third-World Marxist, once said, "I don't advocate abolishing prison. What are we going to do with the Rockefellers and the Nixons and shit?"[47]

Dalou's provocation compels a retheorization of abolitionist ethics under battlefield conditions. His claim that prisons are necessary stems not from his investment in the state's monopoly over legitimate violence, nor in the moral validity of the prison in an abstract sense, but from his tactical calculation that in order for a besieged population to endure in the face of determined opposition, liabilities and antagonists would need to be incapacitated and neutralized. After all, taking the guards hostage and imprisoning them had been the Revolt's condition of possibility, enabling the delimited freedom that had brought them to this point. Attica was an incomplete abolition, not only because it occurred on a temporally and geographically limited scale but also because it necessitated other forms of captivity. Still, Attica represented something worth fighting for. And fight they did, in visible and invisible ways.

THE ATTICA UNDERGROUND

In an untitled essay in *Babylon*, an underground newspaper launched by the Algiers-based International Section of the BPP, two key figures of

New York's radical prison movement argue that "in the United States there exists an undeclared state of war." On one side were the poor and dispossessed masses struggling to eke out an existence across the globe. On the other were the "super-rich," their corporate empires, and their "racist reactionary state machinery." However, a large fraction of the populace, especially those who the authors call "black reform integrationists and white liberals," were confused about the nature of their struggle and the methods needed to win. This confusion was dangerous since the people were running out of time. What was needed was for progressive political forces to accept the terms of war and "transcend all constraint, all restrictions imposed upon us by the enemy."[48]

Written in December of 1971 in the Brooklyn House of Detention, this call to arms was co-authored by Dhoruba bin-Wahad, a leader in the New York chapter of the BPP and a key architect of the Black Liberation Army, and Herbert X Blyden, of the Tombs and Attica rebellions. Its authorship and analysis are indicative of the underexplored relationship between the Long Attica Revolt, the BLA, and the Black Underground more broadly. This relationship has remained largely unknown for multiple reasons. First, underground formations are inherently secretive. Second, many of Attica's revolutionaries have passed away, often violently, either during the September 13 massacre or years after the rebellion, sometimes under questionable circumstances.[49] Third, analysts of slavery and prisons have tended to produce narratives of Black supplication and suffering over those of agentic and militant rebellion.[50] Fourth, evidence of Black militancy gets pruned from historical narratives out of fear that its appearance could be used as a pretext for greater repression. By contrast, my conception of the Long Attica Revolt treats the axiom "repression breeds resistance" as paradigmatic.[51]

The underground is a geographical metaphor for a condition of militant refusal and exteriority to respectability, visibility, governability, and upward mobility under racial capitalism and colonial war. This condition traverses political, cultural, economic, and spatial domains of furtive, often illegal confrontation with the state. When framed through the practical concerns of revolutionary warfare, the underground is a clandestine infrastructure for carrying out politico-military actions. These actions include financial expropriations, prison breaks, transportation of fugitives, and armed offensives against state infrastructure and personnel. The basic premise is that a liberation movement cannot succeed if it does not have an apparatus for engaging in criminalized activities, ideally those that leave no definite links to the aboveground forms of organization it is designed to support.⁵²

The BLA was not a discrete organization, but rather an umbrella term for various decentralized units. Zayd Malik Shakur defined it as a "solid, subterranean apparatus existing here in the United States—an aligned conglomeration of many armed groups that base their credentials on action."⁵³ In her opening statement during a trial for the killing of a New Jersey state trooper, Assata Shakur, perhaps the best-known member of the BLA, described its origins and nature:

> The idea of a Black Liberation Army emerged from conditions in Black Communities: conditions of poverty, indecent housing, massive unemployment, poor medical care, and inferior education. The idea came about because Black people are not free or equal in this country. Because ninety percent of the men and women in this country's prisons are Black and Third World. Because ten-year-old children are shot down in our streets. Because dope has saturated our communities, preying on the disillusionment and frustration of our children. The concept of the BLA arose because of the political, social, and economic oppression of Black people in this country. And where there is oppression, there will be resistance. The BLA is part of that resistance movement. The Black Liberation Army stands for freedom and justice for all people.⁵⁴

The fact that the grievances of the BLA around issues of conditions, poverty, housing, unemployment, medical care, education, freedom, equality, oppression, and state violence are virtually identical to the formal demands issued throughout the jail rebellion, the Auburn rebellion, and Attica disrupts the dominant narrative that Attica was about reforming "poor prison conditions," and instead focuses our attention on the generalized conditions of anti-Black genocide under globalized empire.

More than receptacles for the criminalized poor, prisons were crucibles through which the BLA, as a historically specific articulation of the Black Underground, was forged in blood and bone. Following the Panther 21 frame-up, Kuwasi Balagoon, Dhoruba bin-Wahad, and other New York Panthers were forced underground, organizing themselves into autonomous BLA cells. At the same time, the radicalizing effects of racist state violence combined with militant political education to create a situation in which, according to Assata Shakur, Black revolutionaries were "being manufactured in droves in the ghetto streets, places like attica, san quentin, bedford hills, Leavenworth, and sing sing."⁵⁵ Kareem C'Allah joined the BLA in Auburn and estimates that thirty other men followed the same path, including Woody "Changa" Green, Anthony

"Kimu" White, Henry "Sha Sha" Brown, James "Kato" Dunn, James "Joe Chink" Daniels, Mariano "Dalou" Gonzalez, and Jomo Sekou Omowale.[56] There were also folks like Blyden, Akil Al-Jundi, and many others who never "officially" joined, if such a thing can be said about an underground organization, but were politicized by BLA ideology and who DOCS would label "BLA Associates." BLA actions carried out beyond prison walls often made their connection to Attica explicit. For example, three months after the massacre, a BLA Unit calling itself "The Attica Brigade" claimed responsibility for a grenade attack on an NYPD patrol car.[57]

Although *The Black Panther* begins mentioning the BLA as early as October of 1968, the public became aware of its existence in the spring of 1971, when it claimed responsibility for killing two New York City patrolmen and wounding two more. At roughly the same moment, captives began establishing their own underground formation within Attica's walls. The so-called "Central Revolutionary Format," also known as the Tactical Intelligence and Combat Unit, aimed to build an infrastructure of political radicalization, communication, and military capacity that linked the militant factions of Attica's various political constituencies through a pyramid structure. At the top stood the Chief Tactician, the organization's "sole commander . . . responsible for the arranging and movement of . . . troops [and] . . . the orderly planning of maneuvers." In the middle were tactical Mission Planners, responsible for exchanging information, enforcing discipline, and ensuring the coordination of maneuvers. Finally, there were a network of cells, composed of no more than four "brother-comrades" who had undergone a program of political, economic, and socio-cultural "indoctrination" as well as the study of the "military-industrial complex" and guerrilla warfare.[58]

Mao Tse-Tung's *Little Red Book*, Mikhail Bakunin's *Revolutionary Catechism*, and the writings of Frantz Fanon and George Jackson were required reading.[59] The extent to which this plan for an underground formation was actually realized prior to the Attica rebellion, the identity of its participants, and its impact during the Revolt all remain an open question. But the incubation of this clandestine politico-military apparatus alongside and in dialogue with the BLA significantly reshapes how we think about Attica, revealing it to be an expression of the Black Underground and an articulation of a global, decolonial, abolitionist, revolutionary counter-war.

Of course, not all the rebels in Attica saw the rebellion in these terms, participated in these formations, or identified with radical or revolutionary politics. Bugs represented a sizable fraction of the population that saw themselves, not as revolutionaries, but as gangsters: outlaw capitalists committed to individual financial gain. Bugs approached New York City's huge market for heroin as a path to upward mobility, familial stability, and material comfort within existing capitalist social relations. When I asked him if he was down with the Panthers, he invoked a tone and rhetorical style that reflected his mindset in the early 1970s:

> Panther? What the fuck a Panther? Nigga, I'm a gangster! Fuck I know about that shit? I ain't political, you know, my politics is "I want what's mine every day in my pocket." Shit, yeah I know conditions is bad and we need to do better, but I'm trying to get out of here and go home where I can do better for myself. Shit, you got two million dope fiends in New York, buying dope every day, I'm gonna be one of the dudes that's gonna sell them some, you understand. And that's my outlook. My revolution is gettin' me some money and movin' my family to a nice house, buyin' me a car, dress well, and eat well, yeah. Cause the rest of that shit ain't nothin'. Wind up in a box somewhere with people singin' over your ass, talkin' bout he challenged the power that be.[60]

While espousing revolutionary politics might garner admiration from the people, it was also likely to result in a painful life and a premature death.

Interestingly, however, it was Bugs the gangster and not the revolutionaries who orchestrated one of the most significant guerrilla acts during the Revolt. After the explosion of the chapel, Bugs melded into the D yard assembly, making a concerted effort to keep a low profile and avoid the spotlight, thereby evading the worst of the retaliation he knew was coming. This was key to his survival. While many of the self-described revolutionaries understood the importance of situational awareness, anonymity, deniability, and evasion, so too did putatively apolitical gangsters like Bugs. The porous boundary between acts of outlaw capitalism and radical politics helps explain why the prison was such an effective site of BLA recruitment.

On September 13, when the state assault force descended upon the commune, the rebels, clearly incapable of marshaling effective resistance, surrendered unequivocally. What ensued was not a battle between an underground army and the state, but a massacre, one frequently likened to the Mỹ Lai Massacre of 1968 in which the US military slaughtered, tortured, and raped hundreds of unarmed civilians in the Quảng Ngãi province of South Vietnam.[61] The weapons and forms of ammunition that state actors used to carry out their indiscriminate killings and

FIGURE 9. Part of the arsenal recovered during the aftermath of the rebellion. Photo: New York State Museum.

targeted assassinations have been well documented.[62] However, the existing literature on Attica has either deemphasized or actively avoided elaborating the primitive military capacities developed by the rebels. This is because doing so disrupts the narrative that Attica was a negotiation for expanded rights and privileges within the prison. Rather it suggests that there was a powerful contingent of brothers who, like Bugs, wanted to "blow the joint up," either as a pure expression of Black rage or as a method of conducting revolutionary warfare through the prison.

Across the rebellion's four days, captives employed the limited resources at their disposal to develop defensive and offensive capabilities. After seizing the prison, hundreds of rebels took found objects to the badly damaged but still functional metal shop, where they fashioned them into all manner of bladed weapons, literally sharpening the tips of their spears in anticipation of drawing the enemy's blood. They constructed barricades on catwalks and in underground tunnels, some of which, according to state actors, they attempted to fortify with electrified wire.[63] They dug a series of foxholes and a long trench that was partially lined with punji stakes—sharpened spikes designed to impale anyone who falls inside, a defensive method popular with the National Liberation Front of South Vietnam.⁶⁴

Following the rebellion, investigators with the state police bomb squad identified several objects of interest, including hundreds of Molotov cocktails and what they described as a "cannon-like device" constructed of an empty oxygen cylinder affixed to a wheelbase. In the metal shop they located an explosive device constructed from a fifty-gallon drum filled with toluene, a combustible liquid. Resting on top of the drum was a football helmet, a blanket, a stick, and a clock. The device had been rigged so that when the helmet was moved, a five-second timer would activate after which an electric charge would flow to the toluene through the filament found in a broken light bulb, causing the device to explode. The bomb squad also located what they called a fully operational "antipersonnel device" in the northwest corner of D yard. Likely constructed by Sam Melville, the so-called "Mad Bomber," the device was comprised of a five-gallon turpentine container affixed to a remote firing mechanism.⁶⁵

Many of these munitions were inoperable, and those capable of functioning were never used. The cannon was incapable of launching projectiles. The toluene bomb was connected to an outlet that had no power. The antipersonnel device found in D yard was fully operational, but was not filled with combustible liquid. Similarly, several of the Molotov cocktails contained cottonseed oil. Others were functional but never ignited.⁶⁶ Nevertheless, the existence of these weapons is indicative of the resourcefulness of the brothers within the yard and their martial subjectivity. The rebels were preparing to defend the commune from attack, not to wage an offensive campaign against their keepers.

These battle preparations were not symptomatic of generalized bloodlust, but rather a militant and rational response to the condition of domestic war. The rebels had ample opportunity to amass enemy casualties, had that been their goal. Many were not averse to violence, indeed had committed acts of violence against their own communities. Moreover, they knew from experience that they would be punished, brutalized, and/or killed regardless of how they treated the hostages. However, as we have seen in the preceding chapters, these combatants curbed their powerful urges for revenge. Elected spokesman Richard X Clark later explained how, as soon as the rebels inverted the power relation, transforming the keepers into the kept, the guards' sense of white masculine supremacy evaporated and in its place was terror, humility, and supplication. "I could feel the vulnerability of their position," he

FIGURE 10. Cannon-like device recovered during the aftermath of the rebellion. Photo: New York State Museum.

wrote. "They had treated us like animals, and now the tables were turned."[67] Given this context of totalizing power over enemies who had shown time and time again that they had no respect for the captives' humanity, it is significant that the rebels did not exact revenge.

In 1972, a BLA communique criticized Attica, and specifically its NOI participants, for failing to execute the hostages.[68] Clark responded, in his book *The Brothers of Attica*, that protecting the hostages was not a religious, moral, or metaphysical question, but a pragmatic and political one: "Muslims know that all white men are devils, and we do not protect devils." He saw defending the hostages as a strategic necessity since, "if we kill them, the man will come right in. There's no point in going to the electric chair for killing a devil that can't get away."[69] The rebels might also have found good reason for not killing the hostages in the pages of Fanon's *The Wretched of the Earth*. Though often misread as an apostle of violence, Fanon argues that while violence is necessary to achieve decolonization, it is woefully insufficient, for "the legitimate desire for revenge alone cannot nurture a war of liberation."[70] In fact, if left unchecked, reciprocal violence will only feed on itself, be exploited by opportunistic elements within movements, and forestall the emergence of new, liberated subjects. For Third World Marxists like Dalou, the martial writings of Mao Tse-Tung offered a rationale for treating the hostages civilly. Mao advised guerrilla forces to give lenient treatment to prisoners of war in order to disorient the enemy.[71]

I am suggesting that although Attica had a robust underground military culture, the decision to refrain from retaliatory violence during the rebellion was grounded in revolutionary political theory and was based on a sober assessment of the field of battle. The rebels withheld violence as a tactical calculation necessary for surviving the battle with the understanding that the next battle would likely require reevaluating this necessity. We might further theorize the rebels' refusal to torture or execute the hostages as a pedagogical strategy designed to educate state actors and the world that it was possible to develop a more humane way of treating those over whom one has power. Thus, rather than satisfying their immediate desire for revenge, they engaged in an almost theatrical performance of benevolence toward the hostages. They built a shelter to protect them from the sun; gave them cigarettes, water, fruit, sandwiches, and coffee; and allowed them limited amounts of exercise.[72] Following the rebellion, multiple hostages reported on their humane treatment; one of them said, "When they ate hot meals, we had hot meals. When they had sandwiches, so did we. We had mattresses but they didn't."[73] Their performance led a journalist with the *Village Voice* to proclaim that the rebels "should be thought of as an 'oppressed nation,' one that was more just and less violent than the larger nation outside."[74]

Despite some criticism of their tactical nonviolence, the BLA's response to Attica was overwhelmingly supportive. In a letter to journalist and Attica observer Tom Wicker, Eldridge Cleaver called Attica "the highest expression yet" of the revolutionary politics that the BPP/BLA helped bring into being, while BPP/BLA soldier Sundiata Acoli called it "a milestone in the development of the New Afrikan liberation struggle behind the walls [and] a symbol of the highest development of prisoner multinational solidarity to date."[75] Ashanti Alston said that as bad as it was, the massacre could have been much worse, and probably would have been if the brothers hadn't held back a lot of their anger. Ashanti was among the BPP/BLA soldiers who helped raise funds and organize a massive funeral for slain Attica Brothers in Brooklyn. Mutulu Shakur participated as well and recalls how the Attica Brothers were treated as warriors killed in battle. "We took the mangled and battered bodies and carried them on our shoulders. Long before we became aware of such a tradition in the South African Struggle, it had become a tradition at the funerals of Black Liberation Army heroes."[76]

The very public organization of the Attica commune coexisted with a rich underground culture that preceded the rebellion and had formal and informal links to broader movements. Amid the clandestine development of the commune's defensive and offensive capabilities, the rebels negotiated the proper role of violence just as they did in movements beyond the walls. Ultimately, an assessment of material and environmental conditions caused the rebels to stand down, a decision that was lauded by some and criticized by others. Attica was a space-time of war strategy and tactics, of militant creativity and innovation, of rational planning and conspiration, but war was only the hard outer layer erected to protect something much more sacred. The commune was also a space-time of ecstasy, joy, love, intimacy, pleasure, and collective Black radical becoming.[77] It is to these undertheorized aspects of its intimate social life that I now turn.

"TO LOVE EACH OTHER IN HUMANHOOD"

"We are men! We are not beasts and we do not intend to be beaten or driven as such."[78] These words were passionately orated by L. D. Barkley during a press conference held in D yard on the first night of the rebellion. By asserting their *masculine* humanity in radical defiance of institutionalized dehumanization, the Attica rebels extended a long tradition of Black radical and revolutionary discourse in which figures like David Walker, Frederick Douglass, Marcus Garvey, Claude McKay, and Malcolm X fundamentally linked the attainment of Black liberation to the realization of Black manhood. The politics implicit in this form of rhetoric have been roundly criticized for their alleged neglect and/or hostility toward feminist and queer approaches to liberation, their ostensible endorsement of Black patriarchy, and for enacting an assumptive logic that necessarily disqualifies dehumanized, dominated, and/or feminized subjects from manhood and radicalism.[79] It is certainly true that the Long Attica Revolt emerged out of a social context in which the very real problems of sexism, homophobia, and misogyny undermined the integrity and dynamism of movements.[80]

However, if we understand that Black manhood has never been a stable phenomenon, and that—per Sylvia Wynter—white, Western, bourgeois man "overrepresents itself as if it were the human itself," then we must ask, what kind of men were the Attica rebels proclaiming

FIGURE 11. Attica rebels with their fists up in D yard. Photo: Associated Press.

themselves to be? Following the IBW, who wrote "the men at Attica were different from their captors," I contend that through their praxis of communing, the rebels enacted forms of gendered life that productively disrupted normative conceptions of manhood.[81] They elaborated improvisational and provisional forms of intimate sociality, subjectivity, and human being that fundamentally challenged the foundations of capitalism, patriarchy, and racial-colonial world order.

It is important to note that Attica's captives experienced the normally functioning prison as an apparatus of abjection, anti-Blackness, and gendered dehumanization. Two descriptions of what, reformulating Fanon, we might call the "psychopathologies of the carceral regime" provide the existential ground against which the radically new modes of social being were fashioned in the commune.[82] In a 1972 interview for the Attica Defense Committee, Big Black described the prison as an engine of alienation that obliterates the capacity for independent thought and action: "You no longer think or act or have the right as a human being to express your political beliefs, to be able to talk about and do the things which is in yourself to do."[83] In a letter to his mother, L. D. Barkley narrated his own slow death: "I'm dying here little by little everyday Mom ... You can't imagine what it's like here."[84] In the following chapter, I argue that carceral death machines like Attica are animated by an aspirational logic of white patriarchal mastery, fostered via disavowed practices of ritual violence that are highly sexualized and fundamentally anti-Black. For now, I cite these endogenous narrations of Attica's necropolitical effects in order to juxtapose them with what was said and done in the commune, thereby revealing the magnitude of the transformations the rebellion engendered.

Accounts from surviving Attica Brothers include detailed narrations of the political debates and events that occurred in the yard, but also lavish narrations of what it felt like to be in and of Attica's abolition geography. In an interview for the *Eyes on the Prize* documentary series, Big Black beautifully articulates his exuberant experience:

> The feeling is hard to describe but it's a feeling of like being born again where you didn't have to worry about who you were or what color you were or where you were at, you know, even being in prison, you know, I didn't feel it then. I didn't even feel like I was in Attica State Prison, just to view what was happening in that yard, you know, it's like freedom. And it was a form of freedom. You know, I didn't have, you know, that keeper up on top of me and, and, I felt like whatever I was feeling, whatever I was thinking was running together, my emotions was into my thoughts and my feelings, you know, and I had all of that together and I, and I used that emotion when I was in the yard to bring, to solidify my thoughts and my feelings and that I was thinking what I was feeling. And everybody else was in that kind of vehicle, the way I felt. I felt, I felt good, ya know. I felt relieved. I felt, I guess, liberated.[85]

By destroying existing relations of psychological, social, and spatial domination, the rebellion unlocked new channels of inner mutation, metamorphosis, and self-actualization. It not only birthed an incipient abolition geography, but new subjects who elaborated themselves as they inhabited, explored, and enjoyed their illegal freedom. Endeavoring to describe his inscrutable transformation, Big Black narrates the convergence of his thoughts, and feelings with those of others and with the geography, forming a collective consciousness, such that the brothers were no longer frozen in carceral space. Instead they inhabited a *vehicle*—a conveyance of collective transport to a liberated lifeway, the location of which was entirely uncharted.

Big Black's narration is suggestive of Neil Roberts's contention that freedom is best conceptualized as an ongoing process of marronage rather than the static antithesis of unfreedom. His concept of *sociogenic marronage*—"a non-sovereign state of being whose conception of freedom is shaped by cognition, metaphysics, egalitarianism, hope for refuge, and the experiences of masses in a social and political order"—is useful for understanding how the Attica rebels engaged in flight while remining fixed in cartographic space.⁸⁶ By collectively liberating themselves from a domestic warzone and employing collective praxis to create an abolition geography, they constructed an illicit freedom that was more total than that which liberalism allowed even in the so-called "free world," not only because theirs was not premised on capital, property, and slavery, but also because they fashioned it on their own.

This profound experience of liberation and movement while remaining in place was tied to practices of celestial observation and cosmic communion. Like abolitionist Harriet Tubman, who famously used the North Star to usher enslaved Africans to freedom, the Attica rebels were stargazers. As they lived in rebellion, they stole time to contemplate the immensity of the universe and to become intimate with that immensity. As Dacajeweiah recalls:

> What stunned me most was this one elderly brother who was looking up at the glimmer of silver stars and was sobbing uncontrollably. I asked him, "What's wrong, brother?" He replied, "I am so happy. This is the first time I have seen the stars in 23 years." At that point I understood freedom as more than just free will unobstructed by any external factors but also as an emotional, sensory symbiotic relationship between wo/man and the universe. It was simply gratitude, humble submission to the natural laws of creation and the sense of elation of feeling that connection.⁸⁷

Dominant characterizations of the rebellion as a purely rational interaction between an aggrieved group and repressive agents of the state violently truncate the exuberant and transcendental modes of consciousness, curiosity, and becoming that were nurtured through rebellion. In moments such as these, this consciousness was not preoccupied with the state or even with politics traditionally construed, but rather with a profound desire for genuine connection to other people, the natural environment, and the cosmos.

In his account of the rebellion, Richard X Clark brings to the surface the gendered practices of intimacy and Black masculine care work that have remained largely submerged in discussions of Attica.⁸⁸ Although the text is rife with homophobic and misogynistic language, it describes the erotic life of the commune in ways that suggest the rebels' practices of doing gender outpaced their often deeply problematic rhetoric. For example, in one passage Clark describes what it was like to walk through the yard on the first night of the rebellion:

> So we walked around, talking softly, just rapping. It was the first time we'd ever seen one another at night, and we just walked through the yard checking. We went through each group . . . me and Shockanee and a brother named

Ahmel, who had one arm and walked with a cane and whom I knew from Auburn.... He was a Five Percenter with a beautiful understanding. There were many other brothers walking around that night, in twos and threes, just strolling, like at a picnic or carnival, just relaxing. We talked on memories of good times, of bad times, we got a lot of gossip ... we drank some pineapple juice and orange juice and smoked without worrying and checked on the hostages and talked ... and tucked some brothers in for the night.[89]

Clark's account is evocative of Audre Lorde's notion of the erotic. Writing as a Black lesbian feminist who had been marginalized in phallocentric and heteronormative movement spaces, Lorde, who also theorized Black life as warfare, offered the erotic as a resource from which women could realize their deepest desires and build bridges of mutual understanding across difference. She saw the erotic as a nonrational form of knowledge in which intellect, emotion, and spirituality become indivisible, creating "an internal sense of satisfaction to which, once we have experienced it, we know we can aspire."[90] At first glance, this Black feminist idea may seem ill-suited for the context of the Attica rebellion, but for those who were there, particularly on the first and second nights, the yard was a sanctuary, a picnic, a carnival, a space-time of relaxation, creativity, care, and indeed, the erotic.

The Attica commune embraced homosocial and homosexual intimacy. We can read the evocatively ambiguous last line of Clark's statement—"we tucked some brothers in for the night"—in a number of ways. Literally, we might surmise that after their long walks, he and the brothers made sure their comrades were comfortable and cozy, pulling their sheets above their shoulders and wishing them a good night. Or perhaps they tucked themselves in together and formed a deeper physical connection. At the very least, the statement articulates a sense of compassion and care that upends normative conceptions of Black revolutionary masculinity within and beyond the prison. The McKay Commission claimed that once the rebels got organized, homosexual relations were "outlawed," but the brothers themselves say otherwise. Clark recalls that in response to the "homos" who were initially "going crazy" under blankets and in corners throughout the yard, he made an announcement "that there was a time and place for everything but that this was neither the time nor the place."[91] His announcement was not a prohibition of homosexuality but rather a call for the collective self-discipline necessary to overcome the challenges that lie ahead.

Following the pathbreaking work of Cathy Cohen, I argue that Attica reflected the radical potential of queer politics that "encourages the fluidity and movement of people's sexual lives."[92] According to Bugs, D yard included an authorized place for sexual activity. He explained how, as they remade the yard, Attica's gender rebels appropriated a structure normally used by the guards for surveillance, covered it with white sheets, screwed a red lightbulb into the socket, and began calling it "the red-light district." As he tells it, the "homos" were "taking care of business, engaging in wild sex, fucking and sucking dicks all night."[93] The Revolt entailed a praxis of sensuous, erotic, carnal activities through which rebels unleashed their most radical imaginations while exploring their suppressed desires and capacities. For some this meant exploring each other sexually; for others it meant taking long walks, telling stories, or singing The Delfonics over open fires. "Brothers were embracing all the time," Clark wrote, recalling that he witnessed someone spontaneously break into tears because he could not remember ever being so close to other people.[94]

The plurality of the Revolt crossed lines of race, gender, politics, and ability. Ahmel, the brother who, according to Clark had "one arm" (actually, he had a medical condition called spastic monoplegia), had also participated in the Auburn rebellion and later joined a BLA unit involved in multiple bank expropriations.[95] After Times Square fell to the rebels, sixty-five captives were released from Attica's E block, a small building near the prison hospital that housed people with medically diagnosed intellectual and physical disabilities. Clark's manuscript notes that present in the yard were several elders and people with heart conditions, rheumatism, asthma, diabetes, epilepsy, cerebral palsy, and wooden legs. He claims they wanted to be present in D yard to experience the commune, noting that they were placed near an exit so they could leave at will.[96] However, the killing of Michael Privitera suggests the profound limitations of the rebels' capacity to create space for expressions of intense cognitive diversity.

Perceptive outsiders noticed the rebels transforming themselves into new collective subjects. When he first met Blyden in the commune, observer Tom Wicker asked for his full name, to which Blyden responded, "I am Attica." Wicker later noted the strange way in which the rebels were dressed. They donned football helmets, fashioned their blankets into ponchos, and had obscured their faces with sheets and scarves. Subsequent analysts have read the refusal of many of the rebels to divulge their names and reveal their faces as a rational effort to conceal their identities from the state. Their desire to avoid being singled out for retaliation certainly played a role. At the same time, Wicker wondered if these flourishes might be "more costume than necessity." Black intellectuals at the IBW leaned into this possibility, writing that the rebels "fashion[ed] new garments to symbolize their new identities."[97]

In my reading, "We Are Men" was a capacious declaration of gendered human being articulated by imperfect people who had access to an imperfect language. It is likely that all of the rebels did not identify as men. Yet the manhood that they proclaimed and enacted subverted norms of masculinity rooted in white bourgeois ideology and colonial patriarchy. We can only speculate about how these subjectivities and discourses might have evolved if allowed to continue flourishing. However, we know that for some of the rebels they continued to do just that. By late 1974, Jomo Omowale began to move away from liberated manhood as a rhetorical model. That year he signed off from one of his letters with the salutation, "To Love Each Other in Humanhood."[98]

ABOLITIONIST INTERNATIONALISM

Across the trials, public forums, and journalistic, documentary, and historiographic accounts that trace the rebellion and the massacre, the Attica demand for "speedy and safe transportation out of confinement to a non-imperialistic country" has been generally ignored or brushed off as an immature exercise of revolutionary fantasy. There are several reasons for this. First, the demand was never realized, a fact that has facilitated its relegation to the margins of Attica's politics. Second, three of the outside observers whose subsequent writings and recollections have shaped the dominant conception of the rebellion interpreted the demand as unserious, unrealistic, and relatively unimportant in comparison to the other demands.[99] Third, transportation was not a hegemonic demand. According to the radical lawyer William Kunstler, one of the Attica observers who did support the demand, commitment to it among the rebels never exceeded a "couple hundred" men, out of nearly 1,300.[100] Fourth, the demand was totally ignored by state actors and did not at all figure into the formal negotiations between the rebels and the state for the release of the hostages. Finally, pursuing the implications of this demand's articulation and the networks that supported it unsettles the historical domestication of the rebellion.

However, once we understand that this demand was an internal demand—that those articulating it were not appealing to the imperialist state but to the anti-imperialist Black underground—it becomes legible as a logical, and even a plausible, call for militant audacity. Clark recalls that "some of the brothers, who were more politically aware were very strong on" the expatriation demand. On September 11, 1971, the commune voted against including it in their formal list of demands but agreed to allow those who supported it to continue pursuing the possibility informally. "We took the position that if they were really interested . . . they could be in charge of it and they could do their own thing," Clark wrote.[101]

Thinking critically about the expatriation demand again allows us to see the political multiplicity and the democratic structure of the Revolt at work. While some may have been against internationalism as a concept, it is likely that others withheld support for the demand on tactical rather than ideological grounds. By contrast, people like Akil Al-Jundi saw internationalism as critical. A Tombs and Attica rebel, Al-Jundi framed the transportation demand as a way to connect the struggle of incarcerated and internally colonized subjects in the United States with anticolonial rebels in Angola, Mozambique, and Guinea-Bissau, those "who opposed the rule of colonialism and daily resist Portugal's endeavor to prevent them from gaining national liberation and determining their own course in life." Arguing that global anticolonial struggles were naturally aligned with those of imprisoned radicals in the United States who were fighting empire from within, Al-Jundi wrote, "When they take a stand against imperialism, they're taking a stand for the benefit of prisoners."[102] His conception of domestic prisons as central to global empire embeds the Revolt within broader traditions of anticolonial nationalism that, as Adom Getachew explains, fought against hierarchal social orders within and between nations.[103]

The abolitionist internationalism inherent in the expatriation demand was part of a deeper current running through Black revolutionary politics within and beyond US prisons. Building on a strategy established by the radical Civil Rights Congress two decades earlier, the New York City jail rebels had discussed taking their grievances before the United Nations.[104] At the same time, organizers of the California prison unionization movement were petitioning prisoncrats to apply the Geneva Convention to US political prisoners and to allow those on death row to apply for asylum in communist regimes.[105] As the Auburn rebellion was unfolding, prisoncrats in Elmira, a prison near New York's border with Pennsylvania, intercepted a letter addressed to the United Nations in which captives sought repatriation to Angola in order to fight in their war of liberation against the Portuguese.[106]

Other strands of rebel internationalism were inspired not by hegemonic postwar institutions like the United Nations, but by criminalized forms of transnational fugitivity. In 1970 Eldridge and Kathleen Cleaver were granted political asylum in Algeria where, with the help of a vibrant expat community, they established the International Section of the BPP. Over the next three years the International Section, which obtained formal recognition from the Algerian government, harbored a steady stream of revolutionaries who successfully escaped the clutches of US repression, including Sekou Odinga, Larry Mack, and Cetewayo Tabor of the New York Panther 21.[107] Victor Martinez of the NYC jail rebellion was also believed to have obtained refuge in Algeria. According to Kathleen Cleaver, by 1971, the International Section was essentially a "colony of fugitives."[108] While many found the expatriation demand ludicrous, others pointed to these examples as evidence of its viability.

Although state actors and liberal observers did not take the demand seriously, organizers within the BPP/BLA did. Much has been written about BPP co-founder Bobby Seale's brief and underwhelming appearance in D yard as an Attica observer.[109] However, representatives of the Oakland-based BPP Central Committee were not the only Panthers involved in Attica. When Attica erupted, New York's BPP chapter continued to have an aboveground footprint even though state repression and FBI-facilitated internecine warfare had forced many of the key figures underground. A twenty-one-year-old Panther named Bernice Jones, who would later change her name to Safiya Bukhari, was one of the major figures overseeing these aboveground operations, as well as serving as a link between aboveground and underground activities.

As repression led to increased political imprisonment, Bukhari hurled herself deeper into prisoner support work.[110] Even before Attica, she had been writing to and visiting the Auburn rebels and had helped Ricardo DeLeon and Kato Dunn establish a BPP chapter in Clinton. Upon hearing the Attica demand for transportation, she immediately contacted foreign governments with whom the Panthers in Algeria had developed ties. The precise details of what happened next are unclear. Bukhari claims to have personally secured verbal agreements from government officials willing to harbor the rebels in Cuba, North Vietnam, and North Korea, while Panther 21 member Afeni Shakur listed North Vietnam, North Korea, Algeria, and Congo Brazzaville. Informed through some combination of underground networks, rumor, and imagination, Dacajeweiah and others believed that as many as seventeen countries had agreed to accept them.[111]

At least one contingent of NY BPP/BLA soldiers traveled to Western New York to coordinate the expatriation demand. In a *New York Times* op-ed, Afeni Shakur claimed to have arrived on the evening of September 11, only to be prevented from entering by roadblocks, where heavily armed state agents threated them with assassination. She further claimed that earlier that morning Dr. Curtis Powell, another acquitted member of the 21, had slipped through the roadblocks and unsuccessfully attempted to enter D yard to communicate directly with the rebels.[112] FBI surveillance, meanwhile, claimed that the Panthers' plan was to hold a press conference outside the prison during which they would contact Eldridge Cleaver by phone. Cleaver was then expected to publicly announce the Algerian government's approval of the rebels' asylum.[113]

In his testimony before Congress, Panther lawyer and Attica observer William Kunstler claimed that on Sunday, September 12, he met with Dr. Powell, Kwando Kinshasa, Lumumba Shakur, and another New York Panther that he did not name, but who was likely Afeni Shakur. Although I have found no evidence to support her claim, Afeni wrote in the *Times* that "at the command of the inmates a jet would land at Kennedy Airport to safely transport those inmates to a non-imperialist country." Later that day, during his last trip to D yard, Kunstler was alluding to these BPP/BLA soldiers when he announced that "there are four third world country people across the street from this prison prepared to provide asylum for everyone that wants to leave this country from this prison," a claim that vexed the observers who were trying to convince the rebels to surrender and accept the reform proposals they had drafted with prisoncrats.[114]

Additional support for the expatriation demand came from unexpected places. In a bizarre twist, members of the Jewish Defense League wrote letters to Governor Rockefeller and staged sit-in protests in front of his office and that of democratic presidential candidates, demanding the authorization of their proposal to exchange Attica rebels with Jews imprisoned in the Soviet Union. The far-right Zionist organization claimed to have communicated with Herbert X Blyden, obtaining his agreement to be exchanged for Sylva Zalmanson, who had been confined in a Moldavian gulag since 1970. Little else is known about the plan and whether the Soviets were even aware of its existence. While the Soviet Union could hardly be characterized as a "non-imperialist" regime a decade and a half after the atrocities of Stalinism were exposed, perhaps Blyden believed that his chances of survival were greater behind the Iron Curtain than they were beneath the Stars and Stripes. There is no evidence of any movement on this plan, but the point stands that many people at the time, both inside and outside the prison, took the expatriation demand seriously.[115]

The internationalism of the Revolt was articulated in other ways. Prior to, during, and after the rebellion, the rebels forged symbolic and material ties with anticolonial movements, especially those in Southeast Asia and Cuba. It is well known that the Attica Liberation Faction's "Manifesto of Demands and Anti-Oppression Platform" was adapted from a similar set of demands constructed as part of the Folsom Prison strike in California. It is less well known, however, that at some point after the Faction submitted these demands to New York's prisoncrats, the document was translated into the Vietnamese language and issued to authorities in Tan Hiep, Tu Duc, and the Con Son Island National Prisons in South Vietnam, where CIA-sponsored "Technical Advisors" from the US were aiding the pacification effort through carceral strategies developed at home.[116] During the rebellion, Attica observer Tom Soto of the Prisoners Solidarity Committee gave one of the rebels a ring that was said to be made from the metal of an American bomber shot down by Laotian women in Southeast Asia.[117] These stories indicate that imprisoned combatants in California, New York, and South Vietnam were appropriating each other's cultural production to elaborate a shared critique of imperialist carcerality.

Following the massacre, the Union of North American Residents, an expat community for Black Americans in Cuba, wrote open letters of solidarity to the surviving Attica rebels: "Your conduct, discipline and courage and unswerving determination to carry your actions to their logical conclusion is admired as an example to all who struggle for justice and respect as human beings." The Union forwarded a message of solidarity from a Vietnamese contingent in Cuba: "We are indignant about the brutal prison system in the United States, which we have heard and read about. George Jackson's letters from prison have deeply moved our youth. Angela's example is brilliant. We know that there are thousands of American revolutionaries in US prisons. And although we cannot express our support for them because of the US new blockade, our hearts are always with them. . . . Our victory in Viet Nam is also your victory."[118] Third World movements recognized the prison movement as a legitimate revolutionary struggle. Communicating through the National Lawyers Guild, Attica rebels responded: "You and all those who have taken an active stand against fascism, imperialism, racism and injustice have been our impetus as you've made the concept of liberation a reality. The people in Cuba, North Vietnam, North Korea, the People's Republic of China, the Palestinians, the Mozambicans, Angolans, and those from Guinea-Bissau are our paragons."[119]

These expressions of transnational affinity, solidarity, and common interest did not evolve into a coalition capable of attacking US empire from within and beyond its borders; nor did the aircraft that many hoped would arrive to whisk the rebels to a locale beyond the reach of empire ever materialize. Yet the mere existence of these revolutionary demands, aspirations, and conspiratorial plans unsettles the rights-based framework that has dominated the narration of Attica for the past fifty years. The failure to document and theorize this internationalism has facilitated the rebellion's domestication, shifting it from a repudiation of US empire to a palatable cry for better treatment within its dungeons. For those on the cutting edge of the prison movement, prisons were zones of combat within a historically protracted, geographically diffuse arena of Revolt against patriarchal white supremacy, capitalism, and globalized empire.

I have labored to decarcerate the revolutionary meaning and significance of Attica. Its maximum demands are not to be found in the formal negotiations between captives and the state for improvements to prison conditions but in the living theories and practices of Revolt itself: in modes of militant self-defense, sabotage, and counterviolence; in methods of autonomous self-governance, aboveground and underground organization and worldmaking; in practices of narrative, archival, and epistemic insurgency; in internationalist politics and radical antiracisms; and in the new forms of gendered life, social consciousness, and human being to which the Revolt gave rise. The self-activity of the Revolt's intellectuals, engineers, organizers, and participants marked the disintegration of authoritarian rule and the production of an illegal freedom. They liberated themselves from an acute zone of war and, for a time, lived in a world of their own making. This world was provisional, incomplete, and imperfect, and yet was rooted in radical principles of justice, equality, and mutuality that were more capacious than those of the world beyond the walls. For this reason, the rebellion was interpreted by many not as a temporary rupture of racial-colonial power, but as a revolution, an abolition, a decolonization, a proper condition of existence. More than fifty years later, Attica remains a living example that collectively, ordinary people can be more than the sum of their parts.

PART TWO

Prison Pacification

CHAPTER 4

Gender War

Sexual Revenge and White Masculine Repair

At 9:46 a.m. on September 13, 1971, a National Guard helicopter released thirty-five pounds of tear gas into Attica's D yard. Within seconds, rebelling captives and captured guards were debilitated by its effects: an intense choking sensation, shortness of breath, burning eyes and skin, headaches, dizziness, and vomiting. Had the state intended simply to incapacitate the rebels, rescue the hostages, and recapture the prison, the dispersion of gas and the deployment of ground forces armed with blunt instruments would have sufficed, as no significant resistance was offered. That state actors took a far more spectacular approach indicates that neither basic incapacitation nor the preservation of life were priorities. As thick plumes of white crystalline powder consumed the yard, the assault force—armed with what one survivor called "a fantastic assortment of man-killing weaponry"[1]—indiscriminately fired more than two thousand rounds of ammunition in less than fifteen minutes. When the fusillade ceased, they systematically hunted and assassinated known radicals, including L. D. Barkley, the rebellion's chief spokesman, and Samuel Melville, an anti-imperialist bomb expert, among others. The state killed twenty-nine rebels, most of them Black, and ten white hostages. Additionally, they left more than a hundred survivors with serious physical wounds. It was one of the most lethal encounters in the US settler state since the Wounded Knee massacre of 1890.[2]

Although the Attica massacre has been narrated numerous times, this chapter explores an aspect that remains undertheorized: the pervasive

FIGURE 12. Military helicopter flying over D yard. Photo: Attica Brothers Foundation.

use of rape and other forms of gender-based violence as modes of domination. It argues that at its core, the massacre was a collective act of *sexual revenge* that aimed to punish the rebels and defend the racial breach within normative masculinity. In dialogue with existing conversations exploring how normative conceptions of gender and race are constructed through anti-Black sexual violence,[3] this chapter describes a range of terroristic practices that are likely to be agonizingly familiar because of their centrality to the maintenance of white power across historical regimes. It shows that as a Black masculine insurgency, the Long Attica Revolt hurled the figure of White Man into crisis and divested it of a core pillar: the politically, culturally, and sexually subordinated Black male. In response, state actors, white civil society, and mass media unleashed well-worn rituals of violence that aimed to expel these evildoers from the domain of masculine humanity, while simultaneously revitalizing the ascendancy of White Man.

In an unpublished interview, Roger Champen, an elected spokesman of the rebellion, described the effects of the massacre in the following way: "A psychological operation . . . was performed on those boys. . . . Some got killed. Something happened to those guys. . . . They're not the same kind of people no more. I don't know what has happened to them, but they're not there."[4] I opened this chapter with a description of the state's lethal incursion into Attica, but here Champen calls our attention to a different register of violation. His use of the phrase "psychological operation" has military and medicalized connotations, suggesting that Attica was at once a counterinsurgency *psyop* and a kind of surgical procedure that altered people, such that they remained living but were no longer "there." It is this other kind of killing, the kind that assails the body but truly targets the personality, spirit, soul, that is the focus of this chapter.[5]

Champen's remarks indirectly raise questions of masculinity and sexual violence. His formulation is rife with uncertainty, ambiguity, and perhaps an incapacity to give a precise name to what he struggles to describe. Although he was there, he places rhetorical distance between himself and "those boys" to whom something happened. In other words, that something, whatever it was, did not happen to "us," nor did it happen to "men," but to an infantilized subset of the captive population, who was permanently altered and unmade by it.[6] I do not profess to know what was in Champen's mind at that moment. However, the fact is that sexual violence lies at the core of counterinsurgency, though this fact is often obscured by generic terms such as "torture" and "brutality," which do not immediately conjure sexual violation although they often involve it.[7] If, for Champen, these sexualized dynamics were what constituted the unknowable "something" that happened to "those boys," then his inability to name it and his need to distance himself from it is consistent with the tendency of men to underreport being victimized by sexual violence and to equate sexual victimization with "emasculation."[8] Champen's silence is compounded by a silence in the academic and journalistic literature on Attica in which the state's extensive use of sexual violence remains unnamed and undertheorized. Yet thinking through it is key to understanding the massacre, since sexual violence is how "soul murder," as Nell Irvin Painter described the racial killing that does not kill the body, is carried out.[9]

As previous accounts of Attica have done, I draw heavily from the primary research produced by the New York State Special Commission on Attica (the McKay Commission), a government-appointed investigative body that conducted hundreds of interviews with Attica survivors, prison personnel, and administrators. I also draw on the civil litigation through which Attica survivors successfully sued the state for subjecting them to cruel and unusual punishment.[10] These materials provide an invaluable resource for cataloguing the scale and scope of atrocity.

However, I decenter these duly noted, juridically mediated, and scholastically authorized sources of evidence, focusing instead on "discredited," "inadmissible," and "untrustworthy" modes of knowledge, analysis, and narration. I construct my argument by thinking and theorizing with criminalized Black rebels, both living and dead. What they have to say upends the popular notion that the ongoing refusal of the state to divulge its secrets are what prevent us from fully understanding Attica. Thinking in expansive ways that others might dismiss as "mental illness," these rebels force us to resituate the apocalyptic violence of the state within nonlinear and overlapping space-times of anti-Black violence and rebellion: the slave ship, the plantation, the battlefield, the colony, the way back then and the here and now. Their heretical conceptions of the massacre are an aspect of the Long Attica Revolt, as they demonstrate the incapacity of state violence to divest them of their cognitive autonomy. By reading the state archive against itself and by submerging official sources within the unorthodox frameworks the rebels provide, this chapter excavates a domain of forbidden knowledge that the state has no language to describe. But before plunging into the chapter's three major sections, I analyze prisons for men as zones through which broader notions of racialized masculinity are constituted.

GENDER WAR

Asked why the FBI was so obsessed with Black revolutionary formations such as the Black Panther Party, Dhoruba bin-Wahad offered a psychosexual explanation. He explained that at a concrete level, Black people with guns did not pose an existential threat to a highly militarized US society. However, in the white collective unconscious, the image of armed Black men arouses the terrifying specter of Black male "potency." "One of the things that scares white America is the thought of assertive Black manhood," he explained. "They cannot deal with the threat that it represents to white male supremacy."[11] Dhoruba's remarks call attention to the sexual anxieties structuring racist state repression, those involving the Black male's supposed genital and sexual superiority. And it does not matter that what Tamari Kitossa has termed the "Black Phallic Fantastic" —the idea that Black men are "priapic, hypersexual, prone to rape"—is a product of white invention.[12] The fact that power, authority, and the capacity for violence are concentrated in the White Man's hands forces the world to contend with that which might otherwise only dwell in his mind.

Under capitalist modernity, White (bourgeois, heteropatriarchal) Man is defined over and against other modes of gendered life. These subordinated humanisms include the biologized category of women as well as feminine, queer, and trans socialities. Crucially, though, it also includes colonized and racially marked "men." This means that Blackness is a historically feminized racial category in which Black males are divorced from hegemonic masculinity.[13] In this specific context, "manhood" and "masculinity" refer to structural locations of dominance and entitlement articulated across environmental, economic, political, racial, and sexual domains. The White Man's ongoing effort to maintain racial and gender dominance helps explain why the political repression of Black men often take explicitly sexualized forms.

Participants in the Long Attica Revolt sought to upend a structure of gendered and sexual racism that constantly assailed their humanity. In chapter 2 I discussed the "rectal examination" as a mundane form of state-sanctioned rape employed to humiliate and dehumanize imprisoned people. Examples of similarly violent rituals abound. For years prior to the Revolt, white male prison guards in Attica and elsewhere referred to their black and brown truncheons as "nigger sticks." Not only did they wield these symbols of phallic power against noncompliant, deviant, and/or revolting captive bodies, they also used them to issue nonverbal commands. The captives were not seen as worthy recipients of rational speech, only as inanimate objects controlled by sexualized violence. One tap against the prison's concrete walls meant stop, two taps meant walk, three taps commanded silence.[14] As a medium of communication, the nigger stick demarcated the boundaries between white masculine humanity and ungendered Black nothingness, between those who were men and those who were not.

Capitalist social relations are entangled with these racial-gender dynamics. The orderly functioning of the prison enables those who work in them to support themselves and provide for their families, and therefore to see themselves as men. When the Revolt took place, the New York Department of Corrections (NY DOCS) operated twelve prisons and had an annual budget of over $100 million, most of which was paid out in employee wages.[15] These prisons were (and are even more so today) economic pillars of the communities that surrounded them. Amid a deindustrializing political economy, prison towns like Attica, Dannemora, and Comstock increasingly depended on the state-funded transfer of human bodies from Black urban geographies to function as commodities of industrialized punishment.[16] Racist ideologies engendered what W.E.B. Du Bois termed the "psychological wages of whiteness," preventing most whites from recognizing that the social forces responsible for the overwhelmingly Black captive population were also responsible for closing their factories and mills, creating a landscape in which working in a prison was one of their few economically viable options. In many cases, multiple generations of white male guards earned their living by lording over a seemingly boundless supply of racially othered males convicted of all manner of criminalized acts, constantly reinforcing notions of inherent white male supremacy.

Commonly referred to as "up south," the rural regions of New York State have a long history of organized white supremacy, fascism, and militant anticommunism, all of which are entrenched within the carceral system.[17] News that guards at Eastern Prison in Napanoch, NY, were actively recruiting for the Ku Klux Klan made headlines in 1974, but by then the interconnections between white supremacist organizations and the prison were well-known to captives, who regularly witnessed cross burnings and Klan rallies on prison grounds. Immediately following the massacre, family members and supporters of the rebels spoke of being harassed at state police checkpoints while groups in full Klan regalia were allowed to pass through without incident. After the massacre, the state's prison towns were awash with racist propaganda; one sign likened Black people to cancer and called for them to be summarily cut from the social body.[18]

Encapsulated by their statement "We are MEN! We are not beasts and do not intend to be beaten or driven as such," the Attica rebels asserted a political masculinity, and in so doing repudiated these genocidal logics and bestial dehumanizations. Critical interventions by Black feminist scholars have subjected masculinist formulations such as this to analytical pressure, showing how the dynamism of potentially transformative movements is hampered by patriarchy and how women and gender-nonconforming people were forced to struggle against these logics, both in the broader world and in their own movements.[19] The Revolt was not untarnished by patriarchy, sexism, and homophobia. Not only do phallocentric, sexist, and homophobic discourses litter the archive the rebels left behind, but many of them had committed acts of gender violence against each other and those in their communities, and it is critical that this dynamic be named and condemned for the harm that it caused.

At the same time, their declaration of manhood is more complex than it may initially appear. First, it must be understood within the context of the collective subordination of these "men" within a historical structure of carceral gender violence that destabilizes conventional notions of their gendered positionality. Moreover, as I showed in the preceding chapter, the practices they enacted under the rubric of "manhood" involved emergent forms of inner mutation, intimacy, sensuality, care, queerness, collectivity, and interdependency that defy hegemonic norms. When viewed through this frame, it becomes clear that as a totality, the Revolt was not an attempt to appropriate the trappings of white patriarchal power, to attain parity with White Man, or to become Man at the expense of others' autonomy or dignity.[20] It was an effort to chart a new course for what a revolutionary manhood or "humanhood," as one survivor termed it, could become. The Attica massacre violently disrupted this emergent project. In fact, it sought (unsuccessfully, I might add) to eradicate this very idea.

Unwilling or unable to comprehend the significance of this gender insurgency, state enforcers experienced the Long Attica Revolt as a violent threat to their manhood. While the rebels were still in control of D yard, Executive Deputy Commissioner Walter Dunbar told his subordinates that "he saw an inmate take a sharp instrument, cut out [a hostage's] reproductive organs and take the young man's organs and stuff them in his mouth."[21] After the massacre, when ten prison guards lay dead or dying, Dunbar and his cronies told the press that the rebels had slit their throats. The *New York Times* reported that rebels "emasculated" a hostage, editorializing that their conduct "reflect[ed] a barbarism wholly alien to civilized society."[22] These claims, which also found their way into FBI surveillance reports, were readily accepted because of their compatibility with deeply ingrained ideas about Black male savagery and sexual degeneracy. Moreover, they legitimated the existing social order, demonstrating the importance of containing this civilizational threat by all available means. The problem, however, was that the rebels did not slash the guards' throats, and castrated no one.

I refrain from calling this counterfactual a "lie" since it exposes a disavowed truth. In the symbolic universe of patriarchal white domination, Black rebels did not simply seize a prison, capture hostages, and assert demands. They murdered, mutilated, and sexually violated White Man, exposed his political and sexual impotence, and forced him to autocannibalize the ultimate symbol of his masculine identity. A masculinity contest, a gender war, lay at the heart of their efforts to keep prisons under control, and it was a zero-sum game. One side won by making the other side lose. The winner accumulated masculinity as a finite and privatized resource, while the loser was literally and figuratively unmanned.[23]

The sexualized history of white racial terrorism in the United States suggests that through their castration fable, state actors were projecting their disavowed anxieties and fantasies onto the rebels.[24] The fetishistic dispossession, appropriation, and consumption of Black male genitalia is a vaunted ritual of white sociality.[25] Fanon writes that although his unconscious mind is saturated with "the most immoral instincts and unmentionable desires," the White Man attempts to repudiate his irrationality by transferring his desires to Black males, and labels them the embodiment of evil.[26] It can hardly be considered coincidental that the person Dunbar accused of committing this atrocity was the rebellion's head of security, a dark and physically imposing man named Frank "Big Black" Smith. Fanon continues: "Still on the genital level, isn't the white man who hates Blacks prompted by a feeling of impotence or sexual inferiority? Since virility is taken to be the absolute ideal, doesn't he have a feeling of inadequacy in relation to the Black man, who is viewed as a penis symbol? Isn't lynching the black man a sexual revenge? We know how sexualized torture, abuse, and ill-treatment can be."[27] Let us now return to the Attica massacre and look squarely at this sexual revenge. For it is in these inflictions of violence that we can see a key source from which Man derives his identity, power, and coherence.

"THIS IS ALL A NIGGER IS GOOD FOR"

"You ever seen that picture in that black book in Omaha, Nebraska, from 1919 when they lynched a Black boy?" The question caught me by surprise. Bugs and I had been discussing his "exit interview" with Attica Deputy Warden Karl Pfeil, which occurred a week after the massacre. Although he hadn't been told, Bugs knew then that if he did well on the interview, he would be transferred, but if he failed, he would remain in Attica and be tortured. When asked the pivotal question—"What did you do in the yard?"—Bugs told the truth, but nothing more: "I survived." Pfeil accepted this answer and approved Bugs's transfer to Comstock, a maximum-security prison near the Adirondack Mountains, promising that if he found out Bugs was more involved than he was letting on, he would be brought back to Attica to suffer the same fate as those deemed "militants." It was at this point in his story that he asked me about the lynching picture. I immediately recalled the archival footage of Queen Mother Moore's invocation of lynching during her 1973 speech in Green Haven Prison.

I had seen the photo. It depicts William Brown's lifeless body atop a smoldering pyre. Flames engulf his mutilated head like a terrible halo. His seared flesh is the color of charcoal. The police had arrested him, but a mob kidnapped him from the kidnappers, stripped him naked, hanged him from a lamppost and filled his already lifeless body with bullets. They then tied his remains to the back of a police car and dragged him to a major downtown intersection. They placed him on a pile of wood, doused it with lamp oil, and set it aflame, cooking his flesh to a crisp. Then they tied the desecrated body to the back of a car for a second time and paraded it through the streets of downtown Omaha. Pieces of the noose and probably pieces of his flesh were taken as souvenirs. Upward of twenty thousand people witnessed the spectacle. His corpse was eventually buried in a grave that remained unmarked until 2019. The image is not something one forgets. Dozens of white men are standing shoulder to shoulder around Brown's scorched form. They are respectably dressed in suits, ties, overcoats, and sports caps. A child peers curiously over the shoulders of the men in the front row. Some of them are smiling.[28]

Bugs continued, "Yeah, well imagine on the town hall lawn, that picture being blown up to a church window size and the caption under it says, 'This is all a nigger is good for.' Now as I'm getting on this Corrections Department bus, and I'm shackled and everything, and I stop and I hesitate and I look at that picture." I'm confused by what I am hearing. Was Bugs telling me that a lynching occurred in the town square of Attica, New York, in 1971? Was he asking me to conjure the horror and spectacle of Brown's lynching so that I would have a frame of reference to understand what happened to him and the others? Was he explaining that the response to Attica was performed in a manner specifically designed to communicate that Black people had value only as objects of degradation? His instruction that I "imagine" the photograph suggested that he was making some kind of figurative analogy.

"And where was this picture?," I asked, trying to clarify.

"It's on the town hall lawn."

I repeat back what he is telling me. "They had a blown-up image of a, of a, of a Black man being lynched and burned on the town hall?"

"His charred body was laying there, he had been lynched and set afire. Yes. And the body was like black charcoal, you know, there was all of those townspeople. They had been observers of it, you know?"

I was too disoriented by the way in which his narrative defied a linear temporality, how it ruptured any notion of a progressive teleology, to fully comprehend what Bugs was telling me.

It was August of 2020. People across the United States and beyond were in the streets rebelling against state-endorsed white supremacist terror. Three months earlier George Floyd, a Black man from Minneapolis, had been murdered by a white cop, who kneeled on his neck for over eight minutes. His fellow officers stood idly by as Floyd cried out, "I can't breathe" several times. Eric Garner had cried the same words when an NYPD officer choked him to death in 2014. Both were spectacles of ritual violence that were video-recorded, circulated on social media, and consumed millions of times. The public outcry did nothing to stem the tide of killings of Black men and women by police and other racist vigilantes in between and since these events. I couldn't help but think of this as I was talking with Bugs about the white supremacist terror he experienced in Attica, fifty years earlier. He was answering my questions by invoking an act of white supremacist terror that occurred fifty years before that. I had completely lost track of time. What for me created a profound cognitive dissonance was for Bugs a durable historical artifact: "If I live to be a hundred I'll never forget that scene that's indelibly stamped in my mind."

Bugs was explaining that as he waited to be sent "upriver" in a line of shackled Black men, he saw that a physical reproduction of this infamous photo had been magnified and displayed in the town square. Beneath it someone had written, "This is all a nigger is good for!" White folks in the town of Attica understood the massacre through the moral and libidinal economy of lynching and were empowered enough in this understanding to allow this grotesque commemoration of anti-Blackness to be displayed in the center of their community, just as other white people had done with William Brown's corpse, and with George Floyd, Eric Garner, Michael Brown, ad infinitum.

Although generally associated with what Billie Holiday hauntingly vocalized as "southern trees bearing strange fruit," historian Manning Marable explains that "the form lynching assumes—hanging by the neck, shooting, castration, burning at the stake, or other spontaneous and random forms of violence—is secondary to the actual terror it evokes among the Black masses."[29] Lynching is an American ritual of racial terrorism and spectatorship that emerged as a dominant expression of patriarchal white supremacy following chattel slavery's formal abolition.[30] Authored more than a century ago, Ida B. Wells's analysis of lynching anticipates Fanon's conception of sexual revenge.[31] Challenging the dominant narrative that lynchings responded to the figure of the Black male rapist, Wells argued that through this form of terror, the White Man sought to affirm and repair his masculine self-conception, a self-conception that was imperiled by the specter of Black political, economic, and cultural advancement.[32]

Literary theorist Aliyyah I. Abdur-Rahman argues that lynching is a form of gang rape: "a profound expression of communal sexual-perversion—specifically, one in which the victim is gruesomely violated for the sexualized psychosocial satisfaction of a whole host of participants and spectators."[33] This analytic applies to how the state restored order following rebellions in the New York City jails, Auburn, Attica, and elsewhere. Upon regaining physical control, state actors immediately denuded and sexually violated the rebels. Commonly used in situations of war across cultural and historical contexts, the official rationale for stripping the enemy is to ensure that they cannot smuggle contraband in clothing or bodily orifices. Unofficially, however, "enforced nudity" is a mundane form of sexual violence, a means of publicly humiliating the vanquished, of putting their defeated bodies on display, and of enhancing their vulnerability to other forms of abuse.[34]

Survivors of the Branch Queens and Kew Gardens rebellions disclosed the sexualized nature of their dehumanization. "They herded us like animals and forced us to lie on top of each other while guards made cruel and racist remarks like 'Put that dick in him, nigger.' Prisoners who refused to lie on the other men were beaten mercilessly," reported BPP veteran Albert Woodfox.[35] Several men were commanded to bend over and spread their buttocks only to be prodded and kicked in the rear. Others were told to "try fucking each other," "I want your dick in the man's ass in front of you," or promised that if they could maintain an erection, they would be spared further beatings.[36] Through these inflictions of sexualized torture, objectification, and violent homoeroticism, the guards sought to expel their captives from the domain of masculine humanity while reasserting themselves as dominant White Man.

Similar rituals were performed in prisons where no major rebellions occurred. Panther Ricardo DeLeon reported that two days after the state siege of Attica, DOCS executed a series of "Anti-Radical Raids" against politicized prisoners in Clinton.[37] Captives maintained that prison guards and some of the same state troopers responsible for the bloodshed in D yard wantonly subjected them to gassings, macings, beatings, "strip searches," "rectal examinations," and other forms of sexualized humiliation. One of the victims described how "a dozen or so guards set upon me and literally ripped the clothes from my body until I lay naked on the floor." He further explains that as they "released their tensions on us" through physical violence, they forced the prisoners to kiss their feet and call themselves niggers.[38] Others were told to drop to their hands and knees, bark like dogs, and pronounce themselves "punks," prison sexual vernacular for men who are anally penetrated during homosexual sex.[39] These practices were employed, in one captive's words, "to strip the black man of his pride" and to make it so that "he conforms to the taste of his oppressors," a formulation that evokes an often undisclosed white fetish for the figurative and literal consumption of Black flesh.[40] A prisoner's rights lawyer later told Congress that despite a virtual media blackout, men in Clinton endured "a truly vicious amount of brutalization" until at least April of 1972,[41] revealing the temporality and geography of the massacre to be much broader than has been previously understood.

This brutalization sought to actively produce new gender and racial formations. An Auburn and Attica survivor explained that while torturing their captives, guards were "calling the people niggers, calling brothers white niggers, spanish niggers, black niggers, everybody is a nigger" who had taken part in the rebellion.[42] The capacious use of this phrase coupled with inflictions against people of all hues illuminates the fundamental anti-Blackness of the carceral state formation at the same time that it shows how this violence aimed to reproduce a social order that had been radically destabilized. By classifying all who rebelled "niggers," the assault force legitimized the exposure of phenotypically white bodies to the forms of debasement for which Black people are automatically eligible. This violence was not only aimed at killing, controlling, or debasing "niggers," but at *producing* them. And perhaps most importantly, it sought to purify and reconstruct the transgressed borders of White Man, to restore it as a privileged category of social being, although one for which white skin alone was now insufficient.

As a lynching party and gang rape, the Attica massacre unleashed the sexual charge that simmers just beneath the surface of carceral domination. A survivor recalled a frenzied state trooper running amid the denuded Black forms, yelling "find the big niggers and get their nuts."[43] Big Black, who was accused of castrating a guard, was captured, stripped of his clothing, and forced to lay spreadeagled on a picnic table while his assailants variously cursed him, spit on him, burned his body with cigarettes, and subjected him to Russian roulette. He remained on the table for hours, during which the guards repeatedly attacked his genitals and threatened to castrate him with their bladed weapons. Other victims were anally raped with a variety of foreign objects, including "nigger sticks," gun barrels, a broken bottle, and a screwdriver.[44] These rituals of sexual terror went on for days, even after it became known that neither Big Black nor anyone else had castrated a hostage.[45]

Attica's official body count reflects but a fraction of the casualty, suffering, and loss the massacre produced, not only for those who experienced it directly, but also for their loved ones. Survivors suffered a range of physiological and psychological harms including amputations, malunion fractures, scarring, chronic pain, arthritis, loss of mobility, spinal disorders, hypertension, seizures, cold sweats, recurring nightmares, migraines, uncontrolled rage, fatigue, fevers, flashbacks, swelling, paranoia, hallucinations, speech impediments, insomnia, depression, dizziness, auditory and visual impairments, blackouts, bone disorders, nosebleeds, memory loss, numbness, difficulty around crowds, fear of raincoats, prisons, police, and helicopters, difficulty trusting others, survivor's guilt, suicidal ideation, self-mutilation, hostility toward symbols of authority, and hatred of police. Several survivors of the massacre later died of drug overdoses, cirrhosis of the liver, and alcohol poisoning resulting from chemical dependencies developed after the massacre.[46] Casper Baker Gary, who I discuss in detail below, was one of many whose lives were shortened by mundane acts of cruelty. In 1993, as his body slowly gave way to kidney failure, he confided to a friend that his illness emerged because Attica guards had incessantly kicked him in the back while he was trapped in solitary confinement.[47]

The massacre's genocidal violence produced what anthropologist Christen A. Smith calls *sequelae*, the gendered, reverberating, deadly effects of state terror that infect the affective communities of the dead."[48] Mary Pope, whose husband died of a drug overdose in 1987, revealed that after Attica, he "could not bear to be touched by others."[49] Lana Anderson testified that following the massacre, she watched her husband slowly "slip away."[50] Joan Williams's husband became "extremely impatient, aggressive, and fearful and had difficulty holding jobs."[51] Donna Northrup reported that her husband was "never the same man after what he went through at Attica during the retaking."[52] Charlene Miller testified that after Attica, her father pulled away from his family, began drinking heavily, and that "a light went out in him" that never returned. She testified that her dad told her that he felt like a veteran of war and that "his manhood was taken away from him due to beatings he received in his groin area," which prevented him from performing sexually.[53] George Budd, Jr. testified that his brother, a survivor of Attica, committed suicide on the three-year anniversary of the massacre.[54] In February of 1995, David Galloway, another Attica survivor, hung himself.[55] Nicholas Morales spoke of living death, testifying, "They killed me that day."[56]

Deputy Warden Pfeil, who presided over much of this terror, never discovered that Bugs had done much more than survive during the rebellion. He never learned that during its chaotic opening moments, Bugs had improvised a makeshift bomb that leveled the prison chapel. Bugs told me that after passing his exit interview—as he filed onto the bus bound for Comstock and saw the sneering white faces looming over William Brown's corpse staring back at him—he turned to take one last look at Attica Prison, capturing a mental image that still brings him a small measure of delight: "The chapel was still on fire and thick black smoke was still coming from the top. This is a week later man. They hadn't been able to put the fire out [laughs]. Might still be on fire up there as far as I know, fifty years later, you dig?"

"A BEAUTIFUL OPERATION"

During a recorded phone conversation held just hours after the massacre, Nelson Rockefeller intimated to President Nixon that the assault was "really a beautiful operation."[57] The governor's description of this macabre spectacle of Black death and mutilation as "beautiful" suggests that its visualization was circulated and consumed within broader economies of white culture.[58] Having analyzed the sexualized practices of the massacre as lynching, I now turn to the photographic and representational practices deployed to memorialize and communicate its white supremacist aesthetic to broader audiences. As with the physical violence itself, these visual practices were as much about dehumanizing and ungendering Black men as they were about producing white masculine selfhood. As Maurice O. Wallace explains, through popular photographic practices, "Black men come to embody the inverse picture necessary for the positive self-portrait of white identity."[59]

This violence of representation is exemplified by the cover image of *The Official Report of the New York State Special Commission on Attica*. Published by Bantam Books on the one-year anniversary of the massacre, it depicts what can aptly be described as a twentieth-century slave coffle. A lone state trooper—clad in a bright orange raincoat, helmet, pants, and boots—stands with his feet shoulder-width apart. Clutching a long "nigger stick," which hangs below his knees, he is surrounded by a sea of niggerized bodies, most but not all of which are brown. The bodies are arranged in what appears to be several columns, but which is in fact a single, massive, serpentine line that extends across Attica's A yard. The figures are standing upright, with their hands on top of their heads. They are completely nude, and their genitals and buttocks exposed.

As a semiotic vehicle in the pre-internet era, the cover of the book conveyed white masculine supremacy and Black non-being as common sense, and did so under the insidious guise of an objective white liberal humanism. Clearly shaped by the visual imaginary of white supremacy in which White Man exists over and above his "primitive" wards, the tableau provided publics beyond the walls with a titillating glimpse of the spoils of domestic war. It invited them to identify, not with the denuded, disgraced, and niggerized figures in the coffle, but with the generic stand-in for legitimized white/state power, authority, and domination—the uniformed man with the big stick standing in the center of the frame.

The massacre was under intense visual surveillance. The FBI reportedly obtained 583 black and white photographs, 464 35-millimeter color slides, 331 color photographs, and 6 videotapes captured during the massacre and its aftermath by the New York State Police, the Monroe County Sheriff's Office, and the Niagara Falls Police Department, among other agencies.[60] Additionally, at least one member of the National Guard took it upon himself to photograph the event "as a private citizen" (he then sold some of his photos to the press). Existing discussions have heretofore focused on the degree to which the visual record, which was generously pruned, cropped, and otherwise edited before it was turned over, was useful for identifying assailants for criminal and civil litigation.[61] Although critical, this focus on authorized use-values obscures the covert ways in which visual representations of anti-Black violence circulate as ubiquitous technologies of white subject formation, as sources of covert enjoyment, and as semiotic stabilizers of white civilization.

Before initiating the slaughter, the documentarians were instructed to "capture situations of opportunity."[62] In other words, the men with cameras were afforded the same latitude and creative license as the men with guns. In his testimony before the McKay Commission, an Attica survivor named Francis J. Huen briefly discussed the use of photographic equipment. As the vanquished rebels were being abused, Huen witnessed a trooper yelling "get that [redacted]" and then fire his rifle from the catwalk down into the yard at an indiscernible target, which we can safely assume was a person. He then saw a photographer run toward that very spot in order to shoot with a camera that which had already been shot with a gun. For Huen, who was white and apparently unsympathetic toward the rebellion, the event was "scary, but also reassuring to me [because] they had time to take pictures, they didn't feel they had to be on the defensive." The massacre was a space-time of luxury and indiscretion where a violent mob had occasion to experiment and indulge their delayed longings. The photos served no tactical function. And yet, Huen suspected that these acts were not entirely random, that they were partially choreographed. He recalled that "civilian-dressed people" were positioned on the catwalks, and that they seemed to be "directing things a bit."[63] The beautiful operation was a cinéma vérité of terror.

Officially, state actors recorded the operation for "archival" and "training" purposes, a non-explanation that says little about what they hoped to learn from the visual record and how they understood its value as an archive.[64] Much of the available footage was captured by a New York State Police sergeant. It is notable for its obscured and degraded quality as well as its incompleteness. Interestingly, the trooper narrates what he is recording, allowing viewers to experience the encoding of the dominant narrative as the actual events are unfolding. At one point, he points the camera at a tunnel and, using proto-genocidal language, remarks that captives were constantly "scurrying" between different sections of the prison "like rats." Experimenting with different forms of visualization, Smith shoots some of his video through the scope mounted on his rifle. The reticle pans back and forth across the yard, putting viewers in the position of sharpshooter, a preview of what was to come. At another point, he zeros in on a revolting Black man, referring to him as "the ugliest, blackest negro gentlemen I've even seen in my life," at which point laughter can be heard in the room, indicating what Saidiya Hartman calls "the complicated nexus of terror and enjoyment."[65]

When asked why he was showing the footage to cadets at the Police Academy, John C. Miller, former chief inspector of the New York State Police, admitted that it was not being used to derive lessons from the assault. He testified that "you view something to possibly learn something . . . [but sometimes] it's something that you see that you have done and it doesn't necessarily mean that it's going to improve things or it's going to be changed."[66] This suggests that there was no tactical or strategic reason to show these videos to incoming cadets and that perhaps the footage was screened simply so that they could see what they had done, to appreciate it from an aesthetic point of view. It was to *train* the cadets—that is, to help them develop habits, thoughts, and/or behaviors—in forms of engagement that didn't necessarily have to be improved or changed.

But what of the massacre's unseen, redacted, and deleted visual archive? We can confidently speculate. As several scholars have noted, photographs are central to the ritual of lynching and their primary function is not to further terrorize the victims. Rather, through lynching photos white subjects construct their collective identity and group solidarity upon the substrate of Black subjection. As keepsakes, lynching photographs become an instrument for manipulating time, enabling predators to prolong the ecstatic, fleeting moment of total power lynching rituals allow.[67] Through photography, David Marriott explains, "an image of white identity emerges from a spectacle of annihilation: the lynchers posing, grimly, alongside their black 'trophies.' A moment frozen in time, flash-lit in the heat of subsided passion."[68] Having performed their human sacrifice in the most excessive way possible, the mob stages photographic encounters in which they look at the camera, not with expressions of horror, but with countenances of calm satisfaction, whiteness reborn again and again.

Later, amid the prosaic flow of daily life, participants in the lynch mob can return to that extraordinary moment through the photograph. They show the images to their family and friends who see them standing next to a thing that is clearly not alive, not human, and against this negative, a narrative of their own vitality, dominance, and belongingness to the community of Man is drawn in sharp relief. It is entirely predictable that this is what the unseen Attica photos contained. And if more evidence is required, perhaps that which has not been culled from a putatively bygone era, we need look no further than the US torture camp Abu Ghraib. Not only did the cache of images obtained by the press in 2004 reveal that Muslim men constructed as terrorists and "enemy combatants" were being subjected to the violence of sexual racism, but also that US soldiers and prison guards, both male and female, took pleasure in being photographed while inhabiting postures of dominance over these men.[69] The visualization of this violence reproduces the myth of White Man as the rightful master of the world, covertly undergirding white patriarchy, the modern state form, and US empire.[70]

During our conversation, Bugs shared a recollection that is also a theorization of the entanglements between violence and visuality, punishment and pleasure, anti-Black terror and white sexuality. While standing in the coffle, he explained:

> [The guards] were celebratin', talkin' bout "did you get a nigger." "Yeah I got five" and you know they were slappin' fives, they was even takin' home movies with us as they paraded us around, they got all kinds of cat calls about the genitalia, "ay ay ay nigger pick your third leg up," you know all that kinda shit. I guess they showed 'em at home for they wives, you know,

they have their cocktail parties and they pull out the home movies of [the] Attica massacre. And it was a big sport for them. Hate them bastards.

The reconquest of Attica was a "parade," a "sport," a contest to see who among the mob could most completely obliterate, dominate, and possess the Black male form. The lens, like the gun and the nigger stick, was simultaneously an instrument of violence and a tool of sexualized play. The wielders of these weapons were not only securing the prison and producing evidence for official state functions, they were producing "home movies" intended for circulation and consumption within the sacred spaces of white sociality: cocktail parties, where such novelties might stimulate jealousy among those who were not there, but wished they were; or the bedroom, where the possession of niggerized bodies and "third legs" fueled unspoken white sexual appetites. Fifty years later, recalling these desires to possess and consume Black flesh, Bugs articulates a deep-seated hatred that still seethes within.

James Baldwin has much to say about the sexual charge of white ritual violence. He narrates his short story, "Going to Meet the Man," from the perspective of Jesse, a white deputy sheriff in a small Southern town who sees himself as a "good man." The story opens with Jesse unable to achieve an erection while trying to have sex with his wife. Frustrated, he lies beside her in bed, plumbing the depths of his mind until he arrives at a memory of himself torturing an imprisoned Black man—a civil rights "ringleader," a "bad nigger"—by shocking the man's testicles with a cattle prod. The memory causes Jesse to "hurt all over with that peculiar excitement which refused to be released."[71]

He then probes deeper into his subconscious, recalling how he was ushered into white manhood under the tutelage of his father and his father's friends, who "had been responsible for law and order much longer than him."[72] As a child, sitting on his father's shoulders amid a sea of white faces, he witnessed his first lynching. He saw a Black man being burned alive and castrated and he watched that sea of white faces, including that of his mother, also watching it and being titillated. "He watched the hanging, gleaming body, the most beautiful and terrible object he had ever seen till then."[73] He remembers how they severed the object's large Black penis, and the memory causes Jesse's "nature to return to him again." Fully aroused, Jesse embraces his wife and tells her to "love me just like you'd love a nigger." They engage in passionate sex.[74] Similarly, in *If Beale Street Could Talk*, a novel that revolves around the Manhattan House of Detention, but which is believed to be loosely based on Attica,[75] a male character who was recently released from prison tells his friend that not only was he raped, but that guards derived sexual gratification from his suffering. "I don't believe there's a white man in this country, baby, who can get his dick hard, without he hear some nigger moan," Baldwin writes.[76] Through fiction Baldwin theorizes how white identity, intimacy, desire, and sexuality are constituted through Black suffering.

The insidiousness of the McKay Commission report, with its cover image of denuded and niggerized males, is that it masks while surreptitiously perpetuating violence against the Attica survivors. However, it does not do so alone. The report was nominated for a National Book Award in 1972 and received near-universal praise for its thoroughness, even-handedness, and courage in criticizing the "excesses" of the state. Its pages are filled with salacious descriptions of the homosexual behaviors of captive men—consensual sex as well as rape. However, nowhere does it analyze the profoundly sexualized techniques of carceral management or the various sexual predations enacted upon Attica captives to restore normative order. And yet the coffle image on the cover of the book visually reifies the captives' status as chattel, presenting their vulnerability to sexual violence as a banal social fact. Among myriad available images, the marketing team at Bantam Books chose to adorn the cover with this grotesque image of sexualized Black subjection. Moreover, until now, no one seems to have thought this atrocity was worthy of remark, as I have been unable to find any evidence that any critics discussed the use of this image on the cover.

What I did find was an article in the September 17, 1972, edition of the *New York Times* announcing the release of the report. It prominently features a version of the same photograph, but with a significant modification: the men's penises have been removed.[77] As I have already shown, the "beautiful operation" entailed orgiastic rituals of sexual domination during which anxieties about Black male genitalia and discourse of castration loomed large. The *New York Times* never printed a formal retraction of their false claim that the rebels had castrated a hostage, nor did the newspaper of record renounce the white supremacist theory of ontology that authorized the claim in the first place. The notion that White Man enjoys a natural and exclusive entitlement to masculine humanity is not so clearly stated in their writeup of the McKay Commission report a year later, but it is embedded within the discourse of the article's accompanying image. The staff of the *Times* found this image so irresistible that they circumvented publication standards prohibiting the display of frontal nudity by pictorially castrating at least three Black men located in the bottom right-hand corner of the frame. The denuded profiles of these men are clearly visible but, in the space where their penises are noticeable in other versions of the image, only a void remains. One can only speculate about whether Attica rebel Jomo Omowale was aware of this alteration when he wrote in 1973, "We must not accept any more media-made castrated leaders who quietly retreat when it's time to stand."[78]

Accompanied by the evocative headline "Anatomy of a Prison Riot," the image provided the paper's global readership with a sexualized visualization of racial mastery, while at the same time providing the comforting assurance that the phantasmagoric Black dick was not there; and moreover, that it was rightfully possessed by a higher authority. This absence was also a presence, one that visually communicated the simultaneous military defeat and sexual disarmament of Black male insurgents. It displayed the availability of Black flesh as an ungendered terrain of libidinal experimentation.[79] It bears stating, although I hope this point is obvious, that my symptomatic reading of this image is not an endorsement of the underlying logic of its deployment, a logic that imputes unique agency to cisgendered men with penises. Rather I am explicating the intensely patriarchal logic of white supremacy in which there can be no masculinity except for that which belongs to White Man.[80]

This is the same white supremacist logic that relentlessly assails Black revolutionary possibility, however imperfect and shackled by patriarchy it may be.[81] In fact, the *Times* accompanied this excision of the rebels' bodies with an excision of their politics. The central finding of the report, according to the article, was that in contrast to claims made by state actors such as Nelson Rockefeller and Russell G. Oswald, the rebellion was reformist rather than revolutionary in its orientation. This shows that it was the elite liberal media and not the right-wing lynch mob that realized the fantasies of the rebellion's most ardent antagonists. Through "Anatomy of a Prison Riot," the newspaper simultaneously negated Black revolutionary politics and obliterated the Black penis.

"PETITION FOR CERTIFICATES EXTRAORDINARY"

I have a visceral memory of my first encounter with "Petition for Certificates Extraordinary." I was seated at a microfilm machine in the New York State Archives in Albany, browsing through copies of Attica-related correspondence received by Rockefeller's office in 1972. I was hoping to gain insight into what imprisoned people and their families were writing during the massacre's immediate aftermath to the man who authorized it. The first thing I noticed about the document was its remarkable visuality. Before attempting to decipher its meaning, I appraised its form: its emotive force, its textual density, the fierce intentionality of its organization and its inscriptions. As anthropologist Tim Ingold explains, "In the lines left upon its surface the handwritten page bears witness to gestures that, in their qualities of attentiveness and feeling, embody an intentionality intrinsic to the movement of their production."[82] Written by hand in all caps, the letters of each word, the words of each sentence, and the sentences of each paragraph threaten to suffocate each other. And yet, mirroring the conditions under which they were produced, each character exists in its own tightly controlled space. Each line proceeds across the page with geometric precision, stopping just shy of the edge only to proceed anew on the next row, like a tier of prison cells. As a purely aesthetic form, "Petition for Certificates Extraordinary" conveys a terrifying discipline and a barely contained rage. I found myself imagining that were I able to hold the original document I would be able to feel the deep impressions the author's pen must have left on the page.

The petition's author, Casper Baker Gary, was born in Hamlet, North Carolina, in 1938. He was an artist, an athlete, a leader among his peers, and "always a brilliant kid," his younger brother told me.[83] In the late 1950s, after an undesirable discharge from the US Army, Casper moved to New York City. Shortly thereafter he was arrested for stealing less than $100, resulting in a conviction for first-degree robbery and a stiff sentence of ten years in prison. His time behind the walls was laden with antagonism. Between 1959 and 1969, Casper was shuttled between New York's toughest prisons, accumulating dozens of disciplinary infractions on his record: "does not operate his loom or produce as he should" (8-26-60); "Complaint by [redacted] that Gary has become insistent that he become intimate with him" (3-1-61); "writing a sarcastic & threatening note to P.K. [Principal Keeper] claiming that he was being treated in an inhumanely, uncivilized, barbaric manner" (8-18-61); "Sending a warning note to Warden" (10-3-61); "passing notes out window from HBZ [Attica's solitary confinement unit] to yard" (10-1-63). Each of these infractions was met with punishment: loss of privileges, deferral of parole hearings, solitary confinement, and of course, those unofficial penalties and brutalities that, as a matter of course, are not recorded. These experiences radicalized Casper, who was released from prison in October of 1969 only to be reincarcerated one month later for a parole violation.

As his given name suggests, Casper was very much a spectral figure, a being that defies classification, but one thing is certain: he was mad. Following Therí Alyce Pickens's useful disruption of critical disability studies, I embrace the capacity of "madness" to convey a "lexical range that includes (in)sanity, cognitive disability, anger, and. . . . excess."[84] Indeed, Casper's madness cannot be disentangled from the term's various registers, nor can it be wholly attributed to or divested from his extensive biography of captivity and repression. When the Tombs erupted in rebellion, he was in the Dannemora State Hospital for the Criminally Insane, where he was subjected to electroshock "treatment." The deputy director of that institution accused Casper and his Prisoners Liberation Front of subversion, of intentionally infiltrating the institution for the purpose of disruption. "They [the PLF] were obviously not psychotic, but only faking," he explained in a staff meeting.[85] Evidence suggests that Casper was in the protracted Auburn rebellion at some point between November 1970 and May of 1971, but when Attica erupted he was in Clinton, where, given his antagonism with the administration, he was likely targeted by the sexualized anti-radical raids.

Casper finalized his extraordinary Petition in Green Haven in November of 1972. Its expressed purpose is to persuade Robert R. Douglass—Governor Rockefeller's personal attorney and the highest-ranking government official at Attica during the massacre—to formally endow the PLF with the authority to expose the massacre's perpetrators to "proper legal sanction."[86] The McKay Commission report had recently been released, confirming the captives' suspicions that officials were "whitewashing" their own violence. Over the preceding fourteen months Casper had been conducting his own investigation, during which he claims to have interviewed more than five hundred people, guards and captives alike. Through this process, he claims to have developed a picture of the "actual behavior of the several and various state officers and agents" who partook in the violence.[87]

We can only speculate about whether Casper truly believed that Douglass, a member of Rockefeller's inner circle, would entertain his peculiar request to effectively deputize the PLF, and about what constituted "proper legal sanction" in his eyes. But Casper clearly took the petition seriously and wanted it to be taken seriously by others. It is correctly formatted as a legal writ, signed by Casper, and even notarized. Its language is extremely formal. It is laden with long, complex sentences, exacting word choices, and bewildering verb tenses, but features few spelling or grammatical errors.

To engage "Petition for Certificates Extraordinary" is to wade into an unruly, evasive, and eclectic form of *mad science*. Its mode of study, explanation, and narration defies established notions of time and politics and genres of written communication, begging to be interpreted in myriad ways. Unquestionably, though, the document forces its readers to contend with the violent sexual perversity that saturated the Attica massacre. In ways unlike any other document I have ever encountered, it exposes the world-shattering rituals of ontological warfare that were imposed upon the rebels.

Although the petition is a trenchant critique of violence, my decision to excerpt and analyze it will inevitably be experienced by many readers as a violence of its own.[88] This is a contradiction with which I have grappled, ultimately deciding to reproduce the petition, not as an attempt to invoke sympathy or even outrage, but to demonstrate the enormity of sexual violence at Attica *and* the workings of liberal authorized accounts in sanitizing that violence. This sanitization has facilitated our generalized failure to understand the actually existing dynamics of the prison as war, encumbering the developing of abolitionist ethics and politics.

Casper conveys the primary findings of his research—a catalog of "despicable and savage atrocities"—in language that demands to be quoted at length. To Douglass he writes:

> ... I AM NOW ABLE TO CONFIDENTLY ALLEGE THAT DURING SAID 13 THRU 20 SEPTEMBER 1971 PERIOD AT ATTICA, SOME OF THE PRISONERS (MORE THAN 100) WERE, FROM TIME TO TIME, TAKEN FROM GROUPS, CELL BLOCKS AND COMPANIES, AND CONDUCTED BY A GROUP OF THREE (3) OR MORE STATE POLICEMEN AND/OR PRISON GUARDS, BCI [BUREAU OF CRIMINAL INVESTIGATION], SHERIFF DEPUTIES, ETC. TO ONE OF THE MANY ISOLATED CELLS, ROOMS, YARDS, SHOPS, CORRIDORS, BASEMENTS, ATTICS, ROOFTOPS, AND OTHER ISOLATED PLACES AND THEN AND THERE EACH OF THE SAID PRISONERS, DEPENDING ENTIRELY UPON THE PARTICULAR TASTES AND CHARACTER OF THEIR HAPPENSTANCE TORMENTORS, WERE FORCED, AT GUN-POINT, TO SUBMIT TO AT LEAST ONE, BUT NOT INFREQUENTLY EACH PRISONER WAS COMPELLED TO ENDURE ALL, OF THE FOLLOWING DESPICABLE AND SAVAGE ATROCITIES:
>
> 1. TO BE FORCIBLY RAPED BY EACH OF THE SEVERAL OFFICERS.

STATE OF NEW YORK DEPARTMENT OF GOVERNOR
DEPARTMENT OF EXECUTIVE SECRETARY: MR. ROBERT R. DOUGLASS
OFFICE OF EXECUTIVE COUNSEL: MR. MICHAEL WHITEMAN
OFFICE OF STATE OPERATIONS: DR. T. NORMAN HURD
OFFICE OF SPECIAL STATE PROSECUTOR: MR. ROBERT E. FISCHER

IN THE MATTER OF THE APPLICATION OF CASPER BAKER GARY, SECRETARY-GENERAL, NEW YORK PRISONERS' LIBERATION FRONT, FOR AN AUDIENCE WITH GOVERNOR NELSON A. ROCKEFELLER CONCERNING SOME HIGHLY APPARENT ATROCITIES AGAINST DEFENSELESS ATTICA PRISONERS BY NEW YORK STATE POLICE, PRISON GUARDS, SHERIFF DEPUTIES, BCI, ETC. DURING THE RE-TAKING AND SECURING OF ATTICA PRISON FROM 13 THRU 20 SEPTEMBER 1971.

PETITION FOR CERTIFICATES EXTRAORDINARY

STATE OF NEW YORK
COUNTY OF DUTCHESS
VILLAGE OF STORMVILLE   ss.:
GREEN HAVEN PRISON
PUNITIVE SEGREGATION
TANK ONE, CELL #3

TO: HON. ROBERT R. DOUGLASS, ESQ.
EXECUTIVE SECRETARY, STATE OF NEW YORK
STATE CAPITOL
ALBANY, NEW YORK - 12224

HONORABLE SIR:
I, CASPER BAKER GARY, BEING DULY SWORN, ACCORDING TO LAW, DEPOSES AND SAYS:

I.

THAT THIS IS AN APPLICATION TO YOU, AS EXECUTIVE SECRETARY, AND THROUGH YOUR ADMINISTRATIVE PREROGATIVE IN RESPECT OF THE EXECUTIVE COUNSEL, DIRECTOR OF STATE OPERATIONS, SPECIAL STATE PROSECUTOR, AS WELL AS ALL OTHER THEORETICAL AND ACTUAL DEPARTMENTS, FOR RELIEF IN THE NATURE OF CERTIFICATES EXTRAORDINARY, DERIVED FROM YOUR INHERENT AUTHORITY AND POWER TO GATHER INFORMATION CONCERNING ANY CONCEALMENT OF CRIMINAL COMPLICITY IN PUBLIC BUSINESS BY MEMBERS OF THE EXECUTIVE STAFF, INVESTING ME WITH ALL OF THE POWERS OF EXECUTIVE SECRETARY, EXCEPT THOSE WITHHELD BY LAW, SO THAT I MAY CONDUCT A THOROUGH AND COMPLETE INVESTIGATION OF THE 13-20 SEPTEMBER 1971 EVENTS AT ATTICA PRISON AT MY OWN AND OTHER PRISONERS' EXPENSE, AND REPORT ALL FINDINGS DIRECTLY TO YOU AND THROUGH YOU TO THE GOVERNOR OF THE STATE OF NEW YORK; AND/OR SUCH OTHER AND ADDITIONAL CERTIFICATES AS YOU SHALL BE KIND ENOUGH TO DEVISE TO ME FOR THE AFORESTATED PURPOSE.

II.

THAT IN THE PAST FOURTEEN (14) MONTHS I HAVE SPOKEN WITH MORE THAN FIVE HUNDRED (500) PRISONERS AND CORRECTIONAL OFFICERS (THE EXACT NAMES AND WHEREABOUTS OF WHOM I AM NO LONGER ABLE TO CERTIFY FROM MY OWN KNOWLEDGE AT THIS WRITING), WITH A VIEW TO GET SOME SENSE OF THE ACTUAL BEHAVIOR OF THE SEVERAL AND VARIOUS STATE OFFICERS AND AGENTS DURING THE 13 THRU 20 SEPTEMBER 1971 PERIOD OF THE RE-TAKING AND SECURING OF THE ATTICA CORRECTIONAL FACILITY AT ATTICA, WYOMING COUNTY, NEW YORK; SO THAT I AM NOW ABLE TO CONFIDENTLY ALLEGE THAT DURING SAID 13 THRU 20 SEPTEMBER 1971 PERIOD AT ATTICA, SOME OF THE PRISONERS (MORE THAN 100) WERE, FROM TIME TO TIME, TAKEN FROM GROUPS, CELL BLOCKS AND COMPANIES, AND CONDUCTED BY A GROUP OF THREE (3) OR MORE STATE POLICEMEN AND/OR PRISON GUARDS, BCI, SHERIFF DEPUTIES, ETC. TO ONE OF THE MANY ISOLATED CELLS, ROOMS, YARDS, SHOPS, CORRIDORS, BASEMENTS, ATTICS, ROOFTOPS, AND OTHER ISOLATED PLACES, AND THEN AND THERE EACH OF THE SAID PRISONERS, DEPENDING ENTIRELY UPON THE PARTICULAR TASTES AND CHARACTER OF THEIR HAPPENSTANCE TORMENTORS, WERE FORCED, AT GUN-POINT TO SUBMIT TO AT LEAST ONE BUT NOT INFREQUENTLY EACH PRISONER WAS COMPELLED TO ENDURE ALL OF THE FOLLOWING DESPICABLE AND SAVAGE ATROCITIES:

FIGURE 13. Page 1 of Casper Baker Gary's Petition for Certificates Extraordinary. Photo: New York State Archives.

PETITION FOR CERTIFICATE EXTRAORDINARY (CONT'D) PAGE 2

1. TO BE FORCIBLY RAPED BY EACH OF THE SEVERAL OFFICERS.

2. TO PERFORM FELLATIO ON EACH OF THE SEVERAL OFFICERS.

3. TO KNEEL WITH HIS MOUTH OPEN AS EACH OFFICER TOOK HIS TURN URINATING IN HIS FACE AND/OR MOUTH.

4. TO HOLD HIS MOUTH OPEN AS EACH OFFICER TOOK HIS TURN EXPECTORATING INTO HIS FACE AND/OR MOUTH ALL SUCH MUCOUS AND/OR MUCUS FLUIDS AND SECRETIONS AS COULD BE DRAWN WITH THEIR MOUTHS FROM THEIR LUNG AND NASAL CAVITIES.

5. TO EAT OF THE STOOLS OF EACH OF THE SEVERAL OFFICERS AFTER EACH OFFICER HAD TAKEN HIS TURN UPON THE TOILET, FLOOR, GROUND, ETC.

6. TO HOLD STILL WHILE EACH OFFICER APPLIED A LIGHTED CIGAR, CIGARETTE AND/OR MATCH OR CIGARETTE LIGHTER TO HIS PENIS, TESTICLES, RECTUM, AND OTHER VITAL PARTS OF HIS BODY.

7. AND TO ANY AND ALL OTHER FOUL AND DESPICABLE SAVAGERIES AS CHANCED TO STRIKE THE FANCY OF ANY ONE OF THE SEVERAL OFFICERS.

THE VERY FACT THAT YOU WERE THE HIGHEST-RANKING EXECUTIVE OFFICER PRESENT AT THE ATTICA FACILITY AT THE TIME OF SOME OF THE ABOVE NOTICED ATROCITIES, AND THE FACT THAT YOUR JUDGMENT CARRIES ENORMOUS WALLOPING POWING POWER THROUGHOUT THE STATE, AND THAT YOU ARE SO WELL LOVED BY SO MANY PEOPLE, INCLUDING MYSELF, WE CANNOT, AND INDEED WILL NOT PERMIT ANYONE TO DOUBT YOUR PROFOUND AND ABIDING CONCERN ABOUT THESE AND SUCH WIDE-SPREAD REPORTS.

IN THIS CONNECTION, IT IS NOT ENTIRELY UNWORTHY OF OBSERVATION THAT THE "NEW YORK SPECIAL (McKAY) COMMISSION ON ATTICA" HAS ALREADY IMPLICATED TO THE EXTENT OF BEING WITNESS SEVERAL HIGH OFFICIALS WHO WERE WITH YOU MOST OF THE TIME. THESE OFFICIALS WHO CLAIMED FIRST-HAND KNOWLEDGE OF THESE PROCEEDINGS OR PART OF SAME, AT THE TIME IN QUESTION, INCLUDES ASST. ATTY-GEN. ROBERT E. FISCHER, DEPUTY COMM'R OF CORRECTION WALTER DUNBAR, STATE SENATOR JOHN DUNN, GEN. A.C. O'HARA, MAJ. JOHN MONAHAN, AND DR. T. NORMAN HURD. (SEE "ATTICA", CHAPTER 18, pp. 426-454, CHAPTER A, pp. 455-470).

IT IS TRUE, AND IT GOES WITHOUT SAYING, PEOPLE TEND TO IMPOSE ON OTHERS ONLY THOSE THINGS THAT THEY EXPECT WOULD, OR WOULD DESIRE TO, BE DONE TO THEMSELVES, IF THE CIRCUMSTANCES WERE TO REVERSE AND TURN THE OTHER WAY AROUND. BUT IF WE ARE TO ADMIT AS LEGITIMATE FORMS OF REPRISALS THESE AND ANY SUCH ATROCITIES, THEN, WE CAN BE VERY SURE THAT IT WILL NOT BE LONG BEFORE THE TAIL BEGINS TO WAG THE DOG.

I DO NOT HERE ATTEMPT TO PROJECT THROUGH THE BACK DOOR TO YOU A MORALITY THAT I COULD NOT PRESS HOME THROUGH THE FRONT, INSOFAR AS I ACCOUNT MORALITY AS PROPERLY LEFT THE FINAL DETERMINATION OF EACH INDIVIDUAL MORTAL WITH RULES RESERVED FOR CONDUCT ALONE; BUT WE CANNOT ALLOW "MANHOOD" TO BE CONFUSED WITH "THUGHOOD," NOR CAN UNIFORMS IMPLY IMMUNITY. BECAUSE IF WE SAY THAT "MIGHT IS RIGHT", THEN WE PUT TO BEGGING FOR MISCHIEF YET UNBORN. SUCH A COURSE, SIR, I AM CONFIDENT THAT YOU ARE TOO WISE TO TAKE.

III.

THE ADDITIONAL FORCE PROPELLING ME TO LAY THIS PARTICULAR MATTER BEFORE YOU, RATHER THAN SOMEONE ELSE IS THE VERY GOOD REASON THAT ALTHOUGH YOU CAN BE STONE-WALL STUBBORN IN QUESTIONABLE INTERPRISES, YOU ARE KNOWN TO BE STEEL-TRAP DEPENDABLE IN EVERY CASE WHERE THE MATTER IS VERY SERIOUS. YOU ARE, ACCORDING TO ALBANY LEGEND, THE "ONLY MEMBER OF THE GOVERNOR'S TEAM WHO ALSO PLAYS ALL-SEASON-LONG ON THE TEAM OF HIS FELLOWMEN". IT COMES AS NO SURPRISE AT ALL, THEN, THAT YOU SHOULD TURN OUT TO BE OUR ONLY HOPE IN THE EXECUTIVE TODAY, AND IT REQUIRES NO GREAT COURAGE ON MY PART AT ALL TO ACCEPT THIS ABSOLUTE REALITY. THE ATROCITIES AT ATTICA JUST MUST NOT BE LONG IGNORED. HISTORY HAS GIVEN MUCH OF THE DECISION TO YOU.

FIGURE 14. Page 2 of Casper Baker Gary's Petition for Certificates Extraordinary. Photo: New York State Archives.

> PETITION FOR CERTIFICATES EXTRAORDINARY (CONT'D)   PAGE 3
>
> IV.
>
> THAT FINALLY, I COME TO YOU BECAUSE YOU ARE MY BROTHER AND PROTECTOR IN THE FAMILY, AS WELL AS ONE OF THE KEEPERS OF THE DEEDS, AND THE FUNDAMENTAL AND UNSHAKABLE LOVE THAT BINDS US TOGETHER IS OLDER THAN THE FIRST MOUNTAIN, PRE-DATING BY A BILLION GENERATIONS THE ORDINARY ASSIGNABILITY OF FIBROUS DIFFERENTIATION AND SCALED PIGMENTATION, SO THAT YOU AND I ARE JUST AS ASSUREDLY OF THE MOTHER AND FATHER AS THEY ARE OF THE SAME AND IDENTICAL OCEAN OF LIFE, THAT MAJESTIC COLLECTION OF SUB-MICROSCOPIC PEOPLE WHOSE ETERNAL CHANCE AND DUTY IT IS TO BECOME HUMAN BEINGS. AND SO LONG AS YOU AND I WERE IN THAT BOUNDLESS SUB-MICROSCOPIC UNIVERSE WE SHARED WITH ONE ANOTHER, ASSISTED AND PROTECTED ONE ANOTHER, FOR THERE COULD BE NO DOUBT THAT WE WERE BROTHERS FLESH OF THE SAME FLESH BLOOD OF THE SAME BLOOD, AND BONE OF THE SAME BONE. THE MERE ADDITION OF VARIOUS PARTICLES AND THE INCEPTION OF INCREASED QUANTITIES OF LIGHT RAYS INHERENT IN THE METAMORPHOSIS FROM AUTOCHTHONOUS SEA-BROTHERS TO FELLOWMEN, HAS NO EFFECT WHATSOEVER UPON THE MIGHT WOMB FROM WHICH WE HAVE IN COMMON SPRUNG.
>
> SO THEN, IF YOU HAVE THE POWER TO PROTECT US, AND THE REQUISITE WISDOM TO EFFECT JUSTICE — WHICH YOU INDISPUTABLY DO — THEN YOU HAVE A SOLEMN, SACRED AND UNSHAKABLE DUTY TO ME, YOUR BROTHER EVEN BEFORE THE COMING OF THE WORLD (BUT EVEN MORE SO NOW THAT I INVOKED OUR ETERNAL CONSAGUINITY) TO BESTIR YOURSELF BETIMES AND CONSULT THE LAWS OF THE HUMAN RACE WHICH NO ONE MAY WISELY IGNORE, AND ASCERTAIN FOR YOURSELF HOW SURELY WE ARE BOUND UP AND HELD TOGETHER BY BLOOD, AND THEN YOU SHALL KNOW OF A CERTAINTY THAT IF YOU HAD NOT IN FACT BEEN MY BROTHER BEFORE EVER OUR MOTHERS, I WOULD NEVER HAVE COME TO YOU AT ALL.
>
> THIS, THEN, IS THE WARRANT I SEEK FROM YOU, MY BROTHER:
>
> STATE   OF   NEW YORK
> DEPARTMENT   OF THE EXECUTIVE
> OFFICE   OF   EXECUTIVE SECRETARY
> HON. ROBERT R. DOUGLASS
>
> ## TO WHOM IT MAY CONCERN:
>
> I, ROBERT R. DOUGLASS, EXECUTIVE SECRETARY TO THE GOVERNOR OF THE STATE OF NEW YORK, BY THE POWERS, DUTIES, PREROGATIVES AND PROTOCOLS VESTED IN ME AS AFORESAID, WITH A VIEW TO DISCHARGE ALL MY DUTIES AS EXECUTIVE SECRETARY TO THE GOVERNOR OF THE STATE OF NEW YORK, WHICH REQUIRES OF ME A MOST FIRM AND INEXHAUSTIBLE COMMITMENT TO UPHOLD AND MAINTAIN SECURE THE FUNDAMENTAL CODE OF THE LAWS OF THE HUMAN RACE, DO NOW HEREBY DELEGATE, ASSIGN, COMMISSION, EMPOWER, APPOINT, AUTHORIZE, DECLARE, ANNOUNCE, PROMULGATE AND PROCLAIM THAT CASPER BAKER GARY, SECRETARY-GENERAL, NEW YORK PRISONERS LIBERATION FRONT, MY BROTHER EVEN BEFORE THE COMING OF THE WORLD, SHALL EXERCISE AND ENJOY ALL THE POWERS, PREROGATIVES AND PROTOCOLS OF THE OFFICE OF EXECUTIVE SECRETARY TO THE GOVERNOR OF THE STATE OF NEW YORK, BUT AT THE EXPENSE OF THE NEW YORK PRISONERS LIBERATION FRONT, UNTIL SUCH TIME AS I AM ABLE TO CERTIFY TO THE AFORESAID GOVERNOR THAT THE ATROCITIES PERPETRATED AGAINST THE ATTICA PRISONERS FROM 9 THRU 13 SEPTEMBER 1971 BY MEMBERS OF THE STATE POLICE, PRISON GUARDS, SHERIFF DEPUTIES, BCI, ETC. HAVE BEEN BY THE AFOREMENTIONED CASPER BAKER GARY EXPOSED TO PROPER LEGAL SANCTIONS.
>
> IN WITNESS WHEREOF I HAVE HEREUNTO PLACED MY HAND AND AFFIXED THE SEAL OF THE EXECUTIVE SECRETARY OF THE GOVERNOR OF NEW YORK.
> (SEAL)
>
> STATE OF NEW YORK } ss.:   RESPECTFULLY SUBMITTED,
> COUNTY OF DUTCHESS   BY _____
>   SWORN BEFORE ME THIS   CASPER BAKER GARY
>   3RD DAY OF NOVEMBER, 1972   #18087 · SEC'Y-GEN. NEW YORK PLF
>   BY _____   DRAWER B
>   NOTARY PUBLIC   STORMVILLE, N.Y. - 12582
>
>   CC: HON. ARTHUR O. EVE, ESQ.; HON. ANTONIO G. OLIVIERI, ESQ.; STATE CAPITOL · ALBANY, N.Y.

FIGURE 15. Page 3 of Casper Baker Gary's Petition for Certificates Extraordinary. Photo: New York State Archives.

2. TO PERFORM FELLATIO ON EACH OF THE SEVERAL OFFICERS.
3. TO KNEEL WITH HIS MOUTH OPEN AS EACH OFFICER TOOK HIS TURN URINATING IN HIS FACE AND/OR MOUTH.
4. TO HOLD HIS MOUTH OPEN AS EACH OFFICER TOOK HIS TURN EXPECTORATING INTO HIS FACE AND/OR MOUTH ALL SUCH MUCOUS AND/OR MUCUS FLUIDS AND SECRETIONS AS COULD BE DRAWN INTO THEIR MOUTHS FROM THEIR LUNG AND NASAL CAVITIES.
5. TO EAT OF THE STOOLS OF EACH OF THE SEVERAL OFFICERS AFTER EACH OFFICER HAD TAKEN HIS TURN UPON THE TOILET, FLOOR, GROUND, ETC.
6. TO HOLD STILL WHILE EACH OFFICER APPLIED A LIGHTED CIGAR, CIGARETTE AND/OR MATCH OR CIGARETTE LIGHTER TO HIS PENIS, TESTICLES, RECTUM, AND OTHER VITAL PARTS OF HIS BODY.
7. AND TO ANY AND ALL OTHER FOUL AND DESPICABLE SAVAGERIES AS CHANCED TO STRIKE THE FANCY OF ANY ONE OF THE SEVERAL OFFICERS.[89]

Through thick description and zealous rhetorical precision, Casper's research charges a small detachment of state actors with systematically gang-raping starved and injured men. This devastating accusation viscerally shifts the focus of our interrogation away from the "excessive," yet generally permissible, inflictions of violence that have shaped dominant understandings of the Attica massacre. In their stead we are confronted with a class of sexualized atrocity that has not and *cannot* be fully incorporated into the public discourse because doing so would rupture the myth of White Man and white civilization. Casper forgoes rehashing the generic forms of killing and beating that had already received considerable attention in the official reports and the media, perhaps because the fact is that such killings, woundings, and thrashings, even when applied to a degree believed to be beyond what is "necessary," are authorized and normalized as something that people generally, and the state in particular, can legitimately do to people generally, and revolting Black people especially.

As I have already shown, bodily waste was weaponized by both sides of the struggle. Caged rebels in Auburn resisted state terror by hurling their urine and feces at their armed attackers. However, this defensive practice is incommensurable with what the petition describes: the ritualized execration of utterly powerless human beings under the threat of death. Isolated and held at gunpoint, they were forced to kneel, a position of worship and supplication, and to open their mouths awaiting receipt of their enemy's rancid bodily discharge. These acts of violent white masculinity could have been plucked from the pages of *100 Days of Sodom*, or from Pier Pasolini's depiction of fascism in the film *Salò*. They have precedent in the real-life arsenal of Thomas Thistlewood, the eighteenth-century plantation overseer who devised a punishment he called "Derby's Dose," in which an enslaved person was forced to defecate into the mouth of another, after which the mouth would be sealed shut.[90] Unlike the beatings and killings that made headlines, these atrocities of sexual revenge cannot be written off as the mere "excess" of an otherwise rational system. Rather, the production of excess was clearly the object of these defilements insofar as they fixated on reproductive organs, bodily orifices, and the digestive system, the very parts of human anatomy that produce excess: phlegm, urine, feces, semen.

To be forcibly raped. To perform. To kneel. To hold. To eat. Casper describes acts alleged to have happened in the past, but does so using infinitive tenses and subjunctive grammatical moods, placing these acts in a space-time of rumor, doubt, speculation, and possibility, a space-time in which they could happen, did happen, are happening, and will happen, again and again. I have neither the capacity nor the interest to verify Casper's claims according to positivist standards of Truth. What matters most is that prisons are engines of antihuman violence. While it describes spectacular and exceptional expressions of this condition, Casper's research draws our attention to how a racial-sexual logic of "thingification" undergirds prisons under normal conditions. The patriarchal organization of authority, the institutionalized segregation of the sexes, the regulation of intimacy, the separation from family, the divestment of rights, the condoning of rape, the facilitation of racism, the strip searches, the rectal examinations, the nigger sticks, the vulnerability to violence—the Attica massacre was the logical culmination of the prison's mundane rituals.

The Long Attica Revolt was energized by collective efforts to articulate, enact, and realize modes of being that transcended a liberal humanism that presents itself as universal while hinging on the dehumanization of Others. After elaborating the inconceivable violence of the massacre, Casper engages and extends this conversation. The petition's final section theorizes an alternative ontological schema in which race—as the hierarchical ordering of humanoid species—is rendered obsolete via the recognition of a true human universality. For Casper, Attica was symptomatic of the generalized failure among those masquerading as humans—warmongers, predators, and parasites—to comprehend that at a spiritual and molecular level they are essentially indivisible from those they hunt. To Douglass, who was white and as far as I know a complete stranger, Casper expounds:

> THAT FINALLY, I COME TO YOU BECAUSE YOU ARE MY BROTHER AND PROTECTOR IN THE FAMILY, AS WELL AS ONE OF THE KEEPERS OF THE DEEDS, AND THE FUNDAMENTAL AND UNSHAKABLE LOVE THAT BINDS US TOGETHER IS OLDER THAN THE FIRST MOUNTAIN, PRE-DATING BY A BILLION GENERATIONS THE ORDINARY ASSIGNABILITY OF FIBROUS DIFFERNTIATION AND SCALED PIGMENTATION, SO THAT YOU AND I ARE JUST AS ASSUREDLY OF THE MOTHER AND FATHER AS THEY ARE OF THE SAME AND IDENTICAL OCEAN OF LIFE, THAT MAJESTIC COLLECTION OF SUB-MICROSCOPIC PEOPLE WHOSE ETERNAL CHANCE AND DUTY IT IS TO BECOME HUMAN BEINGS. AND SO LONG AS YOU AND I WERE IN THAT BOUNDLESS SUB-MICROSCOPIC UNIVERSE WE SHARED WITH ONE ANOTHER, ASSISTED AND PROTECTED ONE ANOTHER, FOR THERE COULD BE NO DOUBT THAT WE WERE BROTHERS, FLESH OF THE SAME FLESH, BLOOD OF THE SAME BLOOD, AND BONE OF THE SAME BONE. THE MERE ADDITION OF VARIOUS PARTICLES AND THE INCEPTION OF INCREASED QUANTITIES OF LIGHT RAYS INHERENT IN THE METAMORPHOSIS FROM AUTOCHTHONOUS SEA-BROTHERS TO FELLOWMEN, HAS NO EFFECT WHATSOEVER UPON THE MIGHT WOMB FROM WHICH WE HAVE IN COMMON SPRUNG.[91]

Casper offers a new formulation of human being through a novel architecture of knowledge that blends Western scientific axioms, Abrahamic religiosity, and a deep mysticism. The prism of mad science stretches his temporal frame of reference far beyond recorded history and the geographical coordinates to the scale of the galaxy, inviting us to ponder human being as a totality of space, matter, motion, and light. He urges us to begin at the beginning, "a billion generations" ago, before culture, civilization, and race. He asks us to ponder how it came to be that beings produced by an "unshakable love" that emerged from a single womb, that are constituted by identical sub-microscopic particles, and that only recently metamorphized into their present form, in which only minor differences of "scaled pigmentation" register in the visual field, proceed to cage, kill, defile, and terrorize one another. His invocation of the human as not yet fully incarnate, as deferred potentiality with the "chance" and "duty" to one day realize its full capacity, evokes the "new humanism" of anticolonial theorists like Frantz Fanon and Sylvia

Wynter. For Casper, the tragedy of the human is that it continually proves itself unable to recognize the truly universal qualities that it reflects and embodies.

The fact that I found this petition in the New York State Archives indicates that someone on the governor's staff received and opened the letter, but we can only speculate as to how and why Casper's cry for help, this primal scream, was preserved while simultaneously ignored. Perhaps the functionary who opened it never really looked at it, simply filed it away with the multitude of letters received from the caged and dispossessed. Perhaps they read it but found it so shocking or unbelievable that they ignored it. Or maybe they tried to read it but found it illegible—not visually, for Casper made sure that his words were clear, but conceptually. This is to say, maybe they saw that Casper was mad and therefore, that his claims had little value. Alternatively, they could have read the petition and believed Casper's claims, but felt that no action was warranted because this is what happens, or should be happening, to "those people." Did Douglass ever see the petition? Did Rockefeller himself? The unanswered and unanswerable questions are legion. And will remain so.

In the symbolic universe of White Man, Attica was much more than a prison rebellion. It was what Baldwin called a "upheaval in the universe."[92] In response, state actors, white civil society, and mass media coalesced into a frenzied mob that inflicted world-shattering violence upon the bodies and minds, the very being, of the rebels. These rituals of sexual revenge and soul murder consciously and unconsciously drew from putatively bygone eras of colonial and chattel dominance. Irreducible to tactics, strategy, or political rationality, these rituals conjured a figurative world in which Black beings exist only as objects of white enjoyment and self-actualization. Though officially aimed at "restoring order" within a riotous rural prison in Western New York, these acts of sexual revenge aimed to stabilize a deeper order: the gendered-racial order that upholds capital, nation, empire, and civilization; the racial taxonomy through which the White Man is formed and without which he vanishes into oblivion.

During a recorded phone conversation, President Nixon told Rockefeller that he thought the massacre was "going to have a hell of a salutary effect on future prison riots."[93] The opposite was true. The rebellion and massacre unleashed new expressions of anticarceral militancy. The Weather Underground detonated a bomb at the Albany headquarters of the New York prison system. Captives in a men's jail in Baltimore and a federal women's prison in West Virginia rebelled in solidarity with Attica.[94] More prison rebellions occurred in 1972 than in any other year on record.[95]

On January 27, 1972, the George Jackson Squad of the BLA carried out a gruesome assassination of NYPD officers Gregory Foster and Rocco Laurie. According to the official story, at around 10:30 p.m., as the pair patrolled the East Village, they were ambushed by three Black men who shot them in the back. Foster, who was Black, was subsequently shot through his eyes. Laurie, who was white, was shot twice in the groin, one bullet striking his penis. The NYPD's chief propagandist called it "a crime of such savagery that it was almost incomprehensible." Yet those responsible for these cruel acts contextualized them as retaliation for the Attica massacre and pervasive anti-Black sexual violence: "No longer will black people tolerate Attica and oppression and exploitation and rape of our black community. This is the start of our spring offensive. There is more to come." Reiterating the source of their animus, they signed off, "we remember Attica."[96]

The failure of state violence to quell the Revolt sets the stage for my discussion in the following chapter. There I reveal that the Attica massacre was only the most visible form of repression within a protracted campaign of prison pacification. In the shadow of their spectacular atrocity, the administrators of carceral war implemented a constellation of seductive reforms that promoted the idea that the state was fulfilling the rebels' "reasonable" demands out of a new sense of enlightened benevolence while in reality, they were legitimizing their rule and enhancing their control through a conscious strategy of counterinsurgency. This "reformist counterinsurgency" reshaped prisons as we know them and laid the groundwork for the United States to become a world leader of incarceration.

CHAPTER 5

Hidden War

Four Strategies of Reformist Counterinsurgency

The massacre that occurred in Attica Prison on September 13, 1971, was only the inaugural moment in a multifaceted campaign of prison pacification. The planners and administrators of this campaign strategically co-opted the demands of the prison movement and redeployed them in ways that strengthened their ability to dominate people on both sides of prison walls. Through shrewdly constructed discourses of reform, they created new and improved prisons, bolstered security protocols, augmented their labor force, and legitimized their power, all while appearing to bow to radical demands. As planned, these putatively benign dispensations exploited a key contradiction within the prison movement, ultimately cleaving support from the movement's radical edge while nurturing its accommodationist tendency. Thus, contrary to how they are popularly understood, I conceptualize the post-Attica reforms not as a break with the violence of the massacre but its extension, albeit in a barely perceptible form.

A growing body of scholarship unearths the logics of war that undergird assumptively benevolent domestic reforms. From the education programs of the Reconstruction era to the Community Action Programs of the Johnson administration, scholars have shown that state efforts to pacify populations—to achieve peace without justice—involve the *calibration* of violence with inducements and solicitations.[1] These discussions typically conceptualize the prison as a manifestation of the hard, violent, and repressive side of this dynamic, and indeed it is. As I argued in the introduction, by 1970 state actors increasingly deployed carceral institutions as a means of quelling Black urban rebellion. However, this strategy generated unintended consequences: it gave rise to the Long Attica Revolt.

The intensifying struggle behind the walls made clear that existing techniques of carceral domination—geographically incapacitating populations, fomenting interracial hostility, quarantining "ringleaders," and naked violence—were no longer sufficient to maintain order. Although these overtly repressive measures would remain central in the post-Attica context, they were augmented with a constellation of "modernized," "progressive," and "gentle" techniques, which sought to produce "compliant" and "rehabilitated" subjects in ways that were not immediately recognized as coercive. This new strategy constituted a second layer of domestic war, one that targeted restive incarcerated populations in order to maintain power beyond the prison walls.

While the primary aims of this reformist counterinsurgency were to reassert dominance over the captive population and to isolate radicals, it had auxiliary targets as well. Planners of this campaign used reform to regain legitimacy with prison guards, who had learned through the assault force's killing of their coworkers that their lives were worth little more than those of the prisoners. The reforms were also designed to solicit publics beyond the walls, a large fraction of whom had grown increasingly critical of prisons and developed sympathy, if not solidarity with, the prison movement. Thus, the post-Attica reforms marked a turning point in which prisoncrats began looking beyond the prison, embarking on new efforts to project carceral power and ideology outward.

This chapter demystifies prison reform as a modality of psychological warfare. Also known as psychological operations, or psyops, the US Army defines this modality as "the planned use of propaganda and other measures to influence the opinions, emotions, attitudes, and behavior of hostile, neutral, or friendly groups in such a way as to support the achievement of national objectives."[2] Through the tactical deployment of propaganda and "other measures"—military, political, economic, social, cultural, and so on—planners of this hidden war sought to degrade the rebels' will to struggle while fostering support for their regime among neutral and friendly populations. They sought to incarcerate the horizon of their political aspirations, replace emotions and affects of rebellion with those of compliance, foster investment in the prison's legitimacy, and convince populations that they were not at war. "To subdue the enemy without fighting is the acme of skill," wrote Sun Tzu more than two millennia ago.[3]

Detailed in this chapter is an inherent tension within the prison movement between pragmatic/ameliorative and revolutionary/abolitionist demands. This tension is a crucial part of why the reformist counterinsurgency was so effective. As I will document, carceral planners exploited the tension, cynically co-opting the ameliorative demands in order to marginalize more radical aspirations for social transformation. Building on this, this chapter will analyze four strategies of reformist counterinsurgency: "expansion," "humanization," "diversification," and "programmification." I show that key actors within the state penal hierarchy shaped how the reforms were conceptualized and implemented, arguing that while they were promoted as concessions, their true aim was far more sinister. Through these interlocking reforms, carceral planners sought to disaggregate the captive population, to distribute it across an expanding and diversifying carceral network, and to foster an environment that was less conducive to rebellion, one where new "rehabilitative" programs could take root and flourish with active support from communities on both sides of prison walls. These moves had profound effects. They isolated organizers, demobilized revolutionary organizing, and stabilized the carceral system in a moment of profound crisis. By tracing the inception, implementation, and reception of these carceral innovations, I provide a framework for conceptualizing prisons of today as institutionalized counterinsurgency.

UNPACKING THE CONTRADICTION

Although a central argument of this book is that the Long Attica Revolt articulated an revolutionary abolitionist vision that is irreducible to demands for prison reform, it is also true that throughout the Revolt, incarcerated people and their loved ones enunciated and struggled over pragmatic demands to ameliorate violent prison conditions. The tension between the urgent need to secure reforms to enable the captives' immediate survival as human beings and the equally urgent project of abolishing broader systems of oppression is a central contradiction of the prison movement and the broader Black liberation struggle. While ameliorating harm provides essential relief for those enduring it, such relief can have a stabilizing effect on the predatory systems that generate harm in the first place.[4] At the same time, as I have shown throughout this book, those who engage in militant attacks against the system inexorably face the wrath of the state, often resulting in a painful existence and a premature death.

This internal tension and its implications were on full display during a public hearing of the New York State Select Committee on Correctional Institutions and Programs. Governor Nelson Rockefeller had launched this committee in the weeks after the massacre, a shrewd political move to generate bipartisan support for his prison reform agenda. This panel of so-called experts—lawyers, political elites, and prisoncrats—triangulated the security requirements of the state with carefully selected rebel demands, proposing an array of reforms to "modernize" the prison system "even in light of the State's current serious fiscal situation."[5] Among them were the construction of new prisons, especially at the minimum and medium security levels; improvements to visitation policies, medical care, and the overall institutional "atmosphere"; the implementation of new rehabilitative programs; and the development of "classification capability for determining the types of programs and security needs of the individuals under custody."[6] On February 11, 1972, survivors of the Auburn and Attica rebellions, as well as their family members and supporters, all of whom were organized under the banner of the Prisoners Solidarity Committee (PSC), traveled to downtown Manhattan to force their critiques of these proposals into the public record.[7] Their continued defiance in the face of state power demonstrates that the Long Attica Revolt survived the massacre. However, it also revealed the movement's ideological and tactical heterogeneity, a condition that state actors sought to exploit.

The PSC's bold intervention violated the protocols of courtroom decorum. On the heels of a lengthy testimony claiming that the Nation of Islam was not a legitimate religion, Tom Soto, who had been in Attica during the rebellion as an outside observer, interjected from the audience:

> At this time I would like to state now behind me are Lawrence Killebrew, who was shot three times in Attica, who was marked with an X on his back and I have on my left Sharean of the Auburn 6 who was also in Attica during the rebellion who was gassed at one time for seventeen hours, has been beaten in courtrooms while in chains and shackles and handcuffs, and we also have Carmen Garrigia, the wife of a relative in Attica who was also abused and brutalized. . . . I believe that they should be the next ones to testify.[8]

Soto's brazen introduction of people directly targeted by carceral violence ruptured the progressive facade of the Select Committee, which "was set up as a result of Attica," according to internal documents, but managed to avoid referencing the rebellion or the massacre in its initial report.[9] After a heated argument between Soto and the Select

Committee's chairman, multiple scheduled speakers ceded their time, allowing the PSC to testify.

While the first two speakers described the shocking forms of sexual racism they endured in Auburn and Attica, Carmen Garrigia discussed the subtle and mundane forms of abuse the system inflicted on her whole family. She explained that her husband, James Walker—also a survivor of the Auburn and Attica rebellions—should have been standing by her side, but that, on multiple occasions, his expected release date had been pushed back due to infractions accrued in connection with the rebellions. She further explained that prisoncrats were heavily censoring letters between her husband and their daughter and that because DOCS had few Spanish-language translators, weeks often passed before their letters were delivered. Garrigia outlined the significant costs associated with the eight-hour bus trip from New York City to Attica and inveighed against the invasive searches she endured before and after each visit, explaining how she and her husband tried to maintain some semblance of intimacy by poking their fingers through the wire screen that separated them during visits. She was incensed by the arbitrary restrictions on the kinds of items she was allowed to leave with her husband during these visits. "You can't send honey in," she explained. "They are not allowing toothpaste in there, no fruit juices. How are they supposed to supplement their diet?"[10]

Garrigia's efforts to keep her family whole, maintain an emotional connection with her husband, and introduce items of care that might momentarily sweeten his existence highlight the key role that outside communities, especially women, played in ensuring the survival of those inside. Speaking from her position as caretaker of the family, her testimony challenged the Select Committee's vague language on reforming the prison "atmosphere." Instead, she called for the immediate amelioration of specific material conditions and policies that circumscribed the humanity, dignity, and collective survival of targeted communities. Rebels articulated this category of demand throughout the Long Attica Revolt, from the Tombs rebels, who demanded "as human beings, the dignity and justice that is due to us by right of our birth," to the Auburn demand for Black Studies programs, to "The Fifteen Practical Proposals" the Attica rebels authored after being told that their "Immediate Demands" were unrealistic.[11]

Although achieving "wins" among this class of demands is critical to the long-term sustainability of movements unfolding under conditions of genocide, their pragmatism rendered them vulnerable to co-optation.¹² To co-opt, argues sociologist Robert L. Allen, is "to assimilate militant leaders and militant rhetoric while subtly transforming the militants' program for social change into a program which in essence buttresses the status quo."¹³ As overarching logics of the reformist counterinsurgency, psychological warfare and co-optation intentionally muddled distinctions between victories and defeats. In the words of the US Army's *Counterinsurgency Field Manual*, "Skillful counterinsurgents can deal a significant blow to an insurgency by appropriating its cause."¹⁴

Testifying directly after Garrigia, Joseph Little exposed the imperialist logic undergirding the Select Committee's proposals. Discharged from Attica's hellish walls just ten days earlier, Little excoriated reform and rehabilitation as modes of domination and lambasted the gathering as a "farce." Its so-called experts, Little noted, were regurgitating "the same old bullshit" that prison reformers had been spouting for over a century. Although he could produce "a long dissertation" on the brutalities of prison, however, he was not among the growing chorus of people demanding ameliorative reforms. "Everybody wants to get on the political bandwagon. Everybody is down with penitentiary reform. Let us make the penitentiary like the Holiday Inn. I'm not for no penitentiary reform. I am for abolishing the whole concept of penitentiary reform."¹⁵ Long before abolition was in vogue, Little articulated an abolitionist critique, voicing principled opposition to ameliorative reforms based on an understanding that they would extend the prison's life. His analysis anticipated and radicalized French theorist Michel Foucault's oft-cited observation that prison reform is a constituent element of the prison itself.¹⁶ Not only did Little diagnose the centrality of reform to the prison's core functioning, he asserted a demand for the abolition of reform, which is to say the abolition of the prison itself. As dutifully captured by the court stenographer's remarkable transcript, Little's statements elicited applause from the audience.

Little then denounced "rehabilitation" as propaganda, a disguised attempt to "pacify the inmates," "make them docile citizens," "train them to be like robots," and mold them according to white, ruling-class values. "Am I to be rehabilitated to be like who? To be like the racist guards, the racist administrators who are running this country? To be like Rockefeller? Or the Mellons or any other ruling class? Am I to be like you gentlemen sitting there? Just what constitutes rehabilitation? There is nothing wrong with me. What needs to be rehabilitated is the society we live in."¹⁷ His interrogatory critique inverted standard criminological analytics, which trace criminality to biological, psychological, or cultural defects believed to be internal to those who transgress the law. To the contrary, Little contended that the structure of society is defective, that social life is afflicted by capitalism and white supremacy. In his view, if the committee were truly interested in eliminating violence and crime, they would attack these systems of power, for they produce what Little called a "dog eat dog society," a society that requires crime and prisons.[18]

In a 1973 address to the Fraternal Order of Police, Democratic congressman Richard H. Ichord described an ongoing investigation by the House Internal Security Committee (HISC), of which he was chairman, in the following way: "Our committee has also been conducting a wide-ranging inquiry into the exploitation of prison conditions and unrest by revolutionary groups and organizations in an effort to recruit from behind prison walls and with the aim of tearing down the administration of the penal system as a prelude to destroying the institutions and form of our entire government."[19] Little's unapologetically abolitionist demand for the overturning of the political-economic structure of society is more compatible with this often dismissed theory than it is with liberal reformist analytics that focus on prisoners' rights. As I have already shown, many of the Revolt's combatants, engineers, and elected spokesmen saw themselves as the tip of a revolutionary spear and engaged in anticarceral insurgency with capacious ambitions in mind.

Recognizing the implications of Little's testimony, the vice chairman of the Select Committee asked Little if his political analysis was shared by others. "When the problems at Attica arose, were the people at the proper front of that particular movement fighting for the things that you mentioned before in your testimony? The complete change and not interested in the superficial change that perhaps might have been recommended in a report like this?" he asked.[20] Little neither confirmed nor denied the Revolt's revolutionary impulse. Although he and a few others were now outside the prison walls, they remained targets of carceral state repression. Jury selection in the long-delayed trial of six men criminally charged for their role in the Auburn rebellion had just commenced, and the state's criminal investigation of the Attica rebels was developing rapidly.[21] Moreover, in one of his last public statements before his sudden death, J. Edgar Hoover raised the specter of an "unholy alliance" between "black hardened criminal prison inmates" and "black revolutionary extremists."[22] With the help of HISC, Hoover's secret program to "neutralize" these imprisoned revolutionaries would soon evolve into the Prison Activists Surveillance Program.[23]

It would have been reckless for Little to elaborate on the revolutionary underpinnings of the Attica rebellion within this context of intensifying repression. "It seems as though you might be trying to bait me into [admitting] that I am advocating the overthrow of the government, or something like that . . . but I am no fool," he replied.[24] Little knew state actors were looking for any excuse to further criminalize and pathologize the rebels, which made it tactically necessary for him to de-emphasize Attica's revolutionary politics. Such concealment and obfuscation are central to the conduct of revolutionary warfare. Unfortunately, most scholars and analysts have overlooked this point, taking its outward focus on formal demands at face value. In doing so, they have unwittingly reinforced the reformist counterinsurgency project.

The approaches represented by Garrigia and Little are not necessarily antagonistic. Rather, they existed in productive tension within the PSC, an explicitly abolitionist formation launched by "free world" organizers in support of the Auburn rebels. The same tension existed within individual organizers as well. Throughout the 1960s, Martin Sostre and others launched several successful lawsuits that legally compelled prison authorities to ameliorate dehumanizing conditions.[25] And yet these conditions endured. In "The New Prisoner," an acerbic essay published in 1973, Sostre asserts that Auburn and Attica represented "decades of painful exhaustion of all peaceful means of obtaining redress, of the impossibility of obtaining justice within the 'legal' framework of an oppressive racist society which was founded on the most heinous injustices: murder, robbery, slavery."[26] For Sostre, the fact that what he called the "Attica Reform Demands" were aimed at many of the conditions that his successful litigation should have already resolved demonstrated that captives had no choice but to rebel, seize hostages, and adopt a more revolutionary posture.[27] Sostre saw value in reform and abolition demands, particularly when they were grounded in a revolutionary critique of the social order.

"As the [insurgent] campaign develops, a split is likely to open between the organizers and their followers, and the more successful the campaign the wider will be the split, because the greater the number of concessions granted by the government, the less have the participants to gain from seeing it overthrown," writes counterinsurgency specialist Frank Kitson.[28] In what follows I show how carceral planners followed Kitson's playbook, co-opting ameliorative demands in order to exacerbate the split within the prison movement. As the keynote speaker for the 1971 National Conference on Corrections, US Attorney General

John N. Mitchell laid out the general approach in the prison context. Although the Attica rebellion was perhaps the largest and most dynamic prison rebellion to date, congressional researchers had identified at least seventeen other rebellions in 1971 alone.[29] Like Rockefeller, Hoover, and Ichord, Mitchell believed these eruptions were the work of a "militant hard core among the inmates." To his audience of prisoncrats from across the United States he explained, "If you change the conditions under which the greater majority of them function, you won't have these problems on the massive scales that you have had in a couple of these institutions."[30] Changing the conditions involved four strategies of hidden war: expansion, humanization, diversification, and programmification.

EXPANSION

While no individual is singularly responsible for directing the reformist counterinsurgency, Governor Rockefeller was among its key architects. Although rarely described as such, this heir to the Standard Oil dynasty was a seasoned administrator of hidden warfare. He and his brother David—a former US Army intelligence officer in Algeria and president of Chase Manhattan Bank—were mentored by John and Allen Dulles, who, as the respective heads of the State Department and the CIA during the 1950s, shaped US foreign policy during the height of the Cold War.[31] Prior to becoming the chief executive of the Empire State, Rockefeller used his post as president of the Museum of Modern Art (MoMA) to fight what Frances Stono Saunders calls the Cultural Cold War. In collaboration with the CIA, MoMA elevated "abstract expressionism," an artistic movement favored by Cold War strategists because it allegedly promoted anticommunist values like free enterprise and American exceptionalism. Rockefeller also headed the Office of the Coordinator of Inter-American Affairs, a massive intelligence gathering and propaganda disseminating operation in Latin America, and chaired the Planning Coordinating Group, which used psychological and political warfare techniques to destabilize communist governments. His use of these techniques was consistent with the formative role played by the Rockefeller Foundation in developing the science of propaganda in service of US empire during World War II.[32]

Rockefeller's Cold War outlook informed his approach to the Long Attica Revolt and shaped his understanding of Black rebellion as a threat to Western civilization. He maintained that Attica was caused by the "revolutionary tactics of militants" and, while testifying about Attica, drew an explicit connection between methods employed by Black revolutionaries in the United States and those in Latin America: "One of the most recent and widely used techniques of modern day revolutionaries has been the taking of political hostages and using the threat to kill them as blackmail to achieve unconditional demands and to gain wide public attention to further their revolutionary ends."[33] By suggesting that US prisons were beset with the same political forces that were destabilizing Western imperialism abroad, Rockefeller implicitly justified the massacre and offered a rationale for ongoing counterinsurgency measures. Stressing the existential nature of the threat, he told members of his inner circle, "There was more at stake [in Attica] even than saving lives. There was the whole rule of law to consider. The whole fabric of our society, in fact."[34]

Explorations of Rockefeller's role in forging the carceral state have largely focused on the so-called Rockefeller Drug Laws.[35] Ratified in 1973, they restricted plea bargaining opportunities and imposed "mandatory minimum" sentences for a range of drug offenses.[36] As the 1970s and 1980s wore on and racial criminalization became a key mode of governance, similar laws were replicated throughout the nation, increasing prison populations by prolonging sentence lengths.[37] This intensification of what Nixon, after consulting with Rockefeller, had termed "the war on drugs" is an important aspect of how the United States became the world's foremost jailer.[38] However, in lieu of rehashing this well-worn historical ground, I focus on how Black prison rebellion was also a key driver of prison expansion and how prison expansion fits into a broader framework of counterinsurgency as hidden war.

Expansion is the sine qua non of prison reform, insofar as reforms rarely if ever entail a diminution of the state's capacity to capture and punish targeted populations. When Attica erupted on September 9, 1971, New York State managed a population of 12,500 incarcerated people distributed across twelve major prisons. Auburn, the oldest structure in its network, had opened more than a century and a half earlier, while Green Haven, the newest, opened in 1949.

In the decades after the massacre, the state embarked upon a rapacious experiment with the criminalization and incarceration of targeted populations, namely economically dispossessed Black and Latinx communities, women of color, queer and trans people, and undocumented immigrants. By the year 2000, the peak of its physical carceral capacity, New York boasted seventy-one prisons and a captive population of more than 71,000.[39] The growth of this punitive infrastructure mirrored similar developments nationwide. The total US state and federal captive population exploded by 500 percent between 1971 and 2010.[40] As I will show, Attica was a pivotal moment that gave rise to this unprecedented expansion.

Published in 1970, the American Correctional Association's anti-riot manual provides the basis for understanding prison expansion, modernization, and proliferation as psychological warfare. "Antiquated facilities which are large, drab, overcrowded, and isolated from the community are conducive to the development of frustration and anger," they wrote, while "small, well-designed institutions with individual cells are much more effective in reducing disturbances and tension within the institution."[41] Prison expansion, they claimed, reduced overcrowding. This, of course, is a pernicious myth, given that expanded capacity seems almost inevitably to become inadequate soon after it is made available.[42] Less crowded prisons were said to relieve "tension," "frustration," and "anger," thereby preventing spontaneous rebellions from emerging, while "planned disturbances" could be "neutralized" by removing and isolating "intelligent" and "revolutionary" individuals from the general population, a move requiring flexible carceral capacity.[43] Citing the ACA document, the Select Committee's second report noted that "one of the most desirable and effective methods available is for the system to have a multiplicity of facilities for the difficult agitators. Having alternate facilities provides a means for the inmate to re-establish himself and remove his negative influence in regard to his original peer group."[44]

State actors had been aware of their "need" for more prisons since the beginning of the Revolt. Readers may recall that in the wake of the jail rebellion, the state system was forced to absorb three thousand captives who had been under the city's control. This shift transformed the composition of the prisons, resulting in Auburn having what one administrator called "a critical mass of revolutionaries."[45] Given that these revolutionaries were blamed for the ensuing rebellion in Auburn, it is unsurprising that one of the key ideas guiding the 1973 Multi-Year Master Plan, which laid out the system's capital requirements through 1978, was the need to avoid "critical masses in all facilities." "Smaller, more manageable numbers in the living, eating, working, and recreation areas will decrease the risk of widespread disturbances, while the prospects of a more humane scale are increased," the plan stated.[46] By creating new infrastructure to more effectively isolate revolutionaries, while cultivating an emotional state that was conducive to order, prison expansion was indispensable to counterinsurgency.

This counterinsurgent rationale for expansion has remained central to carceral state development across decades. As a law enforcement union representative told the state legislature in 1985: "Without expansion the entire system is at risk. Without expansion there is increased tension between inmates. Without expansion more inmates who should be classified as being in maximum facilities will be in medium and so on down the line. Without expansion the discipline system breaks down, as we have inadequate numbers of special housing units. As discipline breaks down, so does our control of the system. As you are aware, when control of the system is compromised the potential for a riot or other disturbances are markedly increased."[47] This discourse is notable not only for how tension, breakdowns in discipline, and rebellion are attributed mechanistically to prison infrastructure, but also for how it forecloses the possibility that tension might be lessened by reducing the total captive population through "upstream" interventions such as public investment in education and social services, decriminalization, or arrest diversion. Expansion is a reformist imperative that accepts the permanence of the prison as a given and sees its progression as the only viable option.

The Select Committee's recommendation that "immediate and intensive efforts" be made to expand prison capacity afforded Rockefeller the legislative support he needed to execute his reformist counterinsurgency. In May of 1972, he signed a law that enabled prison expansion to be financed via bond issues while at the same time circumventing the need for voter approval, which normally preceded the accumulation of public debt. Applying a method he used to construct the Empire State Plaza in Albany during the 1960s, Rockefeller built new prisons and renovated existing ones using the "Public Benefit Corporation" (PBC), an entity designed to provide flexible access to state power and capital while partially avoiding both government regulation and the risks of the market.[48] The 1972 law empowered a PBC called the State Dormitory Authority to issue up to $50 million in debt to finance prison construction and renovation (a cap that was later lifted). It then gave another PBC, the Health and Mental Hygiene Facilities Improvement Corporation, responsibility for planning, designing, acquiring, and constructing prisons.[49]

Under the plan, DOCS would continue to run the new prisons, but the Mental Hygiene Facilities Improvement Corporation would hold the titles, at least until DOCS paid off the debt. On its face, the law included a mechanism for balancing the books: prison labor. Since

1953, New York's captive laborers had been remunerated with resources drawn from the Correctional Industry Fund, which accumulated revenues generated from selling the products of their labor. After the passage of the law, state taxpayers started footing the bill for the captives' meager wages, freeing up revenue generated by prison labor to service the PBC's debt. However, according to an annual report from Auburn's Prison Industry Program, one of the most productive such programs in the system, the sale of license plates, highway signs, tobacco, and furniture—all of which, by law, had to be sold to other state agencies—generated revenue barely exceeding $1 million in 1969.[50] If all twelve of the state's major adult prisons pulled in similar numbers—a very big if—their combined revenue would amount to a mere fraction of the Dormitory Authority's debt cap. Thus, the reformed use of the Correctional Industry Fund was an act of propaganda designed to suggest that the impending carceral boom would be financed through fiscally responsible means, when in fact it was to be financed through an undemocratic process that would expand the state's debt.[51]

This massive expansion of carceral capacity was not inevitable. Prison abolition and decarceration were powerful political tendencies during the 1970s, not only among political radicals but within mainstream discourse as well.[52] Rockefeller circumvented a public referendum on an expansion bond issue because he knew its approval was not a foregone conclusion. While diverse constituencies were increasingly concerned about "rising crime," the use of public funds to intensify policing, criminalization, and incarceration had not yet become "common sense" solutions.[53] In 1981, for example, voters rejected Governor Mario Cuomo's $500 million bond issue to fund prison expansion. As geographer Jack Norton has shown, this same "shell game" of laundering tax revenue and public debt through opaque PBC bureaucracies was used to circumvent the will of the voters, facilitating the transformation of much of Upstate New York into a penal colony during the final decades of the twentieth century.[54]

Prison expansion sought to pacify populations on both sides of prison walls. Not only did carceral planners promise that renovated, modernized, and expanded infrastructure would forestall prison rebellion and protect civilization from the scourge of crime, they presented prisons as a form of economic security for residents of the communities where prisons were located. In the 1973 Master Plan, DOCS Commissioner Russell G. Oswald describes economic development as part of the agency's post-Attica expansion strategy: "[The plan] . . . provides the necessary levels of custody and security to safeguard the public, staff and inmates *and maintains the economic integrity and stability in communities and surrounding areas where these facilities have long been a positive factor for employment and economic stability.*"[55] Of the fourteen New York State prisons opened between 1973 and 1979, seven were located in largely white, rural, deindustrializing communities. This dynamic intensified between 1982 and 2000, during which almost all of the thirty-two new prisons were sited upstate. Research has demonstrated that during the 1980s and 1990s, prisons were pitched as de facto jobs programs for unskilled labor, helping to harden white attitudes in favor of the perpetual criminalization and punishment of Black and Latinx populations.[56] As we can see, however, an earlier version of this dynamic emerged directly after Attica, helping to solidify support for prison development among populations who otherwise might have demanded other ways of making a living.

"All this money that they use is designed to kill," noted Sostre, commenting on DOCS's budget, which ballooned from $215,554 in fiscal year 1969–70 to more than $8 million in 1973–74.[57] "It looks like they're getting ready to fight a war."[58] Indeed, days after the massacre, Rockefeller drew $800,000 from the State Emergency Fund to provide DOCS with additional firearms, gas guns, metal detectors, over four thousand gas masks, three thousand helmets, nearly seven hundred sets of face shields and goggles, and new gun towers overlooking Attica's yards.[59] Following the lead of California's prison system, DOCS also developed what they called Correctional Employees Response Teams (CERTs), a prison-based version of police SWAT teams. Equipped with bulletproof vests, riot shields, gas grenades, shotguns, and other martial equipment, these units were designed to rapidly respond to emergencies and, according to DOCS, to suppress "disturbances" using a variety of martial tactics including "carefully controlled offensive strategies."[60]

Despite its apolitical public face as a fiscally responsible means of modernizing the carceral system and relieving tension, post-Attica prison expansion operated simultaneously as political, economic, and psychological warfare. Expansion sought to disperse the population across a wide geographic area, to increase the number of walls dividing captives and eliminate the potential for rebellion. At the same time, it enhanced the prison's repressive capacity such that if rebellion were to emerge, prisoncrats would be prepared to crush it internally, preferably with minimal scrutiny from the outside. Finally, the economic aspect of expansion strengthened support for prison development among rural, white, working-class communities whose survival depended upon the prison's continued existence. Expansion worked hand in glove with another strategy of hidden warfare: the campaign to "humanize" the prisons.

HUMANIZATION

Critical prison studies research has shown how carceral planners couch expansionist and punitive imperatives in terms of care and progressivism as means of legitimating their rule.[61] My analysis extends this conversation by showing that what DOCS called "humanization" was and remains a key rhetoric of reformist counterinsurgency. On its face, humanization invokes a process of relieving oppressive conditions, assumptively through a range of modifications, such as new privileges and programs, better clothing and food, improvements to the physical environment, responsiveness to diversity, and so on. DOCS planners put the term into circulation after Attica forced them to reckon with the violence and racism permeating their prisons. However, as I will show, imprisoned intellectuals, radicals, and rebels conceptualized humanization as either a contradiction or an outright lie, arguing that not only did they leave the system's fundamental inhumanity intact, they were consciously designed to forestall resistance.

Russell G. Oswald assumed leadership of DOCS on January 1, 1971, in the middle of the protracted guerrilla war in Auburn. Three weeks later he sent a harried memo to the governor, complaining that his staff was under constant harassment by "black and white panthers who are bent on the utter destruction of the physical facilities and the correctional 'system'" and that "there are obvious signs of communication with supporters on the outside."[62] In a desperate effort to stabilize the system, he issued a series of memos and directives. He relaxed correspondence and reading-material censorship protocols, ordered the screens removed from prison visiting rooms, announced that showers should be allowed once per day in all facilities, called for the institution of "community-based and community-oriented programming," and placed formal limits on the use of force and gas against captives.[63] Although these humanizing reforms are typically attributed to Attica, they were announced amid the Auburn struggle and reaffirmed during Attica, further demonstrating the importance of the "Long Attica" framework.

Immediately after Rockefeller's massacre, Oswald received intense pressure to actualize these reforms from Council 82, the local representing New York State's law enforcement employees—a seemingly unlikely source. "For the first time in American history a labor union has induced a state government to institute major reforms in its penal and correctional system," announced an article in *82 Review*, the union's periodical. After Attica, guards threatened an illegal strike unless Oswald acceded to their expansionist demands: higher salaries, a larger labor force, more professional training, more security equipment, and the development of "a special institution for incorrigible inmates." However, included in these demands were "improvements in the provision of inmate needs such as adequate clothing, shoes, toilet articles and shower facilities."[64]

Council 82's demand to humanize the system was not an expression of solidarity between the keepers and the kept. Rather, it was an attempt to avert another confrontation in which they might again be taken hostage and/or killed. As historian Rebecca Hill has shown, many within the notoriously reactionary organization felt that "the common enemy is the boss and the inmate."[65] They understood the power of these reforms to assuage some of the hostility and rage welling within and between the captives, improving their own working conditions as a downstream benefit. Conceding to their demands, Oswald attached specific dollar amounts to key reform areas. He pledged $2,134,000 for a new "clothing ration" that would improve "wearability, appearance, and comfort" of the captives' uniforms, while earmarking $689,000 to develop a "nutritious diet" plan.[66]

On the other hand, as I have already shown, imprisoned radicals, rebels, and revolutionaries voiced opposition to humanization. People like Sostre were committed to nurturing rebellion and had therefore come to view brutal prison conditions as politically productive. He and others believed "prisons were the solitary confinement of the ghetto," and that carceral racism and violence were unmediated forms of the oppression that colonized populations experienced daily in the world beyond prison walls.[67] Committed to ending that world and creating a new one, Sostre saw this unmediated violence as a pedagogical tool that aided his ability to politicize and organize captives.[68] He theorized that by incarcerating ever more people within their "dehumanizing cages" and targeting them with "racist-oriented technology," carceral planners were inadvertently spreading the dynamics they aimed to contain. According to Sostre, they were transforming prisons into "revolutionary training camps," accelerating the "cross-fertilization" of political ideologies, and helping to produce "fully-hardened revolutionary cadres" that would "effect the overthrow of your racist-capitalist system."[69]

It was this revolutionary overthrow of the system, and not its incremental reconfiguration, that Sostre desired: "We, the new politically aware prisoner, will soon galvanize the revolutionary struggle in America to its new phase that will hasten the overthrow of your exploitative racist society, recover the product of our stolen slave labor which you now enjoy, and obtain revolutionary justice for all oppressed people."[70]

As part of the attempt to undermine revolutionary struggle, humanization involved the dissemination of propaganda. In Attica's immediate aftermath, DOCS aggressively publicized that they were altruistically improving prison conditions. For example, on the one-year anniversary of the rebellion, the *New York Times* published a story claiming that "Attica Prisoners Have Gained Most Points Made in Rebellion."[71] The article credits DOCS with implementing "expanded amenities" in the form of more access to personal hygiene products, law libraries, and better food. It fails to mention that in mid-July of 1972, just two months earlier, three-fourths of Attica's population had exposed themselves to intense repression by going on strike. The rebels issued a communiqué entitled "Message from the Monster: Attica," which dismissed the "show-case reforms" as subterfuge. "The atmosphere, attitude, and conditions that caused the biggest and bloodiest one day massacre in over a hundred years . . . are back again (twice fold)," wrote Charles "Rabb" Parker, an Auburn rebel and organizer of a formation called the Peoples Party. "I hesitate to use the word 'back' because they never left. They were just suppressed under the fear of death," he continued parenthetically. Rabb was suggesting that the autonomous zones created by militant action—rebellion, hostage-taking, and the threat of assassination—had thus far proven the only means by which Attica's oppressive atmosphere was substantially ameliorated.[72]

Echoing Rabb's notion of "showcase reforms," Sostre impugned humanization as a "smokescreen" designed to sway public attitudes and conceal the administration's new control strategy. Speaking directly to Rockefeller, Oswald, and other the planners of this hidden war, he wrote:

> Listen, pig, are you really that naïve to believe you can fool and pacify us with nightly bribes of ten-cent candy bars and cookie snacks while caging us like animals . . . by removing the wire screen from the visiting room but replacing it with the three foot wide table thrust between our mothers, wives, children and loved ones to maintain your inhuman separation; by changing the color of our uniforms from gray to green (and those of our jailers), while exploiting our slave labor for pennies a day. . . . After Attica?! Well dream on, pig, until the next rude awakening overtakes you.[73]

Sostre believed the administration's "bribes" could not disguise the reality that the "oppressive mentality" and the asymmetries of power that had led to the rebellion remained intact. Moreover, he argued that the potential benefits of each humanizing reform were immediately neutralized by repressive counter-reforms. Oswald removed the screens but replaced them with three-foot tables, "so actually you're further away than you were from your loved ones on the screen," Sostre explained in an interview.[74] Making a similar point, another captive explained that after Attica, they were allowed to spend more time in the yard, but that security protocols were changed so that jogging and exercising were only permitted on an individual basis and gatherings of more than six at a time were criminalized.[75] Roger Champen clarified the lie of humanization in 1973, when he noted that changes had come to the system, yet "there was no change you could point to and say, 'wow, that's better.'"[76]

The state's Multi-Year Master Plan all but explicitly names humanization as a psychological operation. It notes that the process cannot be measured by objective standards, but rather is intended to produce a subjective impact on captives' minds: "Recognition on the part of the offender that he is being treated with at least some regard for his dignity, though his liberty is curtailed, will go a long way in setting the stage for real treatment."[77] This clarifies Sostre's conceptualization of these reforms as "bribes." They were attempts to induce the desired behavior through ultimately frivolous institutional reconfigurations. Although analysts have tended to frame the post-Attica reforms as Attica's "wins," they can in some ways be seen as wins for the state, insofar as they helped stabilize the system and extend its life. As the following section shows, "humanization" is best understood as a process of strategically uneven development, implemented as a behavior-control technique intended to enhance state power.

DIVERSIFICATION

DOCS actualized expansion and humanization as methods of hidden warfare through the strategy of diversification. "The diversification of programs and facilities," notes the Master Plan, "is a response to the reality of diversity within the offender population. The aim of diversification is to turn the differences among the offenders to social advantage by creating a more effective correctional experience."[78] Although pitched as "the ultimate means of achieving a humane correctional environment," my analysis demystifies diversification as a strategy of war.[79] Diversification entails the cultivation of a spectrum of carceral institutions, each with unique infrastructural, staffing, and programmatic capacities, as well as the deployment of these unique capacities to stabilize the overall system. Whereas prior to Attica, individual prisons were populated with "an unplanned mixture of behavioral types and security levels," after Attica, carceral planners strove to disaggregate the population into "homogenous inmate groups" that could be rationally distributed across an expansive and diversified network, making them easier to control.

Diversification is a form of what Foucault famously termed "biopolitics," a technology of power that addresses "a multiplicity of men, not to the extent that they are nothing more than their individual bodies, but to the extent that they form, on the contrary, a global mass that is affected by overall processes. . . ."[80] A footnote buried in the McKay Commission report exemplifies this emergent population-level approach, revealing that among the Attica rebels who were in favor of prolonging the rebellion and remaining in control of the hostages until their demands were met, were "higher percentages of inmates under 30, those convicted of violent crimes, blacks, and single men."[81] Amid the reformist counterinsurgency, carceral planners weaponized this kind of statistical knowledge in order to prevent volatile "critical masses" from forming. Decades later, the late Russell "Maroon" Shoatz, a BPP/BLA political prisoner who spent nearly fifty years behind the walls of Pennsylvania's prison system, analyzed diversification as normalized counterinsurgency. The practice of "separating and transferring the most sophisticated thinkers among the prisoners to other prisons [and] replacing them with a new, younger, less savvy group of prisoners" was a common practice, he explained.[82]

Under the strategy of diversification, prison wardens continued to preside over their institutional fiefdoms but received guidance from centrally located carceral planners, who increasingly had advanced degrees and counterinsurgency expertise. For example, in 1971 DOCS recruited Dr. Robert H. Fosen, a Cornell-trained psychologist, to head its new Division of Research, Planning, and Evaluation. Prior to joining DOCS, Fosen was acting chief of the research division of the California Department of Corrections and then director of the Urban Development Research Program for the American Institutes for Research (AIR), a social and behavioral science think tank that regularly contracted with the Advanced Research Projects Agency, the Central Intelligence Agency, and other mainstays of the national security state.[83]

In 1967, AIR funded *Counter-Insurgency in Thailand*, a study that investigated how psychologists, anthropologists, and other social scientists could aid the state in suppressing anticolonial movements in Southeast Asia. AIR advocated a three-pronged approach to counterinsurgency. First was the use of "threats, promises, ideological appeals, and tangible benefits" intended to cleave support of malleable populations from the insurgency. Second, counterinsurgency should "reduce or interdict the flow of the competing inputs being made by the opposing side by installing anti-infiltration devices, cutting communication lines, assassinating key spokesmen, strengthening retaliatory mechanisms and similar preventative measures." And finally, it had "to counteract or neutralize the political successes already achieved by groups committed to the 'wrong side.'" Critically, the proposal references the "potential applicability" of the project's findings on "disadvantaged sub-cultures" in the United States, suggesting that the similarities between AIR's strategy in Thailand and Rockefeller's campaign in New York is no accident.[84]

Dr. Fosen was instrumental to the establishment of the Adirondack Correctional Treatment Education Center (ACTEC), the nerve center of DOCS' diversification strategy. Planners called it a "specialized facility," one that "offer[s] a spectrum of diagnostic and treatment programs ... includ[ing] individual and group counseling, academic and vocational training, special programming for those unable to adjust to routine institutional environments, and community preparation programs for those soon to be released to the community."[85] Captives from across the state were sent to ACTEC to be studied, classified, diagnosed, experimented upon, and sorted by an international coterie of doctors, behavioral scientists, social workers, and penal experts. No doubt informed by Fosen's research into how different systems of taxonomy and classification could be used to guide complex organizations, his department spearheaded an "offender profile" system that grouped captives into one of eighteen categories and distributed them across the expanding prison system according to set quotas.[86]

While much of the research conducted at ACTEC circulated through opaque institutional channels, some of it appeared in peer-reviewed journals. Such was the case with "Criminosynthesis of a Revolutionary Offender," a psychological profile of a twenty-seven-year-old captive who "identifies with the Black Panthers" and was "similar to the revolutionary offenders involved in the recent Attica rebellion."[87] Published in a 1972 issue of the *British Journal of Social Psychiatry and Community Health*, the study extends the long tradition of pathologizing Black resistance, concluding that the subject had minimal contact with reality, "psychotic tendencies," "high past and present criminal potential," and a "very low rehabilitation potential."[88] Diagnoses such as this were intended to identify "psychopaths" so that they could be incapacitated. However, in a twist of tragic irony, ten years after authoring this article, Dr. A. Steven Giannell reportedly shot and stabbed his two teenaged children to death, and then stabbed himself to death. "Violent End to Life Against Violence," read the headline in the *New York Times*.[89]

The diversification strategy achieved mixed results. Officially, diversification was to occur across maximum, medium, and minimum security levels. The 1973 plan projected that the state's captive population would reach 16,575 by 1978. Fosen's division surmised that 35 percent would be "tractable" enough to be controlled in minimum security, 45 percent could be held in medium security, while 20 percent would require maximum security. It also noted that a small minority, less than two hundred, needed what they called "intensive prescription and control programming," a concept I explore in the final chapter.[90] The ostensible goal of this infrastructural and programmatic diversity was to usher captives through a progressive system of behavioral modification, or as DOCS explained, to "move them upward within the system through a demonstration of responsible behavior."[91] However, this was not achieved in the immediate post-Attica context. As the 1970s wore on, this modernist vision was eclipsed by the lowest common denominator of penal administration: order maintenance. By June 1, 1981, the captive population far exceeded these projections. Only 7 percent were in minimum, 27 percent were in medium, and the majority, 65 percent, continued to be concentrated in the state's aging maximum-security bastilles.[92]

Despite the failure of official diversification, DOCS employed (and continues to employ) unofficial and plausibly deniable forms of this strategy. Captives have noted that in the post-Attica context, individual prisons were more likely to be populated with people who have drastically different sentence lengths and that this was a strategy designed to ensure that no prison would be filled with "lifers" who feel they have little to lose by rebelling against the state.[93] Moreover, within the overall network, certain prisons are known to be more or less "humanized" vis-à-vis population density, geography, program availability, saturation with violence, white supremacy, and so on. Carceral planners cultivate this diversity and employ it to maximize compliance. The recollection of Jacob, a Black man who spent more than a decade incarcerated across various New York prisons throughout the 1970s and '80s, brings this dynamic into sharp relief.

Jacob began his fifteen-year bid in Comstock. Opened in 1911 and officially called Great Meadow, the prison is located in the remote and nearly all-white town of Comstock, nestled in the Adirondack foothills, about 225 miles from New York City, where Jacob is from. Quoting a DOCS official, an FBI memo notes that next to Attica, "Great Meadow is probably the second most guard-oriented facility in the State."[94] During our conversation, Jacob described this "guard orientation" as a seemingly endless nightmare of neglect, abuse, and terror. "It was nothing but cops killing inmates and inmates killing inmates. The tension was so thick you could cut it with a knife." This was no exaggeration. An investigative report notes that in 1975, at least three captives were known to have died in Comstock under questionable circumstances, but possibly more given that DOCS did not consistently report the deaths of those in its custody at this time.[95] In 1983, Comstock guards beat and choked an outspoken Black man named William "Butch" Harvey to death, an act that was subsequently covered up by state investigators.[96]

Jacob's reference to the "thickness" of carceral tension reveals that rather than eliminating rebellion-inducing affects, reformist counterinsurgency displaced and concentrated them in particular carceral sites. Humanization did not reach Comstock, Clinton, or Attica, where conditions were reportedly worse than they were before the rebellion.[97] The FBI warned that throughout 1973, "black extremists" continued to organize around grievances that were supposedly resolved in Attica, and regularly engaged in almost daily confrontations with guards. Disclosing Comstock's function within the diversified network, officials termed it "the garbage heap of the state prison system," a discourse with racist overtones given that Comstock's population was 85 percent Black and Latinx, the highest concentration of any prison at the time.[98] The Bureau also alluded to DOCS' emerging diversification strategy, recording that "a profile system of screening prisoner backgrounds and tendencies" was in the process of development and that "this system will be employed to sort and distribute various types of prisoners."[99]

Jacob vividly remembers the shock he experienced upon being transferred to Green Haven, a reward for compliant behavior during his two years in Comstock. "It was like someone had lifted a curtain of tension off me," he noted.[100] Between 1944 and 1949, Green Haven had been used as a US Army Disciplinary Barracks, where large numbers of "psychotic" World War II soldiers were incarcerated and "treated" using a method known as neuropsychiatry.[101] By the 1970s, under the management of DOCS, Green Haven had become known as the most liberal and forward-thinking prison in the state. While a major reason for this was Green Haven's "programming," a concept I explore next, the prison's progressive reputation also stemmed from the degree of relative freedom, mobility, and access it allowed. "Guys were wearing their own clothes, they were bringing Tupperware to the mess hall and bringing food back to their cells. Men were openly selling loose marijuana cigarettes in the yard. It was like being back in New York City," Jacob recalls.[102] A 1981 report connected Green Haven's permissiveness to Attica. In stark contrast to Comstock's authoritarian atmosphere, it described Green Haven as a "free-for-all," a space where drugs, alcohol, gambling, and sex with female visitors was pervasive. "As long as another Attica was prevented, as long as anyone, inmate or officer, could 'keep a lid on,' various rules and regulations were ignored."[103]

The uneven distribution of punishments and privileges is a fixture of carceral power, yet in the wake of Attica, it was deployed in more conscious and systematic ways. Although promoted as an altruistic effort to "provide more opportunities for inmate self-improvement, in more humane and less restrictive correctional environments," diversification was a strategy of penal counterinsurgency, psychological warfare, and behavior modification.[104] As the Select Committee asked in its first report, "what incentive is there for an inmate to accept the system when it offers little chance for transfer to a facility that grants him materially greater privileges when he has demonstrated his willingness and ability to conform to the rigid rules and philosophy of the maximum-security institution?"[105] It was believed that captives in highly restrictive, geographically remote, intensely violent and racist prisons like Comstock, Clinton, and Attica would be terrorized into submission via the "big stick" of repression and, conversely, that those in relatively "open" prisons like Green Haven, Wallkill, and Sutherland would be induced into compliance via the "carrot" of greater privileges.[106]

Politically astute captives recognized the con. In 1972, Green Haven-based members of the Prisoners Liberation Front, the clandestine politico-military organization that Casper Baker Gary founded in the Tombs, published an essay describing what they called "the latest development of the N.Y. state correctional pacification program," otherwise known as "Oswald-inization" (after Nixon's Vietnamization policy). Entitled "Snacked into Submission!!!," the essay describes a new practice in which each evening prisonrats doled out "a sickening assortment of dime-counter movie treats" to placate the population. It notes that resentment was the initial response, but shortly the sounds of caged men begging for seconds could be heard echoing throughout Green Haven's cellblocks. The PLF further speculated that the ready availability of mind-altering substances was part of the pacification strategy: "Because of the steady flow of enslaving drugs & blinding wine; because of the diversionary ball playing & benevolent racism, the Forces of Liberation get only one response from G.H. inmates, 'Don't mess up this good thing.'"[107] According to the PLF, it was not the militarized and ritualized violence of the massacre that stifled the Long Attica Revolt, but the unevenly distributed humanizing reforms. "As Attica must be a symbol of our first major step toward victory, Green Haven must be symbolic of our last major defeat."[108]

Before moving on to the fourth strategy of reformist counterinsurgency, I am compelled to stress that diversification presents a challenge to what has been called "prison ethnography." Within this growing field of scholarly inquiry, anthropologists, sociologists, and other academics produce research that is largely premised on obtaining administratively approved access to prisons in order to synchronically describe carceral worlds.[109] Although the fraught ethics of this approach have been well documented, the political strategy of diversification raises an epistemological question. How does an understanding of the prison as site of *hidden* warfare against populations on both sides of prison walls reconfigure what is knowable through standard research methodologies?

As I have shown, carceral systems should be understood as complex networks across which constellations of social phenomena—people, infrastructure, knowledge, affects, programs, violence, and so on—are unevenly distributed and circulated as part of a strategic effort to produce particular subjectivities. Adept prisoncrats can grant access to selected carceral zones, while foreclosing access to others, as a way to manage perception. If researchers do not understand and grapple with this dynamic, they risk reproducing logics of counterinsurgency. Elsewhere I have theorized letter-writing as a potential means of circumventing this impasse.[110] However, my broader point is that perhaps the ethnography of prisons, particularly prisons in the United States, should be reconceptualized as the ethnography of war.

PROGRAMMIFICATION

An internal DOCS report from 1991 acknowledges that the Division of Program Services emerged "as a reaction to the 1971 riot at Attica."[111]

Among the division's inaugural concerns was to oversee tactical concessions to key Attica reform demands, specifically the new requirements that DOCS institute "effective rehabilitation programs," "modernize the inmate education system," "reduce cell time," and allow incarcerated people "to be politically active without intimidation or reprisal."[112] Using the DOCS Volunteer Services Program as an example, I show that programmification was intended to co-opt the prison movement, to steer it toward status-quo-oriented institutional politics.[113]

During one of our many conversations, Larry "Luqmon" White, an Auburn rebel and founder of a post-Attica formation called the Green Haven Think Tank, described organizing in prison as a series of battles where captives and the state competed for the support of communities beyond the walls. He explained this dynamic to me using a "political equation" that he had used to politicize his comrades across more than three decades of incarceration. As he saw it, the strategic objective of the prison movement was to achieve "P + C vs. A": Prisoners plus the Community versus the Administration, a balance of forces requiring the incarcerated to first forge solidarity among themselves and to then forge it with political communities on the outside, and in so doing, foster a shared antagonism with the state.

At the same time, the strategic objective of the administration, he explained, was to achieve "A + C vs. P": the Administration plus the Community vs. the Prisoners. Describing state attempts to win the support of "free world" constituencies, Luqmon explained: "After Attica, when they killed all them brothers in there, the community raised hell. And you know what DOCS told them? They said, 'These are the people that were killing you all out in the street. We did that for you. We represent you. We protect you!' We are split from the community and their whole approach to rehabilitation is to expand that split and to keep the community seeing us in a particular light."[114] Although penal rehabilitation is typically assumed to involve the psychological and cultural enrichment of crestfallen citizen-subjects, Luqmon sees the discourse of rehabilitation as a ploy to move populations toward respectability and identification with carceral ideology. His schematization of the prison movement as an ongoing battle between an insurgent force and an established regime for the active support of a broader population constitutes an organic theorization of revolutionary warfare's foundational premise: that the goal is to achieve popular legitimacy.[115]

Established in February of 1972 with federal funds from the Law Enforcement Assistance Administration, the Volunteer Services Program aimed to permanently reconfigure Luqmon's political equation in favor of the state. "More and more," the Master Plan noted only a month later, "correctional professionals are coming to realize that the battle is won or lost not inside the prison, but out on the sidewalks."[116] At the program's launch, hundreds of "housewives, lawyers, psychiatrists, businessmen, entertainers, ministers, teachers, policemen, and firemen" were deployed into New York prisons, facilitating a range of initiatives, including book clubs, recreation programs, street theater groups, music and art classes, Swahili classes, Alcoholics Anonymous groups, typing classes, English as a Second Language classes, group counseling, business classes, and more. DOCS claimed that 5,323 out of 14,000 incarcerated people, or 38 percent of the total population, was enrolled in at least one program by 1973, and that it had 5,000 volunteer service providers by the following year.[117] These statistics were cited as evidence of the system's humanization and progressive evolution, its move away from simply warehousing people in cages.

Although many of these volunteers undoubtedly had altruistic and humanitarian motives, they unwittingly perpetuated counterinsurgency in multiple ways. First, their unwaged labor capacitated the carceral system, enabling it to bolster its capabilities in ways that would have been fiscally unfeasible otherwise. Second, planners surmised that because the volunteers were not employed by DOCS, captives would be more likely to see them as credible messengers who had their best interest in mind and therefore would be "stimulated to accept and participate in a variety of programs and services intended to return [them] to a normal productive life."[118] Third, planners expected that the mere presence of outsiders, many of whom were female, would act as a tension-reducing mechanism, thereby contributing to institutional stability.[119] Fourth, by creating opportunities for "responsible citizens" to enter certain prisons and build relationships with the captives, the volunteer program dislodged, marginalized, and criminalized ongoing efforts by captives to forge relations of solidarity with radical and revolutionary formations that sought to tear down, rather than stabilize, the walls.

The Volunteer Services Program had another core function: to propagandize the general public. The Select Committee referred to it as an aspect of a DOCS "systematic public information program," a program that also included planned prison tours for government officials, media, and select members of the public, as well as the production and distribution of educational films.[120] This public relations offensive intervened in an environment in which "citizens have tended to look upon the [correctional] process with suspicion and, too frequently, have translated this suspicion into a lack of support for programs and facilities."[121] By providing outsiders with the opportunity to enter the prisons and participate in the progressive and productive aspects of carceral power, planners hoped to allay these suspicions, universalize their view of the world, and nurture the public's investment in human caging. In collaboration with DOCS' public relations department, volunteers were aggressively recruited, screened, and put through an extensive orientation process designed, in their words, to "develop community acceptance of the Department's philosophy." A program coordinator told me that a typical volunteer orientation involved "sitting in a room and having the fear of god drilled into you about how dangerous and conniving the criminals were."[122]

Notes from a meeting held in March of 1972 about a potential volunteer-run jobs program in Attica clarifies the kinds of "suspicion" DOCS needed to counteract. Following a presentation by Margarete Appe, the founding Director of the Volunteer Services Program, meeting attendees, most of whom were prominent parishioners of Black churches in the Rochester and Buffalo areas, raised a series of pointed questions: How many Black officials were involved in establishing DOCS policy? How could they ensure that mechanisms for screening volunteers would not exclude poor people and minorities? What was the department doing to address the "malady of white racism" in the prisons? To whom should they forward complaints of brutality communicated to them by prisoners?[123] These questions and concerns reveal that although they were not necessarily aligned with the radical edge of the prison movement, these respectable members of the Black middle class were also not aligned with the priorities of the state. Rather, they represented a target population that needed to be won over if carceral power was to enjoy a semblance of legitimacy. The meeting notes provide no insight into how Appe or other DOCS officials answered these questions in the moment. Yet, a subsequent document nips the question about forwarding complaints of abuse in the bud. Volunteers were not to lead investigations or advocate for reform, the document states. Rather, they were "to provide the services which will supplement and complement that which the Department has set forth to do."[124]

The Metropolitan Applied Research Center (MARC) was one of the first organizations to form a volunteer partnership with DOCS. MARC was founded in 1967 by Dr. Kenneth Clark, a prominent Black social psychologist who envisioned the organization as a Black version of the

RAND Corporation, an eminent counterinsurgency think tank. In a position paper, Clark states that MARC was focused on "Negroes in Northern cities," who eschewed the "disciplined demonstrations" of the Southern civil rights movement in favor of "sporadic and self-destructive social eruptions."[125] In *Black Awakening in Capitalist America*, Robert L. Allen shows that MARC played a key role in steering the Black Power Movement toward integrationist demands and accommodationist modes of political engagement.[126] With financial support from the Ford Foundation, MARC established a fellowship program for middle-class and politically moderate civil rights activists, developed an anti-riot program in Cleveland, Ohio, and helped launch the Joint Center for Political and Economic Studies, a Washington-based think tank that aimed to increase the involvement of Black Americans in electoral politics.

After Attica, MARC spearheaded the publication of "The Awesome Attica Tragedy," a tepid public statement that affirmed some of the reform demands while ignoring the rebellion's challenge to the social order. Signed by prominent members of several civil rights organizations—the National Association for the Advancement of Colored People, the National Conference of Black Lawyers, the Coalition of Concerned Black Americans, the Congress of Racial Equality, and the United Negro College Fund, among others—the statement pressured DOCS to take "seven steps toward prison reform," including recruiting minority prison guards, providing enhanced training to prison personnel, instituting the volunteer program, and enabling religious freedom, although the reform demand for *political* freedom was conspicuously absent.[127]

Programmification was an elegant solution to a growing problem. In a 1971 memo authored five days after George Jackson's assassination, J. Edgar Hoover expressed alarm that "black extremists" were gaining psychological control over prison populations "through the various black studies programs and other so-called educational activity [*sic*] conducted within the prisons by outsiders."[128] Two years later, Raymond Procunier, director of the California prison system, struck a similar chord while discussing the activities of radical organizations like the Prisoners Solidarity Committee and the National Lawyers Guild: "We had all kinds of laws to keep people from breaking out of prison, but we had very little preparation for people breaking into the institution."[129] Through Volunteer Services, DOCS managed to incorporate noncombative and reform-oriented organizations like MARC so that abolitionist formations like the NLG and PSC could be excluded without public objection. Moreover, by framing the program as a humanizing reform, it succeeded in presenting this operation in moral rather political terms.

Through MARC and other volunteer organizations, DOCS encouraged captives to focus their energies toward institutional politics, event planning, and reform-oriented activities, which enhanced the prison's legitimacy, relieved tensions, and eschewed the radical political discourse that produced and was produced by rebellion. Dr. Clark and especially Dixie Moon, MARC's chief administrator, maintained regular contact with various imprisoned groups and individuals. They made several trips to Green Haven and helped organized prison-based events that were open to the public, including picnics, prison reform symposia, and art exhibits. By performing these activities, prison-based groups and formations were able to obtain a modicum of respectability, and some, such as the Think Tank, even secured modest financial sponsorship from the Cummins Foundation, Chase Manhattan Bank, and the South 40 Corporation, a nonprofit established by William H. Vanderbilt.[130] On a much smaller scale, this process was roughly analogous to the philanthropic and corporate penetration of Black politics that the Ford Foundation and MARC helped facilitate beyond the walls.[131]

So-called inmate organization programs worked alongside the volunteer initiative as a key tactic of counterinsurgent programmification. The theory behind this co-optation strategy was elaborated during the 1967 Symposium on Law Enforcement Science and Technology. Alongside papers about "criminal justice information systems," computer hardware configurations, and advance surveillance techniques, a Silicon Valley-based researcher named J. Douglas Grant advocated for deploying incarcerated people as a "correctional manpower resource." Under the auspices of the Institute for the Study of Crime and Delinquency, Grant wrote, "It is becoming clearer that as long as we pour professional services into passive client recipients little modification in behavior results, but when the clients become respected participants in the service functions striking changes take place."[132] Responding to the epidemiological model of prisoner radicalization and rebellion, Grant posited that incarcerated people could be vectors of self-help ideology, a principle he termed "contagion as a principle in behavior change."[133] In the wake of Attica, prisoncrats increasingly adopted this idea as a way to uproot and criminalize autonomous Black Studies programs and inoculate the population against radical ideas. As sociologist Juanita Diaz-Cotto has shown, inmate organizations successfully encouraged incarcerated organizers to participate in an aboveground, formally regulated system of institutionalized politics that made their activities easier to surveil and control.[134]

We can see the inmate organization and volunteer programs working in tandem in post-Attica celebrations of Black Solidarity Day. As I showed in chapter 2, the Auburn rebellion erupted after Black radicals observed Black Solidarity Day in defiance of administrative prohibitions. In 1973, amid the reformist counterinsurgency, DOCS attempted to appease the population by recognizing Black Solidarity Day as an institutional holiday that allowed inmate organizations to organize events with participation from outside volunteers.

Still operational today, the counterinsurgent effects of these programs are evident in a 1989 memo in which a member of the program staff reflects on the activities of an inmate organization called the Black Solidarity Committee. Responding to concerns that a Green Haven event celebrating the achievements of Dr. Martin Luther King Jr. was too militant, the staff member cited the contributions of outside volunteers:

> It is my considered opinion that several members of security on duty during the M.L.K. family event confused the excellent delivery of some of the speakers with the theoretical content of their messages. Some of the speakers spoke with the passion and eloquence of a Black Baptist preacher, but the substance of all of their speeches was conservative and status quo oriented (e.g.: they recommended a strict puritanical lifestyle). In my professional opinion, this is the most effective type of message to disseminate in a penal setting. Furthermore . . . I'm extremely happy to report that not one inmate was removed from the gymnasium for poor disciplinary behavior. Once again, the M.L.K. family event was peaceful and a tremendous asset to the wide array of programs that prevail at Green Haven Correctional Facility.[135]

This scene reveals the cynical logic of programmification, with well-meaning volunteers becoming instruments of pacification, promoting "peace" amid conditions of war. It conjures Saidiya Hartman's notion of "innocent amusements" as, amid the violence of plantation existence, seemingly benign and pleasure-filled diversions become practices of domination and technologies of terror.[136] The fact that "conservative and status quo oriented" discourses were conveyed by people who were familiar with "passionate" Black vernacular traditions was all the better, since this authenticity increased the likelihood that captives would accept and internalize these ideas.

Although I am marshaling a critique of programmification and how it attempted to quell Black rebellion, my intent is not to denounce the incarcerated targets of this hidden war or to second-guess the decisions they were forced to make. The reformist counterinsurgency was effective because it came immediately after the Attica massacre, which demonstrated the state's unmatched capacity to inflict world-shattering terror on rebels. In this moment, imprisoned organizers were faced with three terrible options. They could stop organizing and "do their own time," as the saying goes. They could continue to engage in illegal and antisystemic rebellion, exposing themselves to greater repression. Finally, they could attempt to maneuver within and against the new paradigm of politics, which presented new constraints as well as openings.

Diaz-Cotto cites the Green Haven Think Tank, New York's first formally recognized inmate organization, as a harbinger of the prison movement's generalized decline.[137] While I ultimately concur with this analysis, it is important to acknowledge that given what they were up against, their achievements are remarkable. Originally published in 1976, *Instead of Prison: A Handbook for Abolitionists* credits the Think Tank with establishing an array of higher education, re-entry, counseling, job training, work release, and youth development programs.[138] While these ameliorative endeavors were ultimately appropriated by DOCS and redeployed to stabilize the system, they also helped a besieged population survive the ravages of war. Talk to anyone who was imprisoned in New York during the 1970s, 1980s, and to a lesser extent the 1990s, and chances are they've heard of the Think Tank and personally benefited from their organizing work. Although I have never been incarcerated, this is true for me as well.[139] This book would not exist were it not for Eddie Ellis, Larry White, Hassan Gale, and other Think Tank members who generously and patiently mentored me.[140]

During one of our conversations about this dynamic, Hassan Gale made it plain: "We knew we were tame as an organization, but we also didn't see many other options. After Rockefeller killed his own prison guards, we understood that we wouldn't be able to get anything by taking hostages."[141] His ambivalence about the organization he helped lead mirrors similar autocritiques by those situated within the "nonprofit-industrial complex," universities, and other sites where intellectual and political labor is channeled, captured, and co-opted.[142] However, a critical distinction must be made, as the Think Tank faced this contradiction within a totalizing regime of war.[143]

Interestingly, Hassan's description of the Think Tank as "tame" alerts us to how imprisoned organizers found ways to critique, subvert, and exceed reformist counterinsurgency. His assertion is a direct reference to the 1973 speech delivered in Green Haven by Queen Mother Audley Moore that opened this book. DOCS reluctantly allowed this matriarch of Black radicalism into Green Haven after the Think Tank prevailed in a protracted struggle with the administration, outside volunteers, and other inmate organizations. As we saw, Moore enjoined the population to not lose sight of the fact that as colonized *and* incarcerated subjects, they had been targeted by multiple layers of captivity and war. She then spoke at length about how colonizing forces seek to "tame" Black rebellion through psychological warfare. In this way, Moore's speech situated DOCS's strategy within a much longer genealogy of anti-Black violence and revolt. As the sponsor of her visit, the Think Tank helped sustain the spirit of Revolt, even as they appeared to be going along with the program.

However, when analyzed at the population level, it is clear that DOCS views programmification as a proven, effective means of pacifying the population, and that Attica continued to shape this view for a very long time. During a 1995 hearing about potential cuts to the state prison budget, David Stallone, a representative of more than four thousand non-custodial prison staff, drew an explicit connection between well-funded prison programs and a manageable population. He stressed that "rehabilitation" was only one aspect of programmification's "dual function," the other being security. "We cannot ignore the lessons of Attica without threatening public safety," he said. "Idle time creates a vacuum that is filled by inmates themselves, creating an opportunity for inmates to organize themselves."[144] More than two decades after its eruption, Attica remained a cautionary tale, compelling prisoncrats to view incarcerated people as subjects of risk who are always teetering on the verge of rebellion. One of its key lessons was that, if the state does not organize and program the population, they will do so for themselves, and if this happens, the state will lose control.

It is to the incapacity of counterinsurgency to fully capture, divert, and transform rebellious Black radicalism that the final chapter turns. The interlocking strategies of expansion, humanization, diversification, and programmification targeted the captive majority: those deemed tractable, malleable, and amenable to inducement. These strategies sought to encapsulate the rebels' demands within acceptable parameters while convincing them and the public that the reforms were benign.

However, there was a small but important remainder, the so-called "militant minority," the detritus of counterinsurgency that refused to be swayed by violence or inducements. By centering the experiences of these prisoners of war, an even more obscure aspect of the post-Attica prison pacification campaign is revealed.

CHAPTER 6

The War on Black Revolutionary Minds

Failed Experiments in Scientific Subjugation

"Dear Governor Rockefeller: Please accept my congratulations upon your patience, compassion, courage, and fortitude in dealing with the tragic events at Attica."[1] Thus begins a letter authored four days after the governor had authorized an incursion of Attica Prison during which a state assault force massacred at least twenty-nine rebelling captives and sexually tortured hundreds of others. Its author, Dr. Robert R. J. Gallati, showered Rockefeller with praise even though it had recently been revealed that his armed agents, and not the rebels as had been previously reported, had also killed ten white prison guards who had been taken hostage. Like Rockefeller, Gallati saw this collateral damage as an acceptable loss incurred in the process of quelling an existential threat to civilization. After praising God for the governor's resolute action, Gallati got to the reason for his letter, the notion that "we now have two kinds of prisoners that we must deal with and we need separate programs for each type."

"Our penal operations have been structured around the prisoner who is basically a loyal American and is looking forward to his release from prison in order to return to our kind of society," Gallati wrote. Rooted in liberal notions of rehabilitation, this idea had served penal authorities in the past but had become outmoded. As Gallati saw it, state actors were now dealing with "a new type of totally recalcitrant prisoner," one who "disowns his country and preaches revolution." In his view, Attica illuminated "the grave danger in mixing these two kinds of prisoners." Offering a solution, he suggested that "those who consider themselves 'political' prisoners should be taken at their word and placed among their peers in a special facility. . . ." Asserting the imperative of prison reform, he added that this special facility would "require an entirely new penal approach discretely tailored to meet the custodial requirements of these 'political prisoners.'" A week later, the governor responded, assuring Gallati that his idea would be "studied carefully."[2]

In the previous chapter I analyzed the public-facing, yet woefully misunderstood side of the post-Attica counterinsurgency: the mundane ways state actors targeted the prison's captive majority with solicitous reforms that aimed to cleave popular support from the Revolt's revolutionary edge. Gallati's letter alludes to this strategy, while pointing to the concealed underside of the coin: the carceral techniques aimed at revolutionaries and political prisoners. Although this category—the US political prisoner—does not officially exist, according to the US government, and is internally contested within the revolutionary left, Gallati illuminates its importance, unofficially, for maintaining control. He and others believed this militant minority might hold the key to forestalling future rebellions.

Tip of the Spear's final chapter examines state-orchestrated assaults on Black revolutionary minds. Having already incarcerated insurgent Black bodies, only to learn that physical capture did not equal control, counterinsurgency experts tried and failed to exterminate insurgent Black knowledge, thoughts, feelings, behaviors, and even impulses. They employed techniques that go by a range of imprecise names: behavior modification, coercive persuasion, brainwashing, thought reform, mind control, human programming, and so on.[3] The following pages analyze these clandestine experiments and their mutations across time in ways that reveal how the imperatives behind these initiatives far outlived their official programmatic lives.

I also show how the targets of these experiments—a tight group of revolutionary figures associated with the Black Liberation Army (BLA)—critiqued and resisted this assault. Discussions of prison reform routinely fail to account for the experiences of this class of prisoner because to do so is to sully sanitized narratives of progress. The secret history offered here further illuminates the prison as a domain of warfare. Assailed by multiple layers of captivity and violence, revolutionaries held captive at the tip of the spear refused to allow the state to reduce them to "automatons," "vegetables," "robots," "zombies," and "slaves." Unbroken and undeterred, they continued to pursue the radical aspirations their adversaries strove to eradicate.[4]

Researching and narrating this chapter necessitated a disloyal and rebellious approach to the archive. I draw on a wealth of rarely examined state records stored in academic repositories and released through litigation and FOIA requests, while also comprehending the profound limitations of these sources.[5] Not only are the agents of this war structurally incentivized to lie and omit critical details about their scandalous methods, but their notions of reality are filtered through elitist, patriarchal, and white supremacist epistemologies. For this reason, I interpret official sources through a Black radical interpretive paradigm, submerging these sources within oral history and previously hidden documents produced and archived by Black revolutionaries. By investing incarcerated, criminalized, and pathologized knowledges with a greater degree of epistemic authority than I do the authorized knowledge of the state, I unlock a hidden terrain of struggle at the heart of this war.

I begin by examining the experience of a former political prisoner named Masia A. Mugmuk, who was targeted by the Prescription and Control Program, a.k.a. the Rx Program, after Attica. According to NY DOCS, the Rx Program provided "intensive treatment" to "safety and security threats" with "a history of chronically maladjusted behavior."[6] Although it enjoyed a brief official existence between 1972 and 1973, I reveal the Rx Program's longer history, including its hidden connections to the military-industrial complex and to the CIA, which had been conducting experiments on what agency director Allen Dulles termed "brain warfare" in prisons, hospitals, and beyond, since the inception of the Cold War.[7] According to the CIA Inspector General, "Project MK Ultra"—the most well-known cryptonym for these experiments—was concerned with "the research and development of chemical, biological, and radiological materials capable of employment in clandestine operations to control human behavior."[8] Allegedly developed to defend against Communist brainwashing techniques capable of achieving thought reform, MK Ultra was concretely embedded within the counterinsurgent carceral regime. Long-standing practices of carceral domination helped shape these experiments, which in turn helped shape new technologies of carceral war, technologies currently deployed against captive as well as "free" populations throughout the world.[9]

Next, I show that although the Rx Program was discontinued in 1973, the FBI's Prison Activists Surveillance Program (PRISACTS) emerged shortly thereafter and extended this assault on Black revolutionary minds. Despite the storied institutional rivalry between the CIA and the FBI,[10] archival evidence suggests that the two agencies were to some extent collaborating on this counterrevolutionary project. A 1951 CIA document entitled "Organization of a Special Defense Interrogation Program," a precursor to MK Ultra, indicates that "liaison with the FBI on this subject may be described as 'cooperative,' although somewhat mutually evasive."[11] My findings indicate that this cooperation extended at least into the 1970s, the onset of the massive expansion and proliferation of prisons and penal culture in the United States. However, while the Rx Program and similar behavior modification initiatives strove to directly "program" the minds of individuals, PRISACTS was preoccupied with "neutralizing" revolutionaries who, authorities believed, were able to program others.

I close by examining a hidden contest that extends what I have been calling the Long Attica Revolt into the early 1980s. The struggle involves covert actions employed by New York's PRISACTS administrators to prevent Black radical ideas from seizing hold of the captive majority, forestalling what prisoncrats claimed was a BLA conspiracy to organize "another Attica." By narrating this struggle, I demonstrate that a hidden intelligentsia within the carceral apparatus aimed to decisively conquer the captive population by eradicating the BLA, not as a coherent organization but as an *idea*. Operating on their flawed theory that the "passive majority" was being coercively programmed by the "militant minority," state actors believed that if they could effectively isolate some of the most intelligent and articulate BLA political prisoners, they could assert total control over populations on both sides of the walls. As I demonstrate, they were wrong, and their project failed spectacularly.

It is with some reluctance that I describe these deployments of carceral technology as "failed experiments." The carceral system expanded dramatically in the decades following the period under study, an expansion for which order, at least at the surface level, was a precondition. The technologies analyzed here facilitated that order, enabling the state to wage a campaign of counterinsurgency that was largely unknown to people outside the walls. These technologies inflicted intense forms of individualized and collective punishment, destroyed lives, and in their constant mutation, contributed to the development of newer and even more dystopian carceral technologies, including contemporary supermax prisons and emerging forms of "e-carceration."[12] Moreover, much of what I cover has direct and indirect links to ongoing methods employed in the "Global War on Terror," where techniques that were tested on Black and overwhelmingly Muslim revolutionaries at home were redeployed abroad and vice versa.[13] "Guantanamo Bay is the sum total of what they've been doing to Muslims in US prison for decades," explains BPP/BLA veteran Dhoruba bin-Wahad, a key figure in this chapter.[14]

I opened this chapter with Dr. Gallati's letter to Rockefeller for multiple reasons. First, because its content mobilizes a textbook counterinsurgency rationale: a revolutionary minority must be identified and removed from circulation so as to prevent it from "contaminating" the broader population. Second, because the biography of its author is representative of the class of well-connected, highly educated, yet generally obscure figures who are responsible for waging this one-directional war. Like many of the figures named in this chapter, Gallati cut his teeth in foreign and domestic theaters of imperial conflict. He was a naval officer during the Korean War, where he served as Commander of Military and Industrial Security for the Northeast Area. He spent twenty-seven years with the NYPD, eventually becoming a detective with Special Squad No. 1, an "elite unit" that collaborated with the FBI to counter espionage, sabotage, and subversion. He held four degrees, including a Doctor of Judicial Science from Brooklyn Law School, as well as a certificate from the National Academy of the FBI and lifetime memberships to the National Sheriffs' Association and the International Association of Chiefs of Police, which played a key role in the global circulation of counterinsurgency knowledge.[15]

Gallati helped implement a new tool that enhanced the state's capacity to surveil, capture, punish, kill, and study targeted populations. In 1965, Governor Rockefeller appointed him to serve as inaugural director of the New York State Identification and Intelligence System (NYSIIS), the world's first computer system to be employed in a criminal legal context. Then touted as the largest social science database ever assembled, NYSIIS allowed state actors to aggregate and disseminate intelligence across police, court, prison, probation, and parole agencies. Using the same emerging technologies that powered counterinsurgency operations in Southeast Asia, NYSIIS became the prototype for criminal justice information systems across the United States, including the FBI's National Crime Information Center. It laid what Gallati called "a permanent foundation for a more rational, scientific and truly systemic control of crime and criminals."[16]

Although NYSIIS is not a central aspect of this story, the existence of this emerging technology and its presence within the carceral system is critical to understanding the flawed theory undergirding these experiments in state repression. The theory assumes that human beings can be "scientifically controlled" and programmed like computers. This false idea came into being alongside advances in the computer technology that made NYSIIS possible.[17] "When I give an order to a machine, the situation is not essentially different from that which arises when I give an order to a person," wrote Norbert Wiener in *The Human Use of Human Beings*, a 1950 volume on a field he termed "cybernetics."[18] While this term has fallen into disuse, its imperatives persist, often in unacknowledged ways via "cognitive science," a field that came into being as the events described in this chapter unfolded.[19] The counterinsurgency actors who appear in what follows embraced this mechanistic view of human beings as potential automatons. Rooted in capitalist social relations and patriarchal white supremacy, their ideas stand in direct conflict with those of the Black revolutionaries they targeted, those whose praxis was rooted in collectivized notions of social consciousness, political education, and people's counter-war.

This top-down, unidirectional assault on Black revolutionary minds required its expert administrators to be intimately familiar with the ideas they aimed to annihilate. They paid close attention to developments in Black radical thought both within and beyond prison walls and constantly updated their methods in response to new formations of insurgency. For example, it is plausible that Dr. Gallati drafted his outline for a prison-based counterinsurgency strategy after reading BPP co-founder Huey P. Newton's essay "Prison: Where Is Thy Victory" in the January 3, 1970, edition of *The Black Panther*.[20] Although this cannot be proven, analyzing "subversive literature" was part of Gallati's role as an intelligence operative and the similarities between the two texts are striking.

"There are two types of prisoners," wrote Newton, while jailed for allegedly killing a police officer. "The largest number are those who accept the legitimacy of the assumptions upon which the society is based." The second type were the political prisoners, a minority that rejects those taken-for-granted assumptions and instead believes that "society is corrupt and illegitimate and must be overthrown." Newton argued that the prison as it was then constituted was incapable of achieving "victory" over either type. On the one hand, members of the captive majority, who Newton calls "illegitimate capitalists," learn to participate in prison programs and "say the things that the prison authorities want to hear." They appear "rehabilitated," but continue to engage in criminalized activity upon release. On the other hand, "the prison cannot gain a victory over the political prisoner because he has nothing to be rehabilitated from or to." Ultimately, Newton argued that the prisons of the 1970s were doomed to fail because they were capable only of incarcerating people's bodies, not the ideas that propel movements, ideas which circulate among "all the people, wherever they are."[21]

Whether or not they read this text, Gallati and others responded to this dynamic by placing greater emphasis on the incarceration, manipulation, and elimination of ideas. Across the United States, Canada, and elsewhere, those tasked with keeping recalcitrant populations contained quietly experimented with a variety of scandalous methods including sensory deprivation, electroshock therapy, isolation, hypnotism, chemotherapy, psychosurgery, electrode implantation, and so on.[22] Interestingly, Newton's 1974 essay "The Mind Is Flesh" considers advances in the science of behavioral control and provides a critical revision of his earlier concepts. Citing a number of dystopian counterinsurgency projects developed since 1970, he writes, "In order to prevent ourselves from being enslaved by a minority, the majority of us must vigorously insist that new controls of mind not be applied by the few without the prior conscious consent of the many, both as to technique and objective."[23]

PRESCRIBING PACIFICATION

"They wanted to eliminate freedom fighters, to control us physically and mentally, and to transform us into nonviolent, passive, meek, humble, obedient, modern-day slaves."[24] This is how Masia A. Mugmuk explains the goals of the Rx Program, through which he and others were coerced into becoming test subjects for a wide array of behavior modification technologies during the late 1960s and early 1970s. We were sipping coffee in the living room of his small apartment, where books, archival documents, African art, and primitive weaponry covered every available surface. Although his remarkable story deserves a full accounting, that task exceeds the scope of this chapter. What follows is but a portrait of his bold and excruciating life of rebellion under some of the most intense forms of captivity imaginable. This portrait reveals how far counterinsurgency experts were willing to go to eliminate Black revolutionary thought and behavior, and most importantly, the failure of their experiments and the inviolability of Masia's spirit. After all, despite enduring a panoply of terror, Masia never ceased to resist, was never divested of his cognitive autonomy, and somehow manages to smile often. At the age of eighty, he remains a warrior, a teacher, a walking archive of forbidden knowledge that he dispenses freely, but with great care.

In 1960, at the age of seventeen, Masia, then known as Sylvester Cholmondeley, confessed to raping a white woman. As he tells it, he was leaving a party with a friend when he was accosted by the NYPD, taken to the Rockaway Beach Police Station, tied to a chair, and viciously beaten. He eventually signed a confession that he could not read because he had not learned how. "I did a lot of foul stuff when I was younger," he told me. "I was a street hustler, a gambler, a dope dealer. I used to burglarize rich peoples' houses and I was a bodyguard for a big-time gangster. But I've never raped anyone." He and his family considered fighting the charges, but were dissuaded by a white attorney, who told them he had no chance of winning and reminded them that just five years earlier, Emmett Till, a fourteen-year-old Black boy who had allegedly whistled at a white woman, had been brutally lynched in Mississippi. He followed the advice of his counsel, was found guilty, and was sentenced to fifteen to thirty years in prison, a "legal lynching," as he called it.[25]

In the summer of 1961, while behind the walls of Auburn Prison, Masia joined the Nation of Islam, inaugurating a process of transformation that drew inspiration from Malcolm X.[26] Like Malcolm, Masia taught himself to read by studying the dictionary and became politicized through an intensive collective program of religious, political, economic, and cultural study. He told me a mind-blowing story about how his connection to Malcolm X goes beyond inspiration—that it was a material connection forged through a grassroots conspiracy to subvert penal authority. According to Masia, on more than one occasion Malcolm X traveled to Auburn disguised as a Christian minister in order to gain access to Ned X. Hines, a.k.a. Hekima, a key figure in Auburn's active NOI contingent. Instead of converting Hekima to Christianity, as the authorities believed he was doing, Malcolm would systematically, in his distinctively eloquent way, transmit Black radical ideas to the captive population. Hekima dutifully listened to Malcolm and committed his words to memory. He then returned to his cell and transcribed this "verbal enlightenment" into writing, blending it with knowledge he obtained from the contraband texts of early Black studies scholar J. A. Rogers.[27] Masia and others would then generate handwritten reproductions of Hekima's transcriptions and circulate them throughout Auburn and beyond.

This process constituted an illicit material network of Black revolutionary epistemology that reveals the deep roots of the Long Attica Revolt. Misrecognizing this social infrastructure as a form of fanatical programming, a 1973 study noted that "black extremism" in New York

FIGURE 16. Masia A. Mugmuk being transported to court on June 16, 1976. Photo: Monmouth County (New Jersey) Archives.

prisons was not the result of a "schizophrenic thought disorder," as previously believed, but of "a local cultural system to which these Blacks had been systematically indoctrinated."[28] Such systems of cognitive autonomy would have to be destroyed if the state was ever to truly be in control.

In the wake of Malcolm X's state-facilitated assassination by NOI triggermen,[29] Masia broke with the Nation, developing an eclectic political philosophy that drew from global streams of Black radicalism. After studying *Mau Mau from Within* and other texts, he fashioned himself a Mau Mau behind prison walls, organizing formations of underground resistance that solidified their authority through secret oath-taking practices.[30] Masia's embrace of Kenya's specific brand of anticolonial nationalism is significant given that the British Empire employed a system of prison-based counterinsurgency against the Mau Mau in the 1950s.[31] Moreover, two years after Malcolm's assassination, when J. Edgar Hoover laid out the goals of the Bureau's COINTELPRO against "Black Nationalist Hate Groups," he drew lessons from the British experience in Kenya. This connection is revealed in the program's primary goal, to "prevent the coalition of militant black nationalist groups" because such a coalition "might be the first step toward a real 'Mau Mau' in America, the beginning of a true black revolution."[32]

Masia represented this possibility. Though physically immobilized behind concrete and steel, he and others were engaged in a global struggle against imperialism. That it primarily unfolded on cognitive terrain did not make it any less real or significant.

Masia's combination of Black radical erudition, militant intractability, and charismatic authority represented precisely that which penal authorities aimed to study and eradicate. A psychological evaluation from the early 1970s characterizes him as an "antagonistically inclined individual who is rigidly resistant to authoritarian order," a "rabid racist black power advocate" who displays "open defiance and disdain toward constituted authority."[33] During the same period, the Assistant Attorney General noted that Masia's was "one of the worst, if not the worst disciplinary record ever compiled by a New York State prisoner."[34] When I read these characterizations aloud, Masia released a deep bellowing laugh. These were examples of how the state criminalizes resistance to oppression, he explained.

Between 1961 and his parole in 1975, Masia endured an unfathomable degree of punishment, terror, and degradation: "I've been, chained, whipped, gassed, and put through a whole lot of hell while I was incarcerated." He spent a total of ten years confined in various forms of punitive isolation, much of it in Unit 14, a "Special Housing Unit" that could only be reached by entering Clinton Prison and then taking an elevator that led to rows of underground cages which authorities could access from the front or the rear. Attorneys from the National Lawyers Guild described how this subterranean zone encouraged sadistic guards to satiate their libidinal urges through their captives. "The treatment of men in Unit 14 is not explainable simply by political motivations of prison officials," they wrote. "The guards truly hate the men in their charge and clearly get some kind of sick thrill out of torturing them."[35]

Among the various forms of torture Masia endured was a carceral technology called the "dark hole," a tiny concrete enclosure that, when sealed, is totally devoid of light and in which there is no plumbing and barely enough space to accommodate an average adult. Demonstrating the crouched position he was forced to assume for unknowable lengths of time, often while stripped naked, starved, and forced to experience his own filth, Masia placed both feet on his reclining leather chair and hugged his knees. "This is how I became extreme," he explained, while holding the pose. "I was conditioned by cruel and unusual punishments."

The torture inflicted on Masia and others was part of an evolving regime in which social and behavioral scientists within and beyond the

United States were increasingly looking to "science" for methods of subjugation. Previous research has traced the behaviorist turn in prison management to an April 1961 conference entitled "The Power to Change Behavior," where James V. Bennett, head of the Federal Bureau of Prisons, invited MIT psychologist Edgar Schein to present on his CIA-sponsored research on techniques of "thought reform," "brainwashing," and "coercive persuasion."[36] Exposing this project's orientalist orientation, Schein discussed various "Asian methods" that were said to have cracked the minds of American POWs.[37] "My basic argument is this," he told a group of associate wardens. "In order to produce marked change of behavior and/or attitude, it is necessary to weaken, undermine, or remove the supports to the old patterns of behavior and the old attitudes," a goal that was achievable "either by removing the individual physically and preventing any communication with those whom he cares about, or by proving to him that those whom he respects are not worthy of it and, indeed, should be actively mistrusted."[38]

New York's Dannemora State Hospital for the Criminally Insane (DSH) became a key site for these experiments. In 1966 Governor Rockefeller launched an effort to bolster the institution's status as a research hub by hiring teams of psychological and psychiatric consultants from the State University of New York system, the University of Vermont, and McGill University in Montreal.[39] The latter institution is particularly notable because its psychology and psychiatry programs had received major funding from the Rockefeller Foundation and because under the leadership of Donald O. Hebb and Ewen Cameron, respectively, both have been revealed as important sites of barbaric MK Ultra research.[40]

With the aid of these consultants, the DSH, which was later rebranded the Adirondack Correctional Treatment Education Center (ACTEC), hosted an assortment of behavioral science experiments on incarcerated people. In 1967, Donald G. Forgays, who graduated from McGill in 1950 and went on to chair the Psychology Department at the University of Vermont, was brought on as a co-principal investigator for a multi-year grant entitled "Intensive Treatment Units." Funded by the Department of Health, Education, and Welfare, an MK Ultra conduit that Nelson Rockefeller helmed between 1953 and 1954, topics of investigation included "Muslim and Black Nationalist Groups" and a "psychophysical study of time estimation in hospitalized felons with different degrees of isolation," themes that seem highly relevant to Masia's subjection to the "dark hole."[41]

In 1968, McGill psychologist Ernest G. Poser conducted experiments on whether "sociopaths" and those deemed "hopeless" suffer from an adrenaline deficiency that "retards [their] ability to learn inhibiting impulses from fear-producing experiences." The wording of this inquiry is notable for its Pavlovian specificity, which goes beyond questions of thought and behavior into preconscious impulses elicited from different physiological states.[42] To answer their question, Poser and a graduate student named Deborah G. Sittman injected captives with adrenaline and exposed them to electroshock treatments.[43] By 1969, DSP staff had trained prison guards in hypnosis and aversion therapy techniques, resulting in scenes that an observer called "quite revolting for both for those who watched and those who took part."[44] The director of a think tank called the Narcotic and Drug Research Institute described ACTEC's Therapeutic Community program in ways that are eerily similar to CIA-sponsored efforts to obliterate human consciousness in order to rebuild it anew.[45] It "takes you back to a kind of kindergarten level and then brings you back up," he told Congress.[46]

The DSH/ACTEC was an ideal location for this controversial research. It was located in Dannemora, a small prison town just twenty-five miles from New York's northernmost border with Canada that earned the name "Little Siberia" because of its brutal winters and profound isolation.[47] Moreover, because of an entrenched culture of white supremacy and economic dependence on prisons, Dannemora residents were unlikely to protest illegal or immoral activity perpetrated by prison authorities. Conveniently, DSH/ACTEC was adjacent to Clinton/Unit 14, an arrangement that facilitated the quiet flow of human grist "over the wall" to be used for new experiments. For incarcerated people, these transfers were a site of constant physical and verbal resistance. Dr. Forgays wrote that he frequently "observed black militants brought to the DSH in leg irons and straight jackets, kicking, fighting, cursing, spitting in the faces of guards, and otherwise breaking every rule," adding that these were the types that incited rebellions in San Quentin and Attica.[48] While prisoncrats used the possibility of punitive transfer to Unit 14 as a systemwide threat to produce obedience across the captive population, an even more terrifying threat was that one might be sent to the hospital, where—rumor had it—captives were being lobotomized.[49]

Plans for what became the Rx Program were set in motion during the summer of 1971, during the brief interim between the Auburn and Attica rebellions. According to notes from DOCS' Mental Health Services Task Force, which included prison administrators, representatives from the Department of Mental Hygiene, a State Supreme Court Judge, and academic consultants, including Forgays: "Commissioner Oswald directed that consideration be given to behavior modification, and whether serious thought should be given to segregating the untreatables (militants, for example) so that we can then go about with the constructive programs with the major part of the population."[50] In other words, Oswald's "progressive" and "humanizing" reforms hinged upon the targeted neutralization of these "untreatables."

Officially launched in December of 1972, the Rx Program and ACTEC constituted a post-Attica rebranding of long-standing practices of experimentation. According to the program manual, which Masia and I located amid a massive pile of documents in his bedroom, the initiative aimed to make imprisoned militants easier to control, while producing generalizable knowledge with application beyond prisons. In DOCS' words, its purpose was "controlling and treating inmates who have become clearly unresponsive to the routine correctional experience," while also providing a "base for both Departmental and outside scholarly research as to the nature of aberrant behavior patterns, the etiology of the behavior, delineation of appropriate techniques of treatment, and prevention."[51]

Little about what was taking place in ACTEC was how it appeared on the surface. According to the official count from February 1973, the institution held 455 captives.[52] However, as a "diversified" institution, ACTEC operated myriad programs dispersed across several buildings, each of which contained multiple wards, floors, and wings, ensuring that captives in the same institution could have wildly different experiences. The institutional archive is crammed with letters from captives pleading for transfer *into* ACTEC, specifically its Diagnostic and Treatment Center, which promised to improve one's chances of earning parole. But that program was distinct from Rx, where candidates had to be "nominated" by a program committee based in Albany.

Masia refused his Rx nomination in the spring of 1973. In a letter addressed to him at Clinton, Commissioner Oswald wrote: "I am truly sorry to learn that you view this program as a conspiracy against you and an effort to impede your pending litigation."[53] Masia had evolved into a formidable "jailhouse lawyer" who had a major lawsuit pending against DOCS and who had already succeeded in reducing his maximum sentence to fifteen years, meaning that DOCS would soon be forced to release him. Attempting to dispel "some of the more bizarre rumors," Oswald emphasized that the program "does not include cruel and unusual punishment, does not involve the use of drugs, and will never involve psychosurgical operations to alter behavior." In his reply, Masia restated his position: "Once again, I will not volunteer for the so-called Rx, which in reality, its primary objective is to engender 'marked change' of political prisoners' patterns of behavior and attitude, to systematically undermine the fundamental fibers of their Third World Outlook into which their behavior and attitude patterns are reflected. . . ." He and others would not allow themselves to be transformed into "docile creatures, robot slaves, or neoslaves," he continued.[54]

What happened next could have been taken from the pages of dystopian science fiction. On March 22, 1973, approximately fifteen CERT guards—all of whom were clad in full riot gear and armed with gas guns, shields, and batons—descended on both entrances of Masia's Unit 14 cage. At this point in his narrative, he reminds me that he did thousands of push-ups per day, is skilled in various styles of martial arts, and had defended himself against armed "goon squads" before. He told me he knew that they would be coming for him and that his plan was to subdue his assailants, liberate everyone on the tier, escape from Clinton, flee across the Canadian border, and link up with the Black underground. The militant audacity of his radical imagination and will speaks to why the state went to such lengths to control him.

A DOCS communiqué claims that Masia resisted, forcing the CERT to employ "necessary force" to complete his transfer.[55] However, a signed affidavit by Masia's attorney, published accounts in *The Black Panther*, *Midnight Special*, and *Prisoners Digest International*, and Masia himself claim otherwise. According to these sources, Masia was given no opportunity to resist. Rather CERT agents preemptively fired four canisters of teargas into his cell, one of which would have smashed into his face and caused serious injury had he not dodged it. Unit 14 was soon consumed with gas, causing the entire tier and even the masked assailants to experience intense pain. Masia maintains that normally, the use of gas would not have slowed him down, that "we had been gassed so many times before that we were immune," a claim I have heard from others who endured similar forms of repression. He is certain, however, that in this instance CERT agents used a special compound of military CS gas. "I would rather them shoot me with a shotgun," he told me. "It blinded me, and I couldn't hardly breathe. I was suffocating like I was drowning in water. I became hopeless and helpless. I became like a baby. I couldn't defend myself." His assertion that this chemical weapon made him "helpless . . . like a baby" provides a potential clue into the authoritarian means by which carceral technologists reduced people to "kindergarten level" before attempting to reprogram and reconstitute them anew. It was not until Masia collapsed that the guards entered his cell. As he struggled to yell "Black Power" over and over again, they beat him with their batons, chained his arms and legs to a long metal pole, and rushed him toward the elevator on their shoulders as though he were a hog being taken to slaughter.[56]

Masia's recollections of exactly what happened next—the sequence of events, the names and faces of the people he interacted with, and the particulars of the regimen he was subjected to—are largely inaccessible. They emerge not as a coherent narrative, but as a series of impressions, which I gathered through repeated inquiry. The gaps in his recollection are unsurprising, given that memories are notoriously imperfect, especially across the passage of time and in instances of severe trauma. Moreover, it is entirely plausible that Masia's assailants sought to delete or otherwise manipulate his memories, as this was one of the formative objectives of MK Ultra.[57] It is significant, though, that by combing through state archives I have been able to corroborate much of what he managed to recall.

The next thing Masia remembers is waking up in a cold shower and being referred to by his new designation, "Rx 21," another in a long line of depersonalizing names thrust upon him by the state. He was then told by someone using what he described as a "Chinese accent" not to scrub the particulate residue left by the gas, unless he wanted his skin to peel off. An interdepartmental communication reveals that Masia's interlocutor was Dr. Pablo M. Lomangcolob, a psychiatrist of Filipino descent and a member of the US Army Medical Corps. According to the memo, Dr. Lomangcolob provided Rx 21 with "the proper decontamination treatment," ensuring that "no permanent damage was incurred."[58] Masia was now in Rx Program's "diagnostic phase," a four-to-six-week process during which he would be tested and probed. Depending on the results, he would remain in ACTEC or be transferred to a so-called "open prescription" program amid the general population in a designated maximum-security prison.

As his vision began to recover, a process that took weeks, Masia was able to assess his surroundings. He was inside a small, windowless enclosure that was totally empty, save for a toilet and a bed, which was affixed to the floor. The barrenness of the cell was central to the broader strategy of behavior modification. Like similar programs in the federal prison system, the Rx Program employed an "operant conditioning" model in which conformance to program expectations allowed targets to earn "privileges" like toiletries, additional clothing, writing implements, stationary, stamps, time outside the cell, and social interaction.[59] Operant conditioning, and its Pavlovian counterpart "classical conditioning," where positive as well as negative stimuli are used to induce the desired behavior, have always been part of the arsenal of carceral power. What distinguishes their use in behavior modification regimes is their intensive application on specific individuals as part of an allegedly objective science of social control.[60] As Dr. Edgar Schein explained, "prison managers invented the concept of isolating people long before social scientists got around to documenting effects of such isolation; and the withholding of mail or visiting privileges to blackmail prisoners into 'behaving themselves' is as old as prisons themselves."[61]

Describing his new surroundings as a "spy cell," Masia explained how his captors fastidiously recorded, tracked, and analyzed everything he and others did. This too is corroborated by the state archive. Commenting on the suitability of ACTEC as a site for behavior modification research, Forgays noted that it had "several rooms with one way viewing potential, voice monitoring and recording, and polygraph recording."[62] Program documents show that Rx guards were trained to surveil a wide variety of behaviors on a daily, and sometimes hourly, basis: exercise, sleep, bed making, cleanliness, bathing habits, reading habits, eating habits, bowel movements, use of foul language, and conversations with peers, to name a few. Data points produced by this perverse colonial gaze were then arranged on longitudinal graphs and analyzed for changes over time.[63] Like skilled computer programmers, ACTEC experts aimed to grasp all of their variables.

NOI member Tyrone O'Neal, aka "RX-8," told the local press that prisoncrats were subjecting him to "psychological and psychochemical terror."[64] During a 1973 interview from the Brooklyn House of Detention, Dhoruba bin-Wahad told a reporter that the Rx Program was "geared towards tampering with people's brains, towards using drugs, towards turning people into vegetables."[65] Unsurprisingly, administrators dismissed such accusations as "conspiracy theories" and brushed aside the suggestiveness of the program's name—"Prescription Rx"—as an unfortunate coincidence. They accused the captives of "paranoid thinking," and of "doing battle in a war that doesn't exist."[66]

However, it must be remembered that people incarcerated in more standard carceral institutions had long accused their keepers of employing drugs as a pacification strategy. As I have already shown, captives in

Green Haven were convinced that authorities were facilitating the flow of alcohol, marijuana, and cocaine into prison walls in order to stifle their will to resist. "They allow a certain amount of drugs in prison," explained Auburn and Attica survivor Jomo Omowale, adding that this policy comes "all the way from the White House."[67] Although claims such as Omowale's are rarely taken seriously, high-level government complicity in the flow of drugs across US borders is a matter of public record.[68] Moreover, a surfeit of letters, articles, affidavits, and testimony from across carceral systems accuse prisoncrats of encouraging and pressuring captives to consume mood-altering substances, with forcible injections, and with surreptitiously serving them drugged food and beverages.[69] In his investigation of "the secret drugging of captive America," sociologist Anthony Ryan Hatch argues that these "neurochemical weapons" are so pervasive that the contemporary prison system would be incapable of functioning without them.[70]

Describing his brief encounter with the Rx Program, an Attica Brother named Carlos Roche relayed a story that sounded a lot like MK Ultra. He told me that after refusing to "volunteer," he showed his nomination letter to Elizabeth Fink, an attorney for the Attica Brothers. Fink purportedly showed the letter to Joseph Henderson, a federal judge for the Western District of New York, who investigated the program and, according to Roche, learned that "the Department of Defense gave the Department of Justice a grant to pass down to state prisons to test out this medication on cons that they wanted to use on dudes coming back from Vietnam."[71] This was a startling claim that Roche conveyed to me with certitude and before I mentioned my search for evidence linking the program to the military-industrial complex and the CIA. The preceding chapters have discussed the prison as a zone of active combat, but Roche's recollection illuminates the prison as war in another sense. It suggests that the counterinsurgent state is invented, developed, refined, and reconstituted through its material connection to carceral systems, with the latter serving as a primary locus of Black revolutionary insurgency and therefore a primary locus of state counterinsurgency research and development. Unfortunately, I could not corroborate this statement because Fink and Henderson had already passed away. As we will soon see, however, I later found information that supported this claim.

Masia told me that penal authorities had drugged and attempted to poison him before his stint in ACTEC, and he did not see this common strategy of control as particularly scandalous. For him, it was more important for the world to understand that the Rx Program involved

FIGURE 17. Donald G. Forgays at his desk. Photo: University of Vermont, Silver Special Collections Library.

what he called "sex experiments." Within the prison context, food is always a technology of control, but according to Masia, this was even more evident in ACTEC. He claims that the food was much more enticing than in other prisons, but that it had been infused with specific drugs that caused the population to become "excessively horny," to "masturbate all day," to "turn us into homos," and to "make us want to rape each other." Among Masia's various assertions, the claim that the state was trying to manipulate people's sexual desires strained my credulity. I was especially skeptical given that he claims to have never eaten the food, that he protested his forced transfer by immediately going on a hunger strike, and therefore only witnessed these symptoms or was told about them by others who experienced them. I considered excluding these assertions from the narrative on this basis and because of my own discomfort with Masia's homophobic language and the way that some of these notions play into misguided conceptions of homosexuality as "unnatural" or "pathological." However, given that he was entrusting me with his story, I continued to trust him, and to take him seriously as a chronicler and narrator of his own experience. I scoured the archive for traces of corroborating evidence and what I found astounded me.

Successful grant applications and evaluations reveal that under the leadership of Donald G. Forgays, ACTEC did in fact host sexual experiments. One project involved the study of people imprisoned for what Forgays called "sexual deviancy crimes other than homosexuality," a category that Masia technically fit, his claim of having been framed for rape notwithstanding. Another study was curiously entitled "Sexual Conditioning with Non-dominant Responses." Little else is revealed about this project except that researchers understood that if exposed, they would be "liable to repercussions."[72] Then there was a study entitled "Behavioral Therapy: Homosexuality." According to Forgays, "the basic approach of this project will be to use slides of male and female adult figures, a strain gauge on the penis of the subject and electric shock as the aversive stimulus in a typical operant conditioning paradigm."[73] Similar experiments were being performed at roughly the same time by researchers in California state prisons, specifically Atascadero State Hospital, popularly known as "Dachau for queers," and in Vacaville Medical Facility, which the CIA was forced to admit was an MK Ultra test site.[74]

Using incarcerated deviants, militants, and malcontents as raw material, ACTEC functioned as a laboratory where respected members of the academic community experimented with scientific forms of sexual grooming and rape. After violently reducing them to a childlike state, they subjected those over whom they exercised asymmetrical power to coercive medical and scientific techniques that aimed to cultivate sexual desires, orientations, and practices that were contrary to their will and suited the needs of those who aimed to control them. For Forgays and others, these practices of scientific sexual racism, domination, and violence were inextricable from the political objective of countering insurgency. "It was our conviction," wrote Forgays, "that various groups of inmates in the system, e.g., the overt homosexual, the militant, the non-cooperatives, etc. constituted . . . a set of problems to whose solution mental health and behavior science professionals could possibly contribute."[75] These academic experts aimed to manipulate and remold the most intimate parts of people's personalities. If this could be achieved, perhaps they could also reshape their loyalty, their political affinities, their personal aspirations.[76]

Against the dominant conception of the prison as a site of criminal justice that is marginal to global concerns, these experiments illuminate the prison as a site of incubation for technologies that are central to the reproduction of empire. My research strongly suggests that Dr. Forgays's unethical experiments were carried out on behalf of the CIA. At the very least, the imperatives of his Intensive Treatment Units program were shaped by that agency's global brain warfare agenda. Previous research has revealed that that psychologist Donald O. Hebb, Forgays's mentor at McGill, played a central role in helping the CIA understand the implications of sensory deprivation for manipulating the mind.[77] Between 1955 and 1957, Forgays worked as an Assistant Professor of Psychology, Sociology, and Anthropology at Cornell University during a moment when the Cornell-based Human Ecology Fund functioned as a conduit for MK Ultra research that aimed to weaponize anthropology and related disciplines.[78]

While at the University of Vermont, under the auspices of Project Themis, a Department of Defense effort to draw university-based academics into the Cold War effort, Forgays followed in Hebb's footsteps. In 1968, the DoD awarded Forgays a three-year grant of well over a half-million dollars to perform a study entitled "Isolation and Sensory Communication." Its aim, according to Forgays, was "to study individual differences in the influence of sensory isolation upon psychological and physiological functioning and also to employ the isolatory environment as an appropriate one in which to study other aspects of human functioning," including "subject attitude and personality characteristics." Methods included confining people to water-immersion and air-isolation tanks for as much as a month at a time, while exposing them to forms of "auditory indoctrination" that run "counter to specific subject attitudes."[79] Critically, Forgays and his colleague Robert B. Lawson were conducting this research at the same time they were consulting with DOCS.

Forgays's relationship with the military-industrial complex preceded Project Themis by well over a decade. After completing his PhD in 1950, Forgays did a tour of duty in the Korean War.[80] Throughout that decade, according to his CV, most of his research output circulated as internal memos and technical reports for the RAND Corporation and an innocuous-sounding agency called the Human Resources Research Center, which was located at the Randolph and Lackland Air Force bases in Texas. When I learned this, I immediately remembered what Carlos Roche told me: that Rx Program administrators were testing drugs on incarcerated people on behalf of the Air Force. As if this web of connections was not convincing enough, Forgays was stationed at

Lackland during the early 1950s, at the same time that the base's head of psychiatry was Dr. Louis Jolyon West, a high-level MK Ultra asset.[81]

By tracing these sinuous intellectual and institutional networks, we can see how prisons function as central nodes within global networks of counterinsurgency knowledge production. This knowledge is coercively extracted from captive Black revolutionaries and redeployed in the broader world. Brain warfare initiatives built on already existing practices of colonial domination that had long flourished in and through prisons. As I showed in chapter 4, the Long Attica Revolt presented state actors, mass media, and white civil society with a rare opportunity to intensify and publicly display violent rituals of sexual racism that undergird the social order under normal conditions. The experiments in ACTEC extended the Attica massacre not only because of their counterinsurgent objective, but also because of their intensely sexualized methods. Whether enacted through the brutal intimacy of physical violence or at the scientific remove of a laboratory, these rituals and technologies aimed to penetrate captive bodies, to obliterate their will to resist and fortify patriarchal relations of white supremacy and sexual mastery.

The results of the studies at ACTEC and of this broader research agenda are difficult to ascertain, not least because the powerful administrators of these programs wanted it that way. However, we can safely assert that, at best, the results were mixed. A survey of sensory deprivation research found that isolation enhances people's susceptibility to external influence, essentially starving them of information and "maximizing the impact and the reward value of whatever information *is* made available to him."[82] But it also notes that "subjects of higher intelligence or complexity, if they recognize the manipulative intent of the experimental treatment, exhibit resistance and even a boomerang effect."[83] According to Louis Jolyon West, certain drugs "have been proved effective as reinforcers of desired behavior" and "may also reinforce related or conditional behaviors."[84] This may be true, but when captives throughout New York prisons began to realize their food was drugged with tranquilizers and other substances, they stopped eating it. After going on a hunger strike, one of them told *The Black Panther*, "I started feeling better immediately. The drowsiness went away, and I felt stronger and more alert."[85] To my knowledge, Forgays, who continued to have an illustrious career, never produced any publicly accessible reports discussing how different individuals responded to the "intensive treatment" he exposed them to at ACTEC, or what was done with this knowledge.

One thing is certain: the Rx Program failed to break Masia's mind. On June 29, 1973, he was transferred to the so-called "open prescription" program at Comstock, where he met and became fast friends with Dhoruba bin-Wahad.[86] According to FBI surveillance from this period, Comstock was teeming with "black extremists," who were well-organized and engaged in almost daily confrontations with the authorities.[87] Masia recalls receiving a visit from the FBI shortly before his parole. After arriving by helicopter, bureau agents questioned him about his political philosophy and his post-release plans. He concealed his true thoughts, just as he had done with the Rx analysts who had been probing his mind. And yet Masia knew that they knew that he had not been "rehabilitated," that he still embraced revolutionary politics. Months later, when he and his new wife—Mzuri Mugmuk—were on the outside and working with the BLA, they articulated their political beliefs on their own terms: "We have been and are still, as are a number of other Brothers and Sisters, committed to the Black Liberation Movement, . . . dedicating and activating our lives to the struggle for total liberation, freedom and self-determination of our oppressed people, especially with the revolutionary intent to replace the present social order with a scientific socialist order with which to meet the needs, wants and aspirations of the oppressed people as a stepping stone towards the salvation of all the world's oppressed inhabitants."[88] Masia's ongoing commitment to Black liberation and socialist revolution demonstrate the spectacular failure of these carceral technologies to change his mind.

MUTATIONS OF COGNITIVE WAR

The year 1973 saw the decline of both prison-based behavior modification programs and MK Ultra. On June 20, 1973, NY DOCS announced that it was phasing out the Rx Program.[89] The CIA claimed to have shut down its brain warfare research earlier that year. From its inception, a CIA memo notes, the agency "pursued a philosophy of minimum documentation in keeping with the high sensitivity of some of the projects."[90] However, as the cascading Watergate scandal heightened public scrutiny of domestic US intelligence operations, Richard Helms, director of the CIA, ordered the destruction of the few records that did exist, ensuring that the full scope of the program would never be known.[91] In 1975, when a presidential commission to investigate CIA activity in the United States was established, the person selected to lead it was none other than Nelson Rockefeller, who was then vice president of the United States.[92]

Given the former New York governor's involvement in facilitating prison-based experiments, and his family foundation's ties to key sites of MK Ultra research, it is entirely unsurprising that his commission barely scratched the surface of CIA activities and that no records of his interviews with MK Ultra administrators were maintained for posterity.[93]

It would be a grave error to believe that these experiments in scientific subjugation ended with the formal elimination of these programs. According to Martin Sostre, whose political defense committee succeeded in preventing his transfer to ACTEC, the imperatives of the Rx Program continued operating via normalized prison tactics. "While our legal, political and physical struggle against the Rx Program has forced the enemy to suspend operations at the ACTEC, the plan now is to increase the capacities of special housing units in maximum-security facilities throughout the state," he wrote in September of 1973.[94] Similar to his critique of the transformations wrought after Attica, Sostre theorized that the official termination of the Rx Program was yet another example of a "dehumanizing reform" designed to confuse the prison's critics. This reform, he maintained, would allow DOCS to continue experimenting on nonconformists and revolutionaries "from the safety of the Box," which they had been doing long before concepts like behavior modification became fashionable.[95]

Sostre later authored a letter critiquing the state's flawed theory that human beings could be disassembled, tinkered with, and reprogramed like computers: "Beware of those who seek to subdue the person by dichotomizing the spiritual and the physical—the old game of divide and conquer. Although the spiritual and physical are one, those who seek to robotize us into submission try to project into our collective consciousness their negative racist, and exploitative ethic to place us in conflict with ourselves, our brothers, and sisters, and nature."[96] Sostre believed that counterrevolutionary carceral techniques were doomed to fail because their emphasis on isolation, division, dichotomization, and conquest conflicted with the laws of nature, a yearning for "harmony and unity."[97] My discussion of the Auburn rebellion in chapter 2 showed how political consciousness was produced through a complex and multilayered process of anticarceral struggle that involved physical resistance, writing, and collective practices of care. Against this expansive method of Revolt, the state's project was to isolate specific inputs and outputs in order to manipulate a totality they did not fully comprehend.

Popular resistance to this ongoing assault on revolutionary minds constitutes an elusive terrain of the Long Attica Revolt, one that again illuminates "Attica" as a metonym for a protracted struggle that transcends a specific carceral site and exceeds diminutive notions of prisoners' rights. For prisoncrats, even the memory of Attica threatened their power. On September 13, 1973, captives in Comstock gathered in the yard to hold a memorial on the second anniversary of the massacre. Much like they had during the lead-up to the Auburn rebellion, prisoncrats responded by locking the prison down and isolating those they deemed responsible, including Dhoruba bin-Wahad. In an open letter to *Workers' Power*, the organizers of the Attica memorial analyzed this incident as an example of how the state attempts to "control our compassion for our loved ones and our friends, our beliefs and non-beliefs" and "robotize us and make us stereotypes to appease the jailers' egos."[98] The fact that these forms of what they termed "mind control" did not involve scientists in white coats or advanced technology did not make them any less violent or significant.

A national effort to permanently incarcerate revolutionary ideas came into being on May 10, 1974. On that day, the FBI launched PRISACTS. While the program was officially termed a surveillance "liaison" program and not a behavior modification initiative, state sources provide compelling evidence of deep institutional ties between the two projects. Like the Rx Program, the FBI's "Black Nationalist Hate Groups" COINTELPRO, which directly preceded PRISACTS, was preoccupied with what was on the average Black person's mind. A compelling example can be found in a 1968 memo to J. Edgar Hoover, in which the Special Agent in Charge of the San Francisco Field Office suggested that it would be advantageous for Black youths to aspire to become "a sports hero, a well-paid professional athlete or entertainer," rather than revolutionaries. Emphasizing his point, he wrote candidly, "the negro youth and moderate must be made to understand that if they succumb to revolutionary teaching, they will be dead revolutionaries."[99] This ambition to obtain a strategic advantage by degrading an opponent's morale is psychological warfare. The interest in controlling what Black people want, to whom they feel accountable, and what they fear has deep resonance with the experiments unfolding in ACTEC.

PRISACTS launched three months after the Law Enforcement Assistance Administration terminated its funding for prison-based behavior modification research, including psychosurgery, aversion therapy, and chemotherapy.[100] The program's inaugural memo attributes its emergence to the kidnapping and alleged "brain washing" of a wealthy white teenager named Patricia Hearst by members of an avowedly revolutionary group known as the Symbionese Liberation Army (SLA). While the ordeal is much too convoluted to recount here, a few significant details are worth noting.

After kidnapping Hearst, SLA members, most of whom were white, incarcerated her in a dark closet and subjected her to nearly three months of rape, humiliation, brutalization, threats, and political indoctrination. According to Louis Jolyon West, who gave expert testimony during the legal aftermath of the ordeal, the SLA used methods of "coercive persuasion" comparable to what US POWs underwent in Korea. These techniques were said to have induced a "traumatic neurosis," which—according to West—explained why Hearst subsequently renounced her family, joined the SLA, and participated with them in the commission of several criminalized acts, seemingly of her own free will, but actually under the spell of her programmers.[101] What West failed to mention was that similar techniques were being used against US prisoners, or that he himself was involved in CIA-sponsored research that aimed to scientifically induce mental disorders and trance-like states. He also did not disclose that the SLA had formed in Vacaville Medical Facility, California's equivalent to ACTEC, where the CIA later admitted to sponsoring a wide array of mind manipulation experiments.[102]

If the official narrative of Hearst's kidnapping is to be believed—and there is an equally outlandish counter-explanation[103]—then it would seem that PRISACTS emerged because prison-based behavior modification programs were producing blowback beyond prison walls. This possibility receives further support from another PRISACTS memo, authored on the day of the program's launch. It cites an unnamed Rx Program administrator who had expressed anxiety that their efforts to scientifically control militants might be generating contrary effects: "Some inmates learn the psychological techniques used at the facility to modify inmate behavior and some could use these techniques to manipulate these 'political prisoners' groups."[104] This document is significant for multiple reasons. First, it shows that experiments in ACTEC persisted for at least eleven months after the Rx Program's official termination. Second, it shows that the FBI was to some extent aware of what was happening in ACTEC, that the bureau had established a relationship of cooperation and knowledge exchange with Rx administrators.

Most importantly, it reveals that the flawed theories of knowledge, politics, and humanity that haunted behavior modification programs were also embedded within PRISACTS. Sostre was right that state actors were projecting their technocratic and white supremacist conceptions of power and mastery onto the targets of their control. In doing so, they were unable to comprehend the range of possibilities for why people adopt certain beliefs or make certain choices, given their unique circumstances. Administrators of these counterinsurgency projects are inimically opposed to the idea that ordinary people are capable of thinking for themselves, deciding what is in their own best interest, or autonomously acting on their own thoughts. They saw intelligent, politically revolutionary, and charismatic individuals as vectors of a dehistoricized political contagion that mechanically infected an otherwise healthy social order, and the broader population as mere drones who must be (re)programmed by political and technical elites.

Dhoruba bin-Wahad was a confirmed PRISACTS target, and his description of the program's goals sounds a lot like Masia's description of what the Rx Program aimed to achieve. At a population level, PRISACTS "aimed to destroy the development of revolutionary consciousness within the prisons." At an individual level, it meant to "break" the minds and the spirits of specific targets who belonged to the class of imprisoned revolutionaries. Describing his experience to an interviewer in 1990, he said, "To do this they engaged in constant psychological battles, constant psychological torture, and constant attempts to isolate me from the community and from other prisoners."[105]

Shortly after his 1973 conviction on the attempted cop-killing frame-up, FBI surveillance followed Dhoruba into prison. Upon their instruction, DOCS circulated a memo that rearticulated the bureau's social Darwinist understanding of political education. They stressed that Dhoruba should "be afforded considerably more than average custodial supervision, and that he not be assigned to any area where he might exert undue influence on the weaker element."[106] The memo exposes the bureau's elitist conception that by isolating people like Dhoruba, prison programmers would be able to mold the passive majority like clay.

Although their theory was flawed, state actors were right to be concerned. Dhoruba and others were aware of their strategy and labored to expose it at every turn. A prime example comes in the form of "Message to the Black Movement: A Political Statement from the Black Underground," a pamphlet attributed to NYURBA, but which was written by Dhoruba circa 1976.[107] The pamphlet offers a materialist analysis of the historical conjuncture, including the ramifications of rapidly advancing technological capacity concentrated in the hands of a few and the continued necessity of underground formations such as the BLA. However, it also theorizes what I have called "programmification" as a key tactic in the state's ongoing attempt to control, eliminate, and induce particular ways of being Black.

"As it stands now, Black people cannot even conceive of real freedom, we are afraid of real liberation because we have been programmed to be afraid by racist class oppression," Dhoruba writes.[108] Although aware of behavior modification initiatives like the Rx Program, his critique focuses on more ordinary and thus seductive tactics of thought control. As university-sponsored education programs were flooding the post-Attica prison, he wrote that education has "always been another method of programming black people into the lowest strata of capitalist society, ensuring generations of exploitable and marginal labor."[109] These institutionally sponsored education programs were increasingly competing with the threatening forms of self-directed Black study that gave rise to the Revolt. "In order to break these psychological-class chains of 20th century enslavement, we must build a revolutionary culture . . . that not only programs our minds out of oppression, but at the same time impels us against the enemy class and culture."[110] Revolutionaries were also talking about "programming" the population, but unlike that of the state, theirs was not a paternalistic, elitist top-down approach, but a consensual approach to deprogram and reprogram besieged communities from the bottom up.

In July of 1974, the FBI convened a National Symposium on the American Penal System as a Revolutionary Target. Gathered at the bureau's training academy in Quantico, Virginia, prison officials from across the United States joined representatives from Congress and various federal agencies. Among their topics of discussion were the historical development of various revolutionary movements within and beyond the prison and the practice of guerrilla warfare.[111] PRISACTS codified the prison as war on a national level.

Present at the symposium was Bertram S. Brown, the director of the National Institute of Mental Health. Back in 1961, Brown had attended "The Power to Change Behavior," and after hearing a presentation on coercive persuasion, he issued what amounted to a national mandate for prison administrators to experiment on recalcitrant Black Muslims.[112] Following the Revolutionary Target thirteen years later, Brown issued another experimental mandate. He called for greater research in the field of revolutionary propaganda, with a particular focus on "which of the prisoners were particularly susceptible to this material, which would become radicalized, which would become leaders in [radical movements], and for what reasons." Illuminating the ongoing function

FIGURE 18. Prison administrators and FBI agents gathered at the FBI Training Academy in Quantico, Virginia, for the National Symposium on the American Penal System as a Revolutionary Target. Photo: *FBI Law Enforcement Bulletin.*

of prisons as laboratories for developing methods of control aimed beyond prison walls, Brown explained that the findings of this research would be broadly applicable, since "any understanding of those who do respond to these revolutionary concepts might give us a targeted place to find answers to questions involving our general society."[113] The imperatives of carceral war are never separate from those of empire.

The FBI terminated PRISACTS on August 16, 1976, just over two years after its initiation and just before Dhoruba's lawsuit forced the FBI to disclose the program's existence.[114] Similar to how prison-based behavior modification programs were formally discontinued only to be reconstituted under a new guise, counterrevolutionary FBI methods were absorbed into a series of state agencies with intelligence functions. New York's localized version of PRISACTS was based in the Office of the Inspector General (IGO) and administered in concert with the Bureau of Criminal Investigation (BCI) and the Division of Criminal Justice Services (DCJS), which absorbed NYSIIS in 1972. Established the same year, the IGO was another in a long line of post-Attica reforms that aimed to enhance carceral power through concessions disingenuously disguised as "wins" for anticarceral activists. DOCS initially presented the IGO as a mechanism for ensuring compliance with state and federal law, for investigating incarcerated people's complaints, and for ensuring that agreed-upon reforms were implemented effectively. However, the IGO performed extensive intelligence functions. It tracked the movements, associations, and ideas of political radicals across prison walls and maintained centralized dossiers, which it shared with the NYPD, the New York State Police, the FBI, and what eventually evolved into the Joint Terrorism Task Force.[115]

Not only did this sprawling state intelligence apparatus collect intelligence, it weaponized it. Years after leaving NYSIIS in 1973, Dr. Robert Gallati made this point clear. He explained that emerging computer technology facilitated new counterintelligence methods against "special threats" of organized crime and terrorism, common euphemisms for Black radical struggle. Among these methods were what Gallati termed "*subversion*: tactical actions calculated to breed internal dissention or to create distrust and suspicion" and "*disruption*: concentrated efforts to disrupt or dislocate organized crime activities. . . ."[116] Moreover, Gallati stressed that these methods were best deployed as part of a "flexible" and "imaginative" counterintelligence repertoire that was effective for defense as well as offense.[117] Interestingly, the book in which Gallati describes these methods features a laudatory foreword from William Colby, the former head of the CIA's pacification program in Vietnam who became director of the Central Intelligence Agency in 1973, again presenting us with the absent presence of the CIA in the development of carceral technology.[118]

CARCERAL COUNTER-INTELLIGENCE

As I have described elsewhere, evidence suggests that PRISACTS involved assassinations, most of which seem to have been carried out or attempted soon after a target was released from prison.[119] While this is certainly a critical aspect of state repression, here I am interested in how state actors sought to control the circulation of Black radical ideas, thoughts, desires, and representations through what I call *counter-intelligence*. Commonly unhyphenated, I use the term for two reasons. I want to stress that despite the various nomenclatural reforms, institutional reconfigurations, and administrative devolutions, all of which provide a veneer of plausible deniability, this state-based intelligence apparatus is a descendant of COINTELPRO and related programs of domestic war. Second, counter-intelligence speaks to the tactical imperatives of this war on Black revolutionary minds: how state actors, in a literal sense, attempt to counter the intelligence of incarcerated people, to eliminate their capacity for autonomous action and self-governance, and to criminalize threatening ideas and even nonthreatening ones that are not explicitly permitted by the state.

For prisoncrats, the most threatening idea was that which imprisoned Black revolutionaries understood to be indispensable: the BLA. After gunning down BLA member Twymon Meyers in 1973, the NYPD announced that it "broke the back" of the organization.[120] However, key members maintained that the BLA was not an organization, but rather an idea. As Dhoruba explained in a 1973 interview, "The importance of the BLA lies, not in its size, not in its ability to muster so much firepower or whatever. The importance of it lies in the concept. The concept is basically this: that revolutionary armed struggle is a very vital aspect of any progressive movement for revolutionary change."[121] Asked under oath if he was a member of the BLA, Albert Nuh Washington made a similar point: "All the Black people that struggle for the liberation of their people are members of this organization, but it's a concept more than an actuality."[122] So too did Assata Shakur in her autobiography: "There is, and always will be, until every Black man, woman, and child is free, a Black Liberation Army."[123] BLA combatant-theorists apprehended the historical dynamics of the permanent war within which all Black and colonized people were ensnared, whether they were locked behind prison walls or moving throughout the so-called "free world." After deep study and political engagement, they concluded that it was imperative for the historical victims of this racial-colonial war to develop the capacity to respond to it strategically.

Prisoncrats understood that unless they eradicated this concept, they would never be fully in control, and therefore employed invasive surveillance that aimed to decipher who belonged to what category of prisoner. The problem had grown more complex since Gallati authored his letter to Rockefeller back in 1971. By 1977, New York state prisons confined several BPP/BLA political prisoners, including Dhoruba, Robert "Seth" Hayes, Teddy "Jah" Heath, Elmore "Baba Odinga" Thompson, Nuh Washington, Herman Bell, and Jalil Muntaqim. Moreover, dispersed throughout the system was a much larger and more difficult to identify population of what the IGO called "BLA Associates," those who exhibited "close association" with BLA political prisoners and who were said to be involved in "organizing activities through shared use of couriers and through shielded communications between each other."[124] Finally, there was a large contingent of incarcerated people with direct and indirect ties to the Armed Forces of National Liberation (FALN), a revolutionary formation that caried out a variety of clandestine armed actions to support the Puerto Rican independence movement during the mid-1970s and early 1980s.[125]

It was the responsibility of DOCS' localized PRISACTS infrastructure—the IGO, DCJS, and BCI—to maintain a politically advantageous distribution of this militant minority across Auburn, Attica, Comstock, Clinton, and Green Haven prisons. As I showed in the previous chapter, DOCS' post-Attica prison expansion plan prioritized the construction of minimum- and medium-security prisons in an effort to create carceral spaces where the programmable "weaker element" could be disaggregated from the intractables, radicals, and revolutionaries. While this psychological warfare strategy may have contributed to the reduction of riot-inducing "tensions," as carceral planners intended, it left them with only five maximum-security prisons across which to distribute those who not only seemed impervious to state programming, but were believed to possess the capacity to program others. Further complicating matters was that DOCS maintained an unofficial policy that no two members of the BLA's "upper echelon" could be confined in the same prison at the same time.[126] The result was a frantic strategy akin to a repressive game of musical chairs in which political prisoners were ceaselessly moved in and out of solitary confinement and shuffled between New York's most oppressive prisons. This was achieved using illegal covert actions disguised as disinterested penal administration.

As I have already shown, because of its proximity to New York City, its relatively "loose" atmosphere, and its array of program offerings, Green Haven functioned as an institutional "carrot" when juxtaposed to "ultra-repressive" prisons like Clinton, Comstock, and Attica. However, by the late 1970s, captives began noticing a retrenchment of these programs and an intensification of repression. A telling example occurred in 1978, when the SHU cell of a Sunni Muslim captive named Musa Abdul Mu'Mim mysteriously caught fire and, according to eyewitness accounts, was allowed to burn for several minutes before guards came to his aid. Musa, who witnesses claim was sent to the SHU after observing a KKK meeting involving the guards, later died in the hospital. His death was not an isolated incident. A few days earlier Pedro Arroyo, another Green Haven captive, died after complaining of stomach pains in what many saw as suspicious circumstances, as guards were known to threaten to poison those who got out of line.[127] The IGO opened investigations into these deaths, and another into what was later revealed to be "a broad pattern of corruption and malfeasance" by Green Haven personnel, including the facilitation of extortion, drug distribution, gambling, prostitution, theft, and escapes.[128] However, despite these compounding crises, the intelligentsia's chief priority was to keep BLA political prisoners isolated from the captive majority and banish their revolutionary ideas from the carceral system.

"From the time I arrived in 1979, Green Haven and BLA control were synonymous," recalled Thomas A. Coughlin in a sworn deposition.[129] Immediately after assuming his new role as commissioner of DOCS, the former New York state trooper sat for the first of what would be countless meetings with the IGO, whose "main responsibility to me via Green Haven at the time was to keep me apprised of the activities of the Black Liberation Army and their relationship to radical groups on the street."[130] As the commissioner explained, IGO analysts walked him through "a very complicated mosaic" of intelligence, ultimately convincing him that with support from the FALN, BLA political prisoners had subverted their authority and were using coercion and threats to secretly control the population. Their plan, the authorities claimed, was to set the prison ablaze, seize hostages, and immediately execute them,[131] or as Coughlin explained, to "carry out the overthrow of the institution and create another Attica."[132]

This formulation speaks to the state's flawed theory of knowledge, its disingenuous historical memory, and the indispensability of the "Long Attica" framework advanced throughout this book. Nearly a decade after it occurred, the Attica rebellion and massacre continued to function as a paradigm that shaped political struggle within the walls. For imprisoned revolutionaries, Attica represented a watershed moment in the development of prisoner unity and collective radical struggle against racist and gendered state repression. By contrast, state actors positioned the rebellion as an unwarranted terrorist attack against the state. Their discourse, and that of the elite media, is characterized by a pathological revision that frames Attica as "one of the bloodiest prison riots in US history," or some derivation thereof, conveniently leaving out the fact that it was the state and not the rebels that spilled most of the blood in their ferocious *repression* of the rebellion. Nonetheless, state actors invoke Attica as a reminder of the profound trauma they experienced at losing control of a potent symbol of white power and masculinity. They are obsessed with Attica because of what it meant, and still means, to them.

IGO intelligence framed its struggle against this alleged BLA takeover as a kind of war by proxy. At the center of this struggle was an inmate organization called the Creative Communications Committee (CCC). As stated in their intelligence reports, the CCC began as a "legitimate organization" and pursued the "legitimate purpose" of parole reform. However, by the fall of 1978, when Dhoruba became vice president, the IGO noted "the infiltration of the CCC and possibly its complete takeover by the Black Liberation Army was well underway and possibly complete."[133] This reference to "infiltration" is a tacit admission that a covert war was unfolding. As I have already shown, prisoncrats employed inmate organizations as a means of infiltrating the prison movement, as a Trojan horse meant to disseminate conservative ideology and program the population's embrace of what Queen Mother Moore termed "tame" institutional politics. When Dhoruba became involved in the CCC, prisoncrats grew fearful, not only that militants had infiltrated their infiltration strategy, but that they were countering state programming with programs of their own.

On December 16, 1978, after the state's attempt to pressure CCC members to sever their relationship to Dhoruba failed, prisoncrats shipped him to Unit 14. Four days earlier, an administrator had written, "It is extremely imperative that Richard Moore [Dhoruba's slave name] be transferred from this facility immediately. He is quite gifted in his speech and ability to arouse others into becoming involved in violent behavior. If left unattended at Green Haven he will most definitely organize a front to overtake the facility through violent means."[134] Protesting his treatment in a letter to Robert Nelepovitz, who had been taken hostage during the Auburn rebellion, Dhoruba identified what he saw as the actual reason for his transfer: "to exhibit to all prisoners that my type of 'attitude' will not be allowed to become contagious." Aware of the guards' fragile hold on power, Dhoruba closed his missive by invoking Attica. He wrote that attempts to isolate people like him from the captive majority "only ensure future Atticas and in this sense you are correct to do what you have done."[135]

Pressure from Dhoruba's legal and political support campaign forced prisoncrats to release him into Clinton's general population, creating a new problem. Albert Nuh Washington was already in Clinton. Convicted in 1975 for the slaying of two NYPD patrolmen, Nuh Washington, along with Jalil Muntaqim and Herman Bell, were considered to be among the BLA's "upper echelon." It is unclear what prisoncrats believed would happen if these two men were allowed to be in the same prison at the same time. Perhaps their combined powers of influence would prove too much for DOCS to contain, instantly breaking their spell over the captive majority. We'll never know. A few days after Dhoruba hit the general population, Nuh was warned that he was being set up.[136] Later that day, prisoncrats "discovered" what they claimed was a bomb in his cell. In a June 28 letter to his attorney, Dhoruba explained, "Informal reports on my end indicate that the opposition may have employed BCI in setting him up. Also, all of his legal papers, letters, etc. destroyed, confiscated or copied. Opposition claims ongoing investigation."[137] Although it was later revealed that the mysterious device was not a bomb, Nuh spent six months in Unit 14, where he was effectively quarantined from his comrade and from the general population, a major chess piece removed from the board, a crisis of influence averted.[138]

Meanwhile, Jalil Muntaqim had been in Attica since late 1977. Eleven months later he was accused of organizing the so-called Attica Brigade, an underground formation intent on physically retaliating against abusive guards. Jalil spent two months in solitary confinement before being shipped to Auburn, where he was written up for leading the Muslim population in an illegal outdoor prayer ceremony. In late 1979, he was transferred to Green Haven where, much to the administration's dismay, he was promptly elected to a leadership position in the CCC.[139] Conveniently neglecting the fact that the population had elected Dhoruba and Jalil to leadership positions in the organization, Commissioner Coughlin testified that their assent was achieved via "threats," "strong arm tactics," and internecine violence and that state intervention was necessary to prevent harm to incarcerated people, prison staff, and state property.[140]

Jalil describes the administration's claim that he and Dhoruba were using the CCC to build a secret BLA network that aimed to seize Green Haven and launch a massacre, a flat-out lie intended to "facilitate a PRISACTS agenda" and justify severe repression.[141] At the same time, he acknowledges that he and others were aware that the inmate organization program was "subterfuge" designed to "pinpoint who was organizing in the prison and allow the administration to contain their organizing in a way that was effective for the modus operandi of the prison itself."[142] Based on this understanding, he and others performed their CCC work, while at the same time they used "the official organization for unofficial organizing." Jalil maintains that the underground, unsanctioned objective of the CCC was to organize the population to collectively withhold their labor to protest working conditions and recent curtailments of visitation privileges. This was the extent of their conspiracy, he explained.

However, through the state's war on Black revolutionary minds, the ideas and thoughts behind a given action were prioritized over the action itself. What concerned Coughlin and others was that CCC members were not primarily thinking about parole reform, the official focus of their organization; they were thinking about war, and worse, they were actively concealing their criminalized thoughts. Soon after Jalil assumed leadership in the organization, prisoncrats and the IGO began noticing that captives in multiple Green Haven cellblocks were wearing buttons emblazoned with a new CCC logo. The buttons featured a pyramid with an apex hovering slightly above the base and an "all-seeing eye" in its center, much like the image on the back of a one-dollar bill. Within the pyramid's base were three circles, each featuring a small "c" and a much larger stick-figure character. Decoding the icons with the help of a confidential informant, the IGO eventually realized that they were "replete with BLA iconography and revolutionary symbolism."[143] An intelligence summary pointed out the similarity between the CCC pyramid and the pyramid depicted in the BLA's newly unveiled logo, which unbeknownst to them Dhoruba had drawn a few years earlier while in Green Haven.[144] They further surmised that the stick figures within each circle were positioned in postures resembling letters and that when deciphered, the letters spelled "WAR."[145]

"We wanted to raise the consciousness of our constituents, of our fellow incarcerated men, and help them see that we are engaged in a process of war," Jalil explained after I showed him the IGO's surveillance report.[146] His counter-strategy speaks to the very essence of this psychological war, a confrontation that revolves around concepts, knowledge, and consciousness rather than physical territory. Using various technologies of coercion, manipulation, and programming, the state aimed to pacify the population by mystifying the idea that a war was unfolding, by enveloping its violence within liberal discourses of "progress," "correction," "reform," "education," and "rehabilitation." Imprisoned revolutionaries were trying to help the population cut through these layers of obscurity and reveal that the war was not over, that it had only transformed in sophisticated ways, that violence continued to saturate the system but was unequally distributed throughout the population.

Afflicted with a pathological amnesia regarding the imperialist and white supremacist origins of this war, state actors necessarily interpret oppressed peoples' understandings of war as *declarations* of war against normative peace. Moreover, they project their own genocidal conceptions of war onto the populations they subject to genocide. New York Attorney General Robert Abrams later cited the buttons as evidence that "a hardcore group of inmates, composed of CCC members, radical inmates, and general malcontents were attempting to force, via the use of coercive means, other inmates into supporting a violent confrontation with the prison authorities."[147] Abrams, Coughlin, and the IGO claimed that on July 28, 1980, Jalil and the CCC would launch their carefully planned conspiracy to inaugurate their Attica-like rebellion.[148]

On the morning of July 20, 1980, eight days before this planned rebellion was allegedly set to occur, Green Haven's captive population entered the prison's East and West mess halls, picked up their trays and utensils, but walked through the food line without filling their plates. Instead, they sat at their tables in total silence. This simple act of collectively refusing to eat, a nonviolent protest tactic employed across historical and geographic contexts, filled the prison hierarchy with dread. Actors on both sides of this struggle understood that in the New York prison system, refusing to eat had special significance. It conjured images of the Attica rebellion, which was preceded by a silent fast in honor of George Jackson. Their collective refusal to eat signified a refusal of the state's knowledge and programs and the harboring of secrets, that the state's technologies of surveillance could not access. For the state, this was unacceptable.

The day after the strike, in response to this "seething internal situation"[149] as the Attorney General described it, prisoncrats unleashed the tried-and-true method that had undergirded their mind experiments all along: violence. Under Coughlin's orders, Green Haven was placed on total lockdown and a CERT executed a brutal transfer of forty captives, all of whom, according to the state, were "violence prone, radical CCC and BLA leaders, their more active followers, and other inmate sympathizers and general malcontents. . . ."[150] Depositions from Charles Meriwether and Charles Butler, who were shackled together at the wrist and ankle and shipped to Comstock, offer a glimpse of what the "Green Haven 40," as they came to be known, endured at the hand of the state.

As their bus entered Comstock's main gate, Butler and others beheld "approximately twenty-five to thirty officers standing at the bottom of a hill and all of them had extra-long sticks and they were swinging them as if they were having baseball practice."[151] Perched atop a guard tower, they spotted a sharpshooter who was peering at them through the scope of his rifle, pretending to shoot. Aware of Comstock's reputation for racial terror, Butler "became petrified with fear . . . that they either intended to kill us or beat us so bad that we would wish for death." One by one, pairs of captives were physically dragged from the bus, assailed with racist vitriol, and viciously beaten in full view of the others. Their bruised and bloodied bodies were then carried into the prison, where they were stripped of their clothing and forcibly shaved of their head and facial hair. After being "inspected" by a physician who ignored their fresh wounds, the captives were confined to the SHU. In "A Political Prisoner's Journey through the U.S. Prison System," Jalil Muntaqim, who was transferred a few days later, writes about his similarly brutal dislocation from Green Haven as well as his continued resistance in and out of various isolation units.[152]

Years later, during the Green Haven 40's class-action lawsuit against DOCS, authorities claimed that their pre-emptive action forestalled a rebellion, "sparing the personnel and the inmate population of Green Haven from a potential blood bath."[153] However, Coughlin explained that the ultimate goal of the CCC's organizing was inconsequential. He testified that the central issue was that militants and revolutionaries had control over the thoughts and behaviors of the population, which meant that they *could* have organized a massacre if they wanted to. Echoing theorist Walter Benjamin's assertion that the state will always interpret general strikes as symbolic acts of violence, Coughlin explained that the meal strike "could be construed as a terrorist act."[154] He went on, "When the inmates in a maximum-security prison have enough strength and enough organization to shut down that institution—in other words, make the inmate population do its will, that, in my opinion, is a takeover of that institution. Because it was just at the whim of the leadership that hostages weren't taken, or people weren't killed."[155] Similarly, when pressed to produce a single shred of evidence showing that the BLA or anyone else had done or were planning to do anything illegal under the auspices of the CCC, Assistant Inspector General Paul Garcia testified that "it is unlawful for inmates to organize within the prison system."[156] This was clearly untrue, as captives were actively encouraged to organize in ways that facilitated the state's continued control.

The state's rationalization of its surveillance and repression exposes the ideological continuity running through this constantly mutating assault on Black revolutionary minds. While mind control, behavior modification, and thought reform programs officially belonged to a bygone era, the fact that CCC members were terrorized for committing thought crimes shows that prisoncrats continued to pursue these imperatives under different guises. Administrators of the counterinsurgent prison see physical confinement as insufficient for order. Over and above this minimum condition for control is the imperative of negating the captives' independent will, of subjugating them on physiological, psychological, ideological, affective, and libidinal levels, of rendering them incapable of thinking, feeling, or acting in ways that are not explicitly allowed by the state. Though disguised as disinterested prison administration, DOCS colluded with the national security state to facilitate unethical medical experimentation, illegal covert action techniques, and brutal terror to disrupt their cognitive autonomy and foreclose Black radical futurity.

CONTROL UNITS: A CODA

On November 7, 1975, Masia and Mzuri Mugmuk were captured in Minneapolis by what Masia called "an army of FBI and police gestapo armed to kill."[157] Five years later, in an essay entitled "Profile of a Revolutionary Married Couple," Masia declared that he and Mzuri belonged to the Republic of New Afrika and the Black Liberation Army and had been engaged in "efforts to establish armed clandestine formations throughout the Black colonies within the continent of Euro-America." They were brought to New Jersey to stand trial for the murder of Oscar Lowitt, a store operator who had been fatally shot near the Monmouth Park Race Track on July 5. And yet, because they were under twenty-four-hour surveillance, the state knew the Mugmuks did not carry out this murder, Masia argued. Rather, the charge was part of a conspiracy that aimed to "frame us for whatever crime or crimes conductive to taking us out of revolutionary commission or facing the music of violent death."[158]

Along with a man named O'Neal Davis, Masia and Mzuri were indicted for first-degree murder and conspiracy to commit murder. The state's narrative was that Lowitt's wife hired the trio to assassinate her husband for infidelity. Held on $100,000 bail, the Mugmuks pleaded not guilty. They maintained that they were the targets of a frame-up, Masia for the second time in his life. After a seven-day prosecution that relied on the testimony of Davis, who cooperated in exchange for a drastically reduced sentence, Masia and Mzuri Mugmuk were found guilty and sentenced to life.[159] Granted executive clemency in 1985, Mzuri was paroled in 1988. Masia was less fortunate. He spent the next thirty-three years in the New Jersey prison system, where he endured yet another experiment that would have profound implications for incarcerated people everywhere.[160]

Masia's incarceration in Trenton State Prison occurred shortly after its Management Control Unit (MCU) became operational. Launched in 1975 with BPP/BLA veteran Sundiata Acoli as one of its first victims, this ultra-punitive prison-within-a-prison was designed to perform the counterrevolutionary function that New York prisoncrats had discussed in the immediate aftermath of Attica. A person did not have to violate any rules to land in the MCU. They only needed to be Black and display certain intangible qualities that made them potential "troublemakers," "leaders," or "incorrigibles" in the eyes of the state.[161] As Masia explained, "Whether they was jailhouse lawyers, Afro-centric, Muslims, pan-Africanist, Black nationalists, or whatever their affiliation, brothers was placed in MCU because of their political consciousness."[162] With only a few brief interruptions, Masia was held in the MCU between 1976 and 2000, a total of twenty-four years.

During our conversations about his life behind the walls, Masia's narrations constantly shifted across time and carceral geographies. A story about the Rx Program might seamlessly bleed into a story about the MCU and vice versa. This narrative style accurately situates these programs as the fruit of the same putrid tree. Indeed, activist-scholars have traced the "no-touch" torture techniques employed in MCUs like Trenton, as well as the "enhanced interrogation" techniques currently employed by the national security state as part of the Global War on Terror, to the CIA's brain warfare research.[163] Narratives of sleep deprivation, sensory deprivation, prolonged isolation, stress positions, humiliation, intimidation, exposure to extreme temperatures, perpetual lighting, punishing noise pollution, severely restricted visitation, correspondence, and phone privileges, among other forms of profound trauma, emerge from the testimonials of those who have endured these sites within and beyond US borders.[164]

In 1979, a few months before his co-defendant Assata Shakur escaped prison, Sundiata Acoli, a member of the Panther 21, was transferred from the MCU to Marion Federal Penitentiary in Southern Illinois. Marion was one of the federal prison system's key penal laboratories, where behavior modification experiments similar to those explored in ACTEC, Vacaville, and elsewhere were taking place.[165] Back in 1973, Marion's warden had framed these experiments in explicitly counterrevolutionary terms: "The purpose of the Marion control unit is to control revolutionary attitudes in the prison system and in the society at large."[166] A decade later, federal prisoncrats converted Marion to a "permanent lockdown" institution. "What is needed in the Federal Prison System is an institution which incorporates the latest in technology and program features within its new concepts of control and security," noted a government report describing the transformation.[167] For the next twenty-three years, Marion's entire captive population, many of whom understood themselves and were understood by the state to be political revolutionaries, were subjected to no-touch torture while confined to individual cages for twenty-three hours per day, and sometimes longer.

During the 1980s and 1990s, using the Trenton and Marion Control Units as their template, prisoncrats proliferated similarly repressive carceral sites in virtually every state in the nation.[168] According to the most recent and best available data on US carceral practices, at least 80,000 people are held in some form of solitary confinement on any given day in the United States, an estimated 448,000 people have been isolated in the last twelve months, and these people are disproportionately Black and other people of color, people who are queer, and people with disabilities.[169] These forms of isolation go by a variety of official euphemisms: Management Control Units, Special Housing Units, Secure Housing Units, Communications Management Units, Administrative Maximum Facility, Restrictive Housing, Punitive Segregation, Disciplinary Segregation, and Administrative Segregation, among others. While the names vary, the purpose remains consistent. As Nancy Kurshan, author of *Out of Control: A Fifteen-Year Battle against Control Unit Prisons,* explains: "We reasoned and asserted that just as prisons were to control rebellion in society, control unit prisons were to control other prisons, and that the 'holes' or 'boxes' within control unit prisons were used to control control unit prisons, etc. Just boxes stuffed in boxes."[170] Coupled with severe limits on what incarcerated people can read, listen to, and watch, this statecraft of isolation, torture, and manipulation reflects the chilling ongoingness of this war on the mind, a war that has the Black revolutionary at its center but is promiscuous in its aims.

Epilogue

Brother Tyrone, an Attica survivor, told me a haunting story that exemplifies how conditions inside New York state prisons have changed since the 1970s. It occurred shortly before his release in 1993, a year that marks the moment when Black men incarcerated in the House of Detention for Men on Rikers Island founded a chapter of the United Blood Nation, a street organization that had flourished in California since the early 1970s. The New York Bloods formed in response to highly organized Latinx formations such as the Latin Kings and the Ñetas, who maintained control over telephones, televisions, and other key resources by meting out intense violence against unorganized Black captives.[1] Like wildfire, the organization spread within Rikers, to other city jails, the state prison system, and the outside world. This growth accompanied what Tyrone and many others perceived as an aversion, on the part of oppressed groups, to rebelling against the state and an associated increase in internecine violence among those groups. For many, 1993 was a watershed in the slow disintegration of the prison movement.

While heading to his work-release program, Tyrone witnessed an increasingly common occurrence: an argument between a small group of young people over what to watch on television. While he did not get involved, he struck up a conversation with one of the young people later that night. He learned that his new associate was twenty years old, that he was just beginning a forty-year prison sentence, and that he could not read or write. Back in 1970, when Tyrone first entered the system, underground political organizations would have looked upon this kid as a prime candidate for recruitment, after which they would have helped him become literate and ushered him through a process of ideological development. But in 1993, he was a prime candidate for the Bloods, an organization that embraced what many from Tyrone's generation call the "criminal mentality."[2] Looking forward to beginning a new chapter of his life after spending more than two decades behind the walls, Tyrone offered a few words of advice. He implored the young man to spend his time wisely, to learn to read and write, to educate himself, and to work toward obtaining his freedom by using the law libraries, present in every New York state prison as a result of the Attica rebellion. The kid seemed receptive and motivated to follow Tyrone's advice. However, the next morning, as he was again headed to his work-release program, Tyrone found him sitting in front of the TV in the common area, watching cartoons while sucking his thumb—a literal image of what I have been calling prison pacification.[3]

The primary aim of this book has been to show that US prisons are a site of war. While the story I have told begins in the late twentieth century, I employed a Black radical interpretive framework that locates the origins of this war in the sixteenth century, with the onset of the European trade in enslaved Africans, the rise of capitalism as a world system, and the global project of patriarchal white supremacy that underwrites it. From the time of its formation, the US state has used its monopoly over the legitimate use of violence (via law, policing, and prisons) to reproduce capitalist social relations, a project that is tantamount to permanent race and class war. I have examined a specific moment within this war, one that materialized during the late 1960s, a time when police, prisoncrats, elected officials, national security actors, and academics—many of whom participated in campaigns to pacify anticolonial movements abroad—increasingly looked to US prisons as indispensable to a domestic counterinsurgency against militant social movements. As part of the "hard" and explicitly repressive side of this multifaceted campaign, these agents of the state employed carceral institutions to stifle Black intellectual, cultural, and political development; neutralize autonomous Black radical organization; thwart Black internationalism; eradicate Black rebellion; manipulate Black sexuality; and destroy Black revolutionary minds.

Analyzing what I have termed the Long Attica Revolt, I have also shown that prisons are sites of counter-war, a term that reflects the fact that captive rebels were responding to an antagonism they did not initiate. By subordinating the state archive to criminalized and pathologized

Black epistemologies, I detailed how people behind the walls rebelled in complex and protracted ways that are undertheorized in existing conversations about Black radicalism in general, and the Attica rebellion specifically. I stretched the geography of Attica beyond a single carceral site and showed that it was not a single event that can be contained within linear notions of time, but an unruly structure of Revolt that is inseparable from putatively bygone forms of Black radical struggle. I demonstrated that formal demands for improved prison conditions did not reflect the totality of what the rebels wanted, and that such demands were internally contested by rebels who understood the ease with which a pragmatic political approach rendered their struggle vulnerable to cooptation. In addition to petitioning the war-waging state, imprisoned people engaged in capacious forms of physical, cultural, psychological, epistemic, narrative, spiritual, and affective insurgency that aimed to expose and ameliorate carceral repression while also abolishing the anti-Black class war of which prisons are a part. Imprisoned revolutionaries developed aboveground and underground formations of guerrilla warfare, nurtured intimacies and solidarities that transcended prison walls as well as national boundaries, created illicit infrastructures of Black study and archivization, and engaged in armed and unarmed insurgency against the state.

By tracing the unfolding of this Revolt's collision with constantly mutating technologies of state violence, *Tip of the Spear* clarified the cultural asymmetry of this war. State actors waged an imperialist war, a war of capture and conquest that had the production of slaves as its unspoken object. This invocation of slavery does not depend on critical interpretations of law (the 13th Amendment, *Ruffin v. Commonwealth*, etc.), nor on uneven conditions of labor exploitation within carceral institutions, nor on grand theories of the ontological position of Blackness under Western modernity. Neither does it depend solely on the voices of incarcerated people, who frequently narrate themselves as slaves. Rather, it depends on a critical analysis of imperialist war and counterinsurgency in theory and practice. In his influential *On War*, Prussian General Carl von Clausewitz defines war as "an act of force to compel our enemy to do our will" and clarifies that the immediate aim of war is to disarm the enemy and destroy their capacity for resistance.[4] This ambition to abolish a subject's capacity for autonomy and independent will is tantamount to a desire for absolute mastery over an enslaved population.[5] *Tip of the Spear* has elaborated the various ways that state actors tried and failed to achieve this goal: sadistically inventive forms of physical violence, isolation, psychological and psychiatric assault, sexual terror, propaganda, liberal reformism, and white supremacist science and technology.

As an articulation of Black radical counter-war, the Long Attica Revolt did not pursue an equivalent aim. The rebels struggled for reprieve, autonomy, internal transformation, and diverse visions of collective freedom, liberation, revolution, and abolition. As I demonstrated, they engaged in collective and targeted acts of counter-violence, for which many were labeled "extremists" and "terrorists" even though the physical trauma their resistance produced paled in comparison to that against which it responded. At the same time, I showed that, unlike the violence of the carceral warfare state, political counter-violence from below did not reflect the core of the Revolt. Rather, it was only the outermost layer of a manifold struggle that was ultimately about the capacity for Black radical futurity, the evolution of human being, the preservation of historical consciousness, the development of love and intimacy, and the search for new ways of organizing social life that were not rooted in domination, extraction, or accumulation. Ensnared within the bowels of an anti-human regime that aimed to destroy them in every conceivable way, the dregs of the capitalist social order refashioned themselves into combatant-theorists of a new form of war that nurtured radically new forms of social life through the improvisation of rebellion. Across the preceding chapters, the words and deeds of the protagonists demonstrate this fact again and again.

Theorizing the prison as a site of active combat helps explain the breathtaking proliferation of US prisons over the past five decades. Scholars, activists, and government officials representing diverse perspectives have analyzed and debated the extent to which patterns of criminalization, drug use, racial animus, and policing, as well as shifts in demographics, the labor market, social movements, ideology, and the global political economy have propelled carceral expansion.[6] What has been largely overlooked is the extent to which the prison construction boom of the 1980s and 1990s was a direct response to Black rebellion behind the walls. Erupting on the cusp of the United States' globally and historically unprecedented experiment in human caging, the Long Attica Revolt revealed to actors at the highest levels of state power that to effectively control captive populations they would need more and better prisons. As I showed in chapters 5 and 6, counterinsurgency experts responded to the Revolt by expanding and diversifying carceral networks in ways that facilitated the strategic disaggregation of captive populations across geographies to maximize control. This "diversification" strategy aimed to resolve a crisis that was concentrated inside the prison, the crisis of radical imprisoned intellectuals and combatants whose influence on broader populations within and beyond the walls had to be eliminated. Carceral expansion facilitated this strategy and therefore must be seen as a counterrevolutionary imperative.

To see the prison as an institutionalized form of counterinsurgency is to apprehend how not only spectacular violence, but mundane "progressive" and "humanizing" reforms, are constantly being weaponized against the capacity for radical thought. Incarcerated for the next four decades, unable to read or write, passively sitting in front of a television while soothing himself in an infantile way, the young person Tyrone encountered in 1993 was not simply a wayward youth; he was the target of a war he may not have known was unfolding. Prior to Attica, the few televisions that existed within prison walls were only accessible in common areas during limited times, a situation that forced those interested in stimulating their minds to read, write, and study, often in ways that radicalized them. After Attica, when prisoncrats expanded access to television, movement elders began noticing a pronounced decline in young people's desire to read. "I once spent four months in the box for wanting to read *Soledad Brother* by George Jackson and I saw it in here yesterday in the garbage," explained Auburn and Attica survivor Jomo Omowale during the late 1970s. "These kids have no idea. They have the right to read these things and they can't even read. I walk around with these bullets from Attica in my back. What the hell did I do this for?" he asked his wife.[7] The following decade, NY DOCS initiated a program allowing captives to have TVs in their individual cells. While vocal fractions of the increasingly conservative public interpreted this "privilege" as evidence that prisons were "going soft" on the monsters they were said to contain, an article in a prison trade magazine clarified the paternalistic and counterinsurgent logics of this reform: "Incorrigible criminals are vulnerable to the same disciplinary philosophy as a recalcitrant child. . . . Inmates must spend 24 hours in each day, too, same as everybody else. They can spend it plotting their next flirtation with trouble or they can watch TV."[8]

Today's prison-based tablets are on the cutting edge of carceral war.[9] Privately owned digital communications firms such as Securus Technologies and Global Tel Link (GTL) are increasingly flooding carceral systems with app-filled devices specially designed for prison contexts. Although these tools are publicly marketed as bringing fractured communities together, these companies employ predatory pricing strategies that extract scarce financial resources from already vulnerable communities and are rapidly replacing physical letter writing which, as I have shown, is a central terrain of anti-carceral Revolt. These technologies are also facilitating new forms of surveillance and control.[10] As GTL notes on its website, "Deployed in facilities across the country, tablets offer more than just entertainment. They can help modify behavior, enable communication, and increase facility security, control, and operational efficiencies."[11]

With relative openness, these new carceral technologies aim to perform surveillance and behavior modification functions similar to those covertly tested by NYSIIS, the FBI, and the CIA on imprisoned Black revolutionaries during the 1970s. An investigation from 2018 found that police in Missouri have used Securus tools for the warrantless tracking of nonincarcerated citizens' cellphones, and another from 2021 revealed that recordings of over 1,300 telephone calls between incarcerated people and their attorneys somehow wound up in the hands of New York prosecutors, violating attorney-client privilege and depriving people of their right to a fair trial.[12] According to a 2022 investigation by the American Civil Liberties Union of New York, Securus Technologies' Secure Call Platform "provides live and investigative support for law enforcement, featuring voice recognition technology and identification capabilities, as well as call monitoring, behavioral analysis, suspicious keyword notification, pattern analysis, and even location tracking of the called party."[13]

Increasingly ubiquitous tracking technologies such as electronic ankle shackles emerge from the research of Ralph and Robert Schwitzgebel, a fact that links these so-called "alternatives to incarceration" to the disavowed and experimental underside of this carceral war.[14] Back in 1962, Robert Schwitzgebel published a cross-cultural analysis of sensory deprivation research that compared data collected in the United States and Canada, most likely as part of MK Ultra, with data collected from sensory-deprived "Zulu" and "English" populations in South Africa.[15] Twelve years later, Huey P. Newton cited his brother Ralph Schwitzgebel's research on prison-based methods of "coercive behavior modification" as an example of how state actors were increasingly experimenting with scientific methods of controlling people's minds and bodies.[16] In their co-edited *Psychotechology: Electronic Control of Mind and Behavior*, Robert explains that their collective intellectual project was to discover how to move individuals from one "state of being" to another, while controlling the "vehicle" used to facilitate that movement as well as the "nature of its expected course," a gentle way of describing a total assault on human autonomy.[17] The Schwitzgebels' experiments have continued material relevance to the tens of thousands of people who are subjected to myriad forms of electronic monitoring today.

The fact that these technologies are seamlessly targeting communities on both sides of prison walls forces us to contend with another key insight of this book: prison struggles are never just about prison. "Prisons are really an extension of our communities," wrote BPP/BLA member Zayd Malik Shakur in a 1970 essay entitled "America Is the Prison."[18] He continued, building on the insights of Queen Mother Moore and Malcolm X: "We have people who are forced at gun point to live behind concrete and steel. Others of us, in what we ordinarily think of as the community, live at gun point again in almost the same conditions." This Black radical theory of carcerality as a generalized condition of being in North America productively reframes contemporary debates about "decarceration." Driven by reforms at the state and federal levels, the total number of US adults under some form of "correctional control"—incarceration, probation, parole—has declined from over seven million in 2010 to just over five and a half million at the end of 2020, its lowest point since 1996.[19] Though hailed by many as evidence of incremental progress toward a more just world, this development is underwritten by these emerging carceral technologies that allow state actors to functionally incarcerate people where they live, in what James Kilgore calls "techno-cells" without walls.[20] While disconcerting, this rapidly shifting carceral landscape was in some ways anticipated by people who were fighting against the prison in order to change the world, but whose ideas were criminalized, incarcerated, or discounted.

Journalists and scholars have increasingly argued that in the post-9/11 context, counterinsurgency has reshaped US democracy and contributed to a generalized mode of governance that "we" are presently living through.[21] *Tip of the Spear* shows that the reconfiguration of "national security" discourse and practice after 9/11 reflected the metastasis of a longstanding (anti-Black, anti-radical, anti-communist, anti-Muslim) domestic war. Moreover, it offers the prison as a *method* for analyzing and resisting the relations of power and techniques of rule that shape the broader world. Accordingly, to the extent that valuable lessons can be acquired from thinking with this book, these lessons do not apply only to what has happened and is happening inside prisons, jails, immigrant detention centers, black sites, and other zones of official state captivity. They also apply to what is unfolding beyond them. However, I avoid didactically delineating what I think these lessons are, to encourage communities engaged in progressive, radical, and revolutionary struggle to consider these insights in relation to their material conditions and to reach their own conclusions.

Some may be wondering when the Long Attica Revolt ended. For this I have already provided an answer: "Attica Is." Attica is the Attica Brothers Foundation, an organization led by Attica survivors who are preserving the memory of their struggle.[22] Attica is the 2013 Pelican Bay hunger strike that began when imprisoned members of rival gangs collectively resisted indefinite solitary confinement by communicating through toilet drains.[23] Attica is the movement to free political prisoners and to support their well-being upon release. Attica is the international movement to oppose imperialist war, colonialism, displacement, apartheid, and racist nationalism.[24] Attica is the struggle to develop progressive, radical, and revolutionary Black masculinities that are accountable to Black communities. Attica is the Black Lives Matter organizers who refused to be incorporated into the counterinsurgent nonprofit- and influencer-industrial complex.[25] Attica is the movement to oppose liberal reformist logics that present "gender responsive" and "feminist" jails as viable solutions to gender-based violence.[26] Attica is the collective rebellions against racist police terror and the movement to stop "Cop City," a plan to destroy eighty-five acres of Georgia's South River Forest to construct a facility to train police officers in urban warfare.[27] Attica is Black August Resistance, an annual celebration of Black radical and revolutionary history that grew out of the California prison system. Attica is participatory defense campaigns to free incarcerated people, especially criminalized survivors of sexual violence.[28] Attica is the study groups that seed revolutionary ideas that break through in moments of rupture. Attica is Jailhouse Lawyers Speak, imprisoned people who fight for human rights through political education and who organized unprecedented national prison strikes on September 9 in both 2016 and 2018 to coincide with anniversaries of the Attica rebellion.[29] Attica is a living tradition of criminalized Black radicalism born and nurtured amid conditions of war. Attica is racist state repression. Attica is revolutionary abolition.

Notes

INTRODUCTION

1. "Queen Mother Moore Speech at Greenhaven Prison," in People's Communication Network, *Surveying the First Decade: Volume 2*. For more on Queen Mother Moore, see Farmer and McDuffie, *Palimpsest*.
2. Muhammad Ahmad in conversation with Aukram Burton and author, 2019.
3. Tilly, "War Making and State Making as Organized Crime."
4. For useful engagements with Black radical notions of temporality, see Brand, *A Map to the Door of No Return*; Hartman, *Scenes of Subjection*; Robinson, *Black Marxism*; Sojoyner, "Dissonance in Time"; Myers, *Cedric Robinson*.
5. Scheflin and Opton, "The Mind Manipulators"; Robitscher, "Psychosurgery and Other Somatic Means of Altering Behavior."
6. Egan, "Gramsci's War of Position as Siege Warfare."
7. US Army, *The U.S. Army Marine Corps Counterinsurgency Field Manual*, 2.
8. Robert F. Williams, "USA: The Potential for a Minority Revolution," *The Crusader* 5, no. 4 (May–June 1964), 6, UPA.
9. Burton, "Captivity, Kinship, and Black Masculine Care Work under Domestic Warfare"; Berger, *Captive Nation*; Berger and Losier, *Rethinking the American Prison Movement*; Rodríguez, *White Reconstruction*; James, *Imprisoned Intellectuals*.
10. BPP/BLA member Albert "Nuh" Washington defined Black as "a political condition, a state of oppression and consciousness, a nation seeking to become, a people who hope" (quoted in Balagoon, *Soldier's Story*, 10). Similarly, anarchist BPP/BLA veteran Ashanti Alston writes, "I think of being Black not so much as an ethnic category but as an oppositional force or touchstone for looking at situations differently. Black culture has always been oppositional

and is all about finding ways to creatively resist oppression here, in the most racist country in the world" ("Black Anarchism"). See Myers, *Cedric Robinson*; Sivanandan, *Communities of Resistance*; Vargas, *Never Meant to Survive*; Vargas, *Catching Hell in the City of Angels*; Vargas and James, "Refusing Blackness-As-Victimization."

11. Fernández, *The Young Lords*, 242.

12. William R. Coons, "An Attica Graduate Tells His Story," *New York Times*, October 10, 1971, 27. My analysis focuses on Black, Latinx, and white people because they constituted the three major groups in the prison during the 1970s. However, as I show in chapter 3, New York prisons also contained a small, but important Native population.

13. Rodriguez, *White Reconstruction*; Wynter, "Unsettling the Coloniality of Being/Truth/Power/Freedom."

14. Burton, "The Minimum Demands." This assertion resonates with William C. Anderson's critique of narratives of Black struggle that focus exclusively on voting rights. "We have ancestors who did indeed fight and die for our right to cast votes. We also have ancestors who died for much more. Here again, historical struggles get forced into a single cohesive narrative, where radical efforts and aberrations can be lost" (*The Nation on No Map*, 10).

15. Rodríguez, *White Reconstruction*, 161; Best and Hartman, "Fugitive Justice"; Hartman, *Scenes of Subjection*.

16. Fanon, *The Wretched of the Earth*; McKittrick, *Sylvia Wynter*.

17. Martin Luther King Jr., "The Other America," April 14, 1967, Civil Rights Movement Archive, accessed October 11, 2022, https://www.crmvet.org/docs/otheram.htm.

18. Che Nieves in conversation with author, 2020.

19. For engagement with the visionary forms of organizing and rebellion taking place in and around women's prisons, see Shakur, *Assata*; Bukhari, *The War Before*; Law, *Resistance Behind Bars*; Diaz-Cotto, *Gender, Ethnicity, and the State*; Davis, *The Angela Y. Davis Reader*, ed. Joy James; Thuma, *All Our Trials*; Richie, *Arrested Justice*; Haley, *No Mercy Here*; Kaba, *We Do This 'Til We Free Us*.

20. Burton, "Captivity, Kinship, and Black Masculine Care Work."

21. Burton, "Attica Is"; Saifee, "Decarceration's Inside Partners"; Simes, *Punishing Places*. For more on Eddie's time at *The Liberator*, see Tinson, *Radical Intellect*; Ahmad, *We Will Return in the Whirlwind*.

22. Eddie Ellis in conversation with author, 2014.

23. Shange, "Abolition in the Clutch"; Sojoyner, *First Strike*; Buck, "Centering Prisons"; Vargas, *The Denial of Antiblackness*; Vargas, *Never Meant to Survive*; Li, "Captive Passages"; Harrison, *Decolonizing Anthropology*; Mullings, "Interrogating Racism"; Allen and Jobson, "The Decolonizing Generation"; Mondlane, *The Struggle for Mozambique*; Berry et al., "Toward a Fugitive Anthropology"; Ihmoud and Cordis, "A Poetics of Living Rebellion."

24. Robinson, *The Terms of Order*; Myers, *Cedric Robinson*.

25. Trouillot, *Silencing the Past*, 23.

26. In addition to Trouillot, my approach to historical ethnography builds on Skurski et al., eds., *The Fernando Coronil Reader*; Zeitlyn, "Anthropology in and of the Archives."

27. Thompson, *Blood in the Water*; Wicker, *A Time to Die*; McKay Commission, *The Official Report of the New York State Special Commission on Attica*; Bell, *The Turkey Shoot*; Zahm, *The Last Graduation*; Lichtenstein, *Ghosts of Attica*.

28. Burton, "Diluting Radical History."

29. For critical engagement with the concept of "conspiracy theory" and its relevance to political analysis, see Cribb, "Introduction: Parapolitics, Shadow Governance, and Criminal Sovereignty"; deHaven-Smith, *Conspiracy Theory in America*; Hellinger, "Paranoia, Conspiracy, and Hegemony."

30. Trouillot, *Silencing the Past*, 26.

31. McGivern, "Attica: Its Meaning and Freedom," Box 24, Folder 12, Gary McGivern and Marguerite Culp Papers, LSL.

32. This book largely forgoes the longstanding debate regarding who qualifies as a political prisoner in the United States. For engagement with this debate, see Committee to End the Marion Lockdown, *Can't Jail the Spirit: Political Prisoners in the US, a Collection of Biographies* (1985), http://freedomarchives.org/Documents/Finder/DOC3_scans/3.cant.jail.spirit.1985.pdf; Esquivel, *Let Freedom Ring*; Fujino, *Heartbeat of Struggle*.

33. Fanon, *The Wretched of the Earth*, 81. For an interesting genealogy of the use of the "spearhead" metaphor among Fanon, the BPP, and Michel Foucault, see Vásquez, "Illegalist Foucault, Criminal Foucault," 491–92.

34. Jackson, *Soledad Brother*, 111–12.

35. Jackson, *Soledad Brother*, 335. For more on Jackson's radical mutation, see James, "George Jackson: Dragon Philosopher and Revolutionary Abolitionist."

36. Berger, *Captive Nation*.

37. Childs, *Slaves of the State*; Davis, "From the Prison of Slavery to the Slavery of Prison"; Muntaqim, "The Perverse Slave Mentality."

38. A number of prison studies scholars have argued that popular perceptions of the scale of prison labor exploitation in the United States far exceed the reality: Gilmore, *Golden Gulag*; Gilmore and Kilgore, "Some Reflections on Prison Labor"; Stein, "Trumpism and the Magnitude of Mass Incarceration." For discussions of slavery as a power relation, see Patterson, *Slavery and Social Death*; Hartman, *Scenes of Subjection*; Rodríguez, *Forced Passages*.

39. Patterson, *Slavery and Social Death*.

40. Neocleous, *War Power, Police Power*, 82; Singh, *Race and America's Long War*; Losurdo, *Liberalism*; Marable, *How Capitalism Underdeveloped Black America*.

41. Neocleous, *War Power, Police Power*.

42. Finkelman, *Supreme Injustice*; Jerry Zilg, "War against Black America," *Workers World* (New York, NY), February 16, 1972, 15.

43. Besteman, Biondi, and Burton, "Authority, Confinement, Solidarity, and Dissent."

44. Equiano, *The Interesting Narrative and Other Writings*, 111.

45. Jacobs, "Incidents in the Life of a Slave Girl," 128; Harney and Moten, *The Undercommons*.

46. C. James, *The Black Jacobins*; Du Bois, *Black Reconstruction in America*; Price, *Maroon Societies*; Genovese, *From Rebellion to Revolution*; V.

Brown, *Tacky's Revolt*; Stanford, "Black Guerilla Warfare Strategy and Tactics"; Horne, *The Counter-Revolution of 1776*.

47. Boggs, *Pages from a Black Radical's Notebook*, 111.

48. Gilmore and Petitjean, "Prisons and Class Warfare." Subsequent research has uncovered the unfolding of similar dynamics in New York, Louisiana, and elsewhere: Norton, "Little Siberia, Star of the North"; Pelot-Hobbs, "The Contested Terrain of the Louisiana Carceral State"; Morrell, "The Prison Fix," 2012.

49. Abu-Lughod, *Race, Space, and Riots*; "New Police Laws Scored At Rally," *New York Times*, March 8, 1964, 63.

50. Feagin and Hahn, *Ghetto Revolts*.

51. R. Allen, *Black Awakening in Capitalist America*.

52. R. Allen, "Reassessing the Internal (Neo) Colonialism Theory"; O'Dell, "The July Rebellions and the Military State"; Carmichael and Hamilton, *Black Power*.

53. Umoja, *We Will Shoot Back*; Cobb, *This Nonviolent Stuff'll Get You Killed*.

54. Newton, *The Huey P. Newton Reader*, 137.

55. Donner, *Protectors of Privilege*.

56. Quoted in Select Comm. to Study Governmental Operations, *Intelligence Activities and the Rights of Americans*, 20. COINTELPRO was first initiated in 1956 to attack the Communist Party USA. However, by 1969, according to this report, "the Black Panthers had become the primary focus of the program, and was ultimately the target of 233 of the total 295 authorized 'Black Nationalist COINTELPRO actions'" (188).

57. Select Comm. to Study Governmental Operations, *Intelligence Activities and the Rights of Americans*, 681–732; Rafalko, *MH/CHAOS*; O'Neill, *Chaos*.

58. Schrader, *Badges without Borders*; Murakawa, *The First Civil Right*; Seigel, *Violence Work*.

59. Wilson and Felber, "The Makings of a Forum."

60. Losier, "Against 'Law and Order' Lockup," 5; Churchill and Vander Wall, *Agents of Repression*; kioni-sadiki and Meyer, *Look for Me in the Whirlwind*; O'Reilly, *"Racial Matters"*; Newton, "War against the Panthers."

61. "300 Camden Police Quell Riot in Jail," *New York Times*, February 18, 1969, 30; "Inmates Stage 8-Hour Riot in Minnesota State Prison," *New York Times*, September 6, 1969, 27; Useem and Kimball, *States of Siege*; Burton, "Organized Disorder."

62. Horne, *The Counter-Revolution of 1776*, 23.

63. American Correctional Association (ACA), *Causes, Preventive Measures, and Methods of Controlling Riots and Disturbances in Correctional Institutions*, 37.

64. ACA, *Causes, Preventive Measures, and Methods of Controlling Riots and Disturbances in Correctional Institutions*.

65. ACA, *Causes, Preventive Measures, and Methods of Controlling Riots and Disturbances in Correctional Institutions*, 38–46.

66. Elizabeth Fink was also the lead attorney representing the Attica Brothers in their criminal defense trial and their civil trial against the state.

67. Boyle, "COINTELPRO."
68. Boyle, "COINTELPRO."
69. Best and Hartman, "Fugitive Justice"; Hartman, *Lose Your Mother*; Hartman, "Venus in Two Acts."
70. Trouillot, *Silencing the Past*; Lowe, *Intimacies of Four Continents*.
71. Balcells and Sullivan, "New Findings from Conflict Archives"; Christianson, "The War Model"; Davenport, *Media Bias, Perspective, and State Repression*; Sojoyner, "You Are Going to Get Us Killed."
72. Director, FBI to SAC, "Re: Black Extremist Activities in Penal Institutions," March 9, 1971, FBI Files, DBW Archive.
73. Director, FBI to SAC, "Re: Black Extremist Activities in Penal Institutions; Racial Matters," August 21, 1970, FBI Files, DBW Archive.
74. Masco, *The Theater of Operations*; West and Sanders, *Transparency and Conspiracy*.
75. Burton, "Targeting Revolutionaries."
76. Gomez, "Resisting Living Death at Marion Federal Penitentiary."
77. J. Jackson, *Racial Paranoia*; Hellinger, "Paranoia, Conspiracy, and Hegemony in American Politics."
78. US Army, *The U.S. Army Marine Corps Counterinsurgency Field Manual*, 23.
79. Kitson, *Low Intensity Operations*; M. Shakur et al., *Genocide Waged against the Black Nation*; Thomas J. Deakin, "The Legacy of Carlos Marighella," *Law Enforcement Bulletin* 43, no. 10 (October 1974), 19; "The Police Officer: Primary Target of the Urban Guerrilla," *Law Enforcement Bulletin* 41, no. 2 (February 1972), 21; "Trends in Urban Guerrilla Tactics," *Law Enforcement Bulletin* 42, no. 7 (July 1973), 3; "Prisons – A Target of Revolutionaries," *Law Enforcement Bulletin* 43, no. 9 (September 1974), 11. Most back issues of *Law Enforcement Bulletin* are available at https://leb.fbi.gov/archives.
80. ACA, *Causes, Preventive Measures, and Methods of Controlling Riots and Disturbances in Correctional Institutions*, 25.
81. Williams, "The Other Side of the Coin"; Paschel, *Becoming Black Political Subjects*, 155; M. Francis, "The Price of Civil Rights"; Diaz-Cotto, *Gender, Ethnicity, and the State*; R. Allen, *Black Awakening in Capitalist America*; Moore, "Strategies of Repression against the Black Movement"; Schrader, "To Secure the Global Great Society"; Marable, *Race, Reform, and Rebellion*; Ferguson, *Top Down*; Kohl-Arenas, *The Self-Help Myth*; Táíwò, *Elite Capture*.
82. Trouillot, "Good Day, Columbus," 105.
83. Paul Linebarger quoted in Hunt, "Project Camelot and Military Sponsorship of Social Science Research," 135. See also Linebarger, "Psychological Warfare."
84. Ricardo DeLeon, "How Are Things in Dannemora?," *Village Voice*, October 7, 1971, 79.
85. McKay Commission, *The Official Report of the New York State Special Commission on Attica*, 18.
86. Paul L. Montgomery, "Inmates Romp and Picnic with Sons as Prison Offers Token of Family Life," *New York Times*, August 13, 1973, 57.

CHAPTER 1. SHARPENING THE SPEAR

1. "US Prisoners Riot," film clip from October 1970, downloaded 2017 from http://www.aparchive.com; Gottehrer, *The Mayor's Man*.
2. "Text of Tombs' Inmates' Grievances," *New York Times*, August 11, 1970, 30.
3. Committee on the Judiciary, *Hearings Before Subcommittee No. 3*, statement of William Vanden Heuvel, 26.
4. Burton, "Organized Disorder."
5. Shanahan, *Captives*, 144.
6. Martin Arnold, "Tombs: An Ideal Breeding Ground for Riots," *New York Times*, August 16, 1970, 144.
7. Losier, "Against 'Law and Order' Lockup," 5.
8. President's Commission on Law Enforcement and Administration of Justice, *The Challenge of Crime in a Free Society*, 131.
9. "The Prison Insurrections BB4000," produced by Bob Kuttner and Bruce Soloway, April 8, 1971, PRA; Arnold, "Tombs."
10. Brenda Hyson, "There Is No Prison, Either on an Island. . .," *The Black Panther* 5, No. 11 (Oakland, CA), September 12, 1970, 13.
11. Michael T. Kaufman, "Ex-Prisoner at Tombs Feels Close to Cellmates," *New York Times*, August 19, 1970, 22.
12. Kaufman, "Ex-Prisoner at Tombs Feels Close to Cellmates."
13. John J. McCarthy to Kenneth O'Dell, "RE: Casper Baker Gary," May 11, 1972, Non-Criminal Investigation Files, Box 39, Folder 238-D-3-19, NYSA.
14. Casper Baker Gary, "Prisoners Injustice Resistance and Survival Manual," November 4, 1969, A0795-80, Non-Criminal Investigation Files, Box 39, Folder 238-D-3-19, NYSA, 15.
15. Gary, "Prisoners Injustice Resistance and Survival Manual," 1.
16. Gary, "Prisoners Injustice Resistance and Survival Manual," 2.
17. Barnett and Njama, *Mau Mau from Within*; James, *The Black Jacobins*.
18. Gary, "Prisoners Injustice Resistance and Survival Manual," 15–16.
19. "A Talk with Martinez, Hunted Ex-Inmate," *The Black Panther* 4, no. 29 (Oakland, CA), January 16, 1971.
20. "A Talk with Martinez, Hunted Ex-Inmate," 4.
21. Hyson, "There Is No Prison, Either on an Island," 13.
22. Ray Schultz, "Riot in the Tombs," *East Village Other* (New York, NY), August 18, 1970, 12.
23. "Prisoners in Tombs Riot for Second Day," *New York Times*, August 12, 1970, 1.
24. Newton, *The Huey P. Newton Reader*, 148.
25. Melvin Alston in conversation with author, 2020; Francis X. Clines, "Tombs Prisoners Boycott Hearings," *New York Times*, August 18, 1970, 1.
26. Melvin Alston in conversation with author, 2020.
27. Melvin Alston in conversation with author, 2020.
28. "Jail Guards Push Plan on Security: Mass Resignation Threat Backs Demands to Enter Cells to Seek Weapons." *New York Times*, August 19, 1970, 22.

29. Curtis Brown, interview by Bruce Soloway, *The Tombs Trial/Curtis Brown*, August 21, 1972, PRA.

30. United Press International, "J. Edgar Hoover: Black Panther Greatest Threat to U.S. Security," July 6, 1967, https://www.upi.com/Archives/1969/07/16/J-Edgar-Hoover-Black-Panther-Greatest-Threat-to-US-Security/1571551977068.

31. Churchill, "The Other Kind," 191.

32. Director, FBI to SAC, "Black Extremist Activity in Penal Institutions," August 21, 1970, 1, FBI Files, DBW Archive.

33. Zimroth, *Perversions of Justice*, 23.

34. Shakur, *Assata*, 205.

35. Chevigny, *Cops and Rebels*; Burton, "Revolution Is Illegal"; kioni-sadiki and Meyer, *Look for Me in the Whirlwind*.

36. kioni-sadiki and Meyer, *Look for Me in the Whirlwind*, 497.

37. kioni-sadiki and Meyer, *Look for Me in the Whirlwind*, 497.

38. Mondlane, *The Struggle for Mozambique*, 146.

39. kioni-sadiki and Meyer, *Look for Me in the Whirlwind*, 500; John Sibley, "Prisoners Seize Hostages, Take Over Jail in Queens," *New York Times*, October 2, 1970, 1.

40. Liberation News Service, "Revolt Explodes in City Prisons," *Liberated Guardian*, October 19, 1970.

41. "US Prisoners Riot"; Gottehrer, *The Mayor's Man*; Victor Martinez quoted in Liberation News Service, "Revolt Explodes in City Prisons," 16.

42. Curtis Brown, interviewed by Bruce Soloway.

43. Ricardo DeLeon, "Rebellion in the Tombs: An Inmate's Chronicle," *Village Voice*, November 5, 1970.

44. DeLeon, "Rebellion in the Tombs," 9; Curtis Brown, interviewed by Bruce Soloway.

45. Robert D. McFadden, "Prisoners Rebel in 2 More Jails; 23 Held Hostage," *New York Times*, October 3, 1970, 1.

46. Robert D. McFadden, "Rioting Spreads to a Fourth Jail; 5 Hostages Freed," *New York Times*, October 4, 1970, 1.

47. Mazza and McFadden, "Ask to Form 'Congress of Inmates,'" *New York Daily News*, October 4, 1970, 3; kioni-sadiki and Meyer, *Look for Me in the Whirlwind*, 502.

48. DeLeon, "Rebellion in the Tombs," 11.

49. "The Prison Insurrections BB4000."

50. Untitled letter signed by the Time Men, Valvano et al. v. McGrath et al., NARA.

51. kioni-sadiki and Meyer, *Look for Me in the Whirlwind*, 502.

52. Reese and Sbicca, "Food and Carcerality"; Hatch, "Billions Served."

53. Umoja, "Maroon," 208.

54. Gary, "Prisoners Injustice Resistance and Survival Manual," 15–16.

55. Donald Flynn and William McFadden, "Hostage Lives Threatened, Judge Talks with Inmates," *New York Daily News*, October 3, 1970, 3.

56. Gottehrer, *The Mayor's Man*, 268.

57. Gottehrer, *The Mayor's Man*, 268; *New York Daily News*, "4th Jail Erupts; 26 Hostages Held," October 4, 1970, 126.

58. Gottehrer, *The Mayor's Man*, 268; *New York Daily News*, "4th Jail Erupts."

59. Gerald Lefcourt in conversation with author, 2017; Umoja, "Maroon," 208; kioni-sadiki and Meyer, *Look for Me in the Whirlwind*.

60. Gilberto Jimenez, "We Must Fight to Be Free," *Palante* (New York, NY), October 30, 1970, 15.

61. Jimenez, "We Must Fight to Be Free," 15.

62. Badillo and Haynes, *A Bill of No Rights*, 21.

63. kioni-sadiki and Meyer, *Look for Me in the Whirlwind*, 502.

64. Gerald Lefcourt in conversation with author, 2017.

65. Black, *Radical Lawyers*; Lefcourt, *Law against the People*.

66. Hall, "Gramsci's Relevance for the Study of Race and Ethnicity."

67. Balbus, "Commodity Form and Legal Form," 581.

68. "People's Tribunals," *The Black Panther* (Oakland, CA), June 27, 1970, 12; "Plenary Session," *The Black Panther* (Oakland, CA), September 5, 1970, 11.

69. Dhoruba bin-Wahad in conversation with author, 2020.

70. Unknown incarcerated person quoted in "The Prison Insurrections BB4000."

71. Robinson, *Black Marxism*.

72. Robinson, *Black Marxism*, 168–69.

73. On policing as violence, see Fanon, *The Wretched of the Earth*.

74. Gottehrer, *The Mayor's Man*.

75. Sostre, "The New Prisoner," 253.

76. Gottehrer, *The Mayor's Man*.

77. Robert D. McFadden, "Tombs Prisoners Free 17 as Mayor Warns of Force," *New York Times*, October 5, 1970, 48.

78. Gottehrer, *The Mayor's Man*, 272.

79. "Testimony of Ralph Valvano," Valvano et al. v. McGrath et al., NARA.

80. DeLeon, "Rebellion in the Tombs," 11.

81. Robinson, *Black Marxism*, 168.

82. kioni-sadiki and Meyer, *Look for Me in the Whirlwind*, 509.

83. Fanon, *The Wretched of the Earth*.

84. Woods, *Development Arrested*.

85. kioni-sadiki and Meyer, *Look for Me in the Whirlwind*, 504.

86. Sekou Odinga quoted in Balagoon, *Soldier's Story*, 56; Gilbert and Berger, "Grief and Organizing in the Face of Repression"; Umoja, "Maroon," 56–57; Balagun, "Kuwasi at 60."

87. Bloom and Martin, *Black against Empire*.

88. "Open Letter to Weatherman Underground from Panther 21," *The East Village Other*, January 19, 1971, 20.

89. "Open Letter to Weatherman Underground," 3 and 20.

90. kioni-sadiki and Meyer, *Look for Me in the Whirlwind*, 510.

91. Magistrate's Report, Valvano et al. v. McGrath et al, 17, NARA.

92. "Report of the Special Prosecutor," Valvano et al. v. McGrath et al., 22, NARA; Woodard, *The Delectable Negro*.

93. Derrida, *Archive Fever*; Sutherland, "The Carceral Archive"; Browne, *Dark Matters*.

94. Belew, "Bring the War Home."

95. Report of Magistrate Vincent A. Catoggio, Valvano et al. v. McGrath et al., NARA.

96. "Report of the Special Prosecutor," Valvano et al. v. McGrath et al., 3, NARA.

97. The names of these four dead men were Raymond Lavone Moore, Julio Roldan, Jose Perez, and Anibal Davila. See "Justice Not Genocide," *Palante* (New York, NY), December 11, 1970, 8; Interim Findings and Order, Valvano et al. v. McGrath et al., NARA; Fernández, *The Young Lords*; Mbembe, "Necropolitics."

98. Gerald Lefcourt in conversation with author, 2017.

99. "Open Letter to Weatherman Underground from Panther 21," 20.

100. These tactics were forms of "unarmed militancy." See C. Bjork-James, "Unarmed Militancy."

101. McFadden, "Rioting Spreads to a Fourth Jail; 5 Hostages Freed," 77.

102. Chevigny, *Cops and Rebels*, 201–2.

103. kioni-sadiki and Meyer, *Look for Me in the Whirlwind*; Burton, "Revolution Is Illegal."

104. The Tombs 3 began as the Tombs Seven. This included Herbert X Blyden, Curtis Brown, Louis Cabrera, Ricardo DeLeon, Stanley King, Franklyn Myers, and Nathaniel Ragsdale. Daniel O'Connor was also indicted but was not included in the Tombs Seven because he did not receive a kidnapping charge. A guard, Earl D. Whittaker, was also indicted for encouraging the revolt. See Juan M. Vasquez, "Guard Is Indicted with 8 Prisoners in Riots at Tombs: Guard and 8 Inmates Indicted in October Rioting at the Tombs," *New York Times*, January 26, 1971, 1; Baer and Bepko, "A Necessary and Proper Role for Federal Courts in Prison Reform."

105. Balbus, "Commodity Form and Legal Form"; Balbus, *The Dialectics of Legal Repression*; Zimroth, *Perversions of Justice*; Lefcourt, *Law against the People*; Black, *Radical Lawyers*.

106. Ricardo DeLeon quoted in "Tombs Three Acquittal—Only A Skirmish," *Lumpen Grapevine*, n.d., DBW Archive.

107. Ricardo DeLeon, "How Are Things in Dannemora?," *Village Voice*, October 7, 1971, 79.

108. Balagoon quoted in Umoja, "Maroon," 209; Chevigny, *Cops and Rebels*.

109. Quoted in US Congress, *Revolutionary Activities Directed toward the Administration of Penal or Correctional Systems* (Testimony of Robert J. Henderson), 140; NY DOCS, *Annual Report 1970* (Albany: State of New York Department of Correctional Services, 1970), 16, NYSA; Linda Greenhouse, "Sing Sing Prepares for Tombs Inmates," *New York Times*, August 22, 1970, 35; Arnold H. Lubasch, "Mayor Urges State to Take Sentenced Prisoners," *New York Times*, August 12, 1970, 52; Michael T. Kaufman, "The City Is Quietly Transferring 500 Inmates to Upstate Prisons," *New York Times*, October 12, 1970, 30.

CHAPTER 2. BLACK SOLIDARITY UNDER SIEGE

1. Berger, "Subjugated Knowledges"; Sutherland, "The Carceral Archive"; Sutherland, "Disrupting Carceral Narratives"; Sojoyner, "You Are Going to Get Us Killed."

2. Herre, "The History of Auburn Prison from the Beginning to about 1867," 102.

3. Foucault, *Discipline and Punish*, 179.

4. Hall et al., *Policing the Crisis*, 61.

5. Untitled document, August 20, 1974, Box 5, Folder: Jomo BPP Prison Movement, Jomo Joka Omowale Papers, 1969–2008, DMR.

6. Borges, *Militant Education, Liberation Struggle, Consciousness*, 20; Hall, "Constituting an Archive."

7. Césaire, *Discourse on Colonialism*.

8. Fanon, *The Wretched of the Earth*, 1–20.

9. Césaire, *Discourse on Colonialism*, 73.

10. McKay Commission, *The Official Report of the New York State Special Commission on Attica*; Useem and Kimball, *States of Siege*; Berger and Losier, *Rethinking the American Prison Movement*; Thompson, *Blood in the Water*; Burton, "Diluting Radical History."

11. Charles Leon Hill quoted in Michael T. Kaufman, "Troubles Persist in Prison at Auburn," *New York Times*, May 17, 1971, 44. The statement appears exactly as transcribed by the *Times*.

12. Gramsci, Hoare, and Nowell-Smith, *Selections from the Prison Notebooks*; Egan, "Gramsci's War of Position as Siege Warfare"; Hall, "Gramsci's Relevance for the Study of Race and Ethnicity."

13. Fanon, *The Wretched of the Earth*, 178.

14. Foucault et al., "The Masked Assassination," 141.

15. "Auburn Correction Files 1967–1970" and "Auburn Prison Report of Inspection September 1967," Nelson A. Rockefeller Papers Gubernatorial Records, Office Subject Files, Third Administration, Subseries 37.3, RAC.

16. Leo W. O'Brien, *A Comprehensive Report Relating to the Disturbance at Auburn*, Nelson A. Rockefeller Papers Gubernatorial Records, Counsel's Office, Series 10 (FA358), Subseries 4, Box 44, Folder 464, RAC.

17. Smoake v. Fritz, Affidavit of Harry Fritz, 70 Civ 5103, 2, NARA.

18. Quoted in Michael T. Kaufman, "Rising Protests and Lawsuits Shake Routine in State Prisons," *New York Times*, November 11, 1970, 79.

19. NYS DOC Superintendent's Proceeding for Charles Hill, Box 1, Folder: Attica/Auburn Correction Files, 1970–1972, Jomo Joka Omowale Papers, 1969–2008, DMR.

20. Smoake v. Fritz, Affidavit of Harry Fritz, 70 Civ 5103, 2, NARA.

21. O'Brien, *A Comprehensive Report Relating to the Disturbance at Auburn*, 4, NAR.

22. Smoake v. Fritz, Affidavit of Harry Fritz, 3; New York State Senate Committee on Crime and Correction, *The Hidden Society* (Albany, NY), 1970, 14, NYSL.

23. New York State Senate Committee on Crime and Correction, *The Hidden Society*, 14.

24. New York State Senate Committee on Crime and Correction, *The Hidden Society*, 14; Superintendents Proceeding Formal Charges and Affidavit of Joseph Fornish, Box 1, Folder: Attica Trial 1971–1974, Jomo Joka Omowale Papers, 1969–2008, DMR.

25. Kaufman, "Rising Protests and Lawsuits," 1.

26. Anthropologist David Scott defines counter-memory as "the moral idiom and semiotic registers of remembering against the grain of the history of New World black deracination, subjection, and exclusion" ("Introduction," vi).

27. Prisoners Solidarity Committee, *Prisoners Call Out: Freedom* (New York, NY), 13. In author's possession.

28. Hassan Sharrief El-Shabazz, "Hassan of Auburn 6 Speaks," *Prisoner's Solidarity Committee Newsletter on Attica* #2, September 30, 1971, 4, Box 7, Folder: Workers World Party (3 of 3), House Committee on Internal Security, UVA.

29. "Hassan of Auburn 6 Speaks," 4.

30. *Prisoners Call Out: Freedom*, 13.

31. Interview with Mariano "Dalou" Gonzalez by Michael D. Ryan, Dean Albertson Oral History Collection, USC, 14.

32. "Auburn Is Quiet after Outbreak," *New York Times*, November 6, 1970, 83; "Auburn Prison Under Siege Five Hours," *Citizen Advertiser* (Auburn, NY), November 5, 1970, 1, NYSL; Ronald Maiorana, "Statement by Governor Rockefeller," Press Release, November 4, 1970, Nelson A. Rockefeller Papers Gubernatorial Records, Office Subject Files, Third Administration, Subseries 37.3, RAC.

33. McKay Commission, *The Official Report of the New York State Special Commission on Attica*, 129–30. This narrative is repeated in Useem and Kimball, *States of Siege*.

34. Thompson, *Blood in the Water*, 24.

35. Gloria Gonzalez, "Rebelion en la Prison Auburn," *Palante* (New York, NY), November 20, 1970, 11.

36. Kaufman, "Troubles Persist in Prison at Auburn," 37.

37. "YAWF Prisoners Solidarity Committee Launches Campaign to Abolish Concentration Camps," *Workers World* 13, no. 3, 9; "What Is the Prisoners Solidarity Committee?," *Prisoners Solidarity Committee Newsletter on Attica*, no. 1, September 17, 1971, 3, Box 7, Folder: Workers World Party (3 of 3). House Committee on Internal Security. UVA; Prisoners Solidarity Committee, "Fight for Freedom." Archived issues of *Workers World* are available at the Kenneth Spencer Research Library at the University of Kansas.

38. Robert Henderson Testimony, Revolutionary Activities Directed Toward the Administration of Penal or Correctional Systems," March 29, 1973, 134–35.

39. The official name of this prison is Great Meadow. However, it is popularly known as Comstock after the town in which it is located, and I adopt this convention throughout.

40. O'Brien, *A Comprehensive Report Relating to the Disturbance at Auburn*; "Superintendent Fritz reports on lockup, transfer of inmates." *Citizen Advertiser* (Auburn, NY), November 12, 1970, 3.

41. "Prisoners Cry Out for Justice," *Workers World* 13, no. 2 (1971): 8.

42. "Auburn Prisoners Tell Story of Repression," *Workers World* 13, no. 1 (1971): 15.

43. Luk, *The Life of Paper*.
44. *Prisoners Call Out: Freedom*, "All Power to the People," 19.
45. O'Brien, *A Comprehensive Report Relating to the Disturbance at Auburn*, 7.
46. Alim, "Struggle at Auburn Prison"; "Hearings Before the Select Comm. on Correctional Institutions and Programs," 65–66 (1972) (Testimony James Killebrew and Michael Lewis), NYSL; *Prisoners Call Out: Freedom*.
47. Robert Kareem Clarke, "Dannemora: These Pits of Hell," *Village Voice*, September 30, 1971, 10.
48. *Prisoners Call Out: Freedom*, 20.
49. *Prisoners Call Out: Freedom*, 13.
50. *Prisoners Call Out: Freedom*, 24.
51. Wynter, "No Humans Involved," 110.
52. Fanon, *The Wretched of the Earth*, 42.
53. The New York State Advisory Committee to the US Commission on Civil Rights, *Warehousing Human Beings*, 14.
54. Fanon, *The Wretched of the Earth*, 10.
55. "Rules and Regulations of the BPP," attachment to O'Brien, *A Comprehensive Report Relating to the Disturbance at Auburn*.
56. "To the Commissioner of Correctional Services from Superintendent Harry Fritz, January 12, 1971," Box 1, Folder: Attica Trial 1971–1974. Jomo Joka Omowale Papers, 1969–2008, DMR.
57. Alim, "Struggle at Auburn Prison," 53.
58. Jackson, Wald, and Churchill, "Remembering the Real Dragon," 180.
59. Alim, "Struggle at Auburn Prison."
60. Alim, "Struggle at Auburn Prison."
61. Brother A in conversation with author, 2019.
62. Jackson, *Soledad Brother*, 265.
63. Brother A in conversation with author, 2019.
64. *Ithaca Journal*, "Conditions Chaotic Since Prison Riot?," March 11, 1971, 8.
65. Quoted in "Prisoners Cry out for Justice!," *Workers World*, January 29, 1971, 9.
66. Brother A in conversation with author, 2019.
67. Quoted in "In Solidarity with Attica from Other POWs," *Right On!* 1, no. 6. (New York, NY), n.d. [October 1971], 7.
68. Reyes, "On Fanon's Manichean Delirium."
69. NYSP Surveillance, Non-Criminal Investigation Files, NYSA, A0795080.
70. Kareem C'Allah in conversation with author, 2022; "Inmates State Disturbance in Cayuga Court," *Wellsville Daily Reporter*, February 11, 1971, 10; Emily Hanlon, "Inside a Nazi Court with the Auburn Prisoners," *Workers World* (New York, NY), February 12, 1971. During our conversation, Kareem wondered aloud whether he or George Jackson was the first to fight the authorities in a courtroom during this era.
71. Letter signed by Pamela Bayer, Elizabeth Fisher, Elizabeth Gaynes, Joel Gorham, and Lew Oliver, n.d., Box 1, Attica/Auburn–Department of Correction files; 1970-1972. Jomo Joka Omowale Papers, 1969 – 2008, DMR.

72. Del Ray, "Lewis and Clark Saga Ends," *Democrat and Chronicle* (Rochester, NY), June 16, 1972, 22.

73. O'Brien, *A Comprehensive Report Relating to the Disturbance at Auburn*, 6.

74. "To the Commissioner of Correctional Services from Superintendent Harry Fritz, January 12, 1971." Box 1, Folder: Attica Trial 1971–1974, Jomo Joka Omowale Papers, 1969–2008, DMR.

75. George Jackson, "George Jackson: P.S., On Discipline," *The Black Panther* 6, no. 9, March 27, 1971, 6.

76. Jomo Omowale, Mariano Gonzales, and James "Alsayah Allah" Brown, ministers of the Black Panthers, Young Lords, and Five Percenters, respectively, were transferred to Attica, along with Tommy Hicks, Harold "Blood" Thomas, and others. Two of the ringleaders, Earl Smoake and David Walker, were transferred to Green Haven because they had recently been in Attica where, in July of 1970, they helped organize a labor strike in the metal shop.

77. "Superintendent's Hearing Transcript for Jomo Sekou Omowale," Jomo Joka Omowale Papers, 1969–2008, Box 1, Folder: Attica Trial 1971–1974, DMR.

78. My thinking on this question is deeply informed by Césaire, *Discourse on Colonialism*; Fanon, *Black Skin, White Masks*; Fanon, *The Wretched of the Earth*; McKittrick, *Sylvia Wynter*; Robinson, *Black Marxism*; Robinson, *The Terms of Order*; Wynter, "Unsettling the Coloniality of Being/Power/Truth/Freedom."

79. Best and Hartman, "Fugitive Justice," 9.

80. Wynter, "We Know Where We Are From."

81. Getachew, *Worldmaking after Empire*; Walters, *Pan Africanism in the African Diaspora*.

82. Onaci, *Free the Land*, 83.

83. Emani Davis in conversation with author, 2020.

84. Robinson, *Black Marxism*, 171.

85. Jomo Omowale, "Inner View," *Awakening of a Dragon: Attica Brother Jomo*. Attica Bond to Free Jomo (Buffalo, NY), n.d, IA.

86. Omowale, "Inner View."

87. Spillers, "Mama's Baby, Papa's Maybe," 67; Weheliye, *Habeas Viscus*.

88. Larry White in conversation with author, 2014.

89. Larry White in conversation with author, 2018.

90. *Prisoners Call Out: Freedom*, "First Letter to My Son," 43.

91. *Prisoners Call Out: Freedom*, "First Letter to My Son," 44.

92. Larry White and son in conversation with author, 2018.

93. Ihmoud and Cordis, "A Poetics of Living Rebellion," 814.

94. Robinson, *The Terms of Order*, 38; Mirzoeff, *The Right to Look*; Browne, *Dark Matters*; Fanon, *Black Skin, White Masks*.

95. McKittrick, "Rebellion/Invention/Groove," 81.

96. Redmond, *Anthem*, 1. See also Moten, *In the Break*; Kelley, *Freedom Dreams*; Kelley, *Africa Speaks, America Answers*; Vargas, *Never Meant to Survive*; Ball, *I Mix What I Like*; Woods, *Development Arrested*.

97. L. D. Barkley in Wicker, *A Time to Die*, 319.

98. Fanon, *The Wretched of the Earth*, 28.
99. Myers, *Cedric Robinson*, 187.
100. Woodfox, *Solitary*.
101. W. Kelley, *A Different Drummer*. See also Woodfox, *Solitary*. Interestingly, when it was established in 1969, Carlos Russell, the creator of Black Solidarity Day, drew inspiration from another work of literature, a play entitled "Day of Absence" in which residents of another fictional Southern town vanish, leaving the white majority befuddled and helpless.
102. "Prison Superintendent Lists Changes, Return to Normalcy," *Citizen Advertiser* (Auburn, NY), June 9, 1971.
103. Ricardo DeLeon, "A Letter to the People from inside Maximum," *Right On!*, n.d., 8. Periodicals 001, Box 373, TA; Brother A in conversation with author, 2019; *American Prisons in Turmoil Part II* (Testimony of Herman Schwartz), 1106.
104. "Voices from Inside," Attica Defense Committee, 1972, 24. In author's possession.
105. Sr. Investigator J. E. Connolly to Judge R. E. Fischer, "Interview with Jack Florence re Conspiracy Aspects of the Attica Riot 9/9–13/71," February 16, 1973, Box 5, Folder: Attica Trial/Bobby Seale, Jomo Joka Omowale Papers, 1969–2008, DMR.
106. Berger, *Captive Nation*; Burton, "Targeting Revolutionaries"; Durden-Smith, *Who Killed George Jackson?*
107. Jalil Muntaqim in conversation with author, 2022.
108. Carl Jones-El, "We Are Attica: Interviews with Prisoners from Attica," *Attica Defense Committee*, 1972, in author's possession.

CHAPTER 3. ATTICA IS

1. "Three Categories of Protestors," Hornberger Slides: L2010.23.014.jpg, H-210.30_VF, Attica Collection, NYSM.
2. Burton, "Diluting Radical History."
3. Thompson, *Blood in the Water*, 28.
4. Burton, "Diluting Radical History."
5. Institute of the Black World, *Black Analysis for the Seventies*, 6.
6. "To the People," Box 5, Folder: Attica Trial Misc 1972–1974, Jomo Joka Omowale Papers, 1969–2008, DMR.
7. Wicker, *A Time to Die*.
8. Hill and Ekanawetak, *Splitting the Sky*, 19.
9. Boggs and Boggs, *Revolution and Evolution in the Twentieth Century*, 16–19.
10. "Rockefeller's Mylai," *Worker's World* (New York, NY), September 17, 1971, 13.
11. Allen, *Black Awakening in Capitalist America*; Getachew, *Worldmaking after Empire*; Nkrumah, *Neocolonialism*.
12. Sostre, "The New Prisoner."
13. Melville, *Letters from Attica*, 169.

14. Anderson, *The Nation on No Map*; Samudzi and Anderson, *As Black As Resistance*.

15. Jackson, *Soledad Brother*; Jackson, *Blood in my Eye*.

16. Carl Jones-El interview with Attica Defense Committee, *Voices from Inside: 7 Interviews with Attica Prisoners*, 1972, in author's possession.

17. Marx, *The Civil War in France*, 56.

18. Interestingly, Bugs's friend was the late Eddie Ellis, who was then working as a clerk in Attica's school and who sent me down the path that resulted in this book.

19. Brother A in conversation with author, 2019; Tyrone Larkins in conversation with author, 2019; Larry White in conversation with author, 2019; Sekou Odinga in conversation with author, 2017; Prisoners Solidarity Committee, "Oppressed Bury Their Dead," *Prisoner's Solidarity Committee Newsletter on Attica*, no. 2, September 30, 1971, 2, Box 7, Folder: Workers World Party (3 of 3), House Committee on Internal Security, UVA; Testimony of Leon Jenkins, Appendix I, Akil Al-Jundi v. Vincent Mancussi et al., 63.

20. Hill and Ekanawetak, *Splitting the Sky*, 19. Bugs takes exception to Dacajeweiah's claim of Melville's involvement in the initial moments of the rebellion. He recalls witnessing Melville being released from solitary confinement and joining the rebellion much later. It is possible that Dacajeweiah embellished this detail to heighten the symbolism of multiracial rebellion. Of course, Bugs could have misremembered. Ultimately, the question of Melville's early involvement is of limited historical significance, as it was the state and not the rebels who were to blame for the eruption.. As Richard X Clark, a NOI leader who will soon enter the narrative, explains: "I'll tell you what caused the riot at Attica: Attica . . . The conditions that existed there made it inevitable" (Clark and Levitt, *The Brothers of Attica*, 3).

21. Hill and Ekanawetak, *Splitting the Sky*, 19.

22. McKay Commission, *The Official Report of the New York State Special Commission on Attica*, 187.

23. Fanon, *The Wretched of the Earth*, 6.

24. Bugs in conversation with author, 2020.

25. Haley, *No Mercy Here*, 200.

26. Roger Champen in conversation with Tom Wicker, Box 15, Folder 23, SHC.

27. Interview with Charles Ray Carpenter, McKay Commission Transcript, New York City Public Hearings, April 19, 1972, PM, 653, htttp://www.talkinghistory.org/attica.

28. Testimony of Akil Al-Jundi, Al-Jundi et al. v. Rockefeller et al. Civ 75-132, November 12, 1991, 3620.

29. Testimony of Herbert X Blyden, Al-Jundi et al. v. Rockefeller et al. Civ 75-132, November 7, 1991, 3120.

30. Wicker, *A Time to Die*, 24.

31. Gilmore, "Abolition Geography," 231.

32. Johnston, *Evidence of the Evidence*, 2018.

33. Joy James, "Architects of Abolition," lecture, Brown University, Providence, RI, May 6, 2019, https://www.youtube.com/watch?v=z9rvRsWKDxo.

34. Jomo Omowale, "To the People," Box 5, Folder: Attica Trial Misc 1972–1974, Jomo Joka Omowale Papers, 1969–2008, DMR.

35. Fanon, *The Wretched of the Earth*, 130.

36. Other elected spokesmen included Jerry "The Jew" Rosenberg and Flip Crowley.

37. McKay Commission, *The Official Report of the New York State Special Commission on Attica*, 198–200, 39.

38. McKay Commission, *The Official Report of the New York State Special Commission on Attica*, 197, 265, 87.

39. The concept of Democratic Centralism is attributed to Vladimir Lenin. It involves the facilitation of public participation and debate on issues (democracy) and the implementation of a given course of action via a centralized authority, which delivers decisions binding to all members (centralism). Antonio Gramsci writes, "Democratic centralism offers an elastic formula, which can be embodied in many diverse forms; it comes alive in so far as it is interpreted and continually adapted to necessity" (Gramsci, Hoare, and Smith, *Selections from the Prison Notebooks*, 189). For an internal critique of Democratic Centralism within radical organizations, see Cox, *Just Another Nigger*, 205, and Ervin, *Anarchy and the Black Revolution*, 51–52. While Cox suggests that Democratic Centralism is a good idea in theory, Ervin maintains that it is inherently corrupt and authoritarian.

40. Testimony of Herbert X Blyden, Al-Jundi et al. v. Rockefeller et al. Civ 75-132, November 7, 1991, 3114. Several of the "outside observers" commented on the strength of D yard's democracy. Congressman Arthur O. Eve told the commission that the men in D yard strove to make decisions "totally together"; see New York State Special Commission on Attica, Public Hearings, New York, NY, April 21, 1972, 10:30 a.m., 1028. Law professor Herman Schwartz referred to D yard as a "true democracy"; see New York State Special Commission on Attica, Public Hearings, New York, NY, April 18, 1972, 1:00 p.m., 550. Radical lawyer William Kunstler called it an "Athenian democracy"; see New York State Special Commission on Attica, Public Hearings, New York, NY, April 21, 1972, 2:00 p.m., 1187. All are available at http://www.talkinghistory.org/attica/mckay.html.

41. Jomo Omowale, Untitled 1, Box 4, Folder: Attica Trial—Correspondence 1975–ND, Jomo Joka Omowale Papers, 1969–2008, DMR.

42. Jomo Omowale, Untitled 2, Box 4, Folder: Attica Trial—Correspondence 1975–ND, Jomo Joka Omowale Papers, 1969–2008, DMR.

43. Tyrone Larkins in conversation with author, 2019.

44. Wiggins, "The Truth about Attica by an Inmate," 330.

45. In interviews with Attica survivors it was suggested that while Schwartz and Hess were killed for being traitors, Privitera was murdered because he witnessed the killings and could not be trusted to keep his mouth shut about what he saw. Tyrone Larkins in conversation with author, 2019; Bugs in conversation with author, 2020; "Hour-by-Hour; A Misunderstanding Sparked Attica Prison Uprising," *New York Times*, October 4, 1971, 1; Clark and Levitt, *The Brothers of Attica*, 96–100; Wiggins, "The Truth about Attica by an Inmate."

46. Davis, *Are Prisons Obsolete?*, 8.

47. Mariano "Dalou" Gonzalez, interview by Michael D. Ryan, Dean Albertson Oral History Collection, RSC, 13–14.

48. Blyden and Moore, "Richard Dharuba [sic] Moore," *Babylon*, December 15, 1971, 10,

49. Burton, "Targeting Revolutionaries." People like Tommy Hicks, Sam Melville, and L.D. Barkley, who considered themselves revolutionaries, were assassinated in D yard on September 13. Others, like Dalou Gonzalez, Bernard "Shango" Stroble, and Charles "Rabb" Parker, died under questionable circumstances after being released. Jomo Omowale, Dacajeweiah Hill, Herbert X Blyden, and Akil Al-Jundi have died of natural causes. Many others are still alive and still struggling.

50. Brown, *Tacky's Revolt*.

51. Umoja, "Repression Breeds Resistance."

52. A. Shakur, *Assata*, 227; Muntaqim, *We Are Our Own Liberators*; "Message to the Black Movement: A Political Statement from the Black Underground" (~1976), in Black Liberation Army, 1973-1992. The Black Power Movement Part 3: Papers of the Revolutionary Action Movement, 1963 – 1996. UPA.

53. Zayd Malik Shakur, "Introduction" to *The New Urban Guerrilla*, Box 14, PE036 Orgs., TA.

54. A. Shakur, *Assata*, 169.

55. A. Shakur, *Assata*, 52.

56. Kareem C'Allah in conversation with author, 2022; James "Blood" McCreary in conversation with author, 2021; Dhoruba bin-Wahad in conversation with author, 2020.

57. Robert E. Tomasson, "Grenade Wrecks Police Car Here: Blast Hurts 2 Patrolmen—4 Fugitives Escape," *New York Times*, December 21, 1971, 33; Eric Pace, "Police See More Military Arms in Use," *New York Times*, December 27, 1971, 10.

58. "Writings Confiscated from the Cell of Tyrone Larkins," Tyrone B. Larkins v. Russell G. Oswald. 510 F.2d. 583 (2nd cir 1975), Western District of New York, Georgetown University Digital Repository, http://hdl.handle.net/10822/1049726; Tyrone Larkins in conversation with author, 2019.

59. Tyrone Larkins in conversation with author, 2019.

60. Bugs in conversation with author, 2020.

61. "Rockefeller's Mylai"; "War in Attica," *Time Magazine*, September 27, 1971.

62. Thompson, *Blood in the Water*; Bell, *The Turkey Shoot*; McKay Commission, *The Official Report of the New York State Special Commission on Attica*.

63. Testimony of Jerome O'Grady, Al-Jundi v. Rockefeller, Civ No. 75-132, November 25, 1991, p. 5555.

64. Testimony of Franklin Davenport, Al-Jundi v. Rockefeller, Civ No. 75-132, November 7, 1991, p. 3014.

65. "NYSP Explosives Report," November 12, 1971, NYSM; Attica Transcription: Walter Hornberger, interview by Craig Williams, December 1, 2010, 1, NYSM.

66. "NYSP Explosives Report"; Attica Transcription: Walter Hornberger, interview by Craig Williams, December 1 2010, 1, NYSM; State Trooper Franklin

Paul Davenport testified that the Molotov cocktails he found in D yard were filled with cottonseed oil (Al-Jundi v. Rockefeller, Civ No. 75-132, November 6, 1991, 2923).

67. Clark and Levitt, *The Brothers of Attica*, 31.

68. "Spring Came Early This Year: A Message from the Black Liberation Army," *Right On!*, April 5, 1972.

69. Clark and Levitt, *The Brothers of Attica*, 34, 53.

70. Fanon, *The Wretched of the Earth*, 51, 89, 232.

71. Mariano "Dalou" Gonzalez, interview by Michael D. Ryan, 14; Mao Tse-Tung, "The Present Situation and Our Tasks," https://www.marxists.org/reference/archive/mao/selected-works/volume-4/mswv4_24.htm.

72. Interview with Warren Harry, McKay Commission Transcript, New York City Public Hearings, April 18, 1972, AM, 308, htttp://www.talkinghistory.org/attica.

73. Thomas S. Brown, "Hostage Describes 97 Hour Ordeal," *The Journal* (1971): 9.

74. Jack Newfield, "Attica: The Animals Were Outside," *Village Voice*, September, 23, 1971, 1 and 18.

75. "Letter from Eldridge Cleaver to Tom Wicker," Series 3, Folder 159, Tom Wicker Papers. SHC; Acoli, "An Updated History of the New Afrika Prison Struggle," in kioni-sadiki and Meyer, *Look for Me in the Whirlwind*, 65.

76. Ashanti M. Alston in conversation with author, 2020; Mutulu Shakur quoted in Ferguson and Ferguson, *An Unlikely Warrior*, 284.

77. Vargas, *Never Meant to Survive*.

78. Wicker, *A Time to Die*.

79. Woodard, *The Delectable Negro*, 131; Marable, *How Capitalism Underdeveloped Black America*, 76; Curry, *The Man-Not*; Collins, *Black Feminist Thought*.

80. Ransby, *Ella Baker and the Black Freedom Movement*; Robin D. G Kelley, *Freedom Dreams*; P. Collins, *Black Feminist Thought*; Farmer, *Remaking Black Power*; Bukhari, *The War Before*.

81. Institute of the Black World, *Black Analysis for the Seventies*, 7.

82. Fanon, *Black Skin, White Masks*.

83. Smith, "We Are Attica," Attica Defense Committee, 1972, in author's possession.

84. Quoted in Jack Slater, "Three Profiles in Courage: Mothers Overcome Grief at Deaths of Their Children." *Ebony*, March 1973, 96.

85. Smith, "Interview with Frank Smith (Big Black)."

86. Roberts, *Freedom as Marronage*, 117.

87. Hill and Ekanawetak, *Splitting the Sky*, 20.

88. See Burton, "Captivity, Kinship, and Black Masculine Care Work under Domestic Warfare."

89. Clark and Levitt, *The Brothers of Attica*, 79–80.

90. Lorde, *Sister Outsider: Essays and Speeches*, 54.

91. McKay Commission, *The Official Report of the New York State Special Commission on Attica*, 197; Clark, *The Brothers of Attica*, 55.

92. Cohen, "Punks, Bulldaggers, and Welfare Queens," 439.
93. Bugs in conversation with author, August 2020; McKay Commission, *The Official Report of the New York State Special Commission on Attica*, 197.
94. Clark and Levitt, *The Brothers of Attica*, 75.
95. Kareem C'Allah in conversation with author, 2022.
96. Clark and Levitt, *The Brothers of Attica*, 54. The McKay Commission claims that Attica's disabled captives were "forced to the yard despite chronic ailments." McKay Commission, *The Official Report of the New York State Special Commission on Attica*, 202.
97. Wicker, *A Time to Die*, 47; Institute of the Black World, *Black Analysis for the Seventies*, 3.
98. "Superintendent's Hearing Transcript for Jomo Sekou Omowale," Jomo Joka Omowale Papers, 1969–2008, Box 1, Folder: Attica Trial 1971–1974, DMR.
99. Wicker, *A Time to Die*, 95.
100. "Interview with Kunstler: An Observer Inside Attica," *Los Angeles Free Press*, October 8, 1971, 19.
101. Clark and Levitt, *The Brothers of Attica*, 41.
102. Untitled document, Jomo Joka Omowale Papers, 1969–2008, Box 4, Folder: Attica Trial Misc Correspondence, DMR.
103. Getachew, *Worldmaking after Empire*, 79–87.
104. Horne, *Communist Front?*
105. Cummins, *The Rise and Fall of California's Radical Prison Movement*, 192.
106. Masia A. Mugmuk in conversation with author, 2020.
107. Cleaver goes on to argue, "Later, the Panthers came to realize that their political presence outside the United States also allowed socialist governments to manipulate the Black Panther Party to serve ends that were extraneous to their own goals within America" (*Back to Africa*, 231).
108. Cleaver, *Back to Africa*, 235, 50.
109. Thompson, *Blood in the Water*; Bloom and Martin, "Black against Empire"; Wicker, *A Time to Die*.
110. Bukhari, *The War Before*.
111. Bukhari, *The War Before*, 131; Afeni Shakur, "Go Back Where You Came From," *New York Times*, September 23, 1971, 35; Hill and Ekanawetak, *Splitting the Sky*.
112. Afeni Shakur, "Go Back Where You Came From."
113. FBI Teletype from New York (157-6968) to Director, September 13, 1971, FOIPA Request No.: 1401693-000, p. 88. The surveillance claims that the Panthers arrived on the morning of the 13th, the day after Kunstler's meeting is said to have taken place. This could be a typing error, as the memo makes no mention of the Attica massacre, which would have been taking place as the Panthers arrived if they did indeed arrive on the 13th.
114. US Congress, *American Prisons in Turmoil*, testimony of William Kunstler, 1272.
115. "Letter to Rockefeller from the Jewish Defense League," Nelson Rockefeller personal papers (FA345) Politics, Series J, General Subseries 1, Box 67,

Folder 733—"Attica," 1971, NAR; N.A., "J.D.L. Stages a Sit-In at 6 Candidates' Offices," *New York Times*, February 17, 1972, 23.

116. Bordenkircher, "Prisons and the Revolutionary," 110.

117. "Report from inside Attica," *Prisoners Solidarity Committee Newsletter on Attica*, no. 1, September 17, 1971, 4, Box 7, Folder: Workers World Party (3 of 3), House Committee on Internal Security, UVA.

118. "Attica: International Solidarity," *Midnight Special* 2, no. 8, October 1972, 8, Freedom Archives.

119. "Attica: International Solidarity," 9.

CHAPTER 4. GENDER WAR

1. "Episodes from the Attica Massacre," *The Black Scholar* 4, no. 2 (1972): 38.

2. Interview with John D. Steinmetz, McKay Commission Transcript, New York City Public Hearings, April 26, 1972, PM, 2035-2043, http://www.talkinghistory.org/attica; McKay Commission, *The Official Report of the New York State Special Commission on Attica*, 170, 332-45; Thompson, *Blood in the Water*; Wicker, *A Time to Die*.

3. Razack, "How Is White Supremacy Embodied?"; Hartman, *Scenes of Subjection*; Spillers, "Mama's Baby, Papa's Maybe"; Sharpe, *Monstrous Intimacies*; Haley, *No Mercy Here*; Snorton, *Black on Both Sides*; A. Davis, "Reflections on the Black Woman's Role in the Community of Slaves"; Saleh-Hanna, "Black Feminist Hauntology: Rememory the Ghosts of Abolition?"; Harris, *Exorcising Blackness*; Curry, *The Man-Not*; Foster, *Rethinking Rufus*; Woodard, *The Delectable Negro*.

4. Champen, "A Time to Die," interview with Tom Wicker, Transcript, Tom Wicker Papers 1917–2013, Folder 23, 7.

5. Painter, *Southern History across the Color Line*. See also Fanon, *Black Skin, White Masks*; H. Brown, *Die Nigger Die: A Political Autobiography*; Patterson, *Slavery and Social Death*; Guenther, *Solitary Confinement*.

6. Scarry, *The Body in Pain*.

7. Lazreg, *Torture and the Twilight of Empire*; Khalili, "Gendered Practices of Counterinsurgency."

8. Woodard, *The Delectable Negro*; Foster, *Rethinking Rufus*; Curry, *The Man-Not*; Sabo, Kupers, and London, *Prison Masculinities*; Sivakumaran, "Sexual Violence against Men in Armed Conflict."

9. Painter, *Southern History Across the Color Line*.

10. Al-Jundi v. Mancusi, 75-CV-132 (W.D.N.Y. Aug. 28, 2000).

11. bin-Wahad, Abu-Jamal, and Shakur, *Still Black, Still Strong*, 25–26.

12. Kitossa, "Introduction," *Appealing Because He Is Appalling*, xlii. See also Jordan, *White over Black*, 1550–812.

13. Wiegman, *American Anatomies*; Wallace, *Constructing the Black Masculine*; Curry, *The Man-Not*; Kitossa, *Appealing Because He Is Appalling*; Woodard, *The Delectable Negro*; Connell and Messerschmidt, "Hegemonic Masculinity: Rethinking the Concept"; Cooper, Kimmel, and McGinley, *Masculinities and the Law*; S. Bjork-James, "White Sexual Politics."

14. Clark and Levitt, *The Brothers of Attica*.

15. McKay Commission, *The Official Report of the New York State Special Commission on Attica*, 16.

16. Norton, "Little Siberia, Star of the North."

17. Rubin, *The Forgotten Kapital*; Lay, *Hooded Knights on the Niagara*.

18. "They Pointed Guns at Us," *Prisoner's Solidarity Committee Newsletter on Attica*, no. 1, September 17, 1971, 6, Box 7, Folder: Workers World Party (3 of 3), House Committee on Internal Security, UVA; Hill, "The Common Enemy Is the Boss and the Inmate," 88; N.A., "Klansman-Teacher Is Ousted by State from Prison Post," *New York Times*, December 24, 1974, 42; Wolfgang Saxon, "Prison Teacher Suspended in State Study of K.K.K.," *New York Times*, December 22, 1974, 14; Michael T. Kaufman, "Upstate Prison Teacher Defends His Klan Role," *New York Times*, December 23, 1974, 24; *Smash the Klan: John Brown Anti-Klan Committee—Press Packet* (1977), 9, Freedom Archives, John Brown Anti-Klan Committee (JBAKC) Collection, https://search.freedomarchives.org.

19. P. Collins, *Black Feminist Thought*; Bambara, *The Black Woman*; Ransby, *Ella Baker and the Black Freedom Movement*; Kelley, *Freedom Dreams*; Farmer, *Remaking Black Power*; Taylor, *How We Get Free*; Bukhari, *The War Before*; Spencer, *The Revolution Has Come*.

20. Curry, *The Man-Not*.

21. US Congress, *American Prisons in Turmoil Part II* (Testimony of Arthur O. Eve), 1232.

22. "Massacre at Attica," *New York Times*, September 14, 1971, 40.

23. In his analysis of the psychosexual and racial dynamics of the Revolt, Richard X Clark writes of witnessing a white guard "offering his ass to a black inmate" in exchange for not being held hostage. He continues, "The guards had created a mythical image of the inmates, and now they were living out their own fantasies. They had gone on ripping inmates off anytime they wanted, and because of it they had projected that we would do the same. That same mythical image they had of us—as savages who were kept in cages—was the reason they later were so quick to claim we had cut the throats of six hostages and castrated a seventh. They didn't only make this up to purposefully deceive. They really believed it. The only people they ended up deceiving, though, were themselves" (*The Brothers of Attica*, 33).

24. Fanon, *Black Skin, White Masks*, 167; Harris, *Exorcising Blackness*; Jordan, *White over Black*, 1550–812.

25. Woodard, *The Delectable Negro*.

26. Fanon, *Black Skin, White Masks*, 167; Fanon, *The Wretched of the Earth*, 6.

27. Fanon, *Black Skin, White Masks*, 137.

28. Menard, "Lest We Forget."

29. Marable, *How Capitalism Underdeveloped Black America*, 115.

30. Marable, *How Capitalism Underdeveloped Black America*, 115.

31. Fanon, *Black Skin, White Masks*, 137.

32. Wells-Barnett, *Southern Horrors and Other Writings*; Harris, *Exorcising Blackness*.

33. Abdur-Rahman, *Against the Closet*, 52.
34. Sivakumaran, "Sexual Violence against Men in Armed Conflict."
35. Woodfox, *Solitary*.
36. New York Attorney General's Office of Special Investigation, "Report of the Special Prosecutor," Ralph Valvano, Donald Leroland, and Jonathan Williams, et al. v. Benjamin Malcolm, et al., 27.
37. Ricardo DeLeon, "A Letter to the People from inside Maximum," *Right On!*, n.d., 8, Periodicals.001, Box 373, TA; Ricardo DeLeon, "How Are Things in Dannemora?," *Village Voice*, October 7, 1971, 79.
38. "It Can Happen Here," *Village Voice*, October 21, 1971, 4 and 95.
39. Kunzel, *Criminal Intimacy*, 63–65.
40. Woodard, *The Delectable Negro*.
41. "Prison Superintendent Lists Changes, Return to Normalcy," *Auburn Citizen-Advertiser* (Auburn, NY), June 9, 1971, 3; Akil in conversation with author, September 2019; US Congress, *American Prisons in Turmoil Part II* (Testimony of Herman Schwartz), 1106. For the captives' perspective, see a letter by Auburn 6 member Robert Kareem Clarke, "Dannemora: These Pits of Hell," *Village Voice*, September 30, 1971, 10.
42. "Hearings Before the Select Comm. on Correctional Institutions and Programs," 65–66 (1972) (Testimony James Killebrew), NYSL, 85.
43. Final Decision and Order, Claim of Christopher Lynch, Akil Al-Jundi et al. v. Mancussi et al. 75 Civ-132, August 28, 2000, 108.
44. Final Decision and Order, Claim of Jake Lake, 49; Final Decision and Order, Claim of Lawrence Blair Jr., 52; Final Decision and Order, Claim of Steven Garrett, 109; Final Decision and Order, Claim of Carlos Eugene Brown, 163; Meyer, *Final Report of the Special Attica Investigation*, 37–38; FBI FOIA 1401693-000, 1326.
45. Testimony of Frank Smith, Akil Al-Jundi, on behalf of himself and all others similarly situated v. Vincent Mancussi et al., 43–76; Final Decision and Order, Claim of Christopher Lynch, 108; Final Decision and Order, Claim of Carlos Eugene Brown, 163; Attica Defense Committee, *We Are Attica: Interviews with Prisoners from Attica*; Meyer, *Final Report of the Special Attica Investigation*, 36–38; FBI FOIA 1401693-000, 1326.
46. Final Decision and Order.
47. M.M. in conversation with author, 2020.
48. Smith, "Facing the Dragon," 31.
49. Final Decision and Order, Claim of Lyman Pope, 14.
50. Final Decision and Order, Claim of John Anderson, 20.
51. Final Decision and Order, Claim of James E. Glenn, 23.
52. Final Decision and Order, Claim of Michael Northrup, 76.
53. Final Decision and Order, Claim of Anthony Cerra, 115.
54. Final Decision and Order, Claim of George W. Budd Jr., 17.
55. Final Decision and Order, Claim of David Galloway, 93–94.
56. Final Decision and Order, Claim of Nicholas Goyco Morales, 178-179.
57. Sam Roberts, "Rockefeller on the Attica Raid, from Boastful to Subdued," *New York Times*, September 13, 2011, 2.

58. Wilderson, *Red, White and Black*; Hartman, "Venus in Two Acts"; Woodard, *The Delectable Negro*; Weheliye, *Habeas Viscus*.

59. Wallace, *Constructing the Black Masculine*, 32.

60. FBI FOIA 1401693-000, pp. 88, 405, 427–28.

61. Thompson, *Blood in the Water*; Bell, *The Turkey Shoot*; Kaufman, "Videotape of the Raid Was Made by Troopers"; McKay Commission, *The Official Report of the New York State Special Commission on Attica*, 361.

62. McKay Commission, *The Official Report of the New York State Special Commission on Attica*, 362; Johnston, *Evidence of the Evidence*; Michael T. Kaufman, "Videotape of the Raid Was Made by Troopers," *New York Times*, September 16, 1971, 48; Bell, *The Turkey Shoot*, 59.

63. US Congress, *American Prisons in Turmoil Part II* (Testimony of Francis J. Huen), 1332.

64. Kaufman, "Videotape of the Raid Was Made by Troopers."

65. Hartman, *Scenes of Subjection*, 21. See also Sharpe, *Monstrous Intimacies*.

66. US Congress, *American Prisons in Turmoil Part II* (Testimony of John C. Miller), 1512.

67. Wood, *Lynching and Spectacle*.

68. Marriott, *On Black Men*, 6.

69. Apel, "Torture Culture"; Puar, "Abu Ghraib"; Razack, "How Is White Supremacy Embodied?"; Sexton and Lee, "Figuring the Prison"; S. Smith, *At the Edge of Sight*.

70. Weheliye, *Habeas Viscus*, 110.

71. Baldwin, "Going to Meet the Man," 232.

72. Baldwin, "Going to Meet the Man," 236.

73. Baldwin, "Going to Meet the Man," 247.

74. Baldwin, "Going to Meet the Man," 247.

75. Olivia B. Waxman, "Is *If Beale Street Could Talk* Based on a True Story? The Answer Is Complicated," *Time*, February 22, 2019.

76. Waxman, "Is *If Beale Street Could Talk* Based on a True Story?"

77. Lesley Oelsner, "Anatomy of a Prison Riot: Attica," *New York Times*, September 17, 1972, 1. *The Official Report* actually contains two versions of the coffle image. Inside the book there is an uncropped version in which more of the prison yard and more denuded captives are visible. This version of the image is black and white, as opposed to the color image on the cover. It has also been reversed along the vertical axis.

78. Omowale, "On Leaders in Question," Jomo Joka Omowale Papers, 1969–2008, Box 4, Folder: Attica Trial Misc Correspondence, DMR.

79. Spillers, "Mama's Baby, Papa's Maybe"; Snorton, *Black on Both Sides*.

80. Connell, *Masculinities*; Curry, *The Man-Not*; Fanon, *Black Skin, White Masks*; Wallace, *Constructing the Black Masculine*; Wiegman, Robyn. *American Anatomies*.

81. As Patricia Hill Collins and many others have long argued, Black movements "far too often equate racial progress with the acquisition of an ill-defined manhood" (*Black Feminist Thought*, 7); see P. Collins, *Black Sexual Politics*; "Episodes from the Attica Massacre."

82. Ingold, *Lines*, 143.
83. C. H. in conversation with author, 2020.
84. Pickens, *Black Madness*, 4.
85. HIP Grant Application, "Mental Health Services Taskforce Committee," July 20 and 21, 1971, Folder 13, Box 4, 7, ACTEC Executive Office File, NYSA.
86. Casper also cc'd Arthur O. Eve, a Democratic member of the New York State assembly who was deeply involved in supporting the rebels, and Antonio G. Oliver, a lawyer based in the State Capitol in Albany.
87. Gary, "Petition for Certificates Extraordinary," Nelson Rockefeller Papers 1971–1973, Prisoners Subject File, Reel 18 1368278, 1, NYSA.
88. Hartman, *Scenes of Subjection*.
89. Gary, "Petition for Certificates Extraordinary," 1.
90. Burnard, *Mastery, Tyranny, and Desire*, 35.
91. Gary, "Petition for Certificates Extraordinary," 3.
92. Baldwin, *The Fire Next Time*, 9.
93. Little, "What the Nixon Tapes Reveal about the Attica Prison Uprising."
94. "Attica Is Everywhere." *The Black Panther* (Berkeley, CA), October 16, 1971, 7–8.
95. Useem and Kimball, *States of Siege*.
96. Murray Schumach, "Top Police Officials Believe Black Militants Were the Slayers of Two Policemen on Lower East Side," *New York Times*, January 30, 1972, 35; Daley, *Target Blue*, 415–22.

CHAPTER 5. HIDDEN WAR

1. Ferguson, *Top Down*; Schrader, "To Secure the Global Great Society"; Schrader, *Badges without Borders*; Rodríguez, *White Reconstruction*; Parenti, *Lockdown America*; K. Williams, "The Other Side of the COIN"; R. Allen, *Black Awakening In Capitalist America*; Incite!, *The Revolution Will Not Be Funded*; Ball, *The Myth and Propaganda of Black Buying Power*.
2. US Army, "Field Manual 33-1," H-3.
3. Tzu, *The Art of War*, 77.
4. J. James, "The Womb of Western Theory."
5. Report of the NYS Select Comm. on Correctional Situations and Programs, No. 1. January 24, 1972, NYSL; "For Release," April 6, 1972, Office of Legislative Research Counsel, 30. Series 10, Robert R. Douglass, Subseries 3, Box 7, Folder 73 Corrections-Prisoner Reform, 1972, RAC.
6. Report of the NYS Select Comm. on Correctional Situations and Programs, No. 1, 1.
7. "PSC exposes Rockefeller committee at hearing," *Workers World* (New York, NY), February 16, 1972, 7 and 15.
8. "Hearings Before the Select Comm. on Correctional Institutions and Programs," 65–66 (1972) (Testimony of Tom Sotto), NYSL.
9. "Report of the NYS Select Committee," Office of Legislative Research Counsel, Series 10, Robert R. Douglass, Subseries 3, Box 7, Folder 73, 1972, RAC.
10. "Hearings Before the Select Comm. on Correctional Institutions and Programs," 97–100 (1972) (Testimony of Carmen Garrigia), NYSL.

11. "Text of Tombs' Inmates' Grievances," *New York Times*, August 11, 1970, 30. For a delineation of the Immediate Demands and the Fifteen Practical Proposals, see Wicker, *A Time to Die*.

12. This conversation is in dialogue with Savannah Shange's critique of "winning" in social justice oriented projects (*Progressive Dystopia*, 20).

13. R. Allen, *Black Awakening in Capitalist America*, 17.

14. Nagl et al., *The US Army/Marine Corps Counterinsurgency Field Manual*, 18; Kitson, *Low Intensity Operations*.

15. "Hearings Before the Select Comm. on Correctional Institutions and Programs," 102–3 (1972) (Testimony of Joseph Little), NYSL. Hereafter "Testimony of Joseph Little."

16. Foucault, *Discipline and Punish*, 234.

17. "Testimony of Joseph Little," 102–4.

18. "Testimony of Joseph Little," 102–11.

19. Address of Congressman Richard H. Ichord to the 42nd Biennial Convention of the Fraternal order of Police at the Convention Headquarters, Stardust Hotel, Las Vegas, Nevada, August 6, 1973, B6 Speeches and Interviews, part 2, Staff Directors Files, RG 233, Records of the House Internal Security Committee, 1969–1976, CLA.

20. "Testimony of Joseph Little," 102–11.

21. Nikki Green, "PSC Organizes for Auburn 6 Trial," *Workers World* (New York, NY), February 2, 1972, 9.

22. US Congress, Departments of State, Justice, and Commerce, the Judiciary, and Related Agencies Appropriations for 1973, 92nd Cong. (1972), 922 (Testimony of J. Edgar Hoover).

23. Burton, "Targeting Revolutionaries."

24. "Testimony of Joseph Little," 109.

25. Felber, *Those Who Know Don't Say*.

26. Sostre, "The New Prisoner," 252.

27. Sostre, "The New Prisoner," 247–53.

28. Kitson, *Low Intensity Operations*, 85.

29. Peg Savage Grey, "1971 Prison Disturbances," April 18, 1972, Folder: 1971 Prison Disturbances, Box 88, Attica Commission Investigation Files: 15855-90, NYSA.

30. Mark Brown, "Prison Reform Mitchell Goal," *Sunday Star*, December 5, 1971.

31. Talbot, *The Devil's Chessboard*, 551–52.

32. Glander, *Origins of Mass Communications Research During the American Cold War*, 47; Marchio, "The Planning Coordination Group"; Saunders, *The Cultural Cold War*, 212–34; Seigel, "Nelson Rockefeller in Latin America."

33. Quoted in William E. Farrell, "Rockefeller Sees a Plot At Prison," *New York Times*. September 14, 1971, 1; US Congress, *American Prisons in Turmoil Part II* (Testimony of Nelson A. Rockefeller), 690–92.

34. Quoted in Oswald, *Attica*, 321.

35. Flateau, *The Prison Industrial Complex*; Kohler-Hausmann, *Getting Tough*; Eric Schlosser, "The Prison-Industrial Complex," *Atlantic Monthly*, December 1, 1998; Fortner, *Black Silent Majority*.

36. Scott Christianson, "In 1976: The Lesson Not Learned," *The Nation*, December 4, 1976, 586.

37. Drucker, "Population Impact of Mass Incarceration under New York's Rockefeller Drug Laws."

38. James M. Markham, "President Calls for 'Total War' on U.S. Addiction," *New York Times*, March 21, 1972, 1.

39. Flateau, *The Prison Industrial Complex*; Schlosser, "The Prison-Industrial Complex."

40. The Sentencing Project, "Trends in U.S. Corrections: U.S. State and Federal Prison Population, 1925–2019," https://www.sentencingproject.org/wp-content/uploads/2021/07/Trends-in-US-Corrections.pdf.

41. American Correctional Association, *Causes, Preventive Measures, and Methods of Controlling Riots*, 11.

42. Prison populations are driven by a combination of arrest rates, conviction rates, sentence lengths, parole rates, and death rates, all of which can be manipulated much faster than physical prisons can be constructed.

43. American Correctional Association, *Causes, Preventive Measures, and Methods of Controlling Riots*.

44. NY State Select Committee on Correctional Institutions and Programs, Report No. 2, March 15, 1972, p. 46, NYSL.

45. US Congress, *Revolutionary Activities Directed toward the Administration of Penal or Correctional Systems* (Testimony of Robert J. Henderson), 140.

46. NY DOCS, *Multi-Year Master Plan of the Department of Correctional Services*, 1973, S-4.

47. Testimony of Eliot Seide, "Public Hearing on the Effect of Administration Budget Reductions on the Management of the State Prison System," New York State Legislature Assembly on Committee on Correction, Utica, NY, November 28, 1985, 7–8, NYSL.

48. Norton, "Little Siberia, Star of the North."

49. Chapter 337 10128-B, "An Act to amend the correction law, the public authorities law, the health and mental hygiene facilities improvement act and the state finance law . . .," April 11, 1972, NYSL.

50. Auburn Prison Industries Annual Report (1969–1970), Auburn Volunteer Office Files. B0030-77 Annual Reports, NYSA.

51. Norton, "Little Siberia, Star of the North"; Meunier and Schwartz, "Beyond Attica"; Phillips-Fein, *Fear City*.

52. Prison Research Education Action Project, *Instead of Prisons*; Mitford, *Kind and Usual Punishment*.

53. Forman, *Locking Up Our Own*; Fortner, *Black Silent Majority*; Gilmore, *Golden Gulag*; King, Mauer, and Huling, *Big Prisons, Small Towns*.

54. Norton, "Little Siberia, Star of the North," 41.

55. NY DOCS, *Multi-Year Master Plan of the Department of Correctional Services*, 1973, ii, emphasis added.

56. Norton, "Little Siberia, Star of the North"; Gilmore, *Golden Gulag*; Morrell, "Hometown Prison"; Gottschalk, *Caught*; Hill, "The Common Enemy Is the Boss and the Inmate"; Parenti, *Lockdown America*; King, Mauer, and Huling, *Big Prisons, Small Towns*.

57. Meunier and Schwartz, "Beyond Attica," 924–96.
58. Martin Sostre, interview by Doloris Costello, WBAI, November 6, 1972, PRA.
59. Letter to William Ciuros Jr. from Oswald, October 5, 1971, Series 2, Box 2, Folder 23. Council 82 Collection, MEG; Gould, "The Officer-Inmate Relationship"; Smith, Al-Jundi, and Weiss, "Guest Editor's Interview"; Paul L. Montgomery, "Attica Prisoners Have Gained Most Points Made in Rebellion," *New York Times*, September, 12, 1972, 1.
60. NY DOCS, "New York State Correctional Services Master Plan, 1980–1985," pp. 11 and 21 (1981), NYSA.
61. Schept, "Caring Cages."
62. Russell G. Oswald to Nelson A. Rockefeller, Re: "Progress in Department of Correctional Services," January 25, 1971, Gov. Nelson A. Rockefeller Subject File Reel 17, Subject File 1971–1973, NYSA.
63. New York State Advisory Committee to the US Commission on Civil Rights, *Warehousing Human Beings*, 7-8.
64. "Major New York State Prison Reforms Negotiated by AFSCME Council 82," *82 Review* 2, no. 7 (October 1971), 1 and 3, Council 82 Collection, MEG.
65. Hill, "The Common Enemy Is the Boss and the Inmate."
66. "Major New York State Prison Reforms Negotiated by AFSCME Council 82," 1 and 3.
67. Martin Sostre, interview by Doloris Costello, WBAI, November 6, 1972, PRA.
68. Rodríguez, *Forced Passages*.
69. Sostre, "The New Prisoner," 244.
70. Sostre, "The New Prisoner," 254.
71. Montgomery, "Attica Prisoners Have Gained Most Points Made in Rebellion."
72. "Manifesto from the Monster Attica," in *Hydra Book 2: Earth*, ed. Bill Morehouse, Attica Institute of Human Resources. Subject File Reel 18, 1368278, Governor Rockefeller Papers, 1971–1973, NYSA; Comrade Rabb, "Attica Again?," November 8, 1972, Box 5. Folder Attica Trial Misc 1972 – 1974, Jomo Joka Omowale Papers, 1969–2008, DMR.
73. Sostre, "The New Prisoner," 243.
74. Martin Sostre, interview by Doloris Costello, WBAI, November 6, 1972, PRA.
75. Letter from Hersey Beyer, *Prisoners Digest International* 2, no. 4. (Sept/Oct 1972): 8.
76. Champen interview with Tom Wicker, 33, Folder 23, Subseries 1.1. Tom Wicker Papers, 1917-2013. SHC.
77. NY DOCS, *Multi-Year Master Plan of the Department of Correctional Services*, 1973, 11-1.
78. NY DOCS, *Multi-Year Master Plan of the Department of Correctional Services*, 1973, S-3-4.
79. Meunier and Schwartz, "Beyond Attica," 983.
80. Foucault, *"Society Must Be Defended,"* 242–43.

81. McKay Commission, *The Official Report of the New York State Special Commission on Attica*, 267.

82. Shoatz and Guenther, "Maroon Philosophy," 73.

83. NY DOCS, "Six-Month Operational Digest," June 1971. Auburn Volunteer Office Files, NYSA, 3-21; "State Criminologist to Talk at Chico State," *The Chico Enterprise-Record* (Chico, CA), October 21, 1964, 20. For more on the Advanced Research Projects Agency, see Levine, *Surveillance Valley*.

84. Berreman, "Ethics versus 'Realism' in Anthropology," 48.

85. NY DOCS, *Multi-Year Master Plan of the Department of Correctional Services*, 1973, II-45.

86. Theologus, *Development of a Taxonomy of Human Performance*.

87. Giannell, "Criminosynthesis of a Revolutionary Offender," 230 and 33.

88. Giannell, "Criminosynthesis of a Revolutionary Offender," 230–33; Metzl, *The Protest Psychosis*.

89. Jeffrey Schmalz, "A Life against Violence, and 3 Violent Deaths: Violent End to Life against Violence," *New York Times*, December 28, 1983, 2.

90. NY DOCS, *Multi-Year Master Plan of the Department of Correctional Services*, 1973, I-11.

91. NY DOCS, Annual Report, 1974, 6.

92. "Regarding NYS Prisons Security Levels," August 1981, Folder: Issues, Series 9, Box 8. NYS Coalition for Criminal Justice, MEG.

93. Mechthild, "Prisons, Big Business, and Profit," 377.

94. SAC (157-979) SA Daniel V. Hogan, "Black Extremist Activities at Great Meadow Correctional Facility, Comstock, New York," March 20, 1972, DBW Archive.

95. New York State Commission of Correction, "Great Meadow State Correctional Facility: A Prison in Crisis," June 22, 1976, 8; Jacob in conversation with author, 2017.

96. Edward A. Gargan, "Senator Assails State Panel in Death of a Prison Inmate," *New York Times*, March 19, 1984.

97. Christianson, "In 1976: The Lesson Not Learned," *The Nation*, December 4, 1976, 586; New York State Commission of Correction, "Great Meadow State Correctional Facility: A Prison in Crisis," June 22, 1976, 8; "Attica Is Termed as Bad as before 1971 Rebellion," *New York Times*, July 21, 1976, 1; Jacob in conversation with author, August 2017.

98. SAC (157-979) SA Daniel V. Hogan, "Black Extremist Activities at Great Meadow Correctional Facility, Comstock, New York," April 14, 1973, DBW.

99. SAC (157-979) SA Daniel V. Hogan, "Black Extremist Activities at Great Meadow Correctional Facility, Comstock, New York," March 20, 1972, DBW.

100. Jacob in conversation with author, 2018.

101. Berlien, "Psychiatry in the Army Correctional System," 519–20.

102. Jacob in conversation with author, 2018.

103. New York State Commission of Investigation, *Corruption and Abuses in the Correctional System—The Green Haven Correctional Facility*, 2.

104. NY DOCS, "New York State Correctional Services Master Plan, 1980–1985," p. 11 (1981), NYSA.

105. Report of the NYS Select Comm. on Correctional Situations and Programs, No. 1, 11. NYSL.

106. Richard Dhoruba Moore, "Mass Terror Inside Attica," *Crawdaddy*, October 1976, 61-62.

107. Prisoners Liberation Front, "Snacked into Submission!!!," *Midnight Special* (New York, NY), September 1972. 3.

108. Prisoners Liberation Front, "Snacked into Submission!!!," 3.

109. Cunha, "The Ethnography of Prisons and Penal Confinement"; Wacquant, "The Curious Eclipse of Prison Ethnography in the Age of Mass Incarceration"; Waldram, "Challenges of Prison Ethnography"; Ralph, *Renegade Dreams*; Khan, "The Carceral State."

110. Burton, "Captivity, Kinship, and Black Masculine Care Work."

111. NY DOCS, Division of Program Services Action Plan 1991, in author's possession.

112. Wicker, *A Time to Die.*

113. My analysis is indebted to the work of Juanita Diaz-Cotto in *Gender, Ethnicity, and the State.*

114. Larry White in conversation with author, 2014.

115. Galula, *Counterinsurgency Warfare*; Harcourt, *The Counterrevolution*; Nagl et al., *The U.S. Army Marine Corps Counterinsurgency Field Manual.*

116. NY DOCS, *Multi-Year Master Plan of the New York State Department of Correctional Services*, 1973, S-7, NCJRS.

117. NYS DOCS, Annual Report of the New York State Department of Correctional Services, 1974, 5 and 12, NCJRS; Status Report, Volunteer Service Program, February 1, 1974, Department of Correction Correspondence Files, Reel 10, NYSA.

118. NYS DOCS, "Correctional Volunteer Services Program," February 1972, 1.

119. Larry Mamiya in conversation with author, 2015; Hassan Gale in conversation with author, 2016; NYS DOCS, "Humanizing the System: Report of Operations and Development for 1977." New York State Department of Correctional Services, 27, NCJRS.

120. NY State Select Committee on Correctional Institutions and Programs, Report No. 2, March 15, 1972, 42.

121. "The Correctional Volunteer Service Program—Historical Perspective," 2, Auburn Volunteer Office Files, NYSA,

122. Larry Mamiya in conversation with author, 2015; NYS DOCS, Equity and Justice, 1976, 31, NCJRS.

123. "Correctional Volunteer Services Program," February 1972, Auburn Volunteer Office Files, 4, NYSA.

124. "Correctional Volunteer Services Program Report," March 22, 1972, Auburn Volunteer Office Files, 3–21, NYSA.

125. "THIS IS MARC," Folder: Green Haven Correctional Facility, 1974-1975, Box 302, Kenneth Bancroft Clark Papers, LOC.

126. R. Allen, *Black Awakening in Capitalist America*, 144; Ferguson, *Top Down.*

127. "The Awesome Attica Tragedy," *The Crisis*, November 1971, 299–300.

128. Director, FBI to SAC, Albany. "Black Extremist Activities in Penal Institutions," August 26, 1971, DBW.

129. US Congress, *Revolutionary Activities Directed toward the Administration of Penal or Correctional Systems* (Testimony of Raymond K. Procunier), 1213.

130. Dixie Moon in conversation with author, 2014; Edwin Muller in conversation with author, 2014; Linda Charlton, "'South 40' Tries to Aid Convicts," *New York Times*, April 23, 1972, 62.

131. R. Allen, *Black Awakening in Capitalist America*.

132. Grant, "The Offender as a Correctional Manpower Resource," 229.

133. Grant and Grant, "Contagion as a Principle in Behavior Change." By "epidemiological model," I am refering to the American Correctional Association's belief that riots were contagious (American Correctional Association, *Causes, Preventive Measures, and Methods of Controlling Riots*, 37).

134. Diaz-Cotto, *Gender, Ethnicity, and the State*.

135. Tony Hart to Charles Scully, Green Haven Correctional Facility, January 30, 1989, HG.

136. Hartman, *Scenes of Subjection*, 42.

137. Diaz-Cotto, *Gender, Ethnicity, and the State*.

138. Prison Research Education Action Project, *Instead of Prisons*, 178.

139. Burton, "Captivity, Kinship, and Black Masculine Care Work."

140. Burton, "Attica Is."

141. Hassan Gale in conversation with author, 2018.

142. Incite!, ed., *The Revolution Will Not Be Funded*; Williams, Squire, and Tuitt, *Plantation Politics and Campus Rebellions*; Táíwò, *Elite Capture*.

143. Rodríguez, *Forced Passages*.

144. New York State Legislature Assembly, Comm. on Correction, "Public Hearing on the Effect of Administration Budget Reductions on the Management of the State Prisons" (1995), 125, NYSL.

CHAPTER 6. THE WAR ON BLACK REVOLUTIONARY MINDS

1. R. Gallati to N. Rockefeller, 1971, Folder 170, Box 7, Series P., RG4 (NAR), RAC.

2. N. Rockefeller to R. Gallati, 1971, Folder 170, Box 7, Series P., RG4 (NAR), RAC.

3. Kinzer, *Poisoner in Chief*; Marks, *The Search for the Manchurian Candidate*; Scheflin and Opton, "The Mind Manipulators"; M. Shakur et al., *Genocide Waged against the Black Nation through Behavior Modification Orchestrated by Counterinsurgency and Low-Intensity Warfare in the U.S. Penal System*; Ryan, "Solitude as Counterinsurgency"; Gomez, "Resisting Living Death at Marion Federal Penitentiary, 1972"; Schein, *Brainwashing*; Schein, *Coercive Persuasion*.

4. Scarry, *The Body in Pain*; Lazreg, *Torture and the Twilight of Empire*.

5. Many of the documents cited in this chapter are in my personal collection. I obtained a cache of documents related to the RX Program from Masia A.

Mugmuk and CIA documents from Greg deGiere, the former City Editor for the *Vacaville Reporter*, who FOIAed the CIA in the late 1970s as part of his research on MK Ultra experiments on incarcerated people in Vacaville Medical Facility. His FOIA requests turned up many of the same documents that had already been released to John Marks, which are available at the National Security Archive at George Washington University in Washington, DC. Most of the PRISACTS and DOCS surveillance files were loaned to me by Robert J. Boyle and Dhoruba bin-Wahad, who obtained them as part of their protracted struggle to expose these techniques. I obtained additional files by submitting my own FOIA requests to the FBI and by tracking down old litigation from the National Archives and Records Administration. DeGiere's files are now held in Special Collections at American University.

6. New York State Department of Corrections and Community Supervision, *Multi-Year Master Plan of the Department of Correctional Services*, I-10.

7. Glander, *Origins of Mass Communications Research During the American Cold War*, 63.

8. Marks, *The Search for the Manchurian Candidate*, 223; US Congress, "Project MK Ultra."

9. John Earman, memorandum to Director of Central Intelligence, *Report of Inspection of MK Ultra*, July 26, 1963, 1, GD.

10. O'Reilly, *"Racial Matters,"* 271.

11. Central Intelligence Agency, "Organization of a Special Defense Interrogation Program," June 11, 1951, 4. GD.

12. Kilgore, *Understanding E-Carceration*.

13. Daulatzai, *Black Star, Crescent Moon*; Daulatzai and Rana, *With Stones in Our Hands*; Rana, *Terrifying Muslims*; Khalili, *Time in the Shadows*. As Nancy Kurshan explains, "Indeed, in this day of debate about Guantanamo and Abu Ghraib, it is absolutely essential to realize that a direct line extends from U.S. control units to these so-called 'enhanced interrogation' centers throughout the world" (*Out of Control*).

14. Dhoruba bin-Wahad in conversation with author, 2021.

15. Bottom and Gallati, *Industrial Espionage*. For more on the IACP, see Schrader, *Badges without Borders*. See "Excerpts of remarks prepared for delivery by Secretary of State John P. Lomenzo at dedication of headquarters of NYSIIS, July 29, 1970," FA43B. Subseries 37.3. Reel 22, Department of NYSIIS, RAC.

16. Silbert, "The World's First Computerized Criminal-Justice Information-Sharing System"; Levine, *Surveillance Valley*; Herrmann, *Report to United States Agency for International Development, Office of Public Safety*; Robert R.J. Gallati, "A System in Motion: Annual Report, 1971," New York State Identification and Intelligence System, State of New York, 3. https://www.ojp.gov/pdffiles1/Digitization/16793NCJRS.pdf.

17. Selisker, *Human Programming*, 99–124; Schwitzgebel and Schwitzgebel, *Psychotechnology*, v–vi.

18. Wiener, *The Human Use of Human Beings*, 16.

19. Dupuy and DeBevoise, *The Mechanization of the Mind*; Harnish, *Minds, Brains, Computers*.

20. Huey P. Newton, "Prison: Where Is Thy Victory," *The Black Panther* (Oakland, CA), January 3, 1970, 13. Available at https://www.marxists.org/history/usa/workers/black-panthers.

21. Newton, "Prison: Where Is Thy Victory," 13.

22. US Congress, "Project MK Ultra"; Hornblum, *Acres of Skin*; Gomez, "Resisting Living Death at Marion Federal Penitentiary, 1972"; Scheflin and Opton, "The Mind Manipulators."

23. Newton, *The Huey P. Newton Reader*, 329.

24. Oral history material from Masia A. Mugmuk was collected by author between 2020 and 2022.

25. Respondent's Brief, People v. Cholmondeley, Records & Briefs New York State Appellate Division, 33 AD 2nd, Law Library of the New York Law Institute, MM.

26. For more on the role of Malcolm X and the Nation of Islam in the prison movement see Felber, *Those Who Know Don't Say*.

27. Rogers and Clarke, *World's Great Men of Color*.

28. Forgays and Thorne, "The Special Problem of the Black Extremist in a Correctional Mental Hospital," 264.

29. Kondo, *Conspiracys*.

30. Barnett and Njama, *Mau Mau from Within*.

31. Elkins, *Imperial Reckoning*.

32. FBI writings on urban guerrilla warfare often cite the work of Frank Kitson, who was part of the British counterinsurgency effort in Kenya and Malaya. See for example Thomas J. Deakin, "The Legacy of Carlos Marighella," *Law Enforcement Bulletin* (Washington, DC), October 1974, 19; "Trends in Urban Guerrilla Tactics," *Law Enforcement Bulletin* (Washington, DC), July 1973, 3; Churchill and Vander Wall, *The COINTELPRO Papers*, 8, 110.

33. Quoted in Motion for Preliminary Injunction, Mukmuk [sic] v. Commissioner of DOCS et al., 70 Civ. 3518, 25, MM.

34. David R. Spiegel, affidavit in Support of Motion to Dismiss, Mukmuk v. Commissioner et al., 70 Civ 3518, 2, MM.

35. "Clinton Conditions Condemned," *Midnight Special* 1, no. 1, 9, TA.

36. Scheflin and Opton, "The Mind Manipulators," 96. See also Mitford, *Kind and Usual Punishment*, 131; Gomez, "Resisting Living Death at Marion Federal Penitentiary, 1972"; M. Shakur et al., *Genocide Waged against the Black Nation through Behavior Modification Orchestrated by Counterinsurgency and Low-Intensity Warfare in the U.S. Penal System*.

37. Said, "Orientalism." For more on the orientalism of the brainwashing panic, see Kim, *The Interrogation Rooms of the Korean War*.

38. Quoted in Mitford, *Kind and Usual Punishment*, 131–32.

39. Cormier, *The Watcher and the Watched*; Fink, "A New Way to a New Life."

40. A. Collins, *In the Sleep Room*; McCoy, "Science in Dachau's Shadow"; McCoy, *A Question of Torture*; Oosenbrug, "Building a 'Cross-Roads Discipline' at McGill University."

41. "Intensive Treatment Units," Grant Application to the Department of Health, Education, and Welfare, Folder 2, Box 6, ACTEC Executive Office File, NYSA.

42. NY Gov. Special Comm. Of Criminal Offenders, "The Preliminary Report of the Governor's Special Committee of Criminal Offenders," 18.

43. NY Gov. Special Comm. Of Criminal Offenders, "The Preliminary Report of the Governor's Special Committee of Criminal Offenders," 18. Poser was a colleague of Hebb and a staff member of the Applied Psychology Centre, which Hebb envisioned as a means to access that "untapped supply of contract research and development work for business and the armed services that we have not been able to do anything about" (Oosenbrug, "Building a 'Cross-Roads Discipline," 175–76).

44. "Clinton Project Consultation Report," January 13, 1970, Folder 16, Box 2. ACTEC Executive Office Files, NYSA; O'Connor and Wolstenholme, *Medical Care of Prisoners and Detainees*, 95.

45. Klein, *The Shock Doctrine*, 42.

46. Douglas Lipton testimony in US Congress, *Oversight Hearings on Emerging Criminal Justice Issues*, 362.

47. Forgays and Thorne, "Mission Impossible," 276.

48. Forgays and Thorne, "The Special Problem of the Black Extremist in a Correctional Mental Hospital," 264.

49. While I have found no evidence that psychosurgery was happening in ACTEC, it was certainly happening in prisons during this era. Gobert, "Psychosurgery, Conditioning, and the Prisoner's Right to Refuse Rehabilitation"; Robitscher, "Psychosurgery and Other Somatic Means of Altering Behavior."

50. HIP Grant Application, "Mental Health Services Taskforce Committee," July 20 and 21, 1971, Folder 13, Box 4, ACTEC Executive Office Files, NYSA.

51. NY DOCS, *RX Prescription Correctional and Control Program*, 1972, Albany, NY, MM.

52. Sheridan Lyons, "Prison: No Brainwash, Drugs," *Democrat and Chronicle* (Rochester, NY), February 16, 1973, 6B.

53. Oswald to Cholmondeley, March 13, 1973, 1, MM.

54. Mugmuk to Oswald, March 15, 1973, 1–2, MM.

55. Peter J. Lacy to Carlton D. Marshall, *ACTEC Interdepartmental Communication Monthly Report*, April 3, 1973, 1, F. 45, Box 5, ACTEC Executive Office Files, NYSA.

56. Masia Mugmuk in conversation with author, 2021; Motion for Preliminary Injunction, Mukmuk v. Commissioner of DOCS et al., 70 Civ. 3518, 1, MM; "'Special Care' for New York Activists," *Prisoners' Digest International* II, no. 10 (Iowa City, IA), April 1973, 1; "New Rx Program—'Volunteers' Only," *The Black Panther* (Oakland, CA), June 2, 1973, 7; Lower Gallery Rx Collective, "Intensified Struggle," *Midnight Special* 3, no. 8 (August 1973): 6.

57. Kinzer, *Poisoner in Chief*, 46.

58. "Interdepartmental Communication," Peter J. Lacy to Carlton D. Marshall, April 2, 1973, Folder 45, Box 5, ACTEC Executive Office Files, NYSA.

59. Schwitzgebel, "Development and Legal Regulation of Coercive Behavior Modification," 7.

60. Schwitzgebel, "Development and Legal Regulation of Coercive Behavior Modification"; M. Shakur et al., *Genocide Waged against the Black Nation*

through Behavior Modification Orchestrated by Counterinsurgency and Low-Intensity Warfare in the U.S. Penal System.

61. Edgar H. Schein, "Letter—The Torture Cure," *Harper's Magazine*, November 1973, 128. See also Suedfeld, "Changes in Intellectual Performance," 155.

62. Quoted in Paul C. Agnew, "Intensive Treatment Units," Grant Application to the Department of Health, Education, and Welfare, August 15, 1971, Folder 13, Box 4, ACTEC Executive Office Files, NYSA.

63. Assorted "Behavior Modification Workshop"documents, Prescription Treatment, Box 23, ACTEC Executive Office Files, NYSA.

64. Quoted in Sheridan Lyons, "Prison: No Brainwash, Drugs," 6B.

65. Richard Moore (Dhoruba bin-Wahad) Interview (produced by Mark Schwartz for KPFA). June 16, 1973, Freedom Archives.

66. Quoted in Sheridan Lyons, "Prison: No Brainwash, Drugs," 6B; Cormier, *The Watcher and the Watched*, 10.

67. Jomo Omowale quoted in Davis, Gaynes, and Davis, "Born in Prison," 128.

68. In an essay entitled "A Clinical and Theoretical Overview of Hallucinatory Phenomena," Louis Jolyon West, a high-level MK Ultra operative who will shortly appear in this chapter's narrative, wrote: "The role of drugs in the exercise of internal political control is also coming under increasing discussion. Control can be imposed either through prohibition or supply. The total or even partial prohibition of drugs gives government considerable leverage for other types of control. An example would be the selective application of drug laws permitting immediate search, or 'no knock' entry, against selected components of the population such as members of certain minority groups or political organizations. But a government could also supply drugs to help control a population. This method, foreseen by Aldous Huxley in *Brave New World* (1932), has the governing element employing drugs selectively to manipulate the governed in various ways" (298). See also McCoy, *The Politics of Heroin*; Webb, *Dark Alliance*; Kinzer, *Poisoner in Chief*; Andreas, *Killer High*; Dan Baum, "Legalize It All," *Harper's Magazine*, April 2016, https://harpers.org/archive/2016/04/legalize-it-all.

69. "Affidavit of Antonio Cruz," March 13, 1973, MM; Complaint by Masia A. Mugmuk, May 30, 1974, MM. The ACTEC Executive Office Files list Antonio Cruz as RX-13 and notes that he was transferred into the program on February 23, 1973. For other accounts of forced drugging, see the Assembly Select Committee on Corrections, "An Investigation into the Practice of Forced Drugging/Medication in California's Detention Facilities." December, 1976. Thuma, *All Our Trials*, 113–14; Hatch, *Silent Cells*.

70. Hatch, *Silent Cells*.

71. Carlos Roche in conversation with author, 2021.

72. Meeting notes of the HIP Review Committee, July 15, 1969, Folder 3, Box 5, ACTEC Executive Office Files, NYSA.

73. Quoted in Frederick C. Thorne and Donald G. Forgays, "Intensive Treatment Units," Grant Application to the Department of Health, Education, and Welfare. May 26, 1969, Folder 2, Box 5, ACTEC Executive Office Files, NYSA.

74. Kunzel, *Criminal Intimacy*, 219. Huey P. Newton was incarcerated in Vacaville in 1968. Analyzing the dynamics in the institution, he wrote: "These men were exploited and controlled by the guards and the system. Their sexuality was perverted into a pseudosexuality that was used to control and undermine their normal yearnings for dignity and freedom. The system was the pusher in this case, and the prisoners were forced to become addicted to sex. Love and vulnerability and tenderness were distorted into functions of power, competition, and control" (*Revolutionary Suicide*, 271). According to Stansfield Turner, Director of Central Intelligence between 1977 and 1981, "We also know now that some unwitting testing took place on criminal sexual psychopaths confined at a State hospital and that, additionally, research was done of a knock-out or "K" drug [ketamine, commonly known as a "rape drug"] in parallel with research to develop pain killers for cancer patients" (US Congress, "Project MK Ultra," 7).

75. Paul C. Agnew, "Intensive Treatment Units" Grant Application to the Department of Health, Education, and Welfare. August 15, 1971, Folder 13, Box 4, ACTEC Executive Office Files, NYSA. It is worth noting that in 1994, the US military submitted a proposal to develop a so-called "gay bomb" that would inundate the enemy with "strong aphrodisiacs, especially if the chemical also caused homosexual behavior." The military hoped that this effort would make the enemy lose interest in combat. See Dan Glaister, "Air Force Looked at Spray to Turn Enemy Gay," *The Guardian*, June 13, 2007.

76. A newspaper article from 1958 highlights Forgays as an example of how American men and women were "moving even closer to complete equality at home." The article features an image of Forgays wearing an apron and washing dishes. Given his apparent commitment to gender equality, one can only speculate about how he rationalized his infliction of gender violence against captive Black men. However, the author of the feature provides a potential clue, writing that "today's man of the house is the victim of what Forgays lightly describes as 'perhaps' a form of mild schizophrenia." See "American Males and Females Are Moving Even Closer to Complete Equality in Home," *The Central New Jersey Home News* (New Brunswick, NJ), June 22, 1958, 24.

77. McCoy, *A Question of Torture*, 32; McCoy, "Science in Dachau's Shadow."

78. "Cornellians Get Grants," *The Ithaca Journal* (Ithaca, NY), September 16, 1957, 4; Price, "Buying a Piece of Anthropology"; Price, *Weaponizing Anthropology*.

79. Donald G. Forgays, "Project THEMIS Proposal," Folder 13, Carton B5, Robert T. Stafford Collection. UVM; Goodman and Goodman, *Standing Up to the Madness*, 131.

80. Lawson and Joffe, "Donald G. Forgays (1926–1993)."

81. O'Neill, *Chaos*; O'Neill and Piepenbring, "Inside the Archive of an LSD Researcher with Ties to the CIA's MKULTRA Mind Control Project."

82. Suedfeld, "Changes in Intellectual Performance," 166.

83. Suedfeld, "Changes in Intellectual Performance," 166.

84. West, "A Clinical and Theoretical Overview of Hallucinatory Phenomena," 296.

85. "Napanoch Prisoners Secretly Drugged."

86. "Report of Inmates in Segregation During Month of June 19, 1972," Folder 45, Box 5, ACTEC Executive Office Files, NYSA.

87. SAC (157-979) SA Daniel V. Hogan, "Black Extremist Activities at Great Meadow Correctional Facility, Comstock, New York," March 20, 1972, DBW.

88. "Masia and Mzuri Mugmuk Seek Your Support," 1975, MM.

89. NY DOCS, "New York State Correctional Services Master Plan, 1980–1985," p. 56, NYSA.

90. Marshall S. Carter, "Report of Inspection of MKUltra," Memorandum for Deputy Director/Plans, August 14, 1963, GD.

91. Kinzer, *Poisoner in Chief*.

92. Commission on CIA Activities within the United States, *Report to the President by the Commission on CIA Activities within the United States*.

93. Kinzer, *Poisoner in Chief*; Memo: Information Review Staff, FOIA Request for John D. Marks, IRS 75-2732, July 25, 1975, GD.

94. Martin Sostre, "End to ACTEC?," *Midnight Special* 3, no. 9 (September 1973): 10.

95. Sostre, "End to ACTEC?"

96. Letter from Martin Sostre, April 23, 1974, 1, courtesy of Garret Felber, https://drive.google.com/file/d/1_AZEKmfJlnp4FYdr3Pi6DZudAPSbr_dW/view.

97. Letter from Martin Sostre, April 23, 1974, 2.

98. "Open Letter from Comstock Prison: Remember Attica!," *Workers' Power*, October 19–November 1, 1973, 11.

99. SAC San Francisco to Director, FBI, "Re: Counterintelligence Program; Black Nationalist-Hate Groups; Racial Intelligence," April 4, 1968, 7, DBW.

100. Notably, the LEAA's top administrator explained that these projects would still be eligible for federal funding through the Department of Health, Education, and Welfare, the sponsor of Forgays's research in ACTEC. See Department of Justice, "Law Enforcement Assistance Administration News Release," February 14, 1974, quoted in US Congress, "Individual Rights and the Federal Role in Behavior Modification," 420.

101. Wallace Turner, "Psychiatrist Says He Believes Miss Hearst on Role in Bank Robbery," *New York Times*, February 27, 1976, 12; Louis Jolyon West, "Psychiatrist Pleads for Patty Hearst's Release," *Eugene Register-Guard* (Eugene, OR), December 29, 1978.

102. O'Neill, *Chaos*; Schreiber, *Revolution's End*; Greg deGiere, "The CIA in CMF: A Revealing Report of How Inmates Were Covertly Tested for Effects of Mind-Altering Drugs," *Vacaville Reporter* (Vacaville, CA), August 11, 1976, 1 and 4.

103. Schreiber, *Revolution's End*; Dick Russell, "Who Ran the SLA?," *Ann Arbor Sun* (Ann Arbor, MI), January 22, 1976; Mae Brussells, "Why Was Patricia Hearst Kidnapped?," *The Realist* (New York), February 1974.

104. SA Carl S. Valentine, Re: "Bureau airtel to Albany," May 10, 1974, p. 1, DBW.

105. "Interview with Kiilu Nyasha and Dhoruba Bin-Wahad," May 21, 1990, Freedom Archives.

106. Cited in "Amended Complaint Jury Trial Demanded," Bin-Wahad v. Coughlin et al., 86 Civ. 4112, p. 4. DBW.

107. Bin-Wahad in conversation with author, May 2019.

108. "Message to the Black Movement: A Political Statement from the Black Underground," ca. 1976, p. 1, Black Liberation Army, 1973–1992, the Black Power Movement Part 3: Papers of the Revolutionary Action Movement, 1963–1996, UPA.

109. "Message to the Black Movement" 10.

110. "Message to the Black Movement," 5.

111. "Prisons—A Target of Revolutionaries," *FBI Bulletin*, September 1974, 13.

112. Gomez, "Resisting Living Death at Marion Federal Penitentiary, 1972," 62.

113. US Congress, *Terrorism* (Testimony of Bertram S. Brown), 4197.

114. SAC, Albany to Director, FBI, "Extremist, Revolutionary, Terrorist and Subversive Activities in Penal Institutions (PRISACTS); Extremist Matter," August 16, 1976, DBW.

115. Richard Dhoruba Moore v. Coughlin et al., 86 Civ. 4112; Moore v. FBI; Dhoruba bin-Wahad in conversation with author, 2020; Robert J. Boyle in conversation with author, 2020; New York State Policy Study Group, *Report of the Policy Study Group on Terrorism*; Dunleavy, *The Fertile Soil of Jihad*; Burton, "Targeting Revolutionaries."

116. Bottom and Gallati, *Industrial Espionage*, 245.

117. Bottom and Gallati, *Industrial Espionage*, 246.

118. Bottom and Gallati, *Industrial Espionage*, 246.

119. Burton, "Targeting Revolutionaries."

120. Michael T. Kaufman, "Slaying of One of the Last Black Liberation Army Leaders Still at Large Ended a 7-Month Manhunt," *New York Times*, November 16, 1973, 10.

121. Richard Moore (Dhoruba bin-Wahad), Interview (produced by Mark Schwartz for KPFA), June 16, 1973, Freedom Archives.

122. Albert Washington, "Examination Under Oath," August 9, 1991, 26, DBW.

123. A. Shakur, *Assata*, 52.

124. Testimony of Paul Garcia, June 9, 1987, Meriwether et al. v. Coughlin et al., 80 Civ. 4712, SDNY, 1671, NARA.

125. Awartani, "In Solidarity."

126. J. W. Curran to ES LeFevre, NY DOCS CCF Interdepartmental Communication, March 9, 1978, DBW.

127. "Rally against Intense Repression and Murder of Black and Puerto Rican Inmates at Green Haven Prison," Box 44, Folder 23: Green Haven Prison (Voice of the Struggle), 1977, Yuri and Bill Kochiyama Papers, 1936–2003, CU; Pranay Gupte, "Two Deaths and an Escape Raise Green Haven Tensions," *New York Times*, May 29, 1978, 1.

128. New York State Commission of Investigation, *Corruption and Abuses in the Correctional System*, 1.

129. Deposition of Thomas Coughlin, October 1, 1985, Meriwether v. Coughlin, 80 Civ. 4712, SDNY, 11, DBW.

130. Testimony of Thomas Coughlin, June 11, 1987, Meriwether v. Coughlin, 80 Civ. 4712, SDNY, 2338, NARA.

131. Walter E. Beverly to Watch Commander Edwards, Re: "The Creative Communications Committee," January 28, 1980, DBW.; Beverly to Watch Commander Edwards, NY DOCS Inter-Departmental Communication, July 19, 1980, Meriwether v. Coughlin, 80 Civ. 4712M, SDNY, NARA; Ed Cortune to Watch Commander Edwards, NY DOCS Inter-Departmental Communication, July 21, 1980, Meriwether v. Coughlin, 80 Civ. 4712M, SDNY, DBW.

132. Testimony of Thomas Coughlin, June 11, 1987, Meriwether v. Coughlin 80 Civ. 4712, SDNY, 2348, NARA.

133. Paul Garcia to Brian F. Malone and William G. Bodmer, "RE: CCC GHCF Analysis of Intelligence Data," Meriwether v. Coughlin 80 Civ. 4712, January 25, 1980, 5, NARA.

134. Joseph P. Keenan to Chester Clark, Re: Dhoruba bin-Wahad, NY DOCS Memo, June 12, 1979; Arthur A. Leonardo to William Gard, Re: Richard Moore, June 25, 1979, DBW.

135. Superintendent's Proceeding Report Re: Richard Moore, June 10, 1979; Joseph P. Keenan to Chester Clark, Re: Dhoruba bin-Wahad, NY DOCS Memo, June 12, 1979, Richard Dhoruba Moore v. Coughlin et al., 86 Civ. 4112; NY DOCS Chronological Entry Sheet for Richard Moore, 1978–1978; Moore v. Coughlin et al., 86 Civ. 4112; Letter from Bob Boyle to Gov. Hugh Carey, Re: Richard Dhoruba Moore, September 22, 1979; Letter from R. Dhoruba Moore to Robert Nelepovitz, July 10, 1979, DBW.

136. Albert Washington, "Examination Under Oath," Moore v Coughlin et al., US SDNY, August 9, 1991, 18, DBW.

137. Letter, Dhoruba to Bob (Robert J. Boyle), June 28, 1979, 1, DBW.

138. Robert J. Boyle in conversation with author, October 2022; Albert Washington, "Examination Under Oath," 18.

139. Muntaqim writes that he was transferred to Green Haven in July of 1980 (*We Are Our Own Liberators*, 273–74), but this is incorrect. Based on the available DOCS materials, he was in Green Haven by late 1979.

140. Testimony of Thomas Coughlin, June 11, 1987, Meriwether v. Coughlin 80 Civ. 4712, SDNY, 2345, NARA.

141. Muntaqim in conversation with author, September 2022.

142. Muntaqim in conversation with author, September 2022.

143. Robert Abrams, "Pre-Trial Order," March 22, 1987, Meriwether v. Coughlin 80 Civ. 4712, SDNY, 4, NARA.

144. Bin-Wahad in conversation with author, March 2019.

145. Brian F. Malone, "Analysis of CCC Badge," NYS DOCS, January 21, 1980, Meriwether v. Coughlin 80 Civ. 4712, NARA.

146. Muntaqim in conversation with author, September 2022.

147. Robert Abrams, "Pre-Trial Order," May 22, 1987, Meriwether v. Coughlin, 80 Civ. 4712M, SDNY, 6, NARA; Walter E. Beverly to Watch Com-

mander Edwards, NY DOCS Inter-Departmental Communication, July 19, 1980, DBW.

148. Testimony of Thomas Coughlin, June 11, 1987, Meriwether v. Coughlin 80 Civ. 4712, SDNY, 2348.

149. Abrams, "Pre-Trial Order," 9.

150. Abrams, "Pre-Trial Order," 10.

151. Charles Meriwether and Charles Butler, affidavit in support of claims of physical abuse, Meriwether v. Coughlin.

152. Muntaqim, *We Are Our Own Liberators*.

153. Abrams, "Pre-Trial Order," 12.

154. Benjamin, "Critique of Violence," 240; Deposition of Thomas Coughlin, 14.

155. Deposition of Thomas Coughlin, 21.

156. Testimony of Paul Garcia, Meriwether v. Coughlin 80 Civ. 4712, SDNY, June 9, 1987, 1659–60, NARA.

157. "Masia and Mzuri Mugmuk Seek Your Support," 8; "Wife and 3 Others Are Held in Slaying of Man in Jersey," *New York Times*, December 2, 1975, 79.

158. "Profile of a Revolutionary Married Couple," 1975–1979, 4, MM.

159. "Murder Conspiracy Guilt Plea Entered," *The Daily Register* (Shrewsbury, NJ), March 2, 1976, 4.

160. Executive Clemency—Mzuri Mugmuk aka Vanessa Williams, December 20, 1985, Box 6. Executive Clemency Files, NJSA.

161. Kerness, "The Hidden History of Solitary Confinement in New Jersey's Control Units."

162. Mugmuk in conversation with author, March 2019.

163. Kerness, *The Hidden History of Solitary Confinement in New Jersey's Control Units*; American Friends Service Committee, *Tortured in United States Prisons*, 47; McCoy, *A Question of Torture*.

164. Li, "Captive Passages."

165. Gomez, "Resisting Living Death at Marion Federal Penitentiary, 1972"; M. Shakur et al., *Genocide Waged against the Black Nation through Behavior Modification Orchestrated by Counterinsurgency and Low-Intensity Warfare in the U.S. Penal System*.

166. Quoted in Camp, *Incarcerating the Crisis*, 88.

167. Committee on the Judiciary, *The United States Penitentiary: Marion, Illinois*, 19.

168. Kurshan, *Out of Control*.

169. Kiebala and Rodriguez, "FAQ: Solitary Confinement in the United States"; Lizzie Kane, "No Touching Allowed for Many LGBTQ+."

170. Kurshan, *Out of Control*.

EPILOGUE

1. Soul B, "F.D.S. #96—Soul B—the Big Homie of the Real Big Homies," *Flip daScript*, 2019. https://www.youtube.com/watch?v=FX1MVZhQWNA&t=4498s; Jennifer Gonnerman, "Gangs Behind Bars," *Village Voice*, October 21, 1997, 41–47.

2. Interestingly, as Bloods co-founder Soul B explains in a 2019 interview: "We seen ourselves, when we first founded this thing, as revolutionaries like George Jackson did with the Black Guerilla Family" (F.D.S. #96).

3. Tyrone Larkins in conversation with author, 2019.

4. Von Clausewitz, *On War*, 75–77.

5. Du Bois, *Black Reconstruction*, 9–10.

6. Gilmore, *Golden Gulag*; Murakawa, *The First Civil Right*; Gottschalk, *Caught*; M. Alexander, *The New Jim Crow*.

7. Davis, Gaynes, and Davis, "Born in Prison," 127.

8. NYS DOCCS, "It's Television Time in New York's Prisons," *DOCS TODAY* (Albany, NY), 1988, 3. For another discussion of the legacy of Attica and the introduction of TVs, see Gilbert, "Attica—Thirty Years Later."

9. I. Alexander, "The Carceral Media Regime."

10. Law, "Captive Audience."

11. Quoted in Alexander, "The Carceral Media Regime," 219.

12. Jennifer Valentino-DeVries, "Meant to Monitor Prison Calls, Service Could Track You, Too," *New York Times*, May 11, 2018; Noah Goldberg and John Annese, "NYC Correction Contractor Recorded Thousands More Lawyer-Client Jail Phone Calls Than First Reported," *Daily News* (New York, NY), December 30, 2021.

13. Lisa Laplace to Michael J. Ranieri, "RE: New York Civil Liberties Union's Public Records Request, dated April 27, 2021 (FOIL Number DOCCS-21-04-309)," March 17, 2022, 2, https://www.nyclu.org/sites/default/files/field_documents/letter_to_doccs_voice_recognition_technology.pdf.

14. Kilgore, *Understanding E-Carceration*, 34; Scheflin and Opton, *The Mind Manipulators*, 346–53; Tackwood, *The Glass House Tapes*, 225–26.

15. Schwitzgebel, "A Comparative Study of Zulu and English Reactions to Sensory Deprivation."

16. Newton, *The Huey P. Newton Reader*, 326.

17. Schwitzgebel and Schwitzgebel, *Psychotechnology*, 2.

18. Z. Shakur, "America Is the Prison."

19. Kluckow and Zeng, "Correctional Populations in the United States."

20. McQuade, *Pacifying the Homeland*; Kilgore, *Understanding E-Carceration*, 10; Vitale and Jefferson, "The Emergence of Command and Control Policing in Neoliberal New York."

21. Harcourt, *The Counterrevolution*; Ackerman, *Reign of Terror*; Butler, *Precarious Life*; Brooks, *How Everything Became War*.

22. For more information about the Attica Brothers Foundation, visit https://www.atticabrothersfoundation.org.

23. Fresh Air, "How 4 Inmates Launched a Statewide Hunger Strike from Solitary," *National Public Radio*, March 6, 2014, https://www.npr.org/2014/03/06/286794055/how-four-inmates-launched-a-statewide-hunger-strike-from-solitary.

24. Walia, *Border and Rule*.

25. Rodríguez and Sirvent, "Insurgency and Counterinsurgency."

26. Abby Cunniff, "NYC Activists Push Back against Proposed 'Feminist' Women's Jail in Harlem," *Truthout*, July 2, 2022, https://truthout.org/articles/nyc-activists-push-back-against-proposed-feminist-womens-jail-in-harlem.

27. Kwame Olufemi, Sarah Haley, Stuart Schrader, and Micah Herskind, "The Abolitionist Struggle to Stop Cop City: History, Geography, Intersections," March 14, 2023, https://www.youtube.com/watch?v=hWwJkxxMuhQ&t=3328s.

28. Kaba, *We Do This 'Til We Free Us!*

29. Jared Ware, "'I'm for Disruption': Interview with Prison Strike Organizer from Jailhouse Lawyers Speak," *Shadowproof*, August 16, 2018, https://shadowproof.com/2018/08/16/im-for-disruption-interview-with-prison-strike-organizer-from-jailhouse-lawyers-speak; Jared Ware, "South Carolina Prisoners Demand: 'End prison slavery,'" *Workers World*, August 20, 2018, https://www.workers.org/2018/08/38704.

Bibliography

INSTITUTIONAL ARCHIVAL SOURCES

The Black Power Movement Part 3: Papers of the Revolutionary Action Movement, 1963–1996. UPA Collection from LexisNexis, Bethesda, MD *(UPA)*

The Center for Legislative Archives, Washington, DC (CLA)
Papers of the House Internal Security Committee

Columbia University Rare Books and Manuscript Library, New York, NY (CU)
Yuri and Bill Kochiyama Papers

David M. Rubenstein Rare Book and Manuscript Library, Durham, NC (DMR)
Jomo Joka Omowale Papers, 1969–2008

Eastern Kentucky University, Richmond, KY (EKU)
Correctional Photographs Archive

The Freedom Archives, Berkeley, CA (FA)

Interference Archive, Brooklyn, NY (IA)

Kenneth Spencer Research Library at the University of Kansas (KSR)

Library of Congress, Washington, DC (LOC)
Kenneth Bancroft Clark Papers

274 | Bibliography

Lloyd Sealy Library at John J. College of Criminal Justice, New York, NY (LSL)
Gary McGivern and Marguerite Culp Papers

McKay Commission Talking Archives (Online) (MC)

M. E. Grenader Department of Special Collections and Archives at the University of Albany, Albany, NY (MEG)
Alice P. Green Papers, 1960–2001
Correctional Association of New York Records, 1844–1988
New York State Coalition for Criminal Justice Records, 1971–1986
Council 82 Collection

Monmouth County Archives
DeNucci Photograph Negatives Collection

National Archives and Records Administration, Kansas City, MO (NARA)
Ralph Valvano, Donald Leroland, and Jonathan Williams, et al. v. McGrath [later changed to Benjamin Malcolm] and NYC Department of Corrections Civ 1970-1930, Eastern District of New York
Carter v. McGinnis Civ 1970-539, Southern District of New York
Meriwether v. Coughlin Civ 80-4712, Southern District of New York
Smoake v. Fritz Civ 1970-5103, Southern District of New York
Walker v. Fritz Civ 1970-5104, Southern District of New York

National Criminal Justice Reference Service (NCJRS)

New Jersey State Archives (NJSA)
Executive Clemency Files, 1982–1990

New York City Municipal Archives, New York, NY (NYC MU)
Board of Corrections Files
John V. Lindsay Papers
New York City Jails Files

New York State Archives, Albany, NY (NYSA)
Attica Commission Investigation Files
Adirondack Correctional Treatment and Evaluation Center Executive Office Files, 1965–1975
Auburn Prison Correctional Volunteer Services office files, 1970–1974
Auburn Prison Warden's office files, 1901–1973
Auburn Prison Annual reports of Auburn Prison and Prison for Women, 1919–1974
Governor Malcolm Wilson Central Subject and Correspondence Files, 1973–1974
Governor Nelson A. Rockefeller Central Subject and Correspondence Files, 1959–1973
Inmate Case Files
Non-Criminal Investigations Files

New York State Library, Albany, NY (NYSL)

New York State Museum, Albany, NY (NYSM)
Attica Collection

Pacifica Radio Archives (PRA)

Robert S. Cox Special Collections and University Archives Research Center, University of Massachusetts, Amherst (RSC)
Dean Albertson Oral History Collection

Rockefeller Archive Center, Sleepy Hollow, NY (RAC)
Nelson A. Rockefeller Papers Gubernatorial Records, Office Subject Files, Second Administration, Subseries 37.2
Nelson A. Rockefeller Papers Gubernatorial Records, Office Subject Files, Third Administration, Subseries 37.3
Nelson A. Rockefeller Papers Gubernatorial Records, Office Subject Files, Fourth Administration, Subseries 37.4
Nelson Rockefeller personal papers
Nelson Rockefeller Vice Presidential Records
Rockefeller Foundation Records

Silver Special Collections Library, University of Vermont, Burlington, VT (SSCL)
Robert T. Stafford Papers

The Southern Historical Collection at UNC Chapel Hill, Chapel Hill, NC (SHC)
Tom Wicker Papers, 1917–2013

Tamiment Archives at New York University, New York, NY (TA)
Printed Ephemera Collection on Organizations
Roslyn Payne Collection of Black Panther Party FBI Files

University of Virginia, Charlottesville, VA (UVA)
Committee on Internal Security, 1971–1974.

Orisanmi Burton, US DOJ FOIPA Request 1461616-000 Prison Activists Surveillance Program, March 6, 2020

Russ Kick, US DOJ FOIPA Request 1401693-000 Prison Attica Prison Riot, June 22, 2018

PERSONAL ARCHIVAL SOURCES

Alice Green Collection (AG)
Assorted documents related to NY DOCS and anti-prison organizing

Dhoruba bin-Wahad and Robert J. Boyle (DBW)

Assorted materials related to political prisoners
Assorted materials related to the Black Panther Party and Black Liberation Army
Case files and testimony from *Dhoruba bin-Wahad v. FBI*
Case files and testimony from *Dhoruba bin Wahad v. NY DOCS*
FBI surveillance files
NY DOCS prison files
NYPD surveillance files

Greg deGiere Collection (GD)

Assorted files related to his research and FOIA requests into CIA activities in California's Vacaville Prison during the 1970s

Hassan Gale (HG)

Assorted prison documents

Larry White Collection (LW)

Assorted documents related to the Green Haven Think Tank and inmate organizations

Masia A. Mugmuk (MM)

Assorted prison documents, legal documents, and activism documents

Melvin Alston Collection

Assorted documents related to the Green Haven Think Tank and inmate organizations

CITED INTERVIEWS

Brother A in conversation with author, 2019
Muhammad Ahmad in conversation with Aukram Burton and author, 2019
Kareem C. Allah in conversation with author, 2022
Ashanti M. Alston in conversation with author, 2020
Melvin Alston in conversation with author, 2020
Dhoruba bin-Wahad in conversation with author, 2017–21
Robert Bloom in conversation with author, 2021
Robert J. Boyle in conversation with author, 2017–21
Bugs in conversation with author, 2020–21
C.H. in conversation with author, 2020
Emani Davis in conversation with author, 2020
Eddie Ellis in conversation with author, 2014
Hassan Gale in conversation with author, 2015–21
Jacob in conversation with author, 2017–18
Tyrone Larkins in conversation with author, 2019–20
Gerald Lefcourt in conversation with author, 2017
Larry Mamiya in conversation with author, 2015
Martell in conversation with author, 2020

James "Blood" McCreary in conversation with author, 2021
Dixie Moon in conversation with author, 2014.
Masia A. Mugmuk in conversation with author, 2020–22
Edwin Muller in conversation with author, 2014
Jalil Muntaqim in conversation with author, 2021
Che Nieves in conversation with author, 2020
Sekou Odinga in conversation with author, 2017
Carlos Roche in conversation with author, 2021
Larry White in conversation with author, 2014–21

PUBLISHED SOURCES

Abdur-Rahman, Aliyyah. *Against the Closet*. Durham, NC: Duke University Press, 2012.
Abu-Lughod, Janet L. *Race, Space, and Riots in Chicago, New York, and Los Angeles*. Oxford: Oxford University Press, 2007.
Ackerman, Spencer. *Reign of Terror: How the 9/11 Era Destabilized America and Produced Trump*. New York: Penguin, 2022.
Ahmad, Muhammad. *We Will Return in the Whirlwind: Black Radical Organizations, 1960–1975*. Chicago: Charles H. Kerr Pub. Co., 2007.
Alexander, Ian J. "The Carceral Media Regime: Technologies of Disaggregation, Pacification, and Rebellion in US Prisons." PhD diss., New York University, 2022.
Alexander, Michelle. *The New Jim Crow: Mass Incarceration in the Age of Colorblindness*. New York: New Press, 2012.
Alim, Jalil Abdul. "Struggle at Auburn Prison." *The Black Scholar* 2, no. 10 (1971): 53.
Allen, Jafari S., and Ryan Cecil Jobson. "The Decolonizing Generation: (Race and) Theory in Anthropology Since the Eighties." *Current Anthropology* 57, no. 2 (2016). https://doi.org/10.1086/685502.
Allen, Robert L. *Black Awakening in Capitalist America: An Analytic History*. Trenton, NJ: Africa World Press, 1992.
———. "Reassessing the Internal (Neo) Colonialism Theory." *The Black Scholar* 35, no. 1. (2005): 2–11.
Alston, Ashanti O. "Black Anarchism." Transcript of a speech given at Hunter College on October 24, 2004. https://theanarchistlibrary.org/library/ashanti-omowali-alston-black-anarchism.
American Correctional Association. *Causes, Preventive Measures, and Methods of Controlling Riots and Disturbances in Correctional Institutions*. Washington, DC: American Correctional Association, October 1970.
American Friends Service Committee. *Tortured in United States Prisons: Evidence of Human Rights Violations*. Newark, NJ: American Friends Service Committee, 2011. https://www.afsc.org/document/torture-us-prisons.
Anderson, William C. *The Nation on No Map: Anarchism and Abolition*. Chico, CA: AK Press, 2021.
Andreas, Peter. *Killer High: A History of War in Six Drugs*. Oxford: Oxford University Press, 2019.

Apel, Dora. "Torture Culture: Lynching Photographs and the Images of Abu Ghraib." *Art Journal* 64, no. 2 (2005): 88–100.
Awartani, Sara. "In Solidarity: Palestine in the Puerto Rican Political Imaginary." *Radical History Review*, no. 128 (2017): 199–222. https://doi.org/10.1215/01636545-3857878.
Baer, Harold, Jr., and Arminda Bepko. "A Necessary and Proper Role for Federal Courts in Prison Reform: The Benjamin V. Malcolm Consent Decrees." *New York Law School Law Review* 52, no. 1 (2007): 3–64.
Badillo, Herman, and Milton Haynes. *A Bill of No Rights: Attica and the American Prison System*. New York: Outerbridge & Lazard, 1972.
Balagoon, Kuwasi. *Soldier's Story: Revolutionary Writings by a New Afrikan Anarchist*. Oakland, CA: PM Press, 2019.
Balagun, Kazembe. "Kuwasi at 60." *Monthly Review Online* (December 31, 2006). https://mronline.org/2006/12/31/kuwasi-at-60.
Balbus, Isaac D. "Commodity Form and Legal Form: An Essay on the 'Relative Autonomy' of the Law." *Law and Society Review* 11, no. 3 (1977): 571–88.
———. *The Dialectics of Legal Repression: Black Rebels before the American Criminal Courts*. New York: Russell Sage Foundation, 1973.
Balcells, Laia, and Christopher M. Sullivan. "New Findings from Conflict Archives: An Introduction and Methodological Framework." *Journal of Peace Research* 55, no. 2 (2018). https://doi.org/10.1177/0022343317750217.
Baldwin, James. *The Fire Next Time*. New York: Random House, 1963.
———. "Going to Meet the Man." In *Going to Meet the Man: Stories*. New York: Vintage, 2013.
———. *If Beale Street Could Talk: A Novel*. New York: Vintage, 2006.
Ball, Jared A. *I Mix What I Like!: A Mixtape Manifesto*. Chico, CA: AK Press, 2011.
———. *The Myth and Propaganda of Black Buying Power*. Cham, Switzerland: Springer, 2020.
Bambara, Toni Cade. *The Black Woman: An Anthology*. New York: Signet, 1970.
Barnett, Donald L., and Karari Njama. *Mau Mau from Within: Autobiography and Analysis of Kenya's Peasant Revolt*. New York: Monthly Review Press, 1966.
Belew, Kathleen. *Bring the War Home: The White Power Movement and Paramilitary America*. Cambridge, MA: Harvard University Press, 2018.
Bell, Malcolm. *The Turkey Shoot: Tracking the Attica Cover-Up*. New York: Grove/Atlantic, 1985.
Benjamin, Walter. "Critique of Violence." In *Selected Writings, Volume 1, 1913–1926*, edited by Marcus Bullock and Michael W. Jennings, 236–52. Cambridge, MA: Belknap Press of Harvard University Press, 1996.
Ben-Moshe, Liat. *Decarcerating Disability: Deinstitutionalization and Prison Abolition*. Minneapolis: University of Minnesota Press, 2020.
Ben-Moshe, L., C. Chapman, and A. Carey. *Disability Incarcerated: Imprisonment and Disability in the United States and Canada*. New York: Palgrave Macmillan US, 2014.
Berger, Dan. *Captive Nation: Black Prison Organizing in the Civil Rights Era*. Chapel Hill: University of North Carolina Press, 2014.

———. "Subjugated Knowledges: Activism, Scholarship, and Ethnic Studies Ways of Knowing." In *Critical Ethnic Studies*, edited by Nada Elia, et al., 215–28. Durham, NC: Duke University Press, 2016.

Berger, Dan, and Toussaint Losier. *Rethinking the American Prison Movement.* New York: Routledge, 2017.

Berlien, Ivan C. "Psychiatry in the Army Correctional System." In *Neuropsychiatry in World War II* (Volume 1), edited by Leonard D. Heaton, 491–522. Washington, DC: Department of the Army, 1966.

Berreman, Gerald D. "Ethics verses 'Realism' in Anthropology." In *Ethics and the Profession of Anthropology: Dialogue for a New Era*, edited by Carolyn Fluehr-Lobban, 38–71. University of Pennsylvania Press, 1991.

Berry, Maya J., Claudia Chávez Argüelles, Shanya Cordis, Sarah Ihmoud, and Elizabeth Velásquez Estrada. "Toward a Fugitive Anthropology: Gender, Race, and Violence in the Field." *Cultural Anthropology* 32, no. 4 (2017). https://doi.org/10.14506/ca32.4.05.

Best, Stephen, and Saidiya Hartman. "Fugitive Justice." *Representations*, no. 92 (2005): 1–5.

Besteman, Catherine, Karina Biondi, and Orisanmi Burton. "Authority, Confinement, Solidarity, and Dissent." *PoLAR: Political and Legal Anthropology Review* (October 18, 2018). https://polarjournal.org/2018/10/18/authority-confinement-solidarity-and-dissent-2.

bin-Wahad, Dhoruba, Mumia Abu-Jamal, and Assata Shakur. *Still Black, Still Strong: Survivors of the US War against Black Revolutionaries.* Los Angeles: Semiotext(e), 1993.

Bjork-James, Carwil. "Unarmed Militancy: Tactical Victories, Subjectivity, and Legitimacy in Bolivian Street Protest." *American Anthropologist* 122, no. 3 (2020): 514–27.

Bjork-James, Sophie. "White Sexual Politics: The Patriarchal Family in White Nationalism and the Religious Right." *Transforming Anthropology* 28, no. 1 (2020): 58–73.

Black, Jonathan, ed. *Radical Lawyers: Their Role in the Movement and in the Courts.* New York: Avon Books, 1971.

Bloom, Joshua, and Waldo E. Martin Jr. *Black against Empire.* Oakland: University of California Press, 2013.

Boggs, James. *Pages from a Black Radical's Notebook: A James Boggs Reader.* Detroit, MI: Wayne State University Press, 2011.

Boggs, James, and Grace Lee Boggs. *Revolution and Evolution in the Twentieth Century.* New York: Monthly Review Press, 1974.

Bordenkircher, Donald E. "Prisons and the Revolutionary." Paper presented at the Congress of Correction, Houston, Texas, 1974.

Borges, Sónia Vaz. *Militant Education, Liberation Struggle, Consciousness: The PAIGC Education in Guinea Bissau, 1963–1978.* Frankfurt: Peter Lang Edition, 2019.

Bottom, Norman R., Jr., and Robert R. J. Gallati. *Industrial Espionage: Intelligence Techniques and Countermeasures.* Oxford: Butterworth, 1984.

Boyle, Robert J. "COINTELPRO: The 19-Year Ordeal of Dhoruba bin-Wahad." *Covert Action Information Bulletin*, no. 36. Spring 1991: 12-16.

Brand, Dionne. *A Map to the Door of No Return: Notes to Belonging.* Toronto: Vintage, 2011.
Brooks, Rosa. *How Everything Became War and the Military Became Everything: Tales from the Pentagon.* New York: Simon and Schuster, 2016.
Brown, H. Rap. *Die Nigger Die: A Political Autobiography.* New York: Dial Press, 1969.
Brown, Vincent. *Tacky's Revolt: The Story of an Atlantic Slave War.* Cambridge, MA: Belknap Press, 2020.
Browne, Simone. *Dark Matters: On the Surveillance of Blackness.* Durham, NC: Duke University Press, 2015.
Buck, Pem Davidson. "Centering Prisons: Reframing Analysis of the State, Relations of Power and Resistance." *American Anthropologist* 123, no. 3 (2021). https://doi.org/10.1111/aman.13616.
Bukhari, Safiya. *The War Before: The True Life Story of Becoming a Black Panther, Keeping the Faith in Prison and Fighting for Those Left Behind.* New York: The Feminist Press at CUNY, 2010.
Burnard, Trevor G. *Mastery, Tyranny, and Desire: Thomas Thistlewood and His Slaves in the Anglo-Jamaican World.* Chapel Hill: University of North Carolina Press, 2004.
Butler, Judith. *Precarious Life: The Powers of Mourning and Violence.* New York: Verso, 2004.
Burton, Orisanmi. "Attica Is: Revolutionary Consciousness, Counterinsurgency and the Deferred Abolition of New York State Prisons." PhD diss., University of North Carolina, 2016.
———. "Captivity, Kinship, and Black Masculine Care Work under Domestic Warfare." *American Anthropologist* 123, no. 3 (2021): 621–32.
———. "Diluting Radical History: Blood in the Water and the Politics of Erasure." *Abolition Journal*, January 26, 2017. https://abolitionjournal.org/diluting-radical-history-blood-in-the-water-and-the-politics-of-erasure.
———. "The Minimum Demands." *New York History* 102, no. 1 (2021): 13–16.
———. "Organized Disorder: The New York City Jail Rebellion of 1970." *The Black Scholar* 48, no. 4 (2018): 28–42.
———. "Revolution Is Illegal: Revisiting the Panther 21 at 50." *Spectre: A Marxist Journal* (2020). https://spectrejournal.com/revolution-is-illegal.
———. "Targeting Revolutionaries: The Birth of the Carceral Warfare Project, 1970–1978." *Radical History Review*, no. 146 (May 2023).
Camp, Jordan T. *Incarcerating the Crisis: Freedom Struggles and the Rise of the Neoliberal State.* Oakland: University of California Press, 2016.
Carmichael, Stokely, and Charles Hamilton. *Black Power: The Politics of Liberation.* New York: Random House, 1967.
Césaire, Aimé. *Discourse on Colonialism.* New York: NYU Press, 2001.
Chevigny, Paul. *Cops and Rebels: A Study of Provocation.* New York: Pantheon Books, 1972.
Childs, Dennis. *Slaves of the State: Black Incarceration from the Chain Gang to the Penitentiary.* Minneapolis: University of Minnesota Press, 2015.

Christianson, Scott. "The War Model in Criminal Justice: No Substitute for Victory." *Criminal Justice and Behavior* 1, no. 3 (September 1974). https://doi.org/10.1177/009385487400100.

Churchill, Ward. "The Other Kind: On the Integrity, Consistency, and Humanity of Jalil Abdul Muntaqim." In *Escaping the Prism . . . Fade to Black*. Edited by Jalil Muntaqim, 183-293. Montreal: Kersplebedeb Publishing and Distribution, 2015.

———. *Agents of Repression: The FBI's Secret Wars against the Black Panther Party and the American Indian Movement*, 2nd ed. Boston: South End Press, 2002.

Churchill, Ward, and Jim Vander Wall. *The COINTELPRO Papers: Documents from the FBI's Secret Wars against Dissent in the United States*. Cambridge, MA: South End Press, 2002.

Clark, Richard X., and Leonard Levitt. *The Brothers of Attica*. New York: Links, 1973.

Cleaver, Kathleen Neal. *Back to Africa: The Evolution of the International Section of the Black Panther Party*. Baltimore: Black Classic Press, 1998.

Cobb, Charles. *This Nonviolent Stuff'll Get You Killed: How Guns Made the Civil Rights Movement Possible*. Durham, NC: Duke University Press, 2015.

Cohen, Cathy J. "Punks, Bulldaggers, and Welfare Queens: The Radical Potential of Queer Politics." In *Black Queer Studies*, edited by E. Patrick Johnson and Mae G. Henderson, 21–51. Durham, NC: Duke University Press, 2005.

Collins, Anne. *In the Sleep Room: The Story of CIA Brainwashing Experiments in Canada*. Toronto: Lester & Orpen Dennys, 1988.

Collins, Patricia Hill. *Black Feminist Thought: Knowledge, Consciousness, and the Politics of Empowerment*. New York: Routledge, 2002.

———. *Black Sexual Politics: African Americans, Gender, and the New Racism*. New York: Routledge, 2004.

Commission on CIA Activities within the United States. *Report to the President by the Commission on CIA Activities within the United States*. Washington, DC: Government Printing Office, June 6, 1975.

Committee on the Judiciary. *Hearings Before Subcommittee No. 3 of the Committee on the Judiciary*. Washington, DC: Government Printing Office, 1971.

———. *The United States Penitentiary, Marion, Illinois*. US House of Representatives. Washington, DC: Government Printing Office, December 1984.

Connell, R.W. *Gender and Power: Society, the Person and Sexual Politics*. New York: John Wiley & Sons, 2014.

———. *Masculinities*. 2nd ed. Berkeley: University of California Press, 2005.

Connell, R.W., and James W. Messerschmidt. "Hegemonic Masculinity: Rethinking the Concept." *Gender and Society* 19, no. 6 (December 2005): 829–59.

Cooper, Frank Rudy, Michael Kimmel, and Ann C. McGinley. *Masculinities and the Law: A Multidimensional Approach*. New York: NYU Press, 2012.

Cormier, Bruno M. *The Watcher and the Watched*. New York: Tundra Books, 1975.

Cox, Don. *Just Another Nigger: My Life in the Black Panther Party*. Berkeley, CA: Heyday Books, 2019.
Cribb, Robert. "Introduction: Parapolitics, Shadow Governance and Criminal Sovereignty." In *Government of the Shadows: Parapolitics and Criminal Sovereignty*, edited by Eric Wilson. London: Pluto Press, 2009.
Cummins, Eric. *The Rise and Fall of California's Radical Prison Movement*. Stanford, CA: Stanford University Press, 1994.
Cunha, Manuela. "The Ethnography of Prisons and Penal Confinement." *Annual Review of Anthropology* 43, no. 1 (2014): 217–33.
Curry, Tommy J. *The Man-Not: Race, Class, Genre, and the Dilemmas of Black Manhood*. Philadelphia: Temple University Press, 2017.
Daley, Robert. *Target Blue*. New York: Delacorte Press, 1973.
Daulatzai, Sohail. *Black Star, Crescent Moon: The Muslim International and Black Freedom beyond America*. Minneapolis: University of Minnesota Press, 2012.
Daulatzai, Sohail, and Junaid Rana. *With Stones in Our Hands: Writings on Muslims, Racism, and Empire*. Minneapolis: University of Minnesota Press, 2018.
Davenport, Christian. *Media Bias, Perspective, and State Repression: The Black Panther Party*. Cambridge, UK: Cambridge University Press, 2009.
Davis, Angela Y. *The Angela Y. Davis Reader*. Edited by Joy James, Joy. Malden, MA: Blackwell, 1998.
———. *Are Prisons Obsolete?* New York: Seven Stories Press, 2003.
———. "From the Prison of Slavery to the Slavery of Prison: Frederick Douglass and the Convict Lease System." *The Angela Y. Davis Reader* (1998): 74–95.
———. "Reflections on the Black Woman's Role in the Community of Slaves." *Massachusetts Review* 13, no. 1/2 (1972): 81–100.
Davis, Jomo, Elizabeth Gaynes, and Emani Davis. "Born in Prison." *Grand Street*, no. 54 (1995): 109–28.
deHaven-Smith, Lance. *Conspiracy Theory in America*. Austin: University of Texas Press, 2013.
Derrida, Jacques. *Archive Fever: A Freudian Impression*. Chicago: University of Chicago Press, 1996.
Diaz-Cotto, Juanita. *Gender, Ethnicity, and the State: Latina and Latino Prison Politics*. Albany: SUNY Press, 1996.
Donner, Frank. *Protectors of Privilege: Red Squads and Police Repression in Urban America*. Berkeley: University of California Press, 1992.
Drucker, Ernest. "Population Impact of Mass Incarceration under New York's Rockefeller Drug Laws: An Analysis of Years of Life Lost." *Journal of Urban Health Bulletin of the New York Academy of Medicine* 79, no. 3 (2002): 434–35.
Du Bois, W. E. B. *Black Reconstruction in America, 1860–1880*. New York: Simon and Schuster, 1999.
Dunleavy, Patrick T. *The Fertile Soil of Jihad: Terrorism's Prison Connection*. Washington, DC: Potomac Books, 2011.
Dupuy, Jean-Pierre, and M. B. DeBevoise. *The Mechanization of the Mind: On the Origins of Cognitive Science*. Princeton, NJ: Princeton University Press, 2000.

Durden-Smith, Jo. *Who Killed George Jackson? Fantasies, Paranoia and the Revolution*. New York: Knopf, 1976.

Egan, Daniel. "Gramsci's War of Position as Siege Warfare: Some Lessons from History." *Critique* 44, no. 4 (2016): 435–50.

Elkins, Caroline. *Imperial Reckoning: The Untold Story of Britain's Gulag in Kenya*. New York: Macmillan, 2005.

"Episodes from the Attica Massacre," *The Black Scholar* 4, no. 2 (1972): 34–39.

Equiano, Olaudah. *The Interesting Narrative of the Life of Olaudah Equiano and Other Writing*. Revised ed. New York: Penguin Classics, 2003.

Esquivel, Adolfo Perez. *Let Freedom Ring: A Collection of Documents from the Movements to Free US Political Prisoners*. Oakland, CA: PM Press, 2008.

Fanon, Frantz. *Black Skin, White Masks*. Grove Press, 2008.

———. *The Wretched of the Earth*. Translated by Richard Philcox. New York: Grove Press, 2004.

———. *The Wretched of the Earth*. Translated by Constance Farrington. Harmondsworth, UK: Penguin Books, 2001.

Farmer, Ashley D. *Remaking Black Power: How Black Women Transformed an Era*. Chapel Hill: University of North Carolina Press, 2017.

Farmer, Ashley D., and Erik S. McDuffie. *Palimpsest* (Albany, NY) 7, no. 2 (2018).

Feagin, Joe, and Harlan Hahn. *Ghetto Revolts: The Politics of Violence in American Cities*. New York: Macmillan, 1983.

Felber, Garrett. *Those Who Know Don't Say: The Nation of Islam, the Black Freedom Movement, and the Carceral State*. Chapel Hill: University of North Carolina Press, 2020.

Feldman, Allen. *Formations of Violence: The Narrative of the Body and Political Terror in Northern Ireland*. University of Chicago Press, 1991.

Ferguson, Iyaluua, and Herman Ferguson. *An Unlikely Warrior: Evolution of a Black Nationalist Revolutionary*. North Carolina: Ferguson-Swan Publications, 2011.

Ferguson, Karen. *Top Down: The Ford Foundation, Black Power, and the Reinvention of Racial Liberalism*. Philadelphia: University of Pennsylvania Press, 2013.

Fernández, Johanna. *The Young Lords: A Radical History*. Chapel Hill: University of North Carolina Press, 2019.

Fink, Ludwig. "A New Way to a New Life: A Conference on Criminal Rehabilitation." Social Sciences Occasional Paper no. 1 (1969).

Finkelman, Paul. *Supreme Injustice: Slavery in the Nation's Highest Court*. Cambridge, MA: Harvard University Press, 2018.

Flateau, John. *The Prison Industrial Complex: Race, Crime and Justice in New York*. Brooklyn, NY: Medgar Evers College Press, 1996.

Forgays, Donald G., and Frederick C. Thorne. "Mission Impossible: The Conflicts Underlying Modern Penology." In "A Study of the Mental Health Services of a Correctional Mental Hospital," special issue, *Journal of Community Psychology* 1, no. 3 (July 1973): 271–77.

———. "The Special Problem of the Black Extremist in a Correctional Mental Hospital." In "A Study of the Mental Health Services of a Correctional

Mental Hospital," special issue, *Journal of Community Psychology* 1, no. 3 (July 1973): 263–70.

Forman, James, Jr. *Locking Up Our Own : Crime and Punishment in Black America*. New York: Farrar, Straus and Giroux, 2017.

Fortner, Michael Javen. *Black Silent Majority: The Rockefeller Drug Laws and the Politics of Punishment*. Cambridge, MA: Harvard University Press, 2015.

Foster, Thomas A. *Rethinking Rufus: Sexual Violations of Enslaved Men*. Athens: University of Georgia Press, 2019.

Foucault, Michel. *Discipline and Punish: The Birth of the Prison*. New York: Pantheon Books, 1977.

———. *"Society Must Be Defended": Lectures at the Collège de France, 1975–1976*. New York: Picador, 2003.

Foucault, Michel, Catherine Von Bulow, Daniel Defert, and Sirene Harb. "The Masked Assassination." In *Warfare in the American Homeland: Policing and Prison in a Penal Democracy*, edited by Joy James, 140–58. Durham, NC: Duke University Press, 2007.

Francis, Megan M., "The Price of Civil Rights: Black Lives, White Funding, and Movement Capture." *Law and Society Review* 53, no. 1 (2019): 275–309.

Fujino, Diane Carol. *Heartbeat of Struggle: The Revolutionary Life of Yuri Kochiyama*. Minneapolis: University of Minnesota Press, 2005.

Galula, David. *Counterinsurgency Warfare: Theory and Practice*. Westport, CT: Greenwood Publishing Group, 2006.

Genovese, Eugene D. *From Rebellion to Revolution: Afro-American Slave Revolts in the Making of the Modern World*. Baton Rouge: Louisiana State University Press, 1992.

Getachew, Adom. *Worldmaking after Empire: The Rise and Fall of Self-Determination*. Princeton, NJ: Princeton University Press, 2019.

Giannell, A. Steven. "Criminosynthesis of a Revolutionary Offender." *British Journal of Social Psychiatry and Community Health* 6, no. 3 (1972): 229–33.

Gilbert, David. "Attica—Thirty Years Later." In *The New Abolitionists: (Neo) Slave Narratives and Contemporary Prison Writings*, ed. Joy James. Albany: SUNY Press, 2005.

Gilbert, David, and Dan Berger. "Grief and Organizing in the Face of Repression: The Fight against AIDS in Prison." In *Rebellious Mourning: The Collective Work of Grief*, edited by Cindy Milstein, 273–97. Chico, CA: AK Press, 2017.

Gilmore, Ruth Wilson. "Abolition Geography and the Problem of Innocence." In *Futures of Black Radicalism*, ed. Gaye Theresa Johnson and Alex Lubin, 225–40. New York: Verso, 2017.

———. *Golden Gulag: Prisons, Surplus, Crisis, and Opposition in Globalizing California*. Berkeley: University of California Press, 2007.

Gilmore, Ruth Wilson, and James Kilgore. "Some Reflections on Prison Labor." *The Brooklyn Rail*, June 2019.

Gilmore, Ruth Wilson, and Clément Petitjean. "Prisons and Class Warfare: An Interview with Ruth Wilson Gilmore." *Verso* blog, August 2, 2018. https://www.versobooks.com/blogs/3954-prisons-and-class-warfare-an-interview-with-ruth-wilson-gilmore.

Glander, Timothy. *Origins of Mass Communications Research During the American Cold War: Educational Effects and Contemporary Implications.* London: Routledge, 1999.
Gobert, James J. "Psychosurgery, Conditioning, and the Prisoner's Right to Refuse 'Rehabilitation.'" *Virginia Law Review* 61 (1975): 155–96.
Goodman, Amy, and David Goodman. *Standing Up to the Madness: Ordinary Heroes in Extraordinary Times.* New York: Hyperion, 2008.
Gomez, Alan Eladio. "Resisting Living Death at Marion Federal Penitentiary, 1972." *Radical History Review* 96 (2006): 58–86.
Gottehrer, Barry. *The Mayor's Man.* New York: Doubleday, 1975.
Gottschalk, Marie. *Caught: The Prison State and the Lockdown of American Politics.* Princeton, NJ: Princeton University Press, 2014.
Gould, Robert E. "The Officer-Inmate Relationship: It's Role in the Attica Rebellion." *Journal of the American Academy of Psychiatry and the Law* 2, no. 1. 1974: 34–45.
Governor's Special Committee of Criminal Offenders. *The Preliminary Report of the Governor's Special Committee of Criminal Offenders.* New York, 1968.
Gramsci, Antonio, Quintin Hoare, and Geoffrey Nowell-Smith. *Selections from the Prison Notebooks of Antonio Gramsci.* London: Lawrence & Wishart, 1971.
Grant, J. Douglas. "The Offender as a Correctional Manpower Resource." Paper presented at the First National Symposium on Law Enforcement Science and Technology, Washington, DC, 1967.
Grant, J. Douglas, and Joan Grant. "Contagion as a Principle in Behavior Change." In *Behavioral Intervention in Human Problems*, edited by H. C. Rickard. Oxford: Pergamon Press, 1971.
Guenther, Lisa. *Solitary Confinement: Social Death and Its Afterlives.* Minneapolis: University of Minnesota Press, 2013.
Haley, Sarah. *No Mercy Here: Gender, Punishment, and the Making of Jim Crow Modernity.* Chapel Hill: University of North Carolina Press, 2016.
Hall, Stuart. "Constituting an Archive." *Third Text* 15, no. 54 (2001): 89–92.
———. "Gramsci's Relevance for the Study of Race and Ethnicity." *Stuart Hall: Critical Dialogues in Cultural Studies* (1996): 411–40.
Hall, Stuart, Chas Critcher, Tony Jefferson, John Clarke, and Brian Roberts. *Policing the Crisis: Mugging, the State and Law and Order.* London: Macmillan International Higher Education, 2013.
Harcourt, Bernard E. *The Counterrevolution: How Our Government Went to War against Its Own Citizens.* New York: Basic Books, 2018.
Harney, Stefano, and Fred Moten. *The Undercommons: Fugitive Planning and Black Study.* Wivenhoe, UK: Minor Compositions, 2013.
Harnish, Robert M. *Minds, Brains, Computers: An Historical Introduction to the Foundations of Cognitive Science.* Malden, MA: Blackwell Publishers, 2002.
Harris, Trudier. *Exorcising Blackness: Historical and Literary Lynching and Burning Rituals.* Bloomington: Indiana University Press, 1984.

Harrison, Faye V., ed. *Decolonizing Anthropology: Moving Further toward an Anthropology of Liberation*. Arlington, VA: Association of Black Anthropologists, American Anthropological Association, 1997.

Hartman, Saidiya V. *Lose Your Mother: A Journey through the Atlantic Slave Route*. New York: Farrar, Straus and Giroux, 2006.

———. *Scenes of Subjection: Terror, Slavery, and Self-Making in Nineteenth-Century America*. New York: Oxford University Press, 1997.

———. "Venus in Two Acts." *Small Axe* 12, no. 2 (2008): 1–14.

Hatch, Anthony Ryan. "Billions Served: Prison Food Regimes, Nutritional Punishment, and Gastronomical Resistance." In *Captivating Technology: Race, Carceral Technoscience, and Liberatory Imagination in Everyday Life*, ed. Ruha Benjamin, 67–84. Durham, NC: Duke University Press, 2019.

———. *Silent Cells: The Secret Drugging of Captive America*. Minneapolis: University of Minnesota Press, 2019.

Hellinger, Daniel. "Paranoia, Conspiracy, and Hegemony in American Politics." In *Transparency and Conspiracy: Ethnographies of Suspicion in the New World Order*, edited by Harry G. West and Todd Sanders, 204–32. Durham, NC: Duke University Press, 2003.

Herre, Ralph S. "The History of Auburn Prison from the Beginning to about 1867." PhD diss., Pennsylvania State College, 1950.

Herrmann, William W. *Report to United States Agency for International Development, Office of Public Safety*. Santa Monica, CA: System Development Corporation, July 12, 1967.

Hill, John Bonocore, and Bruderer, Sandra. *Splitting the Sky: From Attica to Gustafsen Lake, Unmasking the Secrets of the Psycho-Sexual Energy and the Struggle for Orignal Peoples' Title*. Chase, BC: Splitting the Sky, 2001.

Hill, Rebecca. "'The Common Enemy Is the Boss and the Inmate': Police and Prison Guard Unions in New York in the 1970s–1980s." *Labor: Studies in Working-Class History of the Americas* 8, no. 3 (2011): 65–96. https://doi.org/10.1215/15476715-1275244.

Hornblum, Allen M. *Acres of Skin: Human Experiments at Holmesburg Prison; A True Story of Abuse and Exploitation in the Name of Medical Science*. New York: Routledge, 1998.

Horne, Gerald. *Communist Front? The Civil Rights Congress, 1946–1956*. Rutherford, NJ: Fairleigh Dickinson University Press, 1988.

———. *The Counter-Revolution of 1776: Slave Resistance and the Origins of the United States of America*. New York: NYU Press, 2014.

Hunt, Ryan. "Project Camelot and Military Sponsorship of Social Science Research: A Critical Discourse Analysis." PhD diss., Duquesne University, 2007.

Ihmoud, Sarah, and Shanya Cordis. "A Poetics of Living Rebellion: Sociocultural Anthropology in 2021." *American Anthropologist* 124, no. 4 (2022): 813–29.

Incite! Women of Color Against Violence, ed. *The Revolution Will Not Be Funded: Beyond the Non-Profit Industrial Complex*. Cambridge, MA: South End Press, 2007.

Ingold, Tim. *Lines: A Brief History*. New York: Routledge, 2016.

Institute of the Black World. *Black Analysis for the Seventies*. Atlanta, GA: IBW Press, 1971–72.
Jackson, George L. *Blood in My Eye*. Baltimore, MD: Black Classic Press, 1990.
———. *Soledad Brother: The Prison Letters of George Jackson*. Chicago: Chicago Review Press, 1994.
Jackson, George L., Karen Wald, and Ward Churchill. "Remembering the Real Dragon—an Interview with George Jackson May 16 and June 29, 1971." In *Cages of Steel: The Politics of Imprisonment in the United States*, edited by Ward Churchill and J.J. Vander Wall, 174-188. Washington, DC: Maisonneuve Press, 1992.
Jackson, John, Jr. *Racial Paranoia: The Unintended Consequences of Political Correctness*. New York: Basic Civitas Books, 2010.
Jacobs, Harriet. *Incidents in the Life of a Slave Girl*. Mineola, NY: Dover, 2001.
James, C. L. R. *The Black Jacobins: Toussaint L'Ouverture and the San Domingo Revolution*. London: Penguin, 2001.
James, Joy. "George Jackson: Dragon Philosopher and Revolutionary Abolitionist." *Black Perspectives*, August 21, 2018. https://www.aaihs.org/george-jackson-dragon-philosopher-and-revolutionary-abolitionist/.
———, ed. *Imprisoned Intellectuals: America's Political Prisoners Write on Life, Liberation, and Rebellion*. Lanham, MD: Rowman and Littlefield, 2003.
———. "The Womb of Western Theory: Trauma, Time Theft, and the Captive Maternal." *Carceral Notebooks* 12 (2016): 253–96.
Johnston, Alexander, dir. *Evidence of the Evidence*. Rifle Baby Productions, 2017.
Jordan, Winthrop D. *White over Black: American Attitudes toward the Negro, 1550–1812*. Chapel Hill: University of North Carolina Press, 2013.
Kaba, Mariame. *We Do This' Til We Free Us: Abolitionist Organizing and Transforming Justice*. Chicago: Haymarket Books, 2021.
Kane, Lizzie. "No Touching Allowed for Many LGBTQ+." *Solitary Watch*, 2021. https://solitarywatch.org/2021/09/16/no-touching-allowed-for-lgbtq-people-in-prison.
Kelley, Robin D. G. *Africa Speaks, America Answers: Modern Jazz in Revolutionary Times*. Cambridge, MA: Harvard University Press, 2012.
———. *Freedom Dreams: The Black Radical Imagination*. Boston: Beacon Press, 2003.
Kelley, William Melvin. *A Different Drummer*. New York: Anchor, 1989.
Kerness, Bonnie. "The Hidden History of Solitary Confinement in New Jersey's Control Units." *Solitary Watch*, 2013. https://solitarywatch.org/2013/03/13/the-hidden-history-of-solitary-confinement-in-new-jerseys-control-units.
Khalili, Laleh. "Gendered Practices of Counterinsurgency." *Review of International Studies* 37, no. 4 (2011): 1471–91.
———. *Time in the Shadows: Confinement in Counterinsurgencies*. Stanford, CA: Stanford University Press, 2012.
Khan, Aisha. "The Carceral State: An American Story." *Annual Review of Anthropology* 51 (2022): 49–66.

Kiebala, Valerie, and Sal Rodriguez. "FAQ: Solitary Confinement in the United States." *Solitary Watch*, November 5, 2018. https://solitarywatch.org/wp-content/uploads/2019/05/Solitary-Confinement-FAQ-2018-final.pdf.

Kilgore, James. *Understanding E-Carceration: Electronic Monitoring, the Surveillance State, and the Future of Mass Incarceration*. New York: New Press, 2022.

Kim, Monica. *The Interrogation Rooms of the Korean War: The Untold History*. Princeton, NJ: Princeton University Press, 2019.

King, Ryan S., Marc Mauer, and Tracy Huling. *Big Prisons, Small Towns: Prison Economics in Rural America*. Washington, DC: Sentencing Project, 2003.

Kinzer, Stephen. *Poisoner in Chief: Sidney Gottlieb and the CIA Search for Mind Control*. New York: St. Martin's Griffin, 2019.

kioni-sadiki, déqui, and Matt Meyer, eds. *Look for Me in the Whirlwind: From the Panther 21 to 21st-Century Revolutions*. Oakland, CA: PM Press, 2017.

Kitossa, Tamari, ed. *Appealing Because He Is Appalling: Black Masculinities, Colonialism, and Erotic Racism*. Edmonton: University of Alberta Press, 2021.

Kitson, Frank. *Low Intensity Operations: Subversion, Insurgency and Peacekeeping*. London: Faber and Faber, 1971.

Klein, Naomi. *The Shock Doctrine: The Rise of Disaster Capitalism*. New York: Metropolitan Books, 2007.

Kluckow, Rich, and Zhen Zeng. *Correctional Populations in the United States, 2020—Statistical Tables*. Washington, DC: Bureau of Justice Statistics, US Department of Justice, March 2022.

Kohl-Arenas, Erica. *The Self-Help Myth: How Philanthropy Fails to Alleviate Poverty*. Berkeley: University of California Press, 2015.

Kohler-Hausmann, Julilly. *Getting Tough*. Princeton, NJ: Princeton University Press, 2017.

Kondo, Zak A. *Conspiracys: Unravelling the Assassination of Malcolm X*. Washington, DC: Nubia Press, 1993.

Kunzel, Regina. *Criminal Intimacy: Prison and the Uneven History of Modern American Sexuality*. Chicago: University of Chicago Press, 2008.

Kurshan, Nancy. *Out of Control: A Fifteen-Year Battle against Control Unit Prisons*. San Francisco, 2013. Available at Freedom Archives, https://freedomarchives.org/out-of-control-is-now-available.

Law, Victoria. "Captive Audience: How Companies Make Millions Charging Prisoners to Send an Email." *Wired*, August 3, 2018. https://www.wired.com/story/jpay-securus-prison-email-charging-millions.

———. *Resistance Behind Bars: The Struggles of Incarcerated Women*. Binghamton, NY: PM Press, 2012.

Lawson, Robert B., and Justin M. Joffe. "Donald G. Forgays (1926–1993)." *American Psychologist* 50, no. 2 (1995): 104.

Lay, Shawn. *Hooded Knights on the Niagara: The Ku Klux Klan in Buffalo, New York*. New York: NYU Press, 1995.

Lazreg, Marnia. *Torture and the Twilight of Empire: From Algiers to Baghdad*. Princeton, NJ: Princeton University Press, 2016.

Lefcourt, Robert, ed. *Law against the People: Essays to Demystify Law, Order and the Courts*. New York: Vintage Books, 1971.

Levine, Yasha. *Surveillance Valley: The Secret Military History of the Internet.* New York: PublicAffairs, 2018.
Li, Darryl. "Captive Passages: Geographies of Blackness in Guantánamo Memoirs." *Transforming Anthropology* 30, no. 1 (2022): 20–33.
Lichtenstein, Brad, dir. *Ghosts of Attica.* A Lumiere production in association with Antidote Films and Crawford Communications. Brooklyn, NY: Distributed by Icarus Films, 2015.
Linebarger, Paul M. A. "Psychological Warfare." *Naval War College Information Service for Officers* 3, no. 7 (1951): 19–47.
Little, Becky. "What the Nixon Tapes Reveal about the Attica Prison Uprising." History.com, September 11, 2019. https://www.history.com/news/nixon-tapes-attica-prison-uprising.
Lorde, Audre. *Sister Outsider: Essays and Speeches.* Berkeley: Crossing Press, 1984.
Losier, Toussaint. "Against 'Law and Order' Lockup: The 1970 NYC Jail Rebellions." *Race and Class* 59, no. 1 (2017): 3–35.
Losurdo, Domenico. *Liberalism: A Counter-History.* London: Verso, 2014.
Lowe, Lisa. *Intimacies of Four Continents.* Durham, NC: Duke University Press, 2015.
Luk, Sharon. *The Life of Paper: Letters and a Poetics of Living Beyond Captivity.* Oakland: University of California Press, 2018.
Marable, Manning. *How Capitalism Underdeveloped Black America: Problems in Race, Political Economy, and Society.* Cambridge, MA: South End Press, 2000.
———. *Race, Reform, and Rebellion: The Second Reconstruction and Beyond in Black America, 1945–2006.* Jackson: University of Mississippi Press, 2007.
Marchio, James. "The Planning Coordination Group: Bureaucratic Casualty in the Cold War Campaign to Exploit Soviet-Bloc Vulnerabilities." *Journal of Cold War Studies* 4, no. 4 (2002): 3–28.
Marks, John D. *The Search for the "Manchurian Candidate": The CIA and Mind Control, The Secret History of the Behavioral Sciences.* New York: W. W. Norton, 1991.
Marriott, David. *On Black Men.* New York: Columbia University Press, 2000.
Marx, Karl. *The Civil War in France and Other Writings on the Paris Commune.* Chicago: Charles H. Kerr, 1998.
Masco, Joseph. *The Theater of Operations: National Security Affect from the Cold War to the War on Terror.* Durham, NC: Duke University Press, 2014.
Mbembe, Achille. "Necropolitics." *Public Culture* 15, no. 1 (2003): 11–40.
McCoy, Alfred W. *The Politics of Heroin: CIA Complicity in the Global Drug Trade.* Chicago: Lawrence Hill Books, 2003.
———. *A Question of Torture: CIA Interrogation, from the Cold War to the War on Terror.* New York: Metropolitan Books, 2007.
———. "Science in Dachau's Shadow: Hebb, Beecher, and the Development of CIA Psychological Torture and Modern Medical Ethics." *Journal of the History of the Behavioral Sciences* 43, no. 4 (2007): 401–17.
McKay Commission. *The Official Report of the New York State Special Commission on Attica.* New York: Bantam Books, 1972.

McKittrick, Katherine. "Rebellion/Invention/Groove." *Small Axe: A Caribbean Journal of Criticism* 20, no. 1 (2016): 79–91.

———. *Sylvia Wynter: On Being Human as Praxis*. Durham, NC: Duke University Press, 2015.

McQuade, Brendan. *Pacifying the Homeland: Intelligence Fusion and Mass Supervision*. Berkeley: University of California Press, 2019.

Mechthild, Nagel. "Prisons, Big Business, and Profit: Whither Social Justice?" In *Diversity, Multiculturalism and Social Justice*, edited by Seth N. Asumah and Ibipo Johnston-Anumowonwo, 361–83. Binghamton, NY: Global Academic Publishing, 2002.

Melville, Samuel. *Letters from Attica*. New York: William & Morrow Company, 1972.

Menard, Orville D. "Lest We Forget: The Lynching of Will Brown, Omaha's 1919 Race Riot." *Nebraska History* 91 (2010): 152–65.

Metzl, Jonathan M. *The Protest Psychosis: How Schizophrenia Became a Black Disease*. Boston: Beacon Press, 2010.

Meunier, Paul D., and Howard D. Schwartz. "Beyond Attica: Prison Reform in New York State, 1971–1973." *Cornell Law Review* 58 (1972): 924–1034.

Meyer, Bernard S. *Final Report of the Special Attica Investigation*. State of New York Department of Law, October 27, 1975. https://ag.ny.gov/pdfs/MeyerReportVol2And3.pdf.

Mirzoeff, Nicholas. *The Right to Look*. Durham, NC: Duke University Press, 2011.

Mitford, Jessica. *Kind and Usual Punishment: The Prison Business*. New York: Knopf, 1973.

Mondlane, Eduardo. *The Struggle for Mozambique*. Baltimore: Penguin Books, 1969.

Moore, Dhoruba. "Strategies of Repression against the Black Movement." *The Black Scholar* 12, no. 3 (1981): 10–16.

Morrell, Andrea. "Hometown Prison: Whiteness, Safety, and Prison Work in Upstate New York State." *American Anthropologist* 123, no. 3 (2021): 633–44.

Moten, Fred. *In the Break: The Aesthetics of the Black Radical Tradition*. Minneapolis: University of Minnesota Press, 2003.

Mullings, Leith. "Interrogating Racism: Toward an Antiracist Anthropology." *Annual Review of Anthropology* 34, no. 1 (2005): 667–93.

Muntaqim, Jalil. "The Perverse Slave Mentality." *Journal of Prisoners on Prisons* 15, no. 2 (2007): 87–90.

———. *We Are Our Own Liberators*. Portland, OR: Arissa Media Group, 2010.

Murakawa, Naomi. *The First Civil Right: How Liberals Built Prison America*. New York: Oxford University Press, 2014.

Myers, Joshua. *Cedric Robinson: The Time of the Black Radical Tradition*. Cambridge, UK: Polity, 2021.

Nagl, John A., James F. Amos, Sarah Sewall, and David H. Petraeus. *The US Army/Marine Corps Counterinsurgency Field Manual*. Chicago: University of Chicago Press, 2008.

Neocleous, Mark. *War Power, Police Power*. Edinburgh, UK: Edinburgh University Press, 2014.

Newton, Huey P. *The Huey P. Newton Reader*. New York: Seven Stories Press, 2011.
———. *Revolutionary Suicide*. New York: Penguin Books, 2009.
———. "War against the Panthers: A Study of Repression in America." PhD diss., University of California, Santa Cruz, 1980.
New York State Advisory Committee to the US Commission on Civil Rights. *Warehousing Human Beings: A Review of the New York State Correctional System*. Washington, DC: US Commission on Civil Rights, 1974.
New York State Commission of Investigation. *Corruption and Abuses in the Correctional System: The Green Haven Correctional Facility*. Albany, 1981.
New York State Policy Study Group. *Report of the Policy Study Group on Terrorism*. Division of Criminal Justice Services. Albany, 1985.
Nkrumah, Kwame. *Neocolonialism: The Last Stage of Imperialism*. New York: International Publishers, 1965.
Norton, Jack. "Little Siberia, Star of the North: Prisons, Crisis, and Development in Rural New York, 1968–1994." PhD diss., City University of New York, 2019.
NY DOCS. *Multi-Year Master Plan of the Department of Correctional Services*. New York State Department of Correctional Services. Albany, April 1, 1973.
———. "New York State Correctional Services Master Plan, 1980–1985." 1981. https://www.ojp.gov/ncjrs/virtual-library/abstracts/new-york-state-correctional-services-master-plan-1980-1985.
O'Connor, Maeve, and Gordon Ethelbert Ward Wolstenholme. *Medical Care of Prisoners and Detainees*. Hoboken, NJ: John Wiley & Sons, 2009.
O'Dell, Jack. "The July Rebellions and the 'Military State.'" *Freedomways* 7, no. 4 (1967): 288–301.
Onaci, Edward. *Free the Land: The Republic of New Afrika and the Pursuit of a Black Nation-State*. Chapel Hill: University of North Carolina Press, 2020.
O'Neill, Tom. *Chaos: Charles Mason, The CIA, and the Secret History of the Sixties*. Boston: Little, Brown, & Company, 2019.
O'Neill, Tom, and Dan Piepenbring. "Inside the Archive of an LSD Researcher with Ties to the CIA's MKULTRA Mind Control Project." *First Look Institute*, 2019, https://theintercept.com/2019/11/24/cia-mkultra-louis-jolyon-west.
Oosenbrug, Eric. "Bulding a 'Cross-Roads Discipline' at McGill University: A History of Early Experimental Psychology in Postwar Canada." PhD diss., York University, Toronto Ontario, 2020.
O'Reilly, Kenneth. *"Racial Matters": The FBI's Secret File on Black America, 1960–1972*. New York: Free Press, 1989.
Oswald, Russell G. *Attica: My Story*. New York: Doubleday, 1972.
Painter, Nell Irvin. *Southern History across the Color Line*. Chapel Hill: University of North Carolina Press, 2002.
Parenti, Christian. *Lockdown America: Police and Prisons in the Age of Crisis*. London: Verso, 2000.
Paschel, Tianna. *Becoming Black Political Subjects: Movements and Etho-Racial Rights in Colombia and Brazil*. Princeton, NJ: Princeton University Press, 2018.

Patterson, Orlando. *Slavery and Social Death*. Cambridge, MA: Harvard University Press, 1982.

Pelot-Hobbs, Lydia. "The Contested Terrain of the Louisiana Carceral State." PhD diss., City University of New York, 2019.

People's Communication Network. *Surveying the First Decade: Volume 2*. Chicago: Video Data Bank, 1973.

Phillips-Fein, Kim. *Fear City: New York's Fiscal Crisis and the Rise of Austerity Politics*. New York: Metropolitan Books, 2017.

Pickens, Therí Alyce. *Black Madness: Mad Blackness*. Durham, NC: Duke University Press, 2019.

President's Commission on Law Enforcement and Administration of Justice. *The Challenge of Crime in a Free Society: A Report by the President's Commission on Law Enforcement and Administration of Justice*. Washington, DC: Government Printing Office, 1967.

Price, David H. "Buying a Piece of Anthropology Part 1: Human Ecology and Unwitting Anthropological Research for the CIA." *Anthropology Today* 23, no. 3, 2007: 8–13.

———. *Weaponizing Anthropology: Social Science in Service of the Militarized State*. Chico, CA: AK Press, 2011.

Price, Richard. *Maroon Societies: Rebel Slave Communities in the Americas*. Baltimore: John's Hopkins University Press, 1996.

Prison Research Education Action Project. *Instead of Prisons: A Handbook for Abolitionists*. Oakland, CA: Critical Resistance, 2005.

Puar, Jasbir K. "Abu Ghraib: Arguing against Exceptionalism." *Feminist Studies* 30, no. 2 (2004): 522–34.

Rafalko, Frank. *MH/CHAOS: The CIA's Campaign against the Radical New Left and the Black Panthers*. Washington, DC: Naval Institute Press, 2011.

Ralph, Laurence. *Renegade Dreams: Living through Injury in Gangland Chicago*. Chicago: University of Chicago Press, 2014.

Rana, Junaid. *Terrifying Muslims: Race and Labor in the South Asian Diaspora*. Durham, NC: Duke University Press, 2011.

Ransby, Barbara. *Ella Baker and the Black Freedom Movement: A Radical Democratic Vision*. Chapel Hill: University of North Carolina Press, 2003.

Razack, Sherene H. "How Is White Supremacy Embodied? Sexualized Racial Violence at Abu Ghraib." *Canadian Journal of Women and the Law* 17, no. 2 (2005): 341–63.

Redmond, Shana L. *Anthem: Social Movements and the Sound of Solidarity in the African Diaspora*. New York: NYU Press, 2014.

Reese, Ashanté M., and Joshua Sbicca. "Food and Carcerality: From Confinement to Abolition." *Food and Foodways* (2022): 1–15.

Reyes, Alvaro. "On Fanon's Manichean Delirium." *The Black Scholar* 42, no. 3-4 (Fall-Winter 2012): 13–20.

Richie, Beth E. *Arrested Justice: Black Women, Violence, and America's Prison Nation*. New York: NYU Press, 2012.

Roberts, Neil. *Freedom as Marronage*. Chicago: University of Chicago Press, 2015.

Robinson, Cedric J. *Black Marxism: The Making of the Black Radical Tradition*. Chapel Hill: University of North Carolina Press, 2000.

———. *The Terms of Order: Political Science and the Myth of Leadership*. Chapel Hill: University of North Carolina Press, 2016.

Robitscher, Jonas B. "Psychosurgery and Other Somatic Means of Altering Behavior." *Journal of the American Academy of Psychiatry and the Law Online* 2, no. 1 (1974): 7–33.

Rodríguez, Dylan. *Forced Passages: Imprisoned Radical Intellectuals and the US Prison Regime*. Minneapolis: University of Minnesota Press, 2006.

———. *White Reconstruction: Domestic Warfare and the Logics of Genocide*. New York: Fordham University Press, 2020.

Rodríguez, Dylan, and Sirvent, Roberto. "Insurgency and Counterinsurgency: An Interview with Dylan Rodriguez." Black Agenda Report, 2022. https://www.blackagendareport.com/insurgency-and-counterinsurgency-interview-dylan-rodriguez.

Rogers, J. A., and John Henrik Clarke. *World's Great Men of Color*. New York: Touchstone, 1996.

Rubin, Jay L. *The Forgotten Kapital: The Ku Klux Klan in Binghamton, New York, 1923–1928*. Binghamton, NY: Bundy Museum Press, 2016.

Ryan, Mike. "Solitude as Counterinsurgency." In *Cages of Steel: The Politics of Imprisonment in the United States*, edited by Ward Churchill and Jim Vander Wall, 83–109. Washington, DC: Maisonneuve Press, 1992.

Sabo, Donald F., Terry Allen Kupers, and Willie James London. *Prison Masculinities*. Philadelphia: Temple University Press, 2001.

Said, Edward. *Orientalism*. New York: Pantheon Books, 1978.

Saifee, Seema. "Decarceration's Inside Partners." University of Pennsylvania Law School, Public Law Research Paper, no. 22–24 (2022).

Saleh-Hanna, Viviane. "Black Feminist Hauntology: Rememory the Ghosts of Abolition?" *Champ Pénal/Penal Field* 12 (2015). https://doi.org/10.4000/champpenal.9168.

Samudzi, Zoé, and William C. Anderson. *As Black As Resistance: Finding the Conditions for Liberation*. Chico, CA: AK Press, 2018.

Saunders, Frances Stonor. *The Cultural Cold War: The CIA and the World of Arts and Letters*. New York: New Press, 2013.

Scarry, Elaine. *The Body in Pain: The Making and Unmaking of the World*. New York: Oxford University Press, 1987.

Scheflin, Alan W., and Edward M. Opton. *The Mind Manipulators: A Non-Fiction Account*. New York: Paddington Press, 1978.

Schein, Edgar H. *Brainwashing*. Cambridge: Massachusetts Institute of Technology, Center for International Studies, 1960.

———. *Coercive Persuasion: A Socio-Psychological Analysis of the "Brainwashing" of American Civilian Prisoners by the Chinese Communists*. New York: W. W. Norton, 1971.

Schept, Judah. "Caring Cages: Troubling Progressive Punishment." *Social Justice* 44, no. 3–4 (2017): 190–96.

Schrader, Stuart. *Badges without Borders: How Global Counterinsurgency Transformed American Policing*. Berkeley: University of California Press, 2019.

———. "To Secure the Global Great Society: Participation in Pacification." *Humanity: An International Journal of Human Rights, Humanitarianism, and Development* 7, no. 2 (2016): 225–53.
Schreiber, Brad. *Revolution's End: The Patty Hearst Kidnapping, Mind Control, and the Secret History of Donald Defreeze and the SLA.* New York: Skyhorse, 2016.
Schwitzgebel, Ralph K. "Development and Legal Regulation of Coercive Behavior Modification Techniques with Offenders." Public Health Service Publication No. 2067, National Institute of Mental Health, February 1971.
Schwitzgebel, Robert L. "A Comparative Study of Zulu and English Reactions to Sensory Deprivation." *International Journal of Social Psychiatry* 8, no. 3 (1962): 220–25.
Schwitzgebel, Robert L., and Ralph K. Schwitzgebel. *Psychotechnology: Electronic Control of Mind and Behavior.* New York: Holt, Rinehart and Winston, 1972.
Scott, David. "Introduction: On the Archaeologies of Black Memory." *Small Axe* 12, no. 2 (2008): v–xvi.
Seigel, Micol. "Nelson Rockefeller in Latin America: Global Currents of US Prison Growth." *Comparative American Studies: An International Journal* 13, no. 3. (2015): 161–76.
———. *Violence Work: State Power and the Limits of Police.* Durham, NC: Duke University Press, 2018.
Selisker, Scott. *Human Programming: Brainwashing, Automatons, and American Unfreedom.* Minneapolis: University of Minnesota Press, 2016.
Sexton, Jared, and Elizabeth Lee. "Figuring the Prison: Prerequisites of Torture at Abu Ghraib." *Antipode* 38, no. 5 (2006): 1005–22.
Shakur, Assata. *Assata: An Autobiography.* Chicago: Hill Books, 2001.
Shakur, Mutulu, Anthony X. Bradshaw, Malik Dinguswa, Terry D. Long, Mark Cook, Mateos Adolpho, and James Haskins. *Genocide Waged against the Black Nation through Behavior Modification Orchestrated by Counterinsurgency and Low-Intensity Warfare in the U.S. Penal System.* 1988. Available at Freedom Archives, https://search.freedomarchives.org.
Shakur, Zayd. "America Is the Prison." In *Off the Pigs! The History and Literature of the Black Panther Party*, edited by G. Louis Heath, 274–80. Metuchen, NJ: Scarecrow, 1976.
Shanahan, Jarrod. *Captives: How Rikers Island Took New York City Hostage.* London: Verso, 2022.
Shange, Savannah. "Abolition in the Clutch: Shifting through the Gears with Anthropology." *Feminist Anthropology* 3, no. 2 (2022): 187–97.
———. *Progressive Dystopia: Abolition, Antiblackness, and Schooling in San Francisco.* Durham, NC: Duke University Press, 2019.
Sharpe, Christina. *Monstrous Intimacies: Making Post-Slavery Subjects.* Durham, NC: Duke University Press, 2010.
Shoatz, Russell "Maroon," and Lisa Guenther. "Maroon Philosophy: An Interview with Russell 'Maroon' Shoatz." In *Death and Other Penalties: Philosophy in a Time of Mass Incarceration*, edited by Geoffrey Adelsberg, Lisa Guenther, and Scott Zeman, 60–75. New York: Fordham University Press, 2015.

Silbert, Jeffrey M. "The World's First Computerized Criminal-Justice Information-Sharing System: The New York State Identification and Intelligence System (NYSIIS)." *Criminology* 8, no. 2 (1970): 107–28.

Simes, Jessica T. *Punishing Places: The Geography of Mass Imprisonment.* Oakland: University of California Press, 2021.

Singh, Nikhil Pal. *Race and America's Long War.* Oakland: University of California Press, 2017.

Sivakumaran, Sandesh. "Sexual Violence against Men in Armed Conflict." *European Journal of International Law* 18, no. 2 (2007): 253–76.

Sivanandan, A. *Communities of Resistance: Writings on Black Struggles for Socialism.* New York: Verso, 1990.

Skurski, Julie, Gary Wilder, Laurent Dubois, Paul Eiss, Edward Murphy, Mariana Coronil, and David Pedersen, eds. *The Fernando Coronil Reader.* Durham, NC: Duke University Press, 2019.

Smith, Christen A. "Facing the Dragon: Black Mothering, Sequelae, and Gendered Necropolitics in the Americas." *Transforming Anthropology* 24, no. 1 (2016): 31–48.

Smith, Frank. "Interview with Frank Smith (Big Black)." Interview by Sam Pollard. *Eyes on the Prize II: America at the Racial Crossroads, 1965 to 1985.* December 9, 1988. Washington University Libraries, Film and Media Archive, Henry Hampton Collection.

Smith, Frank, Akil Al-Jundi, and Robert Weiss. "Guest Editor's Interview." *Social Justice* 18, no. 3 (1991): 84–91.

Smith, Shawn Michelle. *At the Edge of Sight: Photography and the Unseen.* Durham, NC: Duke University Press, 2013.

Snorton, C. Riley. *Black on Both Sides: A Racial History of Trans Identity.* Minneapolis: University of Minnesota Press, 2017.

Sojoyner, Damien M. "Dissonance in Time: (Un)Making and (Re)Mapping of Blackness." In *Futures of Black Radicalism*, edited by Gaye Theresa Johnson and Alex Lubin. London: Verso Books, 2017.

———. *First Strike: Educational Enclosures in Black Los Angeles.* Minneapolis: University of Minnesota Press, 2016.

———. "You Are Going to Get Us Killed: Fugitive Archival Practice and the Carceral State." *American Anthropologist* 123, no. 3 (2021): 658–70.

Sostre, Martin. "The New Prisoner." *North Carolina Central Law Review* 4, no. 2 (1973): 242–54.

Spencer, Robyn C. *The Revolution Has Come.* Durham, NC: Duke University Press, 2016.

Spillers, Hortense J. "Mama's Baby, Papa's Maybe: An American Grammar Book." *diacritics* 17, no. 2 (1987): 65–81.

Stanford, Max. "Black Guerilla Warfare Strategy and Tactics." *The Black Scholar* 2, no. 3 (1970):30-38.

Stein, David. "Trumpism and the Magnitude of Mass Incarceration." *Black Perspectives*, February 16, 2017. https://www.aaihs.org/trumpism-and-the-magnitude-of-mass-incarceration.

Stoler, Ann Laura. *Along the Archival Grain: Epistemic Anxieties and Colonial Common Sense.* Princeton, NJ: Princeton University Press, 2009.

Suedfeld, Peter. "Changes in Intellectual Performance and Susceptibility to Influence." In *Sensory Deprivation: Fifteen Years of Research*, edited by John P. Zubek, 126–66. New York: Appeleton-Century-Crofts, 1969.

Sutherland, Tonia. "The Carceral Archive: Documentary Records, Narrative Construction, and Predictive Risk Assessment." *Journal of Cultural Analytics* 4, no. 1 (2019). https://doi.org/10.22148/16.039.

———. "Disrupting Carceral Narratives: Race, Rape, and the Archives." *Open Information Science* 4, no. 1 (2020): 156–68.

Tackwood, Louis. *The Glass House Tapes*. New York: Avon, 1973.

Táíwò, Olúfẹ́mi O. *Elite Capture: How the Powerful Took Over Identity Politics (and Everything Else)*. Chicago: Haymarket Books, 2022.

Talbot, David. *The Devil's Chessboard: Allen Dulles, the CIA, and the Rise of America's Secret Government*. New York: HarperCollins, 2015.

Taylor, Keeanga-Yamahtta. *How We Get Free: Black Feminism and the Combahee River Collective*. Chicago: Haymarket Books, 2017.

Theologus, George C. *Development of a Taxonomy of Human Performance: A Review of Biological Taxonomy and Classification*. Washington, DC: American Instiutes for Research, 1969.

Thompson, Heather Ann. *Blood in the Water: The Attica Prison Uprising of 1971 and Its Legacy*. New York: Pantheon Books, 2016.

Thuma, Emily L. *All Our Trials: Prisons, Policing, and the Feminist Fight to End Violence*. Chicago: University of Illinois Press, 2019.

Tilly, Charles. "War Making and State Making as Organized Crime." In *Collective Violence, Contentious Politics, and Social Change*, edited by Ernesto Castañeda and Cathy Lisa Schneider. New York: Routledge, 2017.

Tinson, Christopher M. *Radical Intellect: Liberator Magazine and Black Activism in the 1960s*. Chapel Hill: University of North Carolina Press, 2017.

Trouillot, Michel-Rolph. "Good Day, Columbus: Silences, Power, and Public History (1492–1892)." *Public Culture* 3, no. 1 (1990): 1–24.

———. *Silencing the Past: Power and the Production of History*. Boston: Beacon Press, 1995.

Tzu, Sun. *The Art of War*. Translated by Samuel B. Griffith. Oxford: Oxford University Press, 1971.

Umoja, Akinyele O. "Maroon: Kuwasi Balagoon and the Evolution of Revolutionary New Afrikan Anarchism." *Science and Society* 79, no. 2 (April 2015): 196–220.

———. "Repression Breeds Resistance: The Black Liberation Army and the Radical Legacy of the Black Panther Party." *New Political Science* 21, no. 2 (1999): 131–55.

———. *We Will Shoot Back: Armed Resistance in the Mississippi Freedom Movement*. New York: NYU Press, 2013.

US Army. "Field Manual 33-1: Psychological Operations Techniques and Procedures." *Department of the Army Headquarters*. 1994.

———. *The U.S. Army Marine Corps Counterinsurgency Field Manual*. Chicago: University of Chicago Press, 2007.

US Congress. House. *American Prisons in Turmoil Part II*. Hearings Before the Select Committee on Crime. Washington, DC: US Government Printing Office, 1972.

———. *Departments of State, Justice, and Commerce, the Judiciary, and Related Agencies Appropriations for 1973*. Washington, DC: House of Representatives, 1972.

———. Oversight Hearings on Emerging Criminal Justice Issues. Hearings Before the Subcommittee on Criminal Justice. Washington, DC: US Government Printing Office, 1990.

———. *Revolutionary Activities Directed toward the Administration of Penal or Correctional Systems*. Hearings Before the House Committee on Internal Security. Washington, DC: US Government Printing Office, 1973.

———. *Terrorism Part 4*. Hearings Before the House Committee on Internal Security. Washington, DC: US Government Printing Office, 1974.

US Congress. Senate. Individual Rights and the Federal Role in Behavior Modification. A Study Prepared by the Staff of the Subcommittee on Constitutional Rights. Washington, DC: US Government Printing Office, 1974.

———. Senate. Project MKUltra, The CIA's Program of Research in Behavioral Modification. Joint Hearing Before the Select Committee on Intelligence and the Subcommittee on Health and Scientific Research. Washington, DC: US Government Printing Office, 1977.

———. Senate. Select Committee to Study Governmental Operations with respect to Intelligence Activities. *Supplementary Detailed Staff Reports on Intelligence Activities and the Rights of Americans*, Book III. Washington, DC: US Government Printing Office, 1976.

Useem, Bert, and Peter Kimball. *States of Siege: US Prison Riots, 1971–1986*. Oxford: Oxford University Press, 1991.

Vargas, João H. Costa. *Catching Hell in the City of Angels: Life and Meanings of Blackness in South Central Los Angeles*. Minneapolis: University of Minnesota Press, 2006.

———. *Never Meant to Survive: Genocide and Utopias in Black Diaspora Communities*. Lanham, MD: Rowman and Littlefield, 2010.

Vargas, João Costa, and Joy James. "Refusing Blackness-as-Victimization: Trayvon Martin and the Black Cyborgs." *Pursuing Trayvon Martin: Historical Contexts and Contemporary Manifestations of Racial Dynamics*, edited by George Yancy and Janine Jones, 193–204. Lanham, MD: Lexington Books, 2012.

Vásquez, Delio. "Illegalist Foucault, Criminal Foucault." *Theory and Event* 23, no. 4 (2020): 935–72.

Vitale, Alex S., and Jordan Jefferson. "The Emergence of Command and Control Policing in Neoliberal New York." In *Policing the Planet: Why the Policing Crisis Led to Black Lives Matter*, edited by Jordan T. Camp and Christina Heatherton, 157–72. London: Verso, 2016.

von Clausewitz, Carl. *On War*. Edited and translated by Michael Howard and Peter Paret. Princeton, NJ: Princeton University Press, 1976.

Wacquant, Loïc. "The Curious Eclipse of Prison Ethnography in the Age of Mass Incarceration." *Ethnography* 3, no. 4 (2002): 371–97.

Waldram, James B. "Challenges of Prison Ethnography." *Anthropology News* 50, no. 1 (2009): 4–5.

Walia, Harsha. *Border and Rule: Global Migration, Capitalism, and the Rise of Racist Nationalism*. Chicago: Haymarket Books: 2021.

Wallace, Maurice O. *Constructing the Black Masculine: Identity and Ideality in African American Men's Literature and Culture, 1775–1995*. Durham, NC: Duke University Press, 2002.

Walters, Ronald W. *Pan Africanism in the African Diaspora: An Analysis of Modern Afrocentric Political Movements*. Detroit: Wayne State University Press, 1997.

Webb, Gary. *Dark Alliance: The CIA, the Contras, and the Crack Cocaine Explosion*. New York: Seven Stories Press, 1998.

Weheliye, Alexander G. *Habeas Viscus: Racializing Assemblages, Biopolitics, and Black Feminist Theories of the Human*. Durham, NC: Duke University Press, 2014.

Wells-Barnett, Ida B.. *Southern Horrors and Other Writings: The Anti-Lynching Campaign of Ida B. Wells, 1892–1900*. Edited by Jacqueline Jones Royster. Boston: Bedford Books, 1997.

West, Louis Jolyon. "A Clinical and Theoretical Overview of Hallucinatory Phenomena." In *Hallucinations: Behavior, Experience, and Theory*, edited by Ronald K. Siegel and Louis Jolyon West, 287–311. New York: John Wiley & Sons, 1975.

West, Harry, and Todd Sanders. *Transparency and Conspiracy: Ethnographies of Suspicion in the New World Order*. Durham, NC: Duke University Press, 2003.

Wicker, Tom. *A Time to Die*. New York: Quadrangle/New York Times Book Company, 1975.

Wiegman, Robyn. *American Anatomies*. Durham, NC: Duke University Press, 1995.

Wiener, Norbert. *The Human Use of Human Beings: Cybernetics and Society*. New York: Da Capo Press, 1988.

Wiggins, Frederick. "The Truth about Attica by an Inmate." *National Review*, March 31, 1972.

Wilderson, Frank B., III. *Red, White and Black: Cinema and the Structure of US Antagonisms*. Durham, NC: Duke University Press, 2010.

Williams, Bianca C., Dian D. Squire, and Frank A. Tuitt. *Plantation Politics and Campus Rebellions: Power, Diversity, and the Emancipatory Struggle in Higher Education*. Albany: SUNY Press, 2021.

Williams, Kristian. "The Other Side of the COIN: Counterinsurgency and Community Policing." In *Life during Wartime: Resisting Counterinsurgency*, edited by Kristian Williams, Lara Messersmith-Glavin, and William Munger, 83–110. Chico, CA: AK Press, 2013.

Wilson, Stephen, and Felber, Garret. "The Makings of a Forum: Imprisoned Black Radical Tradition." *Black Perspectives*, August 24, 2020. https://www.aaihs.org/the-makings-of-a-forum-imprisoned-black-radical-tradition/

Wood, Amy Louise. *Lynching and Spectacle: Witnessing Racial Violence in America, 1890–1940*. Chapel Hill: University of North Carolina Press, 2011.

Woodard, Vincent. *The Delectable Negro: Human Consumption and Homoeroticism within US Slave Culture*. New York: NYU Press, 2014.
Woodfox, Albert. *Solitary: Unbroken by Four Decades in Solitary Confinement. My Story of Transformation and Hope*. New York: Grove Press, 2019.
Woods, Clyde Adrian. *Development Arrested: The Blues and Plantation Power in the Mississippi Delta*. London: Verso, 2017.
Wynter, Sylvia. "'No Humans Involved': An Open Letter to My Colleagues." *Voices of the African Diaspora* 8, no. 2 (1992): 12–16.
———. "Unsettling the Coloniality of Being/Power/Truth/Freedom: Towards the Human, after Man, Its Overrepresentation—an Argument." *CR: The New Centennial Review* 3, no. 3 (2003): 257–337.
———. "We Know Where We Are From: The Politics of Black Culture from Myal to Marley." Paper presented at the Houston Conference, November 1977. In CLR James Collection, Africana Studies Department, Brown University.
Zahm, Barbara. *The Last Graduation: The Movement for College Programs in New York State Prisons after Attica*. DVD. Deep Dish Television, 1997.
Zeitlyn, David. "Anthropology in and of the Archives: Possible Futures and Contingent Pasts. Archives as Anthropological Surrogates." *Annual Review of Anthropology* 41, no. 1 (2012): 461–80.
Zimroth, Peter L. *Perversions of Justice: The Prosecution and Acquittal of the Panther 21*. New York: Viking Press, 1974.

Index

Italic page numbers indicate figures.

Abdur-Rahman, Aliyyah I., 129
abolition geography, 91
abolitionism. *See* revolutionary/abolitionist goals of prison insurgency
Abrams, Robert, 217–18
Abu Ghraib, 135, 261n13
Acoli, Sundiata, 103, 220–21
ACTEC (Adirondack Correctional Treatment Education Center), 169, 193, 194. *See also* Rx Program
Activist, The, 57
Adolescent Remand Shelter (Rikers Island), 40
Algeria, 112
alienation. *See* dehumanization
Alim, Jalil Abdul, 64–65
Al-Jundi, Akil, 98, 111, 247n49
Allen, Robert L., 155, 177
Alston, Ashanti, 103, 231–32n10
Alston, Melvin, 29
amelioration/revolution tension: Attica rebellion and, 157; bail review hearing and, 37–38; New York City jail rebellions and, 31–33; reformist counterinsurgency and, 152, 154–55. *See also* reform demands; revolutionary/abolitionist goals of prison insurgency
"America Is the Prison" (Shakur), 229
American Civil Liberties Union (ACLU), 228

American Correctional Association (ACA), 14–15, 17, 33, 40, 160, 260n133
American Institutes for Research (AIR), 168–69
Anderson, Lana, 131
Anderson, William C., 232n14
Antelope case (1825), 11
anti-Black sexual violence: carceral narratives ignoring, 121, 141; counterinsurgency strategies and, 121; dehumanization and, 129, 146; during Attica massacre, 119–20, 121, 132–33, 137–38, 253n77; lynching as, 129; maintenance of white hegemonic masculinity and, 120, 129, 136–37, 138, 148; military-industrial complex and, 135; "Petition for Certificates Extraordinary" on, 138–46, 254n86; prison pacification regime and, 106, 123, 146; as psychological warfare, 120–21; reprisals for rebellions and, 65; shame and, 121; targeting of revolutionary captives and, 129–30; visual representation and, 132–36
anticolonialism: Black American renaming customs and, 70; Branch Queens rebellion and, 31; counterinsurgency operations against, 191, 262n32;

301

anticolonialism *(continued)*
  emergent forms of Black masculinity and, 62; insurgent counter-humanism and, 53, 62, 147–48; internationalism and, 111, 114; revolutionary/abolitionist goals and, 23, 24, 81, 114, 159, 192; self-governance and, 31, 83; urban rebellions (1964–72) and, 12; violence as insurgent strategy and, 42, 44, 63. *See also* colonialism/imperialism
Appe, Margarete, 176
archival war, 15–16, 45–46, 185. *See also* carceral narratives
Armed Forces of National Liberation (FALN), 212–13, 214
Arroyo, Pedro, 213
Atascadero State Hospital, 201
Attica Brigade, 216
Attica Brothers Foundation, 230
Attica massacre: anti-Black sexual violence during, 119–20, 121, 132–33, 137–38, 253n77; assassinations during, 119, 247n49; BLA retaliation for, 149; carceral narratives on, 52, 80, 132–34, 183, 214, 253n77; colonialism/imperialism and, 3; emergent forms of Black masculinity and, 125; events of, 119, 120; Hicks and, 85; inside/outside solidarity and, 174; insurgent narratives and, 122; Moore's analysis of, 2–3; Mỹ Lai Massacre and, 99–100; physical and psychological impact on survivors, 131; press coverage, 137–38; proliferation of carceral rebellions after, 148–49; as psychological warfare, 120–21; as public exhibition of carceral violence, 40; revolutionary deaths in, 96, 119, 247n49; survivor litigation, 121, 133; warrior funerals and, 103–4; white supremacist environment and, 124, 127, 128
Attica Prison: Auburn rebels transfer to, 60, 69, 73, 76–77, 243n76; captive political organizing, 77; conditions in, 245n20; metal shop strike, 243n76; programmification in, 176; targeting of revolutionary captives and, 213. *See also* Attica massacre; Attica rebellion
Attica rebellion: anticolonialism and, 114; carceral narratives on, 8, 77, 79–80, 93–94; carceral narratives on lessons of, 68, 181, 206; continuation of, 153; emergent forms of Black masculinity and, 104–5, 110, 125; exit interviews, 126; expatriation demands, 110–11, 112–13; fantasies of Black sexual violence and, 125–26, 138, 251n23; guard vulnerability, 86, 101–2; guerrilla warfare and, 83, 98, 99, 100–101; initiation of, 84, 85–89, 89, 245n20; inside/outside solidarity and, 103–4, 112–13, 254n86; insurgent narratives on memory of, 230; internationalism and, 110–12, 114; George Jackson memorial and, 77, 218; legal aftermath, 94; meal strike and, 218; multiracial narratives of, 85, 245n20; rage and, 88, 100; reform demands, 81, 82, 154, 157; revolutionary/abolitionist goals of, 80, 81, 82–83, 87, 89–90, 115, 156–57; sabotage and, 87–88, 89; self-governance during, 83, 90–95, 109, 246n40, 249n96; sexism and homophobia and, 124; significance of, 82, 115; state investigations of, 93; surrender, 104; as threat to white hegemonic masculinity, 5, 120, 125, 214; white captives and, 90, 94–95. *See also* Attica massacre; Attica rebellion social experience
Attica rebellion social experience, 105, 106–10; costume and, 109–10; disability and, 109, 249n96; emergent forms of Black masculinity and, 104–5, 110; erotic and, 108; freedom and, 106–7; homosexuality and, 108–9; intimacy/care and, 83–84, 107–8, 109
Attica Underground, 83, 96, 97–98, 104. *See also* Black Liberation Army; Black Underground
Auburn 6, 57, 59
Auburn 80, 60, 64–65
Auburn Prison, 60; age of, 159; as carceral archive, 50; jail rebel transfers to, 49, 160; Nation of Islam in, 190; prison labor in, 162; targeting of revolutionary captives and, 213
Auburn rebellion: captive political organizing and, 71; carceral narratives on, 52, 54–55, 56–57, 71; Casper Baker Gary and, 140; guerrilla warfare and, 65; Hicks and, 85; inside/outside solidarity, 57–58, 58, 59, 61, 67; insurgent counter-humanism and, 51, 52–53, 56, 63, 68, 73, 76; insurgent narratives and, 53, 55–56, 57–59, 62–63; intimacy/care and, 53; knowledge communication and, 72; leadership transfers, 60, 69, 73, 76–77,

243n76; legal aftermath, 57, 59, 67, 68–69, 242n70; mental health and, 65–66; Oswald DOCS leadership and, 164; reform demands, 55, 154; reprisals for, 56–57, 59–60, 61–62, 64–65, 72–73; revolutionary/abolitionist goals and, 52, 56; roof SHU (Auburn 80), 60, 64–66, 67–68, 72–73; self-realization and, 72–73, 106; survivor litigation, 69, 77

"Awesome Attica Tragedy, The" (MARC), 177

Baba Odinga. *See* Thompson, Elmore "Baba Odinga"
Babylon, 95–96
bail system, 24–26, 35–38
Bakunin, Mikhail, 98
Balagoon, Kuwasi: Black Liberation Army and, 49, 97; on inside/outside solidarity, 47; masculinity and, 43; New York City jail rebellions and, 31, 34–35, 37; on violence as insurgent strategy, 42–43, 44
Balbus, Isaac D., 37
Baldwin, James, 136–37, 148
Barkley, L. D., 92, 92, 104, 105, 119, 247n49
Battle Acts, 57
behavioral science experiments, 16–17; carceral violence and, 192–93; counterinsurgency strategies and, 185, 199, 202–3; dehumanization and, 197; diversification and, 170; drugs and, 198, 202, 203; electronic monitoring and, 228–29; insurgent narratives on, 189; insurgent resistance to, 184, 185, 189, 194, 195–97, 203, 205; as intrinsic to prison pacification regime, 185, 198, 205; Marion Federal Penitentiary and, 221–22; MCUs and, 221; memory manipulation and, 197; military-industrial complex and, 185, 197, 201–3, 207, 264n68; Queen Mother Audley Moore on, 3; official concealment of, 17, 184, 198; operant conditioning model in, 197–98; PRISACTS and, 185–86, 206, 207; reformist counterinsurgency and, 184, 195; results of, 203–4; revolutionary use of, 206–7; Rx Program plans, 194–95; Rx Program precursors, 193–94, 195, 198, 263n43; Rx Program termination, 204, 205, 206–7; sexual manipulation and, 199–201, 203, 265nn74–76; surveillance and, 198; termination of, 206–7; white supremacist environment and, 194. *See also* Rx Program
Bell, Herman, 212, 215
Benjamin, Walter, 219
Bennet, James V., 193
Best, Stephen, 69
bin-Wahad, Dhoruba: on behavioral science experiments, 198; Black Liberation Army and, 97, 212, 217; Black Underground and, 96; Comstock Attica memorial and, 206; Charles Leon Hill and, 62; litigation by, 15, 210; Masia Mugmuk and, 204; PRISACTS and, 208, 210, 211; on state repression, 122; targeting of revolutionary captives and, 215; on war on terror, 186–87
biopolitics, 168
Black August Resistance, 230
Black Awakening in Capitalist America (Allen), 177
Black Commune, 83. *See also* self-governance
Black Liberation Army (BLA): assassinations by, 149; Attica Underground and, 83, 96, 97–98; Kuwasi Balagoon and, 49, 97; as idea, 97, 212; importance of, 212; inside/outside solidarity and, 103–4; Masia Mugmuk and, 204; outlaw capitalism and, 99; resistance to behavioral science experiments and, 184; on tactical nonviolence, 102, 103; targeting of revolutionary captives and, 186, 212, 213, 214–16, 217; violence as insurgent strategy and, 39, 44
Black Lives Matter, 230
Black masculinity: Black feminist analyses of, 124, 253n81; emergent forms of, 7, 43, 62, 104–5, 110, 124–25; insurgent violence as assertion of, 43; intimacy/care and, 124–25; rebellion as assertion/reclaiming of, 7, 42, 43; sexual victimization as threat to, 121
Black noise, 69
Black Panther, The, 28, 31, 98, 188, 196, 203
Black Panther Party (BPP), 234n56; Auburn rebellion and, 54, 55, 243n76; Black Liberation Army and, 97; captive political organizing and, 26, 76; expatriation demands and, 112–13, 249n113; inside/outside solidarity and, 47, 48, 112–13, 249n113; International Section, 95–96, 112, 249n107; martial

Black Panther Party (BPP) *(continued)*
training and, 64; mini-Panther trial, 30–31, 33, 48; Panther 21 trial impact on, 48; People's Tribunals, 38; political prisoners from, 212; revolutionary/abolitionist goals and, 38; Revolutionary People's Constitutional Convention, 38; self-governance and, 83; state repression of, 30–31, 43, 48, 234n56; tensions within, 43; violence as insurgent strategy and, 43. *See also* Panther 21

Black Power Movement, 177

Black radical tradition: Black political consciousness and, 4, 39, 62, 71, 231n10; embodiment and, 72; pathologization of, 169–70; philanthropic/corporate penetration of, 178; prison as war and, 12; proliferation of carceral rebellions and, 13–14; renaming customs and, 70; restraint and, 39; revolutionary nationalism, 12–13; think tanks, 177; as threat to white hegemonic masculinity, 128; urban rebellions (1964–72), 12, 13; voting rights and, 232n14; Western inability to comprehend, 76. *See also* anticolonialism; Black Liberation Army; Black Panther Party; state repression; violence as insurgent strategy

Black Scholar, The, 57, 64–65

Black Solidarity Day, 54, 56, 69, 70, 72, 179, 244n101

Black Underground, 95–98, 110–11, 112

Blood. *See* Thomas, Harold "Blood"

Blood in the Water: The Attica Uprising and Its Legacy (Thompson), 79

Bloods, 223–24, 270n2

Blyden, Herbert X, 28, 92, 92, 98, 113, 239n104, 247n49

Boggs, Grace Lee, 81

Boggs, James, 12, 81

Borges, Sonia Vaz, 51

Boyle, Robert J., 15

Branch Queens: court boycott, 29; Tombs rebels transfer to, 30. *See also* Branch Queens rebellion

Branch Queens rebellion, 32; amelioration/revolution tension and, 31–33; bail review hearing and, 35–38; inside/outside solidarity and, 34–35, 46–47, 46; revolutionary/abolitionist goals of, 23–24; suppression of, 41, 42, 44–45, 46–47

Brave New World (Huxley), 264n68

Brooklyn House of Detention (BHD) rebellion, 33, 40–41, 47–48

Brothers of Attica, The (Clark), 102

Brown, Bertram S., 209–10

Brown, Curtis, 30, 33, 34, 48, 239n104

Brown, Henry "Sha Sha," 98

Brown, Michael, 128

Brown, William, 126–27, 128, 132

Budd, George, Jr., 131

"Bugs": Attica rebellion initiation and, 84, 85, 86, 87–88, 132, 245n20; on Attica rebellion social experience, 109; Eddie Ellis and, 245n18; exit interview, 126, 132; guerrilla warfare and, 99; on lynching, 126, 127, 128, 132; outlaw capitalism and, 99

Bukhari, Safiya (Bernice Jones), 112

Butch. *See* Harvey, William "Butch"

Butler, Charles, 218

Cabrera, Louis, 239n104

California prison system, 201

C'Allah, Kareem, 67, 97–98, 242n70

Cameron, Ewen, 193

capitalism: crisis of, 12, 123; mechanistic views of humans and, 188

captive litigation: Attica massacre survivors, 121, 133; Auburn rebellion survivors, 69, 77; bin-Wahad, 15, 210; Masia Mugmuk and, 195; New York City jail rebellion survivors, 41, 45; *Sostre v. Rockefeller*, 56, 69, 157

captive political organizing: Attica transfers and, 77; Attica Underground and, 98; Auburn rebellion and, 71; Clinton Prison, 76–77; decline of, 223–24, 227; drugs as barrier to, 34; Casper Baker Gary and, 26–27; Green Haven Prison, 76; Inmates Liberation Front, 28; inside/outside solidarity and, 174; Jackson memorial and, 77; knowledge communication and, 27, 28, 50–51; New York City jail rebellions and, 26, 28; preventive detention and, 50–51; PRISACTS as attempt to prevent, 208; prison as war and, 217; Prisoners Liberation Front, 26–28, 140, 172–73; programmification as co-optation of, 174, 177–79, 181, 209, 215, 219; sound and, 75. *See also* inmate organization programs; knowledge communication

carceral counter-intelligence. *See* revolutionary captives, targeting of carceral narratives: anti-Black sexual violence and, 121, 141; as archive, 50; on Attica massacre, 52, 80, 132–34, 183, 214, 253n77; on Attica rebellion, 8, 77, 79–80, 93–94; on Attica rebellion social experience, 108; Attica Underground and, 96; on Auburn rebellion, 52, 54–55, 56–57, 71; carceral violence fetishization and, 39; on disability, 249n96; epidemiological model of rebellion and, 14, 33, 178, 260n133; extremism and, 66; fantasies of Black sexual violence and, 125–26, 138, 251n23; on humanization, 166; ignoring of carceral violence, 45–46; on insurgent knowledge communication, 190–91; internationalism and, 115; on lessons of Attica rebellion, 68, 181, 206; prison as war and, 217–18; prison conditions and, 100, 115; rebellious archival approaches and, 15–16, 45–46, 185; on reform demands, 5, 8, 23–24, 100, 115; on reformist counterinsurgency, 184; revolutionary/abolitionist goals and, 14, 52, 80, 82, 138; on self-governance, 93–94, 246n40, 249n96; tablets and, 227–28; targeting of revolutionary captives and, 215, 216–17

carceral rebellions: epidemiological model of, 14, 33, 178, 260n133; as reclaiming of Black masculinity, 7; as result of state repression, 13–14, 31. *See also* Attica rebellion; Auburn rebellion; New York City jail rebellions

carceral regime. *See* prison pacification regime

carceral state: anti-Blackness of, 1, 44, 97, 130; broad reach of, 1, 4, 44, 97, 229–30; dehumanization and, 2; prison expansion and, 159, 161. *See also* prison pacification regime; state repression

carceral violence: Attica massacre as public exhibition of, 40; behavioral science experiments and, 192–93; captive litigation and, 41; carceral narratives ignoring, 45–46; carceral narratives justifying, 46, 63; as cause of rebellions, 165–66, 171; colonialism/imperialism and, 63; diversification and, 171; fetishization of, 39; guards as culpable for, 38–39; health impacts of, 70–71; hostages as expendable and, 15, 40, 151, 180; insurgent narrative and, 62–63; as intrinsic to prison pacification regime, 71–72; legal norms and, 38; Masia Mugmuk's subjection to, 192–93; patriarchy and, 105–6; press coverage and, 39–40; PSC testimony on, 154; reform demands on, 25, 67; reformist counterinsurgency and, 150; Rx Program transfers and, 196–97; sexualization and, 106, 123; targeting of revolutionary captives and, 218–19; Unit 14 and, 48, 192, 194; white supremacy and, 46. *See also* anti-Black sexual violence; Attica massacre; rebellion suppression; reprisals for rebellions

Césaire, Aimé, 52
Champen, Roger, 89–90, 92, 92, 93, 120–21, 167
Changa. *See* Green, Woody "Changa"
Chase Manhattan Bank, 178
Cholmondeley, Sylvester. *See* Mugmuk, Masia A.
CIA (Central Intelligence Agency): behavioral science experiments and, 3, 185, 193, 194, 199, 202, 207, 221; behavioral science experiment termination announcements, 204–5; PRISACTS and, 185–86, 211. *See also* MK Ultra
Civil Rights Congress, 111
civil rights organizations, 177
Clark, Kenneth, 176–77, 178
Clark, Richard X, 92, 92, 101–2, 107–8, 109, 245n20, 251n23
classical conditioning, 198
classical liberal theory, 11
Cleaver, Eldridge, 62, 103, 112, 113
Cleaver, Kathleen, 112
Clinton Prison: anti-Black sexual violence, 129–30, 140; Auburn rebels transfer to, 60; behavioral science experiments and, 194; Black Panther Party in, 112; captive political organizing, 76–77; carceral violence in, 48, 192, 194; Casper Baker Gary in, 140; targeting of revolutionary captives and, 48, 192, 213; Unit 14, 48, 192, 194, 196, 215
Coalition of Concerned Black Americans, 177
Cohen, Cathy, 108–9
COINTELPRO, 9, 13, 17, 30, 191, 206, 211, 234n56
Colby, William, 211

Cold War, 17, 158, 185–86
Collins, Patricia Hill, 253n81
colonialism/imperialism: Attica massacre and, 3; behavioral science experiments and, 203; carceral violence and, 63; Queen Mother Audley Moore on, 2; Western liberal humanism and, 51–52. *See also* anticolonialism; counterinsurgency strategies; military-industrial complex
Coltrane, Alice, 75
communication. *See* insurgent narrative; knowledge communication
Community Day events, 18
community support. *See* inside/outside solidarity
Comstock Prison: Attica memorial in, 206; Attica rebels transfer to, 126; Auburn rebels transfer to, 60; diversification and, 171; Masia Mugmuk's transfer to, 204; name of, 241n39; riot (1963), 85; targeting of revolutionary captives and, 213
Congress of Racial Equality, 177
co-optation, 17, 154–55, 174, 178–79
"Cop City," 230
Cordis, Shanya, 74
Coughlin, Thomas A., 214, 216, 217, 218, 219
Counterinsurgency Field Manual (US Army), 155
Counter-Insurgency in Thailand (AIR), 169
counterinsurgency strategies: behavioral science experiments and, 185, 199, 202–3; co-optation and, 17, 155; drugs and, 264n68; operations against anticolonialist movements and, 191, 262n32; post-9/11 governance and, 229; prison as war and, 4; sexual violence and, 121; state repression and, 13, 169, 191; targeting of revolutionary captives and, 183–84, 187. *See also* MK Ultra; prison pacification regime; reformist counterinsurgency; revolutionary captives, targeting of
counter-memory, 55, 241n26
court boycotts, 29
Creative Communications Committee (CCC), 214–15, 216–17, 218
criminal justice discourses, 25
"Criminosynthesis of a Revolutionary Offender," 169–70
Cruz, Antonio, 264n69

Cuba, 114
Cummins Foundation, 178
Cuomo, Mario, 162

Dacajeweiah. *See* Hill, John "Dacajeweiah"
Dalou. *See* Gonzalez, Mariano "Dalou"
Daniels, James "Joe Chink," 98
Dannemora State Hospital for the Criminally Insane (DSH), 66, 193, 194. *See also* ACTEC; Rx Program
Davenport, Franklin Paul, 247–48n66
Davila, Anibal, 239n97
Davis, Angela, 83, 114
Davis, Emani, 70–71
Davis, O'Neal, 220
"Day of Absence" (Ward), 244n101
dehumanization: anti-Black sexual violence and, 129, 146; behavioral science experiments and, 197; colonialism and, 81; prison pacification regime and, 105–6, 124, 146. *See also* insurgent counter-humanism
DeLeon, Ricardo: on anti-Black sexual violence, 129–30; Black Panther Party and, 112; on Clinton Prison captive political organizing, 76–77; legal aftermath and, 48, 239n104; New York City jail rebellions and, 33–34, 41–42, 48, 49; on nomenclatural reform, 17
demands: bail system and, 24–25; expatriation, 110–11, 112–13; insurgent counter-humanism and, 56; knowledge communication and, 31; neutral observers, 31; press conferences, 32; *Sostre v. Rockefeller* and, 157. *See also* reform demands; revolutionary/abolitionist goals
Democratic Centralism, 246n39
Department of Health, Education, and Welfare, 193, 266n100
"Derby's Dose," 146
Detroit Rebellion (1967), 81
Diaz-Cotto, Juanita, 178–79, 180
Different Drummer, A (Kelley), 75–76
discursive insurgency. *See* insurgent narratives
diversification, 167–73, 226–27
Douglass, Frederick, 104
Douglass, Robert R., 140, 147
drugs: as barrier to captive political organizing, 34; behavioral science experiments and, 198, 202, 203; prison pacification regime and, 66, 198–99; war on, 159

Du Bois, W. E. B., 123–24
Dulles, Allen, 158, 185
Dulles, John Foster, 158
Dunbar, Walter, 125, 126
Dunn, James "Kato," 66, 98, 112

Eastern Prison, 124
East Village Other, The, 43
e-carceration, 186, 228–29
education, 209. *See also* programmification
electronic monitoring, 186, 228–29
Ellis, Eddie, 7, 180, 245n18
"enhanced interrogation" techniques, 221
epistolary praxis. *See* insurgent narrative; letter writing
Equiano, Olaudah, 11
Eve, Arthur O., 246n40, 254n86
exception clause (13th Amendment), 10
expatriation demands, 110–11, 112–13
Eyes on the Prize, 106

Fanon, Frantz: on dehumanization, 105; on insurgent counter-humanism, 53, 62, 147–48; on reciprocity of violence, 63, 66, 68; on self-governance, 92; on sexual revenge, 126, 128; on sound, 75; on tactical nonviolence, 102; "tip of the spear" phrase and, 9; on violence as insurgent strategy, 42, 44, 63, 66, 68, 87; on Western liberal humanism, 51–52; on white fantasies of Black sexual violence, 126
FBI (Federal Bureau of Investigation): Attica massacre and, 133; on Black sexual violence, 125; BPP internal tensions and, 43; CIA collaboration, 185–86; counterinsurgency strategies and, 13, 187; masculinity and, 122; National Crime Information Center, 187; National Symposium on the American Penal System as a Revolutionary Target, 209, 210; New York City jail rebellions and, 45; Rx Program and, 207; targeting of revolutionary captives and, 16; white supremacy and, 46. *See also* PRISACTS; state repression
Fifteen Practical Proposals (Attica rebellion), 81, 154
Fight for Freedom: It Is the Only Thing Worth Fighting For!, 58, 61
Fink, Elizabeth, 15, 199, 234n66
"First Letter to My Son" (White), 73–74, 75, 76
Five Percenters, 54, 243n76

Floyd, George, 127–28
Folsom Prison strike, 114
Ford Foundation, 177
Forgays, Donald G., 193, 194, 195, 198, 200, 201, 202–3, 265n76
Fosen, Robert H., 168, 169, 170
Foster, Gregory, 149
Foucault, Michel, 50, 155, 168
French Revolution, 27, 83
Fritz, Harry J., 54, 59–60, 61, 62, 64, 68

Gale, Hassan, 180, 181
Gallati, Robert R. J., 183–84, 187, 189, 211, 212
Galloway, David, 131
gangs, 223–24, 270n2
Garcia, Paul, 219
Garner, Eric, 128
Garrigia, Carmen, 153, 157
Garvey, Marcus, 2, 104
Gary, Casper Baker: on anti-Black sexual violence, 138–47, 254n86; Attica massacre and, 131; Auburn rebellion and, 140; background of, 26, 139–40; on insurgent counter-humanism, 146–48; madness of, 140, 148; Prisoners Liberation Front founding and, 26–28, 172; on self-governance, 35; targeting of revolutionary captives and, 48
gender-based violence, 230
Geneva Convention on the Treatment of Prisoners of War, 29, 111
genocide: carceral narratives and, 134; carceral violence as, 39; colonialism/imperialism and, 81; internationalism and, 29; prison as war and, 217; rebellion suppression and, 45; reform demands, 154; Western liberal humanism and, 52. *See also* carceral state; carceral violence; colonialism/imperialism
Getachew, Adom, 70, 111
Giannell, A. Steven, 170
Gilmore, Ruth Wilson, 12, 91
Global Tel Link (GTL), 227
"Going to Meet the Man" (Baldwin), 136
Golden Gulag (Gilmore), 12
Gonzalez, Mariano "Dalou," 56, 93, 95, 98, 103, 247n49
Gramsci, Antonio, 37, 246n39
Grant, J. Douglas, 178
Great Meadow Prison. *See* Comstock
Green, Woody "Changa," 97

Green Haven 40, 218–19
Green Haven Prison: age of, 159; Attica rebels transfer to, 1; Auburn rebels transfer to, 60, 73, 76, 243n76; captive political organizing, 76; corruption in, 213–14; diversification and, 171–73; meal strike (1980), 218, 219; Queen Mother Audley Moore memorial address, 1–3; programmification in, 172, 178, 179, 180, 181; targeting of revolutionary captives and, 213, 214–15, 216–19, 268n139; violence as insurgent strategy and, 64
Green Haven Think Tank, 7, 76, 174, 178, 180, 181
Guantanamo, 186–87, 261n13
guards: corruption and, 213–14; culpability of, 38–39; as expendable, 15, 40, 151, 180, 183; post-Attica strike threat, 165; reformist counterinsurgency and, 151; vulnerability of, 86, 101–2; white supremacy among, 124, 213. *See also* carceral violence
guerrilla warfare, 4, 65, 83, 98, 99, 100–101
Guevara, Che, 62

Haley, Sarah, 88
Hanson, Warren, 93
Hartman, Saidiya, 69, 134, 179
Harvey, William "Butch," 171
Hatch, Anthony Ryan, 199
Haudenosaunee (Iroquois) Confederacy, 91
Hayes, Robert "Seth," 212
Hearst, Patricia, 206–7
Heath, Teddy "Jah," 212
Hebb, Donald O., 193, 202, 263n43
Hekima. *See* Hines, Ned X. "Hekima"
Helms, Richard, 204
Henderson, Joseph, 199
Hess, Kenneth, 94–95
Hicks, Tommy "Kilimanjaro," 84–85, 243n76, 247n49
Hill, Charles Leon, 52–53, 62, 73–74
Hill, John "Dacajeweiah," 81, 85, 86, 107, 112, 245n20, 247n49
Hill, Rebecca, 165
Hines, Ned X. "Hekima," 190
Hines, Thomas "Shorty," 46
Hogan, Frank, 36
Holiday, Billie, 128
homosexuality: Attica rebellion social experience and, 108–9; behavioral science experiments and, 200, 201, 265n75

Hoover, J. Edgar: on Black Panther Party, 30; COINTELPRO and, 13; counterinsurgency strategies and, 191; PRISACTS and, 15, 156, 206; on programmification, 177; targeting of revolutionary captives and, 16
House Internal Security Committee (HISC), 156
Huen, Francis J., 133–34
Hughes, Thomas, 94
Human Ecology Fund, 202
humanization, 14, 18, 164–67, 172
Human Resources Research Center, 202
Human Use of Human Beings, The (Wiener), 188
Huxley, Aldous, 264n68

Ichord, Richard H., 156
Idle Company, 84, 85
If Beale Street Could Talk (Baldwin), 136–37
IGO (Office of the Inspector General), 210–11, 212, 214–15, 217, 218
Ihmoud, Sarah, 74
ILF (Inmates Liberation Front), 28, 36
incarceration alternatives, 228
Ingold, Tim, 139
inmate organization programs, 178–79, 214–18, 219, 268n39. *See also* captive political organizing
Inmates Forum, The, 28
Inmates Liberation Front (ILF), 28, 36
inside/outside solidarity: Attica massacre and, 174; Attica rebellion and, 103–4, 112–13, 254n86; Auburn rebellion, 57–58, 58, 59, 61, 67; captive political organizing and, 174; civil rights organizations and, 177; community volunteers and, 175–76; Inmates Liberation Front and, 28, 36; New York City jail rebellions and, 34–35, 36, 46–48, 46; radical lawyers and, 37; rebellion suppression and, 47–48; reformist counterinsurgency and, 151; rehabilitation and, 174; revolutionary/abolitionist goals and, 18, 47; state conciliation and, 39–40, 47; targeting of revolutionary captives and, 214; Young Lords Party and, 36, 46, 47. *See also* Prisoners Solidarity Committee
Instead of Prison: A Handbook for Abolitionists (Prison Research Education Action Project), 180

Institute for the Study of Crime and Delinquency, 178
Institute of the Black World (IBW), 80, 82
insurgent counter-humanism: anticolonialism and, 53, 62, 147–48; Auburn rebellion and, 51, 52–53, 56, 63, 68, 73, 76; intimacy/care and, 53, 70; "Petition for Certificates Extraordinary" on, 146–48; reciprocity of violence and, 68; violence as insurgent strategy and, 63, 68, 226
insurgent narratives: Attica massacre and, 122; Auburn rebellion and, 53, 55–56, 57–59, 62–63; on behavioral science experiments, 189; Black noise and, 69; carceral violence and, 62–63; carceral violence impacts on, 70–71; as counter-memory, 55, 241n26; difficulties of, 60–61; insurgent counter-humanism and, 51, 63, 73; intimacy/care and, 70–71, 73–74; letter writing and, 56, 57–59; Long Attica Revolt framework and, 8–9; on memories of Attica rebellion, 230; as poetics of living rebellion, 74–75; on programmification, 208–9; on rehabilitation, 155–56; on reprisals for rebellions, 46, 61–62, 64–65; research focus on, 8; revolutionary/abolitionist goals and, 55–56; silence and, 68–69, 70, 71; sound and, 74, 75; state study of, 188–89; tablets and, 228. *See also* knowledge communication
International Association of Chiefs of Police, 187
internationalism: asylum and, 111–12, 249n107; Attica rebellion and, 110–12, 114; Black Panther Party and, 95–96, 112, 249n107; carceral narratives ignoring, 115; expatriation demands and, 110–11, 112–13; New York City jail rebellions and, 29
intimacy/care: insurgent counter-humanism and, 53, 70; insurgent narratives and, 70–71, 73–74; social life during rebellions and, 83–84
Iroquois (Haudenosaunee) Confederacy, 91
isolation. *See* solitary confinement

Jackson, George: assassination of, 15, 77, 177; background of, 10; Cuba and, 114; on extremism, 66; on guerrilla warfare, 65; litigation and, 242n70; memorial for, 77, 218; political arc of, 62; on prison as war, 10; on reciprocity of violence, 68; on self-governance, 83; on slavery, 11
Jacobs, Harriet, 11
Jah. *See* Heath, Teddy "Jah"
Jailhouse Lawyers Speak, 230
James, Joy, 91
Jewish Defense League, 113
Jimenez, Gilberto, 36, 37
Joe Chink. *See* Daniels, James "Joe Chink"
Johnson, Lyndon, 13
Joint Center for Political Studies, 177
Joint Terrorism Task Force, 211
Jomo. *See* Omowale, Jomo Sekou
Jones, Bernice. *See* Bukhari, Safiya

Kato. *See* Dunn, James "Kato"
Kelley, William Melvin, 75–76
Kilgore, James, 229
Kilimanjaro. *See* Hicks, Tommy "Kilimanjaro"
Killebrew, Lawrence, 153
Kimu. *See* White, Anthony "Kimu"
King, Martin Luther, Jr., 5, 179
King, Stanley, 239n104
Kinshasa, Kwando, 31, 43, 62
Kitossa, Tamari, 122
Kitson, Frank, 17, 157, 262n32
knowledge communication: Attica Underground and, 98; Auburn rebellion and, 72; captive political organizing and, 27, 28, 50–51; censorship of, 56; demands and, 31; fiction and, 75–76, 244n101; Nation of Islam and, 190–91; sound and, 75; as walking archive, 51. *See also* captive political organizing; insurgent narratives
Ku Klux Klan, 124, 213
Kunstler, William, 110, 113, 246n40, 249n113
Kurshan, Nancy, 222, 261n13

Latin Kings, 223
Laurie, Rocco, 149
Law Enforcement Assistance Administration (LEAA), 13, 206, 266n100
Lawson, Robert B., 202
Lefcourt, Gerald, 36, 46
Legal Aid Society, 25
Lenin, Vladimir I., 246n39
letter writing: Auburn rebellion and, 57–59, 62–63; limitations of, 60–61; *Sostre v. Rockefeller* and, 56; tablets and, 228
liberalism, 11, 17
Lindsay, John, 40, 41, 42

Linebarger, Paul, 17
Little, Joseph, 155, 156, 157
Little Red Book (Mao), 98
Locke, John, 11
Lomangcolob, Pablo M., 197
Long Attica Revolt framework, 3; carceral narratives and, 68, 181, 206; counter-war and, 224–25; humanization and, 164; insurgent narratives on, 8–9; ongoing insurgence and, 230; prison expansion and, 226; targeting of revolutionary captives and, 214; "tip of the spear" phrase and, 9; white hegemonic masculinity and, 214
Lorde, Audre, 108
Losier, Toussaint, 25–26
Low Intensity Operations (Kitson), 17
Lowitt, Oscar, 220
Luqmon. *See* White, Larry "Luqmon"
lynching, 2, 126, 127, 128–29, 132, 134–35, 190

Mack, Larry, 112
mad science, 147
Malcolm X: assassination of, 191; on broad reach of carceral state, 229; knowledge communication and, 190; masculinity and, 104; Queen Mother Audley Moore and, 1; political arc of, 62; struggle names and, 70
Management Control Units (MCUs), 220–22
Mancusi, Vincent, 69
Manhattan House of Detention. *See* Tombs
Mao Tse-tung, 62, 98, 103
Marable, Manning, 128
MARC (Metropolitan Applied Research Center), 176–77, 178
Marion Federal Penitentiary, 221–22
Maroon. *See* Shoatz, Russell "Maroon"
Marriott, David, 135
marronage, 27, 83, 106–7
Marshall, John, 11
martial arts, 64
Martinez, Victor: Algerian asylum and, 112; Branch Queens rebellion and, 31, 32–33, 45; Inmates Liberation Front and, 28; New York City jail rebellions and, 23, 24, 28, 29, 32–33, 45; rebellion suppression and, 45; self-governance and, 35; Tombs rebellion and, 28, 29
Marx, Karl, 83
masculinity, 6–7. *See also* Black masculinity; white hegemonic masculinity

Mau Mau Emergency, 27, 191
Mau Mau from Within (Njama and Hales), 191
McGill University, 193, 194, 202
McGivern, Gary, 9
McGrath, George F., 23, 28, 29
McKay, Claude, 104
McKay Commission: on Auburn rebellion, 56–57; on homosexuality, 108; official report cover image, 132–33, 137–38, 253n77; "Petition for Certificates Extraordinary" and, 140; as research source, 121; on self-governance, 93, 246n40, 249n96; on targeting of revolutionary captives, 168. *See also* carceral narratives
McKittrick, Katherine, 75
Melville, Samuel, 82–83, 85, 101, 119, 245n20, 247n49
Mental Hygiene Facilities Improvement Corporation, 161
Meriwether, Charles, 218
"Message from the Monster: Attica," 166
"Message to the Black Movement: A Political Statement from the Black Underground" (bin-Wahad), 208
Meyers, Twymon, 212
Midnight Special, 196
military-industrial complex: anti-Black sexual violence and, 135; behavioral science experiments and, 185, 197, 201–3, 207, 264n68; behavioral science experiments termination announcements, 204–5; diversification and, 168; knowledge communication on, 98; PRISACTS and, 185–86; prison pacification regime intensification and, 186–87, 210, 261n13; targeting of revolutionary captives and, 183–84, 187. *See also* colonialism/imperialism; counterinsurgency strategies
Miller, Charlene, 131
Miller, John C., 134
"Mind Is Flesh, The" (Newton), 189
mini-Panther trial, 30–31, 33, 48
Mitchell, John N., 157–58
MK Ultra: behavioral science experiments and, 202, 203, 264n68; CIA-FBI collaboration and, 186; drug experiments and, 264n68; memory manipulation and, 197; prison as war and, 199; prison pacification regime and, 185; sites for, 193, 201; termination announcement, 204, 205

Moon, Dixie, 178
Moore, Queen Mother Audley: on broad reach of carceral state, 1, 4, 229; Green Haven memorial address, 1–3, 18; Green Haven Think Tank and, 181; on lynching, 2, 126; on reformist counterinsurgency, 215; revolutionary/abolitionist goals and, 38; on violence as insurgent strategy, 42
Moore, Raymond Lavone, 239n97
Morales, Nicholas, 131
Mugmuk, Masia A., 185, *191*; background of, 190, 191–92; character of, 189; MCU incarceration of, 220–21; resistance of, 189, 195–97, 204; on Rx Program sexual manipulation, 199–201
Mugmuk, Mzuri, 204, 220
Mu'Mim, Musa Abdul, 213
Muntaqim, Jalil, 9, 212, 215, 216, 217, 218, 219, 268n169
Myers, Franklyn, 239n104
Myers, Joshua, 75
Mỹ Lai Massacre, 99–100

National Association for the Advancement of Colored People (NAACP), 177
National Conference of Black Lawyers, 177
National Crime Information Center, 187
National Lawyers Guild, 114, 177, 192
national security state. *See* military-industrial complex
National Symposium on the American Penal System as a Revolutionary Target (1974), 209, *210*
Nation of Islam (NOI): Attica rebellion and, 90, 92, 102; Masia Mugmuk and, 190, 191; New York City jail rebellions and, 34–35; reformist counterinsurgency and, 153
Nelepovitz, Robert, 215
Neocleous, Mark, 11
neoslavery analytic, 10–11. *See also* slavery
Ñetas, 223
"New Prisoner, The" (Sostre), 157
Newton, Huey P., 13, 29, 188–89, 228, 265n74
New York City jail rebellions (1970), 23–49; abolitionist internationalism and, 29; amelioration/revolution tension and, 31–33; antidrug policies and, 34; bail review hearing, 35–38; bail system and, 24–26; BHD rebellion, 33, 40–41, 47–48; Branch Queens rebellion, 23–24, 31–33, 32, 34–38, 41, 42, 44–45, 46; captive political organizing and, 26, 28; carceral narratives on, 23–24; casualties of, 46, 239n97; court boycott, 29; demands of, 24–25, 28, 29, 31–32; inside/outside solidarity and, 34–35, 36, 46–48, 46; internal tensions and, 33–35, 41–42, 44–45; leadership transfers to prisons, 49, 160; legal aftermath, 48, 239n104; Prisoners Liberation Front founding, 26–28; psychological warfare and, 41–42; QHD rebellion, 33, 34, 40, 41, 45, 46; reprisals for, 45, 46, 49, 129, 160, 239n97; revolutionary/abolitionist goals of, 23–24, 28, 29, 32–33; self-governance and, 29, 31, 33, 35, 41–42; state conciliatory approach, 39–40, 47; state repression as cause of, 31; suppression of, 29, 40–43, 44–45, 46–47; survivor litigation, 41, 45; Time Men as neutral, 34; Tombs rebellion, 24–25, 28–29, 33, 41–42; transfer among jails and, 29–30
New York prison system: age of, 159; economic role of, 123–24, 162–64, 194; expansion of, 159–64; Indigenous population in, 232n12; jail rebels transfer to, 49, 160; population manipulation, 256n42; white supremacist environment of, 124, 127, 128, 194
New York State Select Committee on Correctional Institutions and Programs, 153–54, 155, 156, 160, 172, 175
New York State Special Commission on Attica. *See* McKay Commission
New York Times. See press coverage
Nieves, Che, 6
Nixon, Richard M., 148–49, 159, 172
nomenclatural reform, 17–18
Northrup, Donna, 131
Norton, Jack, 162
no-touch torture, 221–22
Nuh. *See* Washington, Albert "Nuh"
NYSIIS (New York State Identification and Intelligence System), 187, 210, 211

Oath Keepers movement, 27
oathtaking, 27
O'Connor, Daniel, 239n104
Odinga, Sekou, 85, 112
"offender profile" system, 169
Oliver, Antonio G., 254n86
Omowale, Jomo Sekou: on anti-Black sexual violence, 138; Attica transfer, 68–69, 77; Black Liberation Army and,

Omowale, Jomo Sekou *(continued)*
  98; on captive political organizing,
  50–51; on carceral violence, 71–72;
  death of, 247n49; on drugs in prison
  pacification regime, 199; masculinity
  and, 110; on self-governance, 93–94;
  silence and, 68–69, 70
Onaci, Edward, 70
O'Neal, Tyrone, 198
100 Days of Sodom, 146
ontological totality, 71
operant conditioning, 197–98
Operation CHAOS, 13
organizational discipline. *See* self-governance
"Organization of a Special Defense Interrogation Program" (CIA), 186
Oswald, Russell G.: Attica self-governance and, 92; behavioral science experiments and, 195–96; carceral narratives based on, 57, 80; diversification and, 172; DOCS leadership, 164; guard strike threat and, 165; humanization and, 164–65, 167; insurgent narratives on, 61; prison expansion and, 162–63; on revolutionary/abolitionist goals, 138
Out of Control: A Fifteen-Year Battle against Control Unit Prisons (Kurshan), 222

Painter, Nell Irvin, 121
Palante, 31, 57
Pan-Africanism, 31, 70
Panther 21: acquittal of, 48; Algerian asylum and, 112; arrest of, 30; Black Underground and, 97; humanism and, 62; on inside/outside solidarity, 47; New York City jail rebellions and, 31, 36, 45; on violence as insurgent strategy, 43–44
Paris Commune, 83
Parker, Charles "Rabb," 166, 247n49
Pasolini, Pier, 146
PBC (Public Benefit Corporation) designation, 161
Pelican Bay hunger strike (2013), 230
Peoples Party, the, 166
People's Tribunals, 38
Perez, Jose, 239n97
"Petition for Certificates Extraordinary" (Gary), 138–48, 142–44, 254n86
Pfeil, Karl, 126
Pfeil, Warden, 132
Pickens, Therí Alyce, 140
political prisoners. *See* revolutionary captives, targeting of

"Political Prisoner's Journey through the U.S. Prison System, A" (Muntaqim), 219
Pope, Mary, 131
Poser, Ernest G., 194, 263n43
Powell, Curtis, 113
"Power to Change Behavior, The" (conference, 1961), 193, 209
precolonial Africa, 83
press coverage: Attica massacre, 137–38; Attica rebellion, 125; Auburn rebellion, 53, 56–57; carceral violence and, 39–40; fantasies of Black sexual violence and, 125, 138; on humanization, 18, 166; New York City jail rebellions, 24–25, 28, 29, 32–33, 39–40, 47; rebellion suppression and, 45
pretrial detainees. *See* bail system
preventive detention: bail system and, 25–26; Black Panther Party and, 30; captive political organizing and, 50–51; crisis of capitalism and, 12; prison transfers and, 49
PRISACTS (Prison Activists Surveillance Program), 156; assassinations and, 211; behavioral science experiments and, 185–86, 206, 207; bin-Wahad litigation and, 15, 210; CIA-FBI collaboration and, 185–86; counterinsurgency strategies and, 17; epidemiological model of rebellion and, 208; goals of, 208; localized versions of, 210, 212; mechanistic views of humans and, 207–8; prison as war and, 209; as psychological warfare, 206, 209–10; termination of, 210
prison as archive, 50–51
prison as war, 9–10, 18; asymmetry of, 3–4, 53, 66, 225; behavioral science experiments and, 184, 199; captive political organizing and, 217; carceral archives and, 16; carceral infrastructure and, 68; carceral narratives and, 217–18; classical liberal theory and, 11; counter-war and, 18, 224–25, 226; diversification and, 168; insurgent counter-humanism and, 52–53, 226; MK Ultra and, 199; PRISACTS and, 209; prison expansion and, 163, 227; rebellion suppression and, 40; reformist counterinsurgency and, 150–51; slavery and, 10–12, 225–26; state initial concealing of, 40; targeting of revolutionary captives and, 217; US historical context, 224; violence as

insurgent strategy and, 44, 226. *See also* prison pacification regime
Prisoners Call Out: Freedom (Hill), 58, 62, 73–74
Prisoners Digest International, 196
"Prisoners Injustice Resistance and Survival Manual" (Casper), 26
Prisoners Liberation Front (PLF), 26–28, 140, 172–73
Prisoners Solidarity Committee (PSC): amelioration/revolution tension and, 157; anticolonialism and, 114; Attica rebellion and, 82; Auburn rebellion and, 57, 58, 59, 61, 67; carceral suspicion of, 177; reformist counterinsurgency and, 153; Select Committee testimony by, 153–54
prison ethnography, 173
prison expansion, 159–64, 213, 256n49
prison insurgency: as guerrilla warfare, 4; law and, 48; People's Tribunals, 38; Provisional Government of the Republic of New Afrika, 38; self-realization and, 72–73, 106; white captives and, 4–5. *See also* amelioration/revolution tension; Long Attica Revolt framework; revolutionary/abolitionist goals of prison insurgency; violence as insurgent strategy; *specific rebellions*
prison/jail conditions. *See* carceral violence; prison pacification regime; reform demands; reformist counterinsurgency
prison labor, 161–62, 233n38
Prison Moratorium Project, 7
prison pacification regime: ACA riot control manual on, 14–15, 17; anti-Black sexual violence and, 106, 123, 146; behavioral science experiments as intrinsic to, 185, 198, 205; captive litigation against, 15, 41, 69, 77, 121, 133, 157, 195, 210; as carceral siege, 3–4; carceral violence as intrinsic to, 71–72; dehumanization and, 105–6, 124, 146; diversification and, 172; drugs and, 66, 198–99; intensification of, 186–87, 210, 261n13; MCUs, 220–22; mental health weaponization and, 66; prison as war and, 225–26; prison expansion and, 163; PSC testimony on, 154; psychosurgery and, 194, 263n49; reform as central to, 155; war on terror and, 186–87. *See also* behavioral science experiments; carceral violence; reformist counterinsurgency
Prisons Information Group, 53–54
prison unionization movement, 111

"Prison: Where Is Thy Victory" (Newton), 188–89
Privitera, Michael, 95, 109
Procunier, Raymond, 177
"Profile of a Revolutionary Married Couple" (Mugmuk), 220
programmification, 173–81; community volunteers and, 174–76, 177–78; as co-optation of captive political organizing, 174, 177–79, 181, 209, 215, 219; diversification and, 172; inmate organization programs, 178–79; insurgent critiques of, 208–9; public relations and, 175–76
Project Themis, 202
propaganda. *See* carceral narratives; psychological warfare; public relations
Provisional Government of the Republic of New Afrika, 38
psychological warfare: ACA riot control manual on, 14; anti-Black sexual violence as, 120–21; New York City jail rebellion suppression and, 41–42; nomenclatural reform as, 17–18; PRISACTS as experiment in, 206, 209–10; reformist counterinsurgency as, 151, 160, 167, 181; Rockefeller and, 158
psychosurgery, 194, 263n49
Psychotechology: Electronic Control of Mind and Behavior (Schwitzgebel and Schwitzgebel), 229–30
psyops. *See* psychological warfare
public relations: New York City jail rebellions and, 39; programmification and, 175–76. *See also* press coverage
Puerto Rican independence movement, 213
punitive isolation. *See* solitary confinement

QHD (Queens House of Detention at Kew Gardens) rebellion, 33, 34, 40, 41, 45, 46
Queens House of Detention, Long Island City branch. *See* Branch Queens
Quinn, William, 84, 86

Rabb. *See* Parker, Charles "Rabb"
radical lawyers, 37
Ragsdale, Nathaniel, 48, 239n104
RAND Corporation, 202
rebellion suppression: carceral narratives centering, 52; inside/outside solidarity and, 47–48; insurgent internal tensions

314 | Index

rebellion suppression *(continued)*
  and, 41–42, 44–45, 168; New York City jail rebellions, 29, 40–43, 44–45, 46–47; survivor litigation, 41, 45, 121, 133; violence as insurgent strategy and, 41–43, 44. *See also* Attica massacre
rebellion vs. revolution, 81
reform demands: Attica rebellion, 81, 82, 154, 157; Auburn rebellion, 55, 154; carceral narratives on, 5, 8, 23–24, 100, 115; carceral violence and, 25; civil rights organizations and, 177; genocide conditions and, 154–55, 255n12; New York City jail rebellions, 24–25, 28, 29; press publication of, 39. *See also* amelioration/revolution tension
reformist counterinsurgency, 149; amelioration/revolution tension and, 152, 154–55; as Attica win, 167; behavioral science experiments and, 184, 195; captive choices in face of, 180; carceral narratives on, 184; co-optation and, 17, 154–55, 174, 177–79, 181; diversification, 167–73, 226–27; humanization, 14, 18, 164–67, 172; IGO and, 210; insurgent resistance to, 153–54, 165, 166, 181–82, 209; militarization and, 163; nomenclatural reform, 17–18; prison as war and, 150–51; prison-based tablets and, 227–28; prison ethnography and, 173; prison expansion and, 159–64, 213, 256n49; programmification, 173–81, 209, 215, 219; as psychological warfare, 151, 160, 167, 181; public opinion on, 162; rehabilitation and, 155–56; television and, 227
rehabilitation: inside/outside solidarity and, 174; insurgent critiques of, 155–56. *See also* programmification
reprisals for rebellions: anti-Black sexual violence and, 65; assassinations and, 46; Auburn rebellion, 56–57, 59–60, 61–62, 64–65, 69, 72–73; insurgent narratives on, 46, 61–62, 64–65; New York City jail rebellions, 45, 46, 49, 129, 160, 239n97
Republic of New Afrika, 220
revolutionary/abolitionist goals of prison insurgency, 5–6, 8; anticolonialism and, 23, 24, 81, 114, 159, 192; Attica rebellion, 80, 81, 82–83, 87, 89–90, 115, 156–57; Auburn rebellion and, 52; capitalism and, 81; captive nonparticipants in, 98–99; carceral narratives and, 14, 52, 80, 82, 138; on carceral violence as cause of rebellions, 165–66; counter-war and, 224–25, 226; engagement and, 85–86; geography of, 91; inside/outside solidarity and, 18, 47; insurgent narratives and, 55–56; internationalism and, 29, 84, 111–12; military capacity and, 100–101, *100*, *102*, 247–48n66; New York City jail rebellions and, 23–24, 28, 29, 32–33; popular legitimacy and, 174; prison unionization movement and, 111; rebellion vs. revolution and, 81; reformist counterinsurgency and, 152, 165; rehabilitation and, 155–56; Rockefeller on, 158–59; Select Committee testimony on, 155–56; state delegitimization and, 37; tactical denial of, 157; tensions within, 95; underground and, 96–97; violence as insurgent strategy and, 87
revolutionary captives, targeting of: anti-Black sexual violence and, 129–30; assassinations and, 16, 211, 213, 247n49; counterinsurgency strategies and, 183–84, 187; diversification and, 168; frame-ups and, 215–16; Green Haven Prison, 213, 214–15, 216–19, 268n139; IGO and, 210–11; inmate organization programs and, 214–18, 268n139; inside/outside solidarity and, 214; mechanistic views of humans and, 187–88, 198, 205; no-touch torture and, 221–22; NYSIIS and, 187, 210, 211; prison expansion and, 160–61, 213, 227; radical organizations and, 212–13; state study of insurgent narratives and, 188–89; "tip of the spear" phrase and, 10. *See also* behavioral science experiments; PRISACTS
Revolutionary Catechism (Bakunin), 98
revolutionary nationalism, 12–13. *See also* anticolonialism
Revolutionary People's Constitutional Convention, 38
Right On!, 57, 66
Rikers Island, 40, 223
Roberts, Neil, 106–7
Robinson, Cedric, 8, 39, 42, 71
Roche, Carlos, 199
Rockefeller, David, 158
Rockefeller, Nelson: on Attica massacre, 132; on Auburn rebellion, 56; carceral

narratives based on, 80; Cold War outlook of, 158–59; Department of Health, Education, and Welfare and, 193; guards as expendable and, 183; insurgent narratives on, 61; jail rebellion reprisals and, 49; New York State Select Committee on Correctional Institutions and Programs and, 153; NYSIIS and, 187; presidential commmission on CIA and, 204–5; prison expansion and, 161, 162; reformist counterinsurgency and, 158; on revolutionary/abolitionist goals, 138; state repression and, 12; targeting of revolutionary captives and, 183–84
Rockefeller Drug Laws, 159
Rockefeller Foundation, 193
Rodríguez, Dylan, 5
Rogers, J. A., 190
Roldan, Julio, 239n97
Ruffin v. Commonwealth, 10, 11
Russell, Carlos, 244n101
Rx Program (Prescription and Control Program), 194–204; drugs and, 198, 202, 203; insurgent resistance to, 189, 194, 195–97, 205; military-industrial complex and, 185, 197, 201, 202, 203; operant conditioning model in, 197–98; phases of, 197; plans for, 194–95; precursors of, 193–94, 195, 198, 263n43; PRISACTS and, 206; results of, 203–4; sexual manipulation and, 199–201, 203, 265nn74,76; surveillance and, 198; termination of, 204, 205, 206–7

sabotage, 87–88, 89
Salò (Pasolini), 146
San Quentin Prison, 77
Saunders, Frances Stono, 158
Schein, Edgar, 193, 198
Schwartz, Barry, 94–95
Schwartz, Herman, 246n40
Schwitzgebel, Ralph, 228–29
Schwitzgebel, Robert, 228–29
Scott, David, 241n26
Seale, Bobby, 112
Securus Technologies, 227, 228
Select Committee. *See* New York State Select Committee on Correctional Institutions and Programs
self-governance: anticolonialism and, 31, 83; carceral narratives on, 93–94, 246n40, 249n96; as democracy, 93, 246nn39–40; during Attica rebellion, 83, 90–95, 109, 246n40, 249n96; geography of, 90–91, 109; homosexuality and, 108; New York City jail rebellions and, 29, 31, 33, 35, 41–42; political order and, 91–92, 93, 246n39; security and, 92, 93, 94; spokesmen and, 92, 92; white captives and, 94–95. *See also* Attica rebellion social experience
self-realization, 72–73, 106. *See also* insurgent counter-humanism
semi-liberated zones, 31, 83
sequelae, 131
Seth. *See* Hayes, Robert "Seth"
sexual revenge, 120, 126, 128, 148
sexual violence. *See* anti-Black sexual violence
Shakur, Afeni, 31, 112–13
Shakur, Assata, 30, 97, 212, 221
Shakur, Lumumba, 31, 43, 46–47
Shakur, Mutulu, 103–4
Shakur, Zayd Malik, 97, 229
Shange, Savannah, 255n12
Shango. *See* Stroble, Bernard "Shango"
"sharpening the spear." *See* captive political organizing
Sha Sha. *See* Brown, Henry "Sha Sha"
Shoatz, Russell "Maroon," 168
Shorty. *See* Hines, Thomas "Shorty"
siege warfare, 3–4
Sittman, Deborah G., 194
slavery: anti-Black sexual violence and, 146; Attica massacre and, 3; marronage and, 83; prison as war and, 10–12, 225–26; programmification and, 179; rebellions and, 11–12, 14, 39
Smith, Christen A., 131
Smith, Frank "Big Black," 92, 92, 105, 106, 126, 130
Smoake, Earl, 243n76
"Snacked into Submission!!!" (Prisoners Liberation Front), 172–73
social Darwinism, 208
sociogenic marronage, 106–7
solitary confinement: Auburn rebellion reprisals and, 57, 60, 62, 64–65, 69, 72–73; behavioral science experiments and, 192–93, 198, 202, 203; Casper Baker Gary and, 139; no-touch torture and, 221–22; prison pacification regime and, 198; targeting of revolutionary captives and, 213, 216, 219, 222
Sostre, Martin: on Attica massacre, 40; on carceral violence as cause of rebellions, 165–66; on humanization, 165, 166–67; on mechanistic views of humans, 205;

Sostre, Martin *(continued)*
    on prison militarization, 163; on reform demands, 82; targeting of revolutionary captives and, 48. See also *Sostre v. Rockefeller*
Sostre v. Rockefeller, 56, 69, 157
Soto, Tom, 114, 153–54
Soul B, 270n2
soul murder, 121, 148
South 40 Corporation, 178
Soviet Union, 113
Special Squad No. 1 (NYPD), 187
speculative production. *See* insurgent narrative
Spillers, Hortense, 72
Stallone, David, 181
state framing. *See* carceral narratives
Statement on the Treatment of Criminal Offenders, 29
state repression: anti-racism protests (2020), 127–28; bin-Wahad litigation on, 15, 210; Black Liberation Army and, 97; Black Panther Party and, 30–31, 43, 48, 234n56; counterinsurgency strategies and, 13, 169, 191; economic role of prisons and, 163; IGO and, 210–11; law and, 48; lynching and, 128; preventive detention and, 12, 25–26, 30, 49, 50–51; proliferation of carceral rebellions and, 13–14, 31; *sequelae* and, 131; white hegemonic masculinity and, 122. *See also* carceral state
state violence. *See* carceral violence; state repression
Stroble, Bernard "Shango," 247n49
Sun Tzu, 151
"surplus populations." *See* preventive detention
Symbionese Liberation Army (SLA), 207
Symposium on Law Enforcement Science and Technology, 178

tablets, 227–28
Tabor, Cetewayo, 112
Tactical Patrol Force (NYPD), 40
techno-cells (electronic monitoring), 228–29
television, 227
Thistlewood, Thomas, 146
Thomas, Harold "Blood," 243n76
Thompson, Elmore "Baba Odinga," 212
Thompson, Eric. *See* Omowale, Jomo Sekou
Thompson, Heather Ann, 57, 79
Till, Emmett, 190

"tip of the spear," 9–10, 24, 44
Tombs: Inmates Liberation Front in, 28; Prisoners Liberation Front founding and, 172; rebellion in, 24–25, 28–29, 33, 41–42
Tombs 3, 48
Tombs Seven, 239n104. *See also* Tombs 3
Trenton State Prison, 220–21, 222
Trouillot, Michel-Rolph, 8, 9
Tubman, Harriet, 67, 107
Turner, Stansfield, 265n74

Union of North American Residents (Cuba), 114
United Blood Nation, 223
United Nations, 29, 111
United Negro College Fund, 177
US intelligence operations. *See* CIA; military-industrial complex

Vacaville Medical Facility, 201, 207, 265n74
Vanderbilt, William H., 178
Vietnam War, 99, 101, 114, 172, 199
Village Voice, 57, 103
violence. *See* carceral violence; violence as insurgent strategy
violence as insurgent strategy: anticolonialism and, 42, 44, 63; as assertion of Black masculinity, 43; Attica rebellion initiation and, 86, 87; Auburn rebellion and, 55, 67–68; bail review hearing and, 36; challenge to legal norms and, 38; guards as culpable for carceral violence and, 38–39; guerrilla warfare and, 65; inside/outside solidarity and, 47; insurgent counter-humanism and, 63, 68, 226; legal aftermath of rebellions and, 67; masculinity and, 43; nonviolence and, 39, 102–3; Panther 21 endorsement of, 43–44; prison as war and, 44, 226; prison training and, 63–64; rebellion suppression and, 41–43, 44; reciprocity and, 63, 66, 68, 86; restraint as pathological and, 39, 42; revolutionary nationalism and, 12–13; white captives and, 94–95
Volunteer Services Program, 174–76, 177–78
von Clausewitz, Carl, 225
voting rights, 232n14

Walker, David, 104, 243n76
Walker, James, 154

walking archives, 51, 189. *See also* knowledge communication
Wallace, Maurice O., 132
Ward, Douglas Turner, 244n101
war of becoming. *See* insurgent counter-humanism
war on drugs, 159
war on terror, 135, 186–87, 221, 229, 261n13
war paradigm. *See* prison as war
Washington, Albert "Nuh," 212, 215–16, 231n10
Watergate scandal, 204
Weathermen, 76
Weather Underground, 83, 85, 148
Wells, Ida B., 128
West, Louis Jolyon, 203, 207, 264n68
Western epistemologies, contestation of: fiction and, 76; individualism and, 6; liberal humanism and, 51–52, 63, 76, 133; masculinity and, 104, 110, 120; methodology and, 8, 69; rebellious silence and, 69–70; sabotage and, 88; self-governance and, 92, 94. *See also* carceral narratives; insurgent narratives
Western liberal humanism, 51–52, 63, 76, 133
White, Anthony "Kimu," 97–98
White, Larry "Luqmon," 72–75, 76, 174–75, 180
White, Todd, 73–74
white captives: Attica rebellion and, 90, 94–95; new racial formations and, 130; prison insurgency and, 4–5
white hegemonic masculinity: anti-Black sexual violence as maintenance of, 120, 129, 136–37, 138, 148; Attica rebellion as threat to, 5, 120, 125, 214; Black exclusion from, 123, 124, 129; dependence on racial repression, 122–23; fantasies of Black sexual violence and, 122, 125–26, 128, 251n23; images of Attica massacre and, 132; new racial formations and, 130; sexualization of racist repression and, 123, 129

White Man: civilization myth of, 145; criminality of, 1–2; dominance preservation goals, 3, 129, 133. *See also* carceral state; white hegemonic masculinity; white supremacy
white supremacy: among guards, 124, 213; behavioral science experiments and, 194; carceral violence and, 46; images of Attica massacre and, 132–34; lynching and, 2, 126, 127, 128–29, 132, 134–35, 190; in upstate New York, 124, 127, 128, 194. *See also* prison pacification regime; state repression
Whittaker, Earl D., 239n104
Wicker, Tom, 103, 109–10
Wiener, Norbert, 188
Williams, Joan, 131
Williams, Robert F., 4
Wilson, Stevie, 13
Women's Bail Fund, 47
Woodfox, Albert, 129
Workers' Power, 206
Worker's World, 57
Wretched of the Earth, The (Fanon), 51–52, 102
Writer for the People. *See* Hill, Charles Leon
Wynter, Sylvia, 52, 83–84, 104, 147–48

X, Malcolm: assassination of, 191; on broad reach of carceral state, 229; knowledge communication and, 190; masculinity and, 104; Queen Mother Audley Moore and, 1; political arc of, 62; struggle names and, 70

Young Lords Party (YLP): Auburn rebellion and, 54, 243n76; captive political organizing and, 26, 28, 76; inside/outside solidarity and, 36, 46, 47; *Palante*, 31. *See also* Martinez, Victor
Youth Against War and Fascism, 47, 57, 58

Zalmanson, Sylva, 113

Founded in 1893,
UNIVERSITY OF CALIFORNIA PRESS
publishes bold, progressive books and journals
on topics in the arts, humanities, social sciences,
and natural sciences—with a focus on social
justice issues—that inspire thought and action
among readers worldwide.

The UC PRESS FOUNDATION
raises funds to uphold the press's vital role
as an independent, nonprofit publisher, and
receives philanthropic support from a wide
range of individuals and institutions—and from
committed readers like you. To learn more, visit
ucpress.edu/supportus.